MW00804230

"*The Lean Education Manifesto* is a radical, spec ideas for transforming education in developin more powerful because it comes from experienc̲e̲ ̲ ̲ ̲ ̲ ̲ ̲ ̲ ̲ ̲ ̲ ̲ ̲ ̲ the existing situation, are willing to question all our basic assumptions, and turn just about everything we know on its head. On top of this their new ideas are specific and comprehensive. The pandemic has discombobulated what was already an ineffective and inefficient education system. I love the boldness and quality of the ideas. Here is a book worth examining closely in the search for brand new solutions."

Emeritus Professor Michael Fullan,
OISE/University of Toronto, Canada

"This book by Hamilton and Hattie, expectedly, is a *tour de force*. The book has multiple aspects that each would have made a substantial stand-alone work. There is of course the over-the-top development of the most extensive database on school outcomes available anywhere. There is the delineation of things that are commonly done that don't match the evidence. There is the clear set of new ideas highlighted by a focus on making economic decisions about the operation of schools. There is practical application of evidence to policy and operations of schools. But to me the key is a willingness to rethink schools, to imagine policies based more on science than on history. Imagine the transformation of the world's schools if this approach catches on."

Professor Eric Hanushek,
Paul and Jean Hanna Senior Fellow at the Hoover
Institution of Stanford University, US

"*The Lean Education Manifesto* comes at a time when many children are not learning despite attending school and the pandemic further exacerbating learning losses and amplifying inequities. It provides prudent advice: we have to rethink education, in some cases radically. Simply throwing money towards "bad buys" is reckless. Hamilton and Hattie offer alternative thinking by drawing on their extensive research to make education work for those that need the most help. The biggest takeaway is that this echoes the thinking that we need to go back to basics with evidence, openness and systemic approach to find alternatives for impact."

Dr Brajesh Panth,
Chief of Education Sector Group,
Asian Development Bank

"*The Lean Education Manifesto* is about learning. Particularly, what works in developing countries that have made great strides in terms of getting children enrolled in school but face formidable challenges in terms of student learning. Synthesizing almost 1000 systematic reviews gives us some answers, but also makes the case that we need more data. It is imperative that we invest in data systems and innovate in school systems. Still, Hamilton and Hattie show us what can be done with current knowledge and resources. This is a must read for policymakers, researchers, and funders of school systems in developing countries."

Dr Harry Patrinos,
Education Practice Manager, World Bank

The Lean Education Manifesto

The global expansion of education is one of the greatest successes of the modern era. More children have access to schooling and leave with higher levels of learning than at any time in history. However, 250 million+ children in developing countries are still not in school, and 600 million+ attend but get little out of it – a situation further exacerbated by the dislocations from COVID-19.

In a context where education funding is stagnating and even declining, Arran Hamilton and John Hattie suggest that we need to start thinking Lean and explicitly look for ways of unlocking more from less. Drawing on data from 900+ systematic reviews of 53,000+ research studies – from the perspective of efficiency of impact – they controversially suggest that for low- and middle-income countries:

- *Maybe* pre-service initial teacher training programs could be significantly shortened and perhaps even stopped
- *Maybe* teachers need not have degree-level qualifications in the subjects they teach, and they *might* not really need degrees at all!
- *Maybe* the hours per week and years of schooling that each child receives could be significantly reduced, or at least not increased
- *Maybe* learners can be taught more effectively and less resource intensively in mixed-age classrooms, with peers tutoring one another
- *Maybe* different approaches to curriculum, instruction, and the length of the school day might be more cost-effective ways of driving up student achievement than hiring extra teachers, reducing class sizes, or building more classrooms
- *Maybe* school-based management, public–private partnerships, and performance-related pay are blind and expensive alleys that have limited influence or impact on what teachers actually do in classrooms.

This groundbreaking and thought-provoking work also identifies a range of initiatives that are worth starting. It introduces the *Leaning to G.O.L.D.* methodology to support school and system leaders in selecting, implementing, and scaling those high-probability initiatives; and to rigorously de-implement those to be stopped. It is essential reading for anyone with an interest in education.

Dr Arran Hamilton is Group Director of Education at Cognition Education. Previously, he has held senior positions at Cambridge University Press & Assessment (formerly Cambridge Assessment), Education Development Trust, the British Council, and a research fellowship at Warwick University.

Professor John Hattie is Emeritus Laureate Professor at the Melbourne Graduate School of Education at the University of Melbourne, co-Director of the Hattie Family Foundation, and chair of the Board of the Australian Institute for Teaching and School Leadership.

The Lean Education Manifesto

A Synthesis of 900+ Systematic Reviews for Visible Learning in Developing Countries

Arran Hamilton and John Hattie

Routledge
Taylor & Francis Group

LONDON AND NEW YORK

Cover image: © Getty Images

First published 2022
by Routledge
4 Park Square, Milton Park, Abingdon, Oxon OX14 4RN

and by Routledge
605 Third Avenue, New York, NY 10158

Routledge is an imprint of the Taylor & Francis Group, an informa business

© 2022 Arran Hamilton and John Hattie

The right of Arran Hamilton and John Hattie to be identified as authors
of this work has been asserted in accordance with sections 77 and 78 of the
Copyright, Designs and Patents Act 1988.

All rights reserved. No part of this book may be reprinted or reproduced or
utilised in any form or by any electronic, mechanical, or other means, now
known or hereafter invented, including photocopying and recording, or in
any information storage or retrieval system, without permission in writing
from the publishers.

Visible Learning® and **Visible Learning**+™ are trademarks of
Corwin Press, Inc. in the U.S. and other countries. "The Lean Education
Manifesto" is an independent publication, and is in no way affiliated with,
or endorsed by, Corwin.

Trademark notice: Product or corporate names may be trademarks or
registered trademarks, and are used only for identification and explanation
without intent to infringe.

British Library Cataloguing-in-Publication Data
A catalogue record for this book is available from the British Library

Library of Congress Cataloging-in-Publication Data
A catalog record has been requested for this book

ISBN: 978–0–367–76297–1 (hbk)
ISBN: 978–0–367–76298–8 (pbk)
ISBN: 978–1–003–16631–3 (ebk)

DOI: 10.4324/9781003166313

Typeset in Bembo and Helvetica Neue
by Apex CoVantage, LLC

Contents

Figures

Author biographies

Dr Arran Hamilton is Group Director of Education at Cognition Education. Previously, he has held senior positions at Cambridge University Press & Assessment (formerly Cambridge Assessment), Education Development Trust, the British Council, and a research fellowship at Warwick University. His core focus is on translating evidence into impact at scale, and he has overseen the design, delivery, and evaluation of education programs across the Pacific Islands, East Asia, the Middle East, the United Kingdom, Australia, and New Zealand.

Professor John Hattie is Emeritus Laureate Professor at the Melbourne Graduate School of Education at the University of Melbourne, co-Director of the Hattie Family Foundation, and chair of the Board of the Australian Institute for Teaching and School Leadership. His areas of interest are measurement models and their applications to education's problems, and models of teaching and learning. He has published and presented over 1,600 papers, supervised 200 thesis students, and published 60 books, including 28 on understanding and applying the Visible Learning research.

Acknowledgements

This is a book about a remarkably simple idea: how to get more out without putting more in. Not in a general sense, but specifically for education systems in the developing countries (a.k.a. the Global South). It's about getting more children to school AND unlocking at least a year's learning growth from a year's teaching input once they are there. And doing so by leveraging existing resource as far as possible: by getting Lean. We also believe that high-income nations would benefit, too, from engaging with these ideas.

COVID-19 was a major catalyst for our Lean thinking. The pandemic resulted in waves of school closures and considerable reductions in economic activity. This in turn ricocheted into significant learning loss for many, gains for some, and a projected decline in medium-term education funding, i.e., the urgent need for more but with less gas in the tank to make it happen. The lockdowns also meant that we had extra time (trapped) at home to think, write, and iterate our thinking on these important issues.

This book started out as a short think-piece, which got longer and longer: growing into a synthesis of 913 systematic reviews of 53,219 studies. Many people contributed to its development. We are particularly indebted to Harry Patrinos, Eric Hanushek, Brajesh Panth, Joseph Wales, Rebecca Spratt, and Phil Coogan, who provided detailed feedback on our early ideas.

Others have thrown valuable mental hand grenades that stopped us in our tracks and propelled us forward in equal measure: thanks be to Sir Michael Barber, Dylan Wiliam, Russell Bishop, Susan Douglas, Hank Levin, Paul Glewwe, Michael Fullan, Yong Zhao, Doug Reeves, Jukka Tulivuori, Mel Sproston, Brian Hinchco, Shaun Hawthorne, Halima Begum, Katelyn Donnelly, and Deborah Rhodes.

We owe a huge intellectual debt to Gene Glass, Robert Marzano, Lant Pritchett, Abraham Wandersman, Paul LeMahieu, Helen Timperley, Viviane Robinson, Sugata Mitra, Rachel Glennerster, Deon Filmer, Rebecca Winthrop, Rukmini Banerji, and Vicky Colbert. We build on your foundations.

To our wives – Mohana and Janet – thank you for your indulgence; and for your (frank) feedback on readability and utility as we pottered away in our respective writing cupboards.

At Routledge, we owe a great debt to our publisher – Bruce Roberts – for seeing something of value in this project, encouraging us to get on with it and telling us when we'd gone too far; to Molly Selby for editorial support; to Helen Strain for overseeing production; and Jess Bithrey for copyediting and enhancing our prose.

But most of all, we thank you for reading this and hope that within you will find warm leads to enhance children's learning in your context, so that they may build a better world.

Naturally, any errors are ours alone and an opportunity to keep on learning.

Arran Hamilton   John Hattie
Kuala Lumpur   Melbourne

Foreword by Sir Michael Barber

Education has always been the key to the future. Never more so than now.

As the global population rises to nine billion by mid-century, from 2.5 billion in the mid-20th century, there are tremendous opportunities to generate wealth and a sustainable way of life for everyone – if, and only if, everyone is well-educated. That means everyone being literate, numerate, well-informed, able to keep learning through life, and grounded in an ethic that enables both diversity (including diversity of perspective) and inclusion (meaning that no one, whatever their life chances at birth, is left behind). That is the task, the moral purpose, facing us.

The alternative, in which vast swathes of people at mid-century are uneducated, would result in a terrifying combination – which we can identify now because it is already looming – of intolerance and hatred, conflict over increasingly scarce resources, and growing divides between the mega-wealthy and the rest.

Improving education in every country is important, and in most it is high on the political agenda, but globally speaking, the biggest challenge of all is improving education across the developing world, for girls as well as boys. There has been significant progress over the last generation. More children and young people have been enrolled in school than ever before. The huge problem though is that very large numbers of them are learning little or nothing. Too often teachers don't even show up and, when they do, they don't have the skills to enhance learning. They often find themselves with poor facilities and learning materials.

For decades now, aid money as well as government money have been poured into education. When the issue of education is raised in global forums, such as at the UN, the World Bank, or the G7, education is often a high priority, especially girls' education, for further rounds of funding. This is right and good. But all too often it is seen as the end of the story. In fact, raising the money is just the start. The central questions then are how it is spent and what it delivers in terms of learning outcomes.

I discovered this again and again in more than 50 visits to Punjab, Pakistan, between 2009 and 2018. Of course, more money was needed and more came, but by far the biggest problem was fixing the system and seeking to ensure that it consistently did what works. And that required a change of mindset among the system's leaders. The then Chief Minister, Shahbaz Sharif, with unshakeable belief in the future, was willing to take the necessary risks. In time, the system followed – enrollment improved, attendance (of teachers as well as students) improved, and, ultimately, learning outcomes measurably improved too. And a good deal of this involved better and more efficient use of the resource and excellence that *already* resided in the system.

This progress depended on taking some conceptually simple and practically challenging steps that were essential in Punjab, a province with around 30 million children:

1 Appointing education officials and teachers on merit – performance not patronage
2 Once good officials were in key posts, ensuring they stayed there for three years or more, replacing a revolving door of comings and goings
3 Communicating with everyone in the delivery chain, from the frontline teachers to the Chief Minister, so they understood what was being attempted and why
4 Training people at the different levels in the required skills
5 Gathering regular data on attendance and learning outcomes
6 Putting the basic facilities in place in every school – and checking them regularly
7 Learning in close to real time what was and wasn't working, and adjusting accordingly
8 And, not least, sticking with it over several years.

It was by no means perfect, but the system improved significantly; there were those measurable outcomes – more children learning, more good teachers, more good schools, and more competent officials. Not to mention more inspiration and more efficiency of impact

What Arran Hamilton and John Hattie have done in this major contribution to the literature is provide, at a level of detail beyond these essential but basic steps, evidence of what works best in classrooms, schools, and systems. Their book provides school and system improvers with a kind of one-stop-shop, a heat map. It synthesizes the findings of 900+ systematic reviews, which between them distill the findings of over 53,000 studies – with a core focus on efficiency of impact. This alone is a significant contribution given how challenging it can be for ministries and program designers to find and then make sense of all these data.

But it does not stop here. Hamilton and Hattie also face up to the question missing in so many education books and reports – "*how do we actually deliver?*"; going on to supply detailed tools and processes to help reformers select appropriate goals and to turn evidence into action in locally appropriate ways. They are also building on an extraordinary track record; over a long and distinguished career, John Hattie has done more than anyone else to synthesize the evidence on what works in education. Arran Hamilton's focus has been on implementation and scale; and together they have produced this important almanac for impact.

Their work could not be more timely. The global education challenge was massive before the pandemic; it is now a crisis of unprecedented scale. We simply can't afford to continue repeating avoidable errors. Many people in the development education field will find their conclusions challenging, possibly even disturbing. My advice is read what they say, look at the evidence they cite, and reflect on the implications and the *opportunities* for your context.

There is a lot of money and emotion invested in the current status quo – but as everyone knows, the status quo is not delivering what we need. Even where there is progress it isn't happening rapidly enough. Often the same people who claim there is a global education crisis then go on to advocate more of the same without even noticing the obvious contradiction. This is unacceptable.

A leading scientist I know says the key to success is to "go into the lab every day with an open mind." With millions of lives and the future of the planet at stake, could we in education emulate that?

Time to learn deep; time to deliver.

BY SIR MICHAEL BARBER
Author of Accomplishment: How Ambitious and Challenging Things Get Done and *How to Run a Government,* both published by Penguin.

Introduction

According to Big Bang theory, our universe started life 13.8 billion years ago as an infinitesimally small singularity that suddenly inflated at a speed faster than light (Planck Collaboration, 2020). It's that bang that apparently led to us being here right now, and to you reading these words. But wind back a mere 300 years and a second local big bang (of sorts) occurred: the rapid global expansion of publicly funded education. The speed at which this has happened – whilst not faster than light – is one of the greatest successes of the modern era.

In less than 300 years, we have moved from very limited schooling to 12 grades of universal education in many parts of the world; and the majority of this has been funded from taxation. But like the actual Big Bang, our local equivalent has led to a patchwork educational universe. Some parts are stable and strong, whilst others are like black holes that suck in matter but give little back in return.

Many such black holes exist in developing/Global South contexts, where there are still 258 million+ children that receive no schooling whatsoever (UIS, 2019, 2020); and an estimated 617 million that attend but get little out of it – leaving the system functionally illiterate (UIS, 2017). This means that around half of the current global school-aged population are entering their adult lives with profound learning poverty (World Bank, 2019). And, as we shall shortly discuss, more recent estimates suggest that the unfolding situation has taken an *extreme* turn for the worse.

This book adds to the (ever) growing pile of monographs, country reports, evaluations, and self-help guides about how we can fill in these black holes, i.e., how we can get more (and more) children into school; and how we can make sure that when they come out the other end they know their onions. Many of the prescriptions and potions suggested in the existing tomes involve addition. *More* money. *More* teacher training. *More* schooling. *More* accountability systems. *More* public–private partnerships. *More* education technology. The logic is that *More* in = *More* out.

But we're sure you've heard the phrase "less is more", which is often attributed to the minimalist architect Ludwig Mies van der Rohe (Johnson, 1947, p. 49).

This book embodies van der Rohe's mantra and suggests that (maybe, just maybe) we need, or at least can get by with, *Less* money; *Less* schooling; *Less* education technology; *Less* teacher training; and so on. Instead, maybe we need to make better and more efficient use of what we've already got. Maybe we need to get Lean; and by doing so, *Less* in becomes *More* out.

If you are a minister or work in the education ministry in a developing country, this book is meant for you. If you are an education specialist working for an international development organization or are a designer of practical, evidence-informed education initiatives, this book aims to be extremely useful to you. If you are a student of development studies, this book may help you pass your exams (but no money-back guarantees). And hopefully after you've earned your scroll, you will join the global legions for change. If you are lucky enough to live in a high-income nation, we also think most of the suggestions, evidence, and tools may be equally applicable to you.

Although, if you are looking for magic beans and simple solutions, you won't find any. But you will find suggested tools and processes to help you interpret the presented evidence from 913 systematic reviews of 53,200+ studies, so that you can build (Lean) local activities to support locally identified priorities. If, after reviewing the research and (properly) using the tools, you conclude you need to add and not subtract, so be it. If you conclude that you need to subtract but that it won't fly in the face of opposition, be bold(er). Current approaches to solve the global learning crisis are simply not working fast enough, so it's about time we shake things up. A lot.

Of course, it's much easier for us to type these words than for you to bring them alive in your respective contexts. And unless you were on silent retreat or hauled up in your private nuclear bunker for the whole of 2020/21, you will have noticed that we are in particularly challenging times. In fact, no doubt, you too were (and continue to be) directly affected by the events we describe below:

1 **The COVID-19 pandemic.** This deadly disease has ravaged the planet and global responses to contain it have involved successive waves of school closures. In 2020, 195 countries implemented nationwide closures (UNESCO, 2020c), impacting 99% of the global school population, or around 1.72 billion children (World Bank, 2021b; UNESCO, 2021).

In mid-2021, the numbers were better, with 'only' 200 million previously enrolled learners now out of school (UNESCO, 2021). No doubt there will be many further twists and turns after this book has gone to the publisher. But, as of July 2021, the cumulative global lost learning time from the start of the pandemic is troubling: India (60 weeks); Myanmar (60 weeks); Argentina (59 weeks); Mexico (57 weeks); Bangladesh (54 weeks). And these are just examples: the tip of a deep and wide iceberg.

Many high- and middle-income countries are focusing on strategies that enable their learners to 'catch-up', through either remedial tuition, summer schools, longer school days, or even grade repetition. Whereas for low-income countries, the risk is that their children simply won't come back at all. And, of course, these national efforts at *more* student 'catch-up', 're-enrollment', or even just contagion control, invariably come with a hefty price tag (Tanaka, 2020).

2 **Global economic uncertainty is awash**. Because of pandemic-related lockdowns, an estimated US$3.7 trillion in wages, and the equivalent of 400 million in jobs, was wiped from the global economy (ILO, 2021). This is so staggering it needs repeating: $3.7 trillion lost; 400 million jobs gone. And this was just between March and December 2020!

To counteract what is (at the very least) the single worst economic crisis since the Great Depression, governments and central banks have committed US$19.5 trillion (and counting) in economic stimulus (IMF, 2020a, 2020b). Governments are also facing declining tax receipts – a consequence of their lost cut of that US$3.7 trillion in economic activity (IMF, 2020c). There is also recognition that the economy that is built back may involve even greater use of technology, with increased demand for high-skilled knowledge workers and correspondingly reduced demand for those with more basic skills (OECD, 2020a). This will mean that there may be greater need to invest in *more* high-quality education but with (potentially) *less* tax base to fund it. We therefore foresee some 'interesting' tensions between ministries of education and ministries of finance over the next half-decade and beyond.

Indeed, by some estimates, governments have already cut their education budgets by an average of 8% since the start of the pandemic, with low-income countries hit hardest (Save Our Future, 2020; see also Al-Samarrai et al., 2021). Other estimates suggest there will be an ongoing shortfall of US$200 billion per annum in education funding across low- and middle-income countries (UNESCO, 2020a).

3 **Declining official development assistance (ODA).** Even before the pandemic, donor investment in developing country education had plateaued, with the Education Commission and UNESCO calculating a US$39 billion per annum shortfall between what low-income countries could collect through domestic taxation vs what they needed (Education Commission, 2016; UNESCO, 2015a). Let alone that now-projected US$200 billion per annum gap (UNESCO, 2020a)!

However, one of the consequences of the global economic uncertainty is that official development assistance levels (a.k.a. international aid) may stagnate yet further as high-income countries potentially divert more public funds to domestic economic stimulus, leaving even less for official development assistance. The United Kingdom was a first high-profile cutter, reducing its aid budget from 0.7% of GNI to 0.5% from 2021 – resulting in £4.5 billion per annum *less* international investment (HM Treasury, 2020). The degree to which this (along with potential cuts from other funders) will affect the size of the future education aid pot is still not yet known. However, UNESCO (2020a) projects that total international aid may decline by 12% by 2022 as a direct consequence of the COVID-19 headwinds – and take several years to recover to even 2018 levels.

At the time of writing (mid-2021), there is still great uncertainty about the long-term consequences of COVID-19 on both the global economy and on children's learning (Zierer, 2021). The reverberations *could* be felt for several years or even decades, and result in more than US$10 trillion in long-term lost economic activity because of reduced human capital development (Azevedo et al., 2020; Psacharopoulos et al., 2021); or, alternatively, everything *could* bounce back very quickly. It is likely, however, that in the next half-decade governments will face tough choices about what to fund and how to fund it. Therefore, developing country ministries of education, international development organizations, and providers of technical assistance and capacity-building may increasingly need to do (and achieve) more with less. In other words, they may need to get Lean – squeezing the pips out of whatever resourcing they can lay their hands on.

Getting Lean

Lean is a specific methodology for generating efficiencies in production processes to unleash greater value for end-users. Its origins can be traced to (at least) 16th-century Venice – where Venetian shipwrights perfected a process that enabled them to assemble a full galley ship in a single day, using *less* materials, *less* motion, and *more* productivity (Davis, 2007). By contrast, it took their European competitors several months to produce a ship of similar size and quality; with a lot more wood and faffing about.

More recently Lean thinking leaped to the automotive industry, with the relentless drive to reduce the number of steps and the amount of waste in car production. Firstly with Henry T. Ford, and latterly with pioneering work at Toyota, which was later popularized (and Westernized) by researchers at MIT (Womak et al., 1990). To our knowledge, very few have yet brought Lean to education in either the 'developed' or developing world (see LeMahieu, Nordstrum & Greco, 2017 for a review of the extremely narrow range of education contexts where Lean has been deployed).

This book is our initial attempt at shining the light on Lean, a sort of work in progress. It involves backwards-mapping through the educational value stream to identify the contribution or learning returns from each ingredient – to see where we should double-down our investments and where we should get (extremely) parsimonious; cutting back on over-processed 'inputs' that add little or nothing to the final 'product'. For the purposes of Parts 1 and 2 of the Manifesto we just want you to think of Lean as a metaphor for achieving more with the same or less, although we do cover the history of Lean in Chapter 2. However, you will have to wait until Part 3 for our suggested processes.

Now, you might be an optimist and think: "COVID-19 is a blip that we will quickly recover from – so let's forget this Lean efficiency nonsense." Or you might be reading these words in 2025 (or later) and reflect that: "Yes, the aftermath of COVID-19 was bad/better than expected [*delete as appropriate] but it's over now – so [again] let's forget this Lean nonsense." However, we also think there are strong moral arguments for thinking Lean – no matter which of these possible futures unfolds.

Public education is funded through taxes, so surely citizens have a right to expect it to be delivered in the most efficient and effective way? Surely, we also have the right to expect that each additional dollar in inputs results in a corresponding additional gain in student achievement. And when the growth in inputs stops leading to a growth in outcomes, we should stop adding more and take a hard look at what we are doing with all the existing nectar.

Using data to get Lean

To think Lean, it helps if you have access to good quality data about the types of education interventions that have been most or least effective in other developing country contexts – so that you can better understand the initiative types that give strong return on investment vs those that are black holes. Here, the good news is that donors have invested heavily over the last two decades in program monitoring, evaluation, and even randomized-controlled trials (RCTs).

But the bad news is that the collective wisdom that emanates from this is less than we might have hoped. We have identified 57 developing country systematic reviews of 3,912 studies (or about 2,500 with duplicates removed). To be fair, these tell us quite a lot about what works to get children into school (what we call the *easier* problem of education). But the collective prescriptions within the 57 for how we translate schooling into high-quality learning are much more underwhelming and tentative (what we call the *hard* problem of education).

Therefore, as well as suggesting that we need to apply Lean principles to the design of education improvement interventions, we also take the opportunity of introducing a new dataset that we believe may help with Lean decision-making. This is the *Visible Learning META*[X], which is the single largest database in the world on what works best in education improvement: a labor of love that John first started compiling in the early 1980s (see *www.visiblelearningmetax.com*). The META[X] synthesizes the findings from 1,700+ meta-analysis of 100,000+ research studies – involving 300 million+ research participants. Although this data was principally collected in high-income nations, we will argue that some of the findings are equally applicable (or at least generate interesting provocations) to developing/Global South contexts.

Lean implications

The meat of the Manifesto takes 107 of the 300+ META[X] data categories (or influences on student achievement) to make tentative suggestions about the Lean implications for how we develop teachers' expertise; equip schools; establish effective governance and accountability systems; and enhance student learning outcomes through use of the most effective pedagogies. We appreciate that some of our (tentative) Lean recommendations are extremely controversial – and deliberately so, as simply doing more of the same needs to be questioned. For example, we suggest that in *some* circumstances:

- *Maybe* pre-service initial teacher training programs can be significantly shortened from the common 1–3-year endeavors and (perhaps) even withdrawn
- *Maybe* teachers need not have degree-level qualifications in the subjects they teach (and they might not really need degrees at all!)
- *Maybe* it would be more cost-effective to select teachers using psychometrics, working memory tests, and observational assessment centers, designed in a manner that is difficult to game
- *Maybe* the hours per week and years of schooling that each child receives could be significantly reduced, i.e., we focus more on quality not quantity
- *Maybe* learners can be taught (more) effectively and (less) resource intensively in mixed-age classrooms, with peers tutoring one another
- *Maybe* different approaches to curriculum, instruction, and the length of the school day might (at least initially) be more cost-effective ways of driving up student achievement than hiring extra teachers, reducing class sizes, or building more classrooms
- *Maybe* education technology is a blind (and expensive) alley
- *Maybe* focusing on school-based management; centralization vs decentralization; corporatized accountability drivers; public–private partnerships; voucher systems; and performance-related pay are also blind alleys that have limited influence or impact on what teachers actually do in their classrooms, with the door shut.

Instead, we suggest that the motherlode is more likely to be found in unlocking teacher collective efficacy, instructional leadership about impact, and through implementation of localized integrated programs that interweave pedagogies that are heavily aligned with what cognitive psychologists tell us about how the brain works.

Too much of the recent international development research sees the answer in terms of another 'brick in the wall', policy document, or structural/accountability driver, instead of enhancing teaching and learning strategies. And, sadly, even those accounts that do acknowledge the importance of the latter tend to treat the interaction between students and teachers in classrooms as a black box; never quite getting to the practical steps for enhancing the *quality* of schooling.

Thankfully, we already know a LOT about how to apply the insights from research on, e.g., memory, attention, forgetting, cognitive load, and willpower to structure and sequence learning experiences into integrated programs that result in *actual* learning (Kirschner & Hendrick, 2020). So, if we want to solve the *hard* problem of education, this is where we should be looking (far more). And the great news is that, to the best of our knowledge, human brains contain the same information processing 'modules' the world over.

If you are in Chennai, Cairo, Cape Town, Caracas, Coventry, or Chicago, yes, you might interpret the world through use of different linguistic systems, with different cultural concepts and points of reference, and attend to different features (Varnum et al., 2010); but, *broadly*, the information storage, retrieval, and processing systems in your brains are the same. This means that effective approaches (like Cognitive Task Analysis; Spaced Practice; Mnemonics; Interleaving; Deliberate Practice, etc.) will help ALL children to get from surface, to deep, to transfer in their learning. Therefore, pedagogy can, will, and must travel. It's just the curriculum and cultural overlay that will vary.

Getting Lean is like a 'game' of educational Jenga

The process of selecting and implementing appropriate Lean initiatives is akin to the game of Jenga. As those who have played it will know, Jenga involves building a tower out of (relatively) uniform rectangular-shaped wooden blocks. Players take turns to remove the blocks as carefully as possible from the lower levels – so that the tower does not topple over; and then to re-affix them at the top – so that the tower expands in height. The idea is to grow the structure through careful, delicate harvesting and re-use of an existing (finite) resource. In Figure 0.1 we

Figure 0.1 The Two Towers

(Authors)

provide an illustration of two towers that are constructed from an identical number of blocks. The first is short, stubby, and over-engineered. The second is almost double the height but stands much more precariously. A gust of wind or floor vibrations will topple it.

However, we can't afford to let the (educational) Jenga tower collapse – so we must be more conservative and diligent in our selection of the blocks to remove. This means that we need access to good quality data about the value and contribution of each of the blocks. But unlike Jenga, we have more options. It's possible to 'hollow out' blocks and put them back in; or even to replace an expensive wooden block with one made of a cheaper composite material that might even be stronger and more durable. And sometimes, it really is necessary to add completely new blocks to the tower. In other words, we can use Lean thinking to enhance the value stream; removing redundant processes, making others more efficient and durable, and, investing in carefully researched and tested new interventions or 'blocks'. We will come back to the Jenga metaphor throughout the book.

—

Now might be a good point for you to pause, make a cup of tea, and reflect on how what we have said so far is relevant to your personal context. For some of you, we will have undoubtedly raised your blood pressure and your sense of incredulity. Beta blockers may be in order. And for others we might be airing thoughts you secretly have but dare not say. Either way, take a moment.

Defining terms; sharing coalface stories; outlining the structure of the book

In this second part of the introduction, we start by going off at an important tangent: addressing the whole notion of 'development'; and introducing a couple of personal coalface stories to illustrate the vast differences in context, wants, and needs across the 'developing world'. We then outline the structure of the book; and, finally, leave you with a few health warnings and indemnity clauses.

Our focus on the 'developing world'/'Global South'

As we have alluded to above, the focus of the Manifesto is on the countries that have *less* life expectancy; *less* economic development; *less* income per capita; *less* calorie intake per capita; *less* access to education; and *less* conversion of schooling into learning. In the old days these were called 'poor' or 'third world' countries (Tomlinson, 2003). Thankfully, these pejorative terms have been (largely) discarded to the dustbin. In modern lingo, countries with *less* are often described as 'developing' and countries with *more* as 'developed'. This, too, has limitations, as it implies that the 'developed' countries have reached the pinnacle of their teleological destiny and have no further to go. Nothing could be further from the truth: every country is (surely) constantly developing (McCowan & Unterhalter, 2015).

Ergo, another set of labels have more recently been doing the rounds: 'Global North' and 'Global South' (Mitlin & Satterthwaite, 2013). Here, the acknowledgement is that more of the countries with *more* are in the Northern Hemisphere and that more of the countries with *less* sit below the equatorial line. Although, confusingly, this means that if you are in the actual North but have *less* – you are part of the Global South and vice versa. To put this in perspective: Australia, where John lives, is in the geographic South but the Global North; whilst Malaysia, where Arran hangs his umbrella, is in the geographic North but Global South! To cut through the spaghetti, others (including the World Bank) have opted for more factual (albeit cumbersome) definitions (Khokhar & Srajuddin, 2015) – dividing nations into high-income, middle-income, and low-income, which are then often abbreviated to (the more unfortunate) HICs, MICs, and LICs.

Personally, we have less problem with the term 'developing' than we do the term 'developed' (where 'more developed' would be closer to the mark). So, you will see 'developing' used as a blanket shorthand for countries with *less* throughout the book. It also happens to be the term that is most widely used and understood. There's even a whole discipline of 'development studies' focused on the notion of becoming more 'developed'. You will also see occasional use of the term 'Global South' – one of us likes this term and the other doesn't, so there has been a continuous cycle of insertion, deletion, and re-insertion! But more often, you will see the more cumbersome High-income, (lower and upper) Middle-income, and Low-income terms used. This reflects the fact that the 'developing' world is not homogenous. Countries at different stages of 'development' confront extremely different types of challenges/goals, requiring different tools in response. Two personal anecdotes illustrate this – first from John, and then from Arran.

John: Postcard from Liberia

John recalls being invited to Liberia in the early 1980s to review the high school examination system into university.

The President, Samuel Doe, had taken power by storming the executive mansion and removing the previous administration from office in a bloody coup. As part of his image rehabilitation, he created 'Samuel Doe scholarships' for any student who gained more than 85 across four exams – and no one had won them. He promised there would be winners but, alas, there were none, so he promised change and I was asked (as a new and naïve academic) to review their system and propose changes. As part of this, I reviewed the following:

- **Curriculum** – it was impressive and put to shame my then-country's syllabus;

- **Examinations** – these were run by the West African Examinations Council based in Nigeria, with many psychometricians from learned-universities supporting, including my own alma mater – the University of Toronto; and
- **Textbooks** – which were very up-to-date and changed each year.

But then I asked to visit some high schools, and in particular one outside Monrovia, the capital. After much stalling, we traveled by convoy (with army personnel kitted with machine guns), but alas, we would not find an open school – because while the teachers were the highest paid in Africa (by legislation), they rarely received an actual paycheck, so they were out in other roles to support their families.

In the city schools, the principals had copies of the exams, textbooks, and curricula, but they were not shared with the teachers (knowledge is power). The exams (based on Nigeria's curricula) had little correspondence to the curricula. There was a healthy market in pre-buying the questions from exam staff and school personnel; and the textbooks were changed each year, which schools had to buy. A relative of a senior official ran the textbook business and was very happy schools had to spend their funds each year on her (highly marked-up) books – which were, allegedly, not then distributed to the students as they had to be returned to be on-sold to another country.

Worse, the 85 was not a percentage (surely they can get 85%, I heard often) but a T-score, which means a student had to be 3.5 standard deviations higher than the mean of 50; and doing this across four subjects meant about 1 student a centenary may accomplish this. I recommended changing it to a percentage and using the newly emerging field of standard setting to set the cut score; and that the textbooks, curricula, and examination be aligned. However, I was then told in no uncertain way that change meant that the winners became losers in the economy of graft. My only saving naivety was agreeing not to submit my report until I returned home, otherwise the consequences could have been dire (so I was told many times before and after leaving Liberia).

For John, this illustrates the perverse incentives that can often be at play in developing country contexts. It also illustrates that governments (from any country) often have very little leverage on what happens in schools and classrooms. Thus, they tend to focus on what they can see, touch, and claim credit for – policy documents; compulsory attendance laws; quantity of school buildings; shiny curricula; and robust assessment systems. While these may be necessary for developing learners, they are not sufficient. And too often, focus on these frameworks and levers detracts from debates about quality in the school, with quality related to the provision of schooling more than the adequacy of learning. This 'adequacy of learning' is more related to teacher and school leader quality – understanding how to develop the skills of learning, the confidence to fail and persevere, and updating professional learning for the adults in the schools.

Arran: Reflections from an Asian nation

Fast forward 35 years and Arran reflects on his involvement in a national transformation initiative in one of the middle-developing Asian nations. In this case Arran does not name the country. All the stakeholders are still alive and still share their ongoing war stories with him, so we spare their blushes.

Not long after I arrived, I toured an assortment of urban and rural schools. Almost all were easy to get to and had electricity, running water, and (most) even broadband. It was rare NOT to see teachers in the classrooms. It was also rare for them NOT to be teaching. This – and their attendance on Saturdays – was even more amazing because it was virtually impossible to get the sack, even for serious misconduct.

Yes, the actual teaching taking place was a bit didactic – lots of teacher talk, lots of students sitting in rows copying things down, and lots of examinations. Teachers tended to see their role as "getting through the curriculum" and ideally finishing early to squeeze in as many exam practice classes as possible. School principals were most likely to be found in their office, dealing with paperwork. They rarely entered the private domain of teachers' classrooms – except for two annually mandated lesson observations. Several principals admitted that they never gave feedback because they didn't want to "hurt anyone's feelings". For sure, teachers and leaders were all invested in their jobs and they seemed to work extremely long hours – ticking off their to-do lists. It was just that this 'busy work' operated in a parallel universe to the learning lives of the kids.

At the national Ministry of Education, the country's (low) ranking in the Organisation for Economic Co-operation and Development's (OECD's) Programme for International Student Assessment (PISA) was the main cause for concern. PISA was perceived as a sort of national virility symbol and it was felt that a higher showing would be a magnet for multinational corporations to set up shop. The self-diagnosis was that there was "too much rote learning" and that children could pass the national exams but they "couldn't think". Although there was a good base to build out from, pretty much all children came to school regularly and 95% left functionally literate.

The ministry brought its best minds together for (many) weeks of national transformation design sessions, and what emerged was a camel built by 20 sub-committees. It wasn't entirely clear which initiatives linked to which (perceived) problems; or how schools, after receiving their memos, would (miraculously) understand, agree with, and implement with fidelity what was being asked of them.

To be fair, some initiatives 'worked' – where the success measure was whether they were being done. Rolling out national primary literacy assessments was well and truly ticked-off. But once student performance was subsequently linked to school accountability rankings a surprising number of children found themselves ('accidentally') locked in storerooms or told to stay home during the assessments. A textbook case of *the law of unintended consequences*.

For Arran, this illustrates that the strategies that get schools built, and get teachers and students to turn up, are often *very* different from those that unleash excellence. And that implementation of multi-pronged initiatives requires great care (and iteration) to have an impact.

Bringing it together

These personal stories from John and Arran highlight two 'developing country' education systems that are very different. John's experiences in Liberia reflect a system where everything looked good on paper but where (often) the schools were not even open; and where, whilst the 'official' purpose was education, the (more important) 'unofficial' purpose seemed to be kickbacks, rent-seeking, and patronage. As John couldn't get inside the classrooms he has no sense of the quality of instruction on the days when things were up and running, or of how many children turned up.

However, 35 years on, Liberia remains an extremely challenging context. Ravaged by long periods of civil war, more than half the school buildings were destroyed, with teachers fleeing or taking up alternative employment (INEE, 2011). After the civil wars ended (note the plural – there was more than one), the country was then hit by a deadly outbreak of Ebola in 2014, resulting in further school closures. And then COVID-19.

By international measures, pre-COVID-19, Liberia already had one of the highest proportions of out-of-school children in the world – with only 54% of children completing primary education (Ministry of Education – Liberia, 2016); whilst the most recent literacy statistics record an adult literacy rate of 48.3% (World Bank EdStats, 2021b). Let's put this in context: in 1460s London the literacy rate is estimated to have been 40% – and that was without *any* formal system of schooling (De Pelijt, 2019). Liberia's education system is only achieving 8.3% more than what can (arguably) be accomplished by doing absolutely nothing!

Ergo, in 2016, the Liberian Ministry of Education attempted a more radical overhaul, launching *Partnership Schools for Liberia*, with non-government operators taking over the management of 185 schools. Whilst early results were promising, progress quickly plateaued and the initiative proved to be not quite the magic bullet that was hoped for (Romero et al., 2020). Indeed, there was much difference in approach and impact between (and within) the operators. No magic diet pills.

Arran's experiences in his middle-income Asian country example could (almost) not be further removed. Whilst it, too, had all the best policies on paper, there was also a reasonable degree of implementation. Schools were open. Teachers and children were in classes. Teaching was taking place. And the teaching was resulting in a (reasonable) degree of learning. There was also very strong investment in inputs (probably too strong). All the teachers had to do a (theory heavy) four-year degree-level program before they were let loose in the classroom. Primary schools were (over-) staffed by subject specialists who sat in the staffroom undertaking complex (and seemingly pointless) admin tasks whilst waiting for the 13 hours a week when it was their turn to be 'on stage'. All quite different to the generalist primary teacher model employed in many high-income nations, where the same teacher stays with the children all day. By Arran's calculation, they had *at least* 100,000 more primary teachers than they really needed, although it was never going to be a vote-winner to implement wholesale Schumpeterian 'creative destruction'. In fact, the teachers were literally a vote-bank that could be counted on to support the dominant governing bloc to remain in power.

The ministry acknowledged it had all the resources it needed: their last hurdle was "changing the mindset" and building the collective efficacy of their teaching army – which was bigger than the actual army. However, the tools they drew on were the same input-oriented ones they had successfully used to build schools, hire teachers, and get children to show up. But these were not the right tools for the new (and much harder) battle of learning, which was all about altering the software of the mind.

The many Global Souths

What these two coalface stories illustrate is that our Lean application of the 'what works best' evidence base must be undertaken and interpreted with extreme caution. Within the Russian doll-like category of 'developing countries' there are many nested figurines of varying shapes and sizes. Some systems exist only on paper. Others operate but dis-functionally, with large numbers of teachers and students missing each day. Yet others have mastered the neat trick of getting teachers and students to turn up and to engage in performative activity, but are still struggling to convert this into high-quality learning. As we illustrate in Figure 0.2, a system's starting point on this continuum affects where it can crawl forward (or backward) to when searching for and implementing Lean-oriented agendas. Again, no magic beans.

Infrastructure Phase	Incentives Phase	Activity Phase	Excellence Phase
Building schools; hiring teachers; process and policy engineering; logistics management; curriculum development	Incentivizing students and teachers to attend regularly; and monitoring/enforcing compliance	Curriculum uniformly delivered to required milestones/timelines; students prepped to pass the test	Teachers as constant evaluators of their own impact; and students as their own lifelong teachers

Figure 0.2 The Many Global Souths

The structure of the Manifesto

Neither of us can abide magical mystery tours, so here (at last) is the roadmap for the rest of the book. Part 1 sets the scene and lays the foundations. We start, in Chapter 1, by reviewing the (200,000-year) history of education – and particularly the phenomenal global progress made during the last 300 years. However, we lament that the last few steps toward high-quality education for all are proving to be the hardest, and are further exacerbated by COVID-19. In Chapter 2 we then explore the thorny issue of education finance; why systems will (likely) need to do more with less; and how we can use Lean thinking to generate better outcomes with the same (or less) resource.

However, to implement Lean initiatives with confidence, we need good quality data about the high probability bets for learning and the Jenga blocks we can remove or hollow out without bringing the whole tower crashing down. In Chapter 3 we take a deep dive into the 57 systematic 'what works' reviews that analyze effective interventions in developing contexts. These cover the 'smorgasbord' of categories outlined in Figure 0.3.

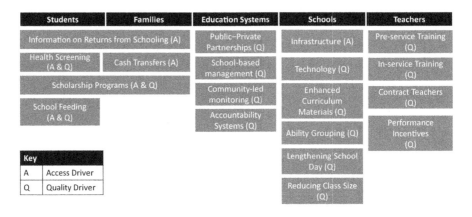

Figure 0.3 Smorgasbord of Education Intervention Categories

And, after concluding that this dataset is not (yet) big enough for us to leverage with confidence, we introduce and explain the META^X dataset in Chapter 4. This includes LOTS of caveats about the tentative (although still, arguably, useful) conclusions that we can draw from research that principally comes from the 'developed' world.

In Part 2 of the Manifesto we get into the meaty detail, surveying the tentative Lean conclusions that can be drawn from combining the META^X data and the 57 developing context systematic reviews in relation to the themes outlined in Figure 0.4.

Chapter 5: Teacher Enhancements	Chapter 6: Structural Enhancements	Chapter 7: Accountability and Motivation Enhancements	Chapter 8: Teaching and Learning Enhancements	Chapter 9: Education Technology Enhancements
This is about how:	*This is about how:*	*This is about how:*	*This is about how:*	*This is about how:*
teachers are selected, trained, and continuously supported to undertake their role	the school operates e.g., its size, finances, building design, and the hours/months of operation	school leadership and governance processes, school accountability drivers, parental choice, performance-related pay and use of public private partnerships impact on student achievement	individual pedagogies can grow student learning; and that these approaches can be combined into programmatic systems for effective teaching and learning	different types of technology can be leveraged to improve the quality of teaching and learning

Figure 0.4 The Part Two Chapter Themes

Finally, in Part 3, we acknowledge that Lean policy recommendations, alone, are not enough. And that we would be doing a great disservice if we simply said: "here you go, we're off now". What folk need are tools that help them to identify initiatives to start, stop, or slow. What works best is also likely to be highly context-specific: what is good for the goose (e.g. a middle-developing Asian country) can be utterly poisonous to the gander (e.g. Liberia).

Therefore, in Chapter 10, we survey the global literature on effective approaches to goal selection, activity/intervention design, implementation, evaluation, iteration, sustainability, and scaling. Then, in Chapter 11, we build these out into an explicit process for crawling forward, to efficiently insert new Jenga blocks, and for crawling backwards, i.e., removing or hollowing out existing planks. We call this framework *Leaning to GOLD* and we provide a teaser of it in Figure 0.5.

G.O.L.D. Improvement				
1. *G*oal Hunting	2. *O*pportunity Searching	3. *L*iftoff	4. *D*ouble-Back	5. *D*^{x}ouble-up
LEAN Improvement				
E. Agree Where To Next	D. Evaluate Future State	C. Pilot Future State	B. Future State Analysis	A. Current-State Analysis

Figure 0.5 The Leaning to GOLD Framework

(Authors)

We also include a *systematic review appendix*, which summarizes the key findings from the 57 developing country reviews that we explore in Chapter 3, and that we continue to interpret in Part 2 of the Manifesto. For the full META^X database of 1,700+ metas of 100,000+ studies, we point you to our global repository: www. visiblelearningmetax.com.

Final health warnings

And now to the cigarette packet health warnings and fine-print indemnity clauses.

Although we call this work a *Manifesto*, it's neither a political or ideological statement of intent nor an attempt to run for public office! We just thought that manifesto sounded catchier than what this book is really about, which is sketching some very preliminary (and tentative) ideas about how we might more systematically go about unlocking stronger educational outcomes – by diverting/redistributing existing funding and not necessarily adding more funding; or how we might even successfully go about doing more with less.

We also forewarn you that some of our early reviewers violently objected to the way that we had set about analyzing and interpreting the data in Part 2. They argued that the thematic areas (or influences on student achievement) we presented were too heavily skewed to what John refers to as the *Politics of Distraction* in his 2015 publication of the same name. These reviewers felt we needed to stop talking about these distractions (i.e., the interventions with high cost and low impact) and instead focus only on the things that *do* work and which could be scaled up cheaply in the low- and middle-income countries. However, we take a more nuanced view.

In developing country contexts where there is little funding, the distractors must be fair game for the axe (or the hollowing out), so that we can then re-harvest the resource and re-focus it on things that do have a higher probability of impact. So, to us, Lean education improvement is *both* about finding things to stop (or reduce) and about finding initiatives with higher impact at lower cost to start, with the caveat that we won't know for sure what the local implications of stopping, reducing, or starting are until we collect evaluation data to know their impact. Within the META^X and the 57 developing country systematic reviews, there are no guaranteed 'silver bullets' that work in all times and places – only probability estimates. So, start small and tread carefully.

Others were critical that we were unable to calculate per student dollar values for the introduction (or removal) of the various treatments we recommended. We agree this is a (BIG) fly in the ointment, but we couldn't report what wasn't recorded in the base data across our 53,000+ studies. Instead, as you use our *Leaning to GOLD* processes to design your own initiatives, we recommend that you calculate the local (financial) cost–benefit analysis for your context and factor this into your decision-making about where to crawl in design space. In other words, we give you the options and you run the numbers yourself.

Some were critical that the base studies within the META^X predominantly focused on student achievement, whereas there are also benefits to children's health; delayed marriage and pregnancy; increased democratic participation and reduced crime, which are not captured by the narrow focus on test scores (see, e.g., Duflo et al., 2021). Again, this is completely fair: but we can only interpret the data we have got. Although we do (attempt to) make links and speculate about those wider benefits within our broader narrative.

And yet, yet others, hated the notion of Lean and felt that it reeked of turning schooling into some sort of car (or galleon) factory. We'll leave you to make your own mind up. And we hope, that despite the controversy, you find something of value in the Manifesto and that, most of all, you buy into our quest to get Lean!

Scene setting

The global massification of education

Writers of amazing fiction often employ a neat trick. They start by painting a picture of an idyllic world and then introduce impending doom in the form of an imminent meteor strike or deadly virus. Then, enter stage left, a band of plucky but under-funded heroes who miraculously save the day. We love this story arc so much that we decided to steal it for this chapter. In the first section we review the global history of education in 3,000 words or less, i.e., the idyllic world of globally moving from near zero to (near) hero in 300 short years – albeit with major bits of plumbing still to sort out. Then in the second section we build and stoke the tension. We explain that access to schooling (which is the *easier* problem of education) is not translating into student learning (the *harder* problem); and that in the fallout of COVID-19 both the *easier* and *harder* problems have become even HARDER. If you are wondering who the plucky but under-funded heroes are, well, that's (probably) you. We hope that the Manifesto gives you the tools and inspiration you need.

The global history of education in >3,000 words

We opened this book by saying that according to the Big Bang Theory, our universe started life 13.8 billion years ago as an infinitesimally small singularity that suddenly inflated at a speed faster than light (Planck Collaboration, 2020). We think this so wondrous that it is worth repeating here. Because it's that great inflation (coupled with Darwinian evolution) that apparently led to us being here right now.

Our ancestral cousins have been around in one form or another for approximately six million years, or about 0.04% of the time the universe has existed. However, the variety that is us (*Homo Sapiens*), has wandered the savannah and latterly the strip mall for a mere 200,000 years (Harari, 2015). Unlike many of our near and distant cousins, we have been generously endowed with prodigious

DOI: 10.4324/9781003166313-3

cognitive capabilities. This gives us the ingenious ability to re-write our operating systems (a.k.a. learn), and enables us to preserve and transmit knowledge across the generations (Tegmark, 2017).

However, for at least 99% of the time humanity has existed there was almost certainly no systemic or centrally organized approach to education. Until approximately 12,000 years ago our ancestors largely operated in nomadic tribal bands numbering no more than 150–200 fluid members. They hunted and foraged the land and once supplies of good grub were exhausted, they moved on (Barker, 2009). Our ancestors had no schoolhouses (or school caves), no semesters or terms, no professional teachers, and no standardized assessments (Diamond, 2012). That does not mean that there was no teaching and learning. It just infers that this occurred informally. It (also) does not mean that there was no 'graduation', although for our ancestors the final 'assessment' was far more likely to be in the form of a hunting trial or an arduous and life-threatening rite of passage rather than a three-hour written examination (Forth, 2018).

Around 10,000 BCE, some bands of humans cottoned on to the idea of planting the land and building long-term farming settlements, rather than foraging and departing; although it took several thousand years for this 'innovation' to spread across the planet (Bocquet-Appel, 2011). The agricultural revolution allowed people to stay put, to build houses, store food, and collect and hoard more private property than what they could carry on their backs. The leap to farming enabled people to trade and for more complex economies to form, with specialization of roles, including advisors, apothecaries, and tutors. And a mere 5,000+ years ago (sometime between 3,400 and 3,100 BCE) some unnamed/unknown forebears invented writing (Chrisomalis, 2009).

Despite all these wondrous advances, there was still no centrally organized, state-controlled schooling (Harris, 1989). Socrates tutored Plato; Plato schooled Aristotle; private tutors taught the Confucian classics to the Chinese so that they could pass the Imperial Examinations and enter the state bureaucracy; master craftsmen trained their apprentices; and parents taught their children. A key catalyst for further change was arguably the invention of the Guttenberg Press in 1440 and its subsequent commercialization, which resulted in a significant increase in the circulation of books and pamphlets (Vincent, 2019).

To interact with this new print-based technology and the knowledge released from it, you needed to be able to read. So, large swathes of people suddenly became extremely motivated to learn their ABCs. In 1460s London, for example, the literacy rate was already as high as 40% without any organized schooling (De Pelijt, 2019). Then, by the 1660s, more than 770 privately endowed secondary schools had sprouted in England; and by 1750 the male literacy rate for the whole of England exceeded 50% (as measured by the proportion of people that could sign their name in a marriage register rather than merely append an X) (Graff, 1995).

In other European countries, informal schools mushroomed to teach the skill of reading, so that people could consume the ever-growing body of printed matter. French peasants organized community classes taught by the most literate in the community; Russian *vol'nye shkoly* (or 'wild' schools) educated rural children; Irish 'hedge schools', which often lacked a school room, literally taught children at the edge of a field, by the hedgerow; and in Prussia and Austria unlicensed *Winkelschulen* (or corner schools) were established by preachers and army veterans to teach the urban poor (Vincent, 2019).

However, by the 18th century a second big bang of sorts occurred: the rise of universal state-funded basic education. The Prussians led the charge as early as 1717 and by the 1830s this had evolved into a national system of free primary schooling that was provided by salaried teachers who had been trained at a specialized college, in publicly funded school buildings, delivering a standardized and secular national curriculum, and with external supervision/inspection to ensure the quality of instruction (Gray, 2013). The system that was pioneered in Prussia is remarkably similar to the schooling model that exists today. And whilst it has become popular in some circles to call this the 'factory model', its origins clearly pre-date the industrial revolution.

After Prussia let the (educational) genie out of the bottle, its schooling model was quickly emulated by its neighbors, who also sought to introduce universal primary education. These included Sweden in 1723, Denmark in 1739, Bavaria in 1771, and the First Polish Republic in 1783. In the aftermath of the French Revolution, ambitious plans for universal schooling were then slowly implemented during Napoleonic era France (Vincent, 2019).

By the early 1800s, as European nation states began to measure their attainments in relation to one another using statistical measures, there was considerable interest in education innovation. Policies were increasingly copied, educational manifestos penned, and transnational fact-finding tours undertaken. In 1843, Horace Mann, who was the secretary of the Massachusetts Board of Education, toured Europe and produced a widely read report on the benefits and mechanics of universal basic education, which was particularly influenced by his observation of the Prussian system (Massachusetts Board of Education, 1844).

Mann's report arguably helped catalyze universal basic education in the United States and the establishment of teacher training colleges (known as Normal Schools). And by 1870, these approaches had also been emulated in the United Kingdom with the passage of the *Elementary Education Act*. This resulted in the establishment of publicly funded school boards that gradually took over the operation of more than 3,000 pre-existing independent schools (Baker, 2001). England's 'monitorial' schools, devised by Andrew Bell and Joseph Lancaster, had classes of students with teachers and monitors (who were the most able older students acting as teaching assistants). These methods are still evident in the structures of schools today, as are remnants of the US and UK 'Dame' schools, which started the move to females dominating the role of teacher in many parts of the world (Barnard, 1961).

The exact confluence of circumstances that resulted in the emergence of state-funded and (generally) state-operated universal primary (and latterly secondary) education varied between nations but seemed to be driven by a mixture of what we call Noble, Grey, and Dark Drivers. We think of Noble Drivers as being altruistic – the motivator being to educate citizens as an end (or moral purpose) in itself. Grey Drivers leverage education primarily for other societal ends, like nation-state building, which can be positive or negative depending on the founding principles of the state. And Dark Drivers, by contrast, are about the personal benefits that education system founders and operators can derive from their management of budgets, appointments, and promotions.

The principal and interlinked Noble Drivers were arguably:

- **Enlightenment values.** By the time that governments had come round to the idea of universal and publicly funded primary education, the philosophical ideas of great Enlightenment thinkers had been percolating for between 50 to 100 years. The works of Emmanuel Kant (1996 [1784]), Jean Jacques Rousseau (1991 [1762]), and David Hume (Hume & Millican, 2007 [1748]) sowed the ideational seeds that humans were malleable and could be improved through education, have human rights, and that those rights include being educated so that we can all unlock our full potential(s). These values were (much) later enshrined in the UN Declarations on Human Rights (1948) and the Rights of the Child (1958).
- **Human capital development.** Equipping children with skills in literacy and numeracy and the general traits and dispositions that support their successful entry to a fulfilling adult life and to employment (Becker, 1993). To our minds (and those of most educators) this is a core purpose of education, but we accept that it might not always have been the prime driver/motivator behind the initial decision of states to fund education through taxation and to deliver it with vast armies of state-employed teachers!

Therefore, these Noble ideals were buttressed by a wide range of Grey Drivers, including:

- **Curtailing the power of the church.** In many European contexts, networks of privately operated schools had already been long-established by (Catholic and Protestant) religious organizations. These schools gave their respective churches considerable power to shape the ideas that went into people's heads when they were at their most malleable (i.e., when they were children). Therefore, in some contexts, governments were (likely) at least partially motivated be the desire to wrestle control of schooling away from the church and firmly into secular state hands (Pritchett, 2013).
- **Nation building.** Many of the countries that first established state-run schooling were relatively young. Prussia was only founded in 1525; the United Kingdom, 1707; the United States, 1776; the French First Republic, 1792; and the Kingdom of Bavaria, 1805. Young countries need a ready mechanism to sow the national mythology, teach the national anthem, collectively salute the flag, standardize the national dialect, build unity, and forge respect for national institutions of government (Anderson, 1991). Schools, with a

uniform curriculum that covers all the above, are arguably relatively effective mechanisms for fostering national unity.

- **The rise of national bureaucracies.** From the late 1700s onwards, many nation states had established large and professionalized civil services. These agencies had become extremely proficient in the art of managing and coordinating (Cornel et al., 2020). With the invention of the telegraph in the 1830s, their reach could also span vast geographic distances. This meant that European and North American governments increasingly had the *capability* to take over the management of independent schools and to found new state-operated schoolhouses – if they so wished – through bureaucratic empire building.
- **Keeping up with the Joneses.** Nation states increasingly compared their successes to those of their neighbors (Pritchett, 2013). It is arguable that from the mid-20th century onwards, there were several boxes that states felt they had to tick in order to have international legitimacy and foster investor confidence. This included having a standing army, a national airline, a radio/TV public service broadcasting network, roads/highways, railways, public sanitation, and a *state-funded education system*. Increasingly, national performance in international benchmarks like the more recent PISA assessments have (arguably) become the 21st-century iteration of that national virility symbol.

There were also likely some Dark Drivers that aligned the personal interests of policymakers with Noble and Grey Drivers, including:

- **Political patronage.** Once school systems are created they require vast armies of teachers and senior functionaries to supervise and monitor what happens in classrooms. For the political and bureaucratic elite this offers an unparalleled opportunity to appoint allies from their support base into public service roles, and to promote them into senior roles in return for their continued political support and services rendered (Kingdon et al., 2014).
- **Rent-seeking.** In many national contexts, education systems (once established) rank within the top-4 spending departments/agencies, endowed with large tax-generated budgets. Ministries of education also often contract with the private sector to build infrastructure (e.g., schools) and to buy goods and support services. This offers the ongoing opportunity for politicians and senior officials to extract personal benefits from private sector organizations in return for contract awards – a.k.a. bribery/kickbacks/facilitation payments/'donations' (Gupta et al., 2000).

Obviously, in public discourse, political leaders were (and are) more likely to frame their decision-making in terms of the Noble Drivers of equality of opportunity, progress, and human rights, than as an attempt to smash the church, consolidate state power, project national virility, and make a (personal) fast buck. However, irrespective of the actual motives of public education system founders

(Noble, Grey, or Dark), the global evidence suggests that the provision of schooling delivers tangible and lifelong benefits for citizens. These include:

1 **Higher lifetime earnings.** Psacharopoulos and Patrinos (2018) aggregated the findings from 1,120 reviews across 139 countries over 60+ years, reporting a strong private (financial) return to schooling. The global average rate of return from one year of extra schooling is around 9% per annum in additional income, and this enhancement remains stable over decades. There is, however, still debate amongst the economists about whether these improved earnings are a result of education directly increasing the skills/human capital of those that attend school or whether it is more of a signaling effect that provides useful hiring information to employers about traits that children already possessed before they entered the classroom. This is the question of whether schools 'polish the diamond' or whether they just 'weigh and certify the gem' (Caplan, 2018).

2 **Reduced participation in crime.** A range of correlational studies have explored the relationship between participation in schooling and the probability of incarceration in the US (e.g., Gould et al., 2002; Hjalmarsson & Lochner, 2012), the UK (Machin et al., 2011), Sweden (Hjalmarsson et al., 2011; Meghir et al., 2011), and Italy (Buonanno & Leonida, 2006). Across all these studies there is a consistent relationship between increased schooling and reduced criminal convictions.

   The precise causal mechanisms are not entirely clear. It could be the *incapacitation effect* (i.e., children cannot be in two places at once and by being in school they are literally incapacitated from committing crime). It might also be due to increased human capital development (i.e., as children attend school, they develop skills that enable legitimate employment). Once in secure employment, they then have a greater stake in society and are therefore less likely to commit crime.

   We should also point out that there is research that explores the benefits of education for those that have embarked on a criminal career. This found that mobsters that had entered illegal enterprises that required high levels of numeracy (e.g., loan sharking, bookmaking, and racketeering) were more likely to be 'successful' if they had completed more years of schooling prior to entering their 'profession' (Campaniello et al., 2016). This would seem to add credence to the human capital development value of their time at school!

3 **Increased health and life expectancy.** A strong body of correlational data also finds a positive relationship between increased education and improved health outcomes. Education seems to reduce participation in activities that risk health and increase the speed with which people access health services in response to medical conditions. Some of the key datapoints include the following: US (Lleras-Muney, 2005) – for individuals born between 1914 and 1939, an additional year of schooling reduced their probability of dying in the next decade by 3.6%; Sweden (Spasojevic, 2003) – of the cohort of men born between 1945 and 1955, an additional year of schooling reduced the incidence of poor health

by 18.5%; and Indonesia (Breierova & Duflo, 2004), which found a correlation between increasing the number of years of schooling during the 1970s and a significant reduction in child mortality rates. A more recent global review of OECD and World Bank data from 1995–2015 found strong positive correlations between increased levels of education, life expectancy, and willingness to have one's own children vaccinated (Raghupathi & Raghupathi, 2020).

We suspect that part of the benefits come from the fact that children are in school rather than work (where there is increased probability of industrial accidents), that children and parents learn about health risks and health behaviors from schooling, and that in adulthood their enhanced education means that they can then undertake less physically dangerous forms of employment and afford better quality healthcare. All these confluences create wave upon wave of virtuous circles.

4　**Better outcomes for girls.** The economic returns from schooling for girls are actually above those of boys. For every additional year of schooling, a woman increases her income by an average of 12% (Schultz, 2002; Psacharo-poulos & Patrinos, 2018). The data also suggest that the higher a girl's level of education the lower the probability that her offspring will die during childhood. For mothers who have secondary-level education, child mortality rates for their children fall by a whopping 49% (Bhalotra & Clarke, 2013). And the higher a woman's education the less likely she is to start a family during her teenage years and the smaller the overall family size she is likely to have (Bhalotra et al., 2013). Across the countries with a high incidence of child marriage, girls with no education are up to six times more likely to become wedded as children than their peers who have attained secondary-level education (ICRW, 2006). In short, education clearly pays off for girls!

Therefore, irrespective of the noble, grey, or dark motivations that have driven political elites to found national and universal public-funded basic education systems, there are major returns for individuals and nations in terms of increased earnings, health benefits, outcomes for girls, and reduced crime rates. But to unlock these benefits, children everywhere need access to high-quality schooling. In the second half of this chapter, we undertake a statistical stock take on how far we have got with this endeavor. We begin by reviewing *access to education* (i.e., getting children into school) and then explore data on the *quality of education* (i.e., ensuring they then actually learn something useful once they are enrolled).

Education statistical stock take

Access to education

When we review the global data on access to education, we can only come to one conclusion: the world-wide expansion of education has been one of the greatest successes of the modern era. Schools have been built; teachers have been hired, trained, and deployed; and both parents and children have been induced to see the benefits of participation.

In Figures 1.1 and 1.2 we show the proportion of school-age primary and secondary students that have attended school, from 1820 to 2010 (derived from Lee &

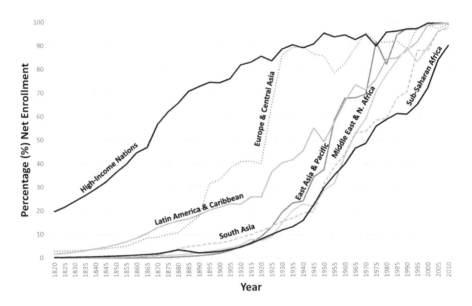

Figure 1.1 Primary School Net Enrollment Percentage (%): 1820–2010

(Adapted from Lee & Lee dataset, 2016)

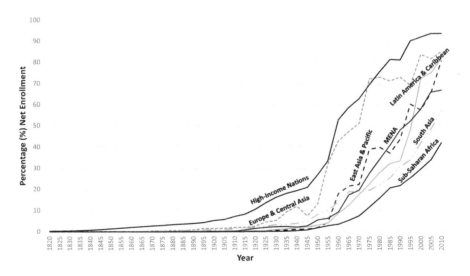

Figure 1.2 Secondary School Net Enrollment Percentage (%): 1820–2010

(Adapted from Lee & Lee dataset, 2016)

Lee, 2016). We can see that global primary school enrollment increased from about 10% in 1850 to 47% in 1940, whilst secondary school enrollments expanded from 0.3% to approximately 8.3% during the same time span. After World War II this trend intensified, so that by 2019 global primary school enrollment exceeded 90% and global rates for lower- and upper-secondary school were around 85% and 65% respectively (UIS, 2020). This growth trajectory has not, of course, been uniform. High-income nations in North America and Western Europe led the charge during the late 18th and early 19th centuries, increasing their primary school enrollments from around 37% in 1850 to approximately 90% by 1940. There was also correspondingly strong growth in secondary enrollments – rising from 1.5% to around 21% over the same timeframe.

Across developing countries we see a similar (albeit slower) growth arc. Primary enrollments increased from a paltry 3% in 1850 to 34% in 1940 and over 90% in 2010. Secondary enrollments were almost at zero in 1850, rose to 4% by 1940 and then reached 68% in 2010. For most developing countries and former colonies in Latin America, Asia, and Africa, the pace of growth in access to education has been slower than for Eastern European states, but there has been growth nonetheless! However, the two geographic regions that stand out as relatively late education adopters are sub-Saharan Africa (e.g., Angola, Burundi, Cameroon, Gabon, Guinea-Bissau, Kenya, Lesotho, Liberia, Malawi, Mozambique, and Rwanda) and South Asia (e.g., Afghanistan, Bangladesh, India, Nepal, and Pakistan).

There has also been a corresponding increase in the duration of schooling. Across 174 countries, the mean average number of years of compulsory schooling was 8.5 years in 2019 vs 5.8 years in the relatively recent 1990 (UNDP HDR, 2020). Although in Bangladesh, Laos, Madagascar, and Myanmar only 5 grades of education are currently provided, and in many sub-Saharan African countries the number is still 7 years or less. However, even this is a significant advancement on the global average of 2 years in 1950 (Barro & Lee, 2013).

Access to education for girls has also been on the up and up (Lee & Lee, 2016). In the case of high-income countries, back in 1870, for every 100 boys at school there were a corresponding 74 girls. By 1940, this had already risen to near parity. The story arcs for Latin America and Eastern Europe started from a lower base than the high-income countries but have reached the same endpoint of near gender parity over that 130-year timespan. The Latin America story is particularly striking, in that it started with only 27 girls per 100 boys at school but had already increased this to 78 girls per 100 boys by 1910! However, there is still some way to go to reach gender parity in sub-Saharan Africa and, to a slightly lesser extent, the Middle East and North Africa, and in South Asian countries.

Data on out-of-school children is represented in Figure 1.3. It shows the (pre-COVID-19) global number of students that were not enrolled/attending school. Yet again, the picture is one of great progress. In 1998, more than 380 million children were not in school and they were disproportionately girls. By 2018, this figure had fallen to 258.4 million (59.1 million children at primary school age; 61.5 million lower-secondary; and 137.8 million upper-secondary). This is still

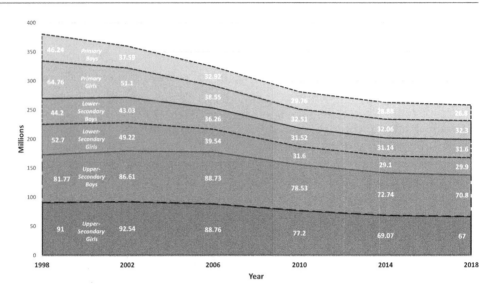

Figure 1.3 Total Number of Out-of-School Children – 1998–2018 (millions)

(UNESCO UIS database, 2020)

extremely high: it is more than the combined populations of Australia, Canada, the UK, France, and Italy – or 53 times the population of New Zealand! It also disproportionally affects sub-Saharan Africa, with 31% of the sub-continent's school-age children being unenrolled in 2019 (UIS, 2020). But the picture for girls has improved – at least in lower- and upper-secondary schooling, where globally they now outnumber boys. And, overall, at primary level we are (almost) within touching distance of universal education for all. Or at least pre-COVID-19 we were.

As we outlined in the introduction, the global dislocations created by the COVID-19 pandemic have had (and will likely continue to have) a profound adverse impact on education outcomes in developing country contexts until at least 2025. In 2020, 195 countries implemented nationwide closures (UNESCO, 2020c), impacting 99% of the global school population or around 1.72 billion children (World Bank, 2021b). As of mid-2021, the cumulative global lost learning time from the start of the pandemic averages more than 66% of a full academic year per child – and counting (UNESCO, 2021). Of which, more than 431 million children could not be reached by either broadcast or digital remote learning solutions (UNICEF, 2020). Whilst the long-term consequences are still being counted, in developing countries we can expect a proportion of those children to never return to school, for these to be disproportionally girls, and with the potential for much worse life outcomes.

Both pre-, during, and post-COVID-19, conflict-afflicted countries also remain the major fly in the ointment of the access to education success story. These territories account for more than one-third of children who are perpetually out of school (UIS, 2020). And, in these challenging contexts, even where children have some access to education, they are 30% less likely to complete primary school and 50% less likely to complete lower secondary (Education Commission, 2016). In short, this means higher dropout rates, higher gender disparities, and significantly poorer literacy outcomes. A further remaining challenge is participation rates for children with special needs. Across 15 sampled lower- and middle-income countries an average 30% of primary-age children with disabilities are out of school; in some individual country contexts the numbers are estimated at above 60% (Mizunoya et al., 2016).

Whilst the fallout from COVID-19, conflict zones, and the under enrollment of children with disabilities remain sizable and significant blots on the educational landscape, from an access perspective, our core message remains that, globally (at least until early 2020), we've never had it so good. Yes, as a consequence of COVID-19 we expect *significant* short-term reversions on the access, retention, and advancement fronts. And there will be many harrowing stories of the human consequences of this tragedy. However, we fully expect governments and communities to pick themselves back up and for the overall levels of access to education to continue to get incrementally better and better. Indeed, one of the consequences of COVID-19 is that countries and individual teachers are having to learn how to provide education at a distance. Some of the lessons from this might also have long-term applications for enhancing education opportunities for children living in remote areas, and for enabling governments to reduce investment in school buildings – as post-COVID-19, children perhaps continue (or start) to undertake some of their learning at home, in the "new normal".

Quality of education

Getting to school is, however, only the first step in the educational process. Children then need to uniformly attain a year's learning growth for a year's teaching input. Let's start with the good news. As we outline in Figure 1.4, in 1900 only 21.4% of the world could be considered *literate*, whereas in 2016 only 14% could be considered *illiterate*. This remarkable increase from just over 20% to over 86% across the world surely should outclass any growth and impact from the Renaissance or the golden days of classical Greece –and this is mainly due to teachers. We have much to celebrate. We surely have richness, quality, and excellence all around us. However, the remaining 14% is still a very large number and is more concentrated in low- and middle-income countries.

Now let's move to the bad news. In the modern knowledge economy, merely being able to read at a basic level and to sign your name rather than append an X is simply not enough. Children need to be primed with learning that scaffolds their entrance into highly technical fields. And this will only grow as robots, AI, and automation eat away at many existing categories of employment. However, even in high-income country contexts, unlocking higher order thinking skills is a considerable challenge.

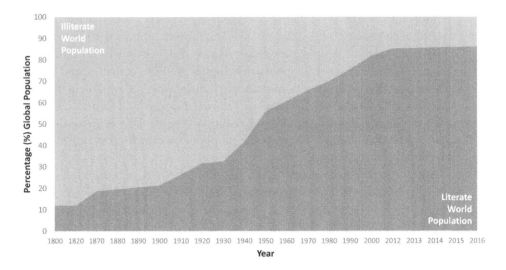

Figure 1.4 Literate and Illiterate World Population Over Age 15 (%): 1800–2016

(Data compiled by Our World in Data based on OECD – How was Life? (2014) & UNESCO Reports (2019) https://ourworldindata.org/grapher/literate-and-illiterate-world-population)

In Figure 1.5, we provide a 2015 high-income country snapshot from the Altinok et al. (2018) dataset, which is the largest globally comparable panel database of education quality. It includes 163 countries, covers 1965–2015, and aggregates assessment data from a range of international assessments (including Programme for International Student Assessment (PISA), Trends in International Mathematics and Science Study (TIMSS), Programme for the Analysis of Education Systems (PASEC), and Progress in International Reading Literacy Study (PIRLS)). Not a single high-income territory meets the 'minimum threshold' level for 100% of their students, which would be the equivalent of all children achieving at least a basic (low/bottom grade) pass in their national student examinations; although Singapore, South Korea, Japan, Hong Kong, and Taiwan come very close. And across these high-income nations, 'only' 81% of students achieved an 'intermediate threshold', which might be considered the equivalent of a good [C] grade. The proportion achieving an 'advanced threshold' (i.e., an excellent grade) averaged 37% across these high-income contexts but with significant disparity between nations/territories.

If we held these high-income jurisdictions up to the highest standards of education success, we should (surely) expect them all to equip a majority (and not a minority) with the skills to achieve at the very highest levels rather than merely an 'intermediate' standard. But we are a long way from this, despite 4%+ of GDP being expended on publicly funded education across developed-country contexts (World Bank EdStats, 2020).

In Figure 1.6, we use the same dataset to shine a light on student learning outcomes in a range of developing countries. The results are even more depressing.

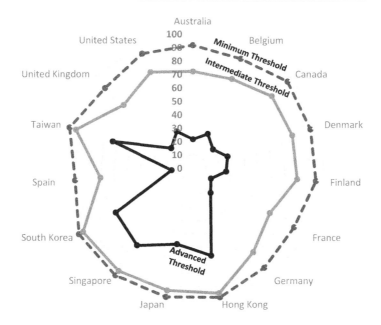

Figure 1.5 Percentage (%) Students Achieving Minimum, Intermediate, and Advanced Assessment Thresholds in Selected High-Income Nations (2015)

(Adapted from Altinok et al. dataset, 2018. Thresholds are benchmarked against PISA, TIMSS, and PIRLS scores)

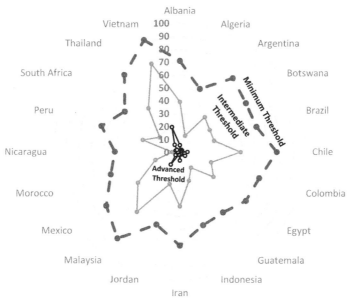

Figure 1.6 Percentage (%) Students Achieving Minimum, Intermediate, and Advanced Assessment Thresholds in Selected Developing Countries (2015)

(Adapted from Altinok et al. dataset (2018). Thresholds are benchmarked against PISA, TIMSS, and PIRLS scores)

Across the selected nations a mere 66% achieved the minimum threshold, 32% the intermediate threshold, and 4.4% the advanced threshold. Vietnam is a clear middle-developing outlier; across the rest, student learning outcomes are extremely shaky.

When we cut the same dataset a different way, highlighting the median percentage of students that achieved a 'minimum threshold' in mathematics and reading at primary school level, the results are harrowing. In low-income countries the number of primary school students that can meet this bedrock standard is a paltry 4.5% for reading and 13.9% for mathematics, whereas for high-income countries the corresponding rates are both over 90%. To put this in context – for mathematics – this means they can (or can't) add or subtract whole numbers (e.g., 1 + 1), recognize and name familiar geometric shapes (e.g., square, circle, etc.), and read simple graphs and tables. For reading it means that they can (or can't) find specific words or phrases within a text (e.g., the cat sat on the mat) and copy/transcribe these (Mullis et al., 2012).

There are also lots of gaps in the global data. Of the 121 countries that we cross-tabulated in the UNESCO Education Statistics database, approximately one-third lacked national reporting data on children's literacy and numeracy levels at the end of primary school (UIS, 2020). By our count, only around half participate in regional or global international assessments for children at the end of lower-secondary school. So, we would not be surprised if the mean average rates of learning in low-income countries are considerably lower than the medians reported above.

When we explore available country-level data, the picture is even more harrowing. In both Malawi and Zambia, 89%+ of students could not read a single word after two full years of schooling (RTI International, 2015). In rural India, fewer than 28% of learners could master double digit subtraction (e.g., 21 minus 10 or 30 minus 11) after three years of primary schooling (ASER Centre, 2017). And when we review data from grade 6 students in West and Central Africa, only 42% have sufficient competency in reading and mathematics to continue their schooling to secondary level (PASEC, 2015).

If schooling isn't producing learning, then what's the point? Parents may as well keep their children at home to work and help support the family. So, we need to understand *why* the quality challenge is so pervasive in low- and middle-income countries so that we can then put countermeasures in place to ensure that children really do get a year's growth for a year's input. In the section below, we outline some potential explanations. Although, beware that we will double back to and question some of these in latter parts of the Manifesto!

Potential explanations for the quality gap

Some of the potential contributing factors for the poor returns from education in low-income and lower-middle-income countries include:

1 **Children not arriving at school primed for learning.** If, for example, children consume insufficient daily calories and suffer malnutrition, live in

unsanitary conditions and suffer dysentery, and/or live in chaotic households where the stress of poverty reduces parental support, we can expect their rate of learning to be hindered, even if they have access to the best teachers. Even in high-income nations, socio-economic status is a major predictor of a child's success at school (Harwell et al., 2017.

2   **Insufficient 'qualified' teachers.** To teach effectively you (arguably) need to have sufficient subject matter knowledge. However, less than 25% of teachers in sub-Saharan Africa have completed secondary education (UIS, 2020), and teachers may not have sufficient pedagogical knowledge. A recent observational study across six sub-Saharan African countries concluded that very few primary school teachers were able to formatively assess their students' progress, and that equally few deployed high-impact instructional approaches (Bold et al., 2017). There are also far higher ratios of students to teachers in developing countries – an average of 45:1 in low-income countries and 33:1 in lower-middle income countries (UIS, 2020).

3   **Low instructional time.** In many low-income country contexts there is a major disparity between the official length of the school day and the amount of time teachers are in their classes teaching – assuming they turn up at all! As Figure 1.7 highlights, in Uganda, teachers are providing instruction for only 42% of their contracted teaching time. And in Mozambique and Ghana the figure is under 40%!

4   **Low teacher self-efficacy.** In some contexts, the data suggest that teachers simply do not *believe* that they can make a difference to the learning lives of

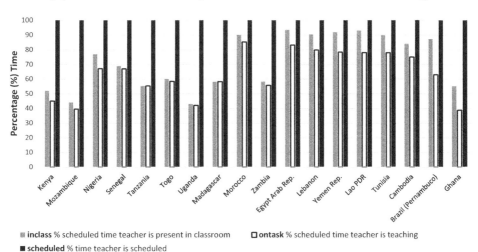

■ **inclass** % scheduled time teacher is present in classroom   ▢ **ontask** % scheduled time teacher is teaching
■ **scheduled** % time teacher is scheduled

Figure 1.7 Teacher Scheduled Teaching Time vs Actual Time in Class vs Actual Teaching Time

(World Bank (2018) World Development Report. This is an adaptation of an original work by the World Bank. Views and opinions expressed in the adaptation are the sole responsibility of the authors of the adaptation and are not endorsed by the World Bank. http://bit.do/WDR2018-Fig_3-10)

their students. Research into teacher mind frames illustrate that in Pakistan, Senegal, and Zanzibar, for example, 50% or more of surveyed teachers agreed that there was little they could do to improve learning outcomes for children from poor backgrounds, and a similar proportion agreed that they could not improve outcomes for children who had already fallen behind (Sabarwal & Abu-Jawdeh, 2017). More recent research also re-confirms these findings (Sabarwal et al., 2021).

Conclusion

In this chapter we have plotted the slow, plodding, and fragmented nature of education provision in the period before the invention of the Guttenberg Press and the educational Big Bang that occurred afterwards. During the last 300 years governments across the globe have embraced responsibility for the provision of state-funded and state-delivered education. And this has grown and grown.

Pre-COVID-19, an estimated 258.4 million children were not in school; however, in percentage terms, this is the lowest unenrolled rate during the whole of human history – so we have much to celebrate. Whilst, yes, the pandemic has thrown up tsunami-strength headwinds that will likely (significantly) reverse this global progress, we have every reason to believe that governments and communities will pick themselves up and build back better. Universal primary education feels almost within touching distance and it is not beyond the realm of possibility that universal (lower) secondary education *could* be achieved in all but the most challenging geographies by 2040. Yes, this is a more conservative date than the 2030 proposed in the UN Sustainable Development Goals, but it factors in those potential COVID-19 headwinds. The *easier* problem is, well, easier. Now onto the *harder* problem.

The mere act of getting children to attend school does not guarantee that they will do any actual learning. Whilst, yes, global literacy rates are undoubtedly the best they have ever been, it is no longer enough. Children everywhere need the knowledge and skills to survive and thrive in a fast-moving and technologically complex world. Even in well-resourced high-income countries, we see considerable variance in the proportion of students that achieve the minimum vs intermediate vs advanced thresholds, and too many children graduate from school with limited employment and social hopes.

When we vector in on low-income and lower middle-income countries, we see an extremely poor transference of schooling into (useful) learning. Given the economic sacrifices that parents in these contexts must often make to get their children into school, this is scandalous. We therefore need to invest in education improvement initiatives to grow the quality of education provision in challenging contexts, because we can't expect this to happen by itself through osmosis.

One of the major messages throughout this book is that waiting 100–150 years for the schooling systems to develop like those in high-income nations is just not acceptable. Disruptive solutions are required; fast tracking of teacher expertise is critical; and an immediate jump to evidence-informed solutions is necessary. However, these things usually come at great (additional) financial cost. In the next chapter we explore this tangled web of educational finance, suggesting that in the aftermath of COVID-19 there may be little in the way of fresh funds to add. Instead, we may all need to learn to do more with less and to get Lean.

2

We need to get Lean

Like football, this chapter is a game of two halves. In the first half, we make the case that whilst education systems need funds, money alone does not make the difference. We also explain that in a post-COVID-19 world, where domestic tax revenues and donor funding are (likely) stagnating, there might not be much more of it to be had anyway. This means that all systems – including those in low- and middle-income contexts – may need to learn to do more with less (a.k.a. get Lean). In the second half, we introduce the Lean methodology, which started life in the automotive industry as a thinking lens to identify educational Jenga blocks that can be removed, hollowed out, or not added in the first place.

Why we need to get Lean

A necessary (but by no means sufficient) condition for enhancing access to and quality of education is the availability of funding. Systems need some level of resource to build and maintain schools; recruit, train and deploy, and continuously improve teachers; develop curriculum, assessment, and quality assurance systems; and to coordinate the whole shebang. Globally, nations have sought to allocate vast sums on this educational enterprise.

Recent estimates suggest that, collectively, governments and private citizens are expending more than US$4.7 trillion per annum on education (UNESCO, 2018). This is almost equivalent to the entire total Gross Domestic Product (GDP) of Japan, which is the third largest economy in the world; or the combined GDPs of Spain, Australia, Korea, New Zealand, and Singapore. The education sector currently employs more than 84 million teachers, which is a near 45% increase since 1993 (World Bank EdStats, 2021a). In fact, education is arguably the world's second largest global 'industry'; according to 2020 data, it is bigger than oil, insurance, automotive, banking, and tourism (IbisWorld, n.d.); second only to healthcare (WHO, 2019).

 DOI: 10.4324/9781003166313-4

Global spending on education has also risen significantly over the last two decades (Al-Samarrai et al., 2019), with per-student expenditure across OECD countries increasing by an average of 24% between 2005 and 2016 alone (OECD, 2021a). On average, each nation expends approximately 4.6% of GDP on education, which works out at around 14.5% of total public expenditure (World Bank EdStats, 2020). However, an obvious and supremely important question is whether this additional money makes a difference. Is there, for example, a clear and unambiguous power-law of continually greater returns to student achievement for each extra dollar of spending? Or, conversely, can systems achieve better (and better) outcomes with the same (or less) budget? In other words, can they get Lean?

To help us answer this question, Figure 2.1 cross-tabulates country averages for the 2018 International PISA Reading Assessments, plotting these against the cumulative expenditure per student. We have also calculated the R^2 value, which is a statistical measure of the proportion of variance in a dependent variable (in our case PISA scores) that can be explained by the independent variable (level of system funding). An R^2 value of 1.0 would mean that student learning outcomes can be explained entirely by the level of funding. An R^2 of 0.0 would mean that there is absolutely no relationship (or at least correlation) between the two variables.

The actual R^2 value for the data in Figure 2.1 is 0.49, which means that (from a correlational point of view, at least) around half of the variance in PISA results are (potentially) explainable by the variance in funding levels across nations. Although,

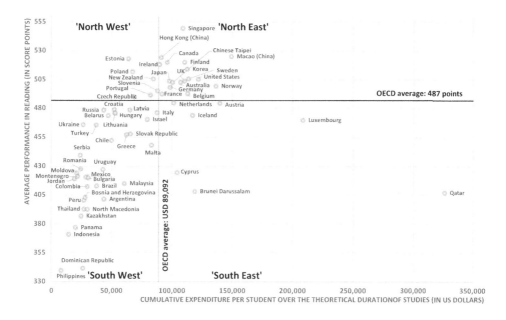

Figure 2.1 PISA Results vs Cumulative Education Expenditure

(Adapted from OECD, PISA 2018 database, Tables I.B1.4 and B3.1.1. https://doi.org/10.1787/888934028406. This is an adaptation of an original work by the OECD. The opinions expressed and arguments employed in this adaptation are the sole responsibility of the authors of the adaptation and should not be reported as representing the official views of the OECD or of its member countries)

with the four outliers in the 'South East' of the graph filtered out (i.e., Qatar, Luxemburg, Brunei, and Cyprus) – each of which invest above average but generate comparatively little – the R^2 increases to 0.74. Money does (*seem to*) matter. However, as we shall go on to explain, the devil is in the detail because correlation is not the same as causation.

The 'North East' and 'North West' systems

Almost all the nations that spend above the OECD average also achieve above average scores on PISA (i.e., those that sit in the 'North East' quadrant in Figure 2.1). But there is significant spread. Brunei, for example, invests around US$8k *more* per student than Finland but achieved more than 100 points *less* in the 2018 PISA Reading assessment. There are also three countries that are firmly in the 'North West' that achieve above average PISA scores for below (OECD) average cumulative student expenditure (i.e., Czech Republic, Poland, and Estonia). They are clearly achieving more with less.

In addition, if you only consider countries and economies where cumulative expenditure is greater than US$50,000 per student, then higher spending on education is not significantly associated with higher scores in the PISA reading test. Those students who had at least two years pre-primary education scored at least 23 points higher in reading at age 15. Early selection into different programs led to lower equity later, and it is the nature of the pre-primary experience that matters much more than later learning: at least two years of developing the concepts about print and number, the social and emotional aspects of learning (perseverance, confidence to take risks, joy of learning), and learning to learn with and through other peers that matters most (OECD, 2020c). Therefore, it is *how and where* we spend the money that matters in these contexts.

In upper-middle- and high-income country contexts that fall within the 'East' and, particularly, the 'South East' quadrants of Figure 2.1, there is a (reasonable) case that too much is spent on 'schooling' and too little on 'learning'. Yes, you need to get students (and teachers) to school to then enact learning, but a major message of the book (and noted by many others) is that the political imperative often seems to stop or slow down once provision of schools, compulsory schooling, or resplendent curricula are devised.

The 'South West' systems

What Figure 2.1 does highlight is that below a certain threshold, money does seem to make a difference. A significant gaggle of middle-income countries languish in the 'South West' quadrant of the table, with relatively limited expenditure per student and significantly lower than average PISA performance. In their econometric analysis of the relationship between PISA scores and system funding, Vegas and Coffin (2015) have calculated that, in mathematics test scores at least, there is a statistically significant correlation between funding levels and student achievement – up to a point. And that point is US$8,000 per annum (in purchasing power parity) per student – after which each additional dollar generates no noticeable improvement in student outcomes (instead it's about what you do with the dollars).

Although even amongst 'South West' systems it is clearly possible for countries to buck the trend. There is wide disparity between what, for example, the Dominican Republic and the Ukraine can achieve with near identical levels of funding (i.e. PISA reading scores of 342 vs 466). This suggests that there might be some circumstances in which Buck Rogers can be unleashed on a shoestring. So, again, *how* we spend also matters.

The 'Deep South West' systems

There are, however, many low-income countries that do not even make it onto Figure 2.1 or feature in Vegas and Coffin's analysis. This is because they do not participate in international student assessments or release (accurate) financial data on their educational expenditure (World Bank, 2018). From the limited data that we do have on these (presumably) 'Deep South West' systems, we know that the funding they are able to collect from taxation (and donor support) often leaves them exceedingly limited wriggle room to invest in skunkworks projects to increase the quality of teaching and learning.

Across all countries, an average of 74% of education funding goes on teacher salary costs; whilst in several sub-Saharan African contexts that figure exceeds 90% (e.g., Central African Republic, Comoros, and Sierra Leone (World Bank, 2018)). In some locales, this means that there are only sufficient remaining resources to pay teachers and undertake basic maintenance of existing school buildings, with little or nothing left to fund new schools or to train teachers, develop curriculum materials, or fund teaching and learning resources. According to Education Finance Watch data (Al-Samarrai et al., 2021), in 2018/19, private contributions from families in low-income countries accounted for 43% of annual education expenditure in their country contexts, versus 16% for households in high-income countries. This means that in low-income nations it disproportionally falls to (poverty stricken) parents to plug the funding gap through additional direct contributions to schools. It seems perverse that those with the least resource should be expected to bootstrap themselves out of poverty!

Even greater ambitions but with declining fiscal headroom (and COVID-19)

In this already challenging context of unevenly distributed education funding, nations are (or at least were) pushing themselves to be more ambitious. Back in 2015, representatives from 184 nations gathered in Incheon, Republic of Korea, to ratify the *UN 2030 Sustainable Development Goals (SDGs) for Education*. Some of the key (although non-legally binding goals) that participating nations agreed to in principle included achieving the following by 2030 (UNESCO, 2015b):

■ Provision of 12 years of free, publicly funded, equitable and quality primary and secondary education; including at least nine years of compulsory education
■ Ensuring that all children have access to quality early childhood development, care, and pre-primary education.

These goals were far more ambitious than the previous Millennium Development Goals that prioritized universal access to primary education, which, as we outlined in Chapter 1, the (pre-COVID-19) world is already (arguably) within touching distance of achieving, with the notable exception of conflict zones and sub-Saharan Africa. The Sustainable Development Goals for education envisage that all children (boys, girls, children of disability) will have access to *at least* primary AND lower secondary education; and that they should actually learn something useful from all this additional schooling!

However, the financial estimates that were built alongside the 2030 targets suggested that sizable increases in education expenditure would be required to achieve the SDGs (Education Commission, 2016; UNESCO, 2015a), including the need for:

■ All nations to increase their level of expenditure on education to *4–6% of GDP and 15–20% of total national public expenditure*; and
■ High-income (donor) nations to ringfence *0.7% of Gross National Income (GNI)* for ODA assistance to lower-income countries.

The initial financial projections compiled by the Education Commission and UNESCO suggested that, on average, an additional US$291 billion per year would need to be invested in low- and lower-middle-income countries to achieve the SDGs. This increased cost reflected both the rising numbers of students (from higher birth rates in lower-income countries) and higher per-student expenditure to expand both the duration and quality of their educational experience. In real terms this would mean that for low-income countries, spending per primary school student would need to increase from US$70 per student per annum in 2015 to US$197 per student per annum by 2030.

UNESCO and the Education Commission's (pre-COVID-19) estimate was that a significant proportion of the required additional funding could be generated if low- and lower-middle-income countries increased the proportion of taxes allocated to education, so that 5.5% of GDP and 20% of public expenditure were allocated for schooling. However, even if these additional funds could be consistently raised by governments, there still remained a projected funding gap of US$39 billion per annum, from 2016 to 2030 (UNESCO, 2015a). This would need to be plugged with additional education aid from the multilateral and bilateral funders.

So, six years on, how did it actually pan out?

First, in the immediate aftermath of Incheon, there was not much movement by nation states to increase the proportion of GDP or public expenditure allocated to education. Education Finance Watch data tell us that the needle has not moved significantly. In 2010/11 government education expenditure as a proportion of GDP was 4.3% in lower-middle-income countries and remained static in 2018/19 (Al-Samarrai, et al., 2021). For low-income countries it increases slightly: from 3.2% to 3.5% of GDP over the same time horizon. These are but averages that hide winners and losers. The latter includes Malawi, whose education expenditure as a proportion of GDP declined from 5.2% to 4.4% over the 2010–2019 time horizon.

Second, there was COVID-19. As we unpacked in the introduction, some of the early economic, social, and educational impacts of the pandemic included an *estimated*:

- US$3.7 trillion in wages wiped from the economy (ILO, 2021)
- 400m global job losses (*ibid.*)
- 4.3% reduction in global GDP (World Bank, 2021a)
- US$19.5 trillion in government and central bank economic stimulus (IMF, 2020a)
- Children losing an average of 66% of a year's schooling due to school lockdowns – and counting (UNESCO, 2021).

Considering the:

- Declining tax revenues/fiscal headroom (IMF, 2020a, 2020c; Al-Samarrai et al., 2021; OECD, 2020d);
- Governmental economic pump priming and eventual required payback (IMF, 2021);
- Difficult decisions that ministries of finance would subsequently have to take about whether to increase taxes to fund their increased borrowing or whether to cut public services (Baker et al., 2020; Al-Samarrai et al., 2021); and
- Lost student learning which may have to be 'remediated' (UNESCO, 2021).

UNESCO went back to its 2015 financial projections, re-ran the numbers, and now believes the education funding gap *could* be nearer to US$200 billion per annum, or five times more than their pre-COVID-19 estimate (UNESCO, 2020a). This means that alternative sources of funding may need to be identified to meet the 2030 Sustainable Development Goals and, in some cases, just to keep the school gates unlocked.

International donors to the rescue?

In the post-World War Two era, a range of multilateral and bilateral institutions were established by high-income nations to support their low-income brethren to develop across a range of sector areas, including education (Unger, 2018). Some of the key multilateral institutions include the World Bank and Regional Development Banks, such as the Asian Development Bank and the Inter-American Development Bank. These organizations provide a mixture of grants and soft loans to low- and lower-middle income countries to finance both capital expenditure and technical assistance.

Several high-income nation states also earmark a proportion of their public expenditure to fund bilateral international aid – a.k.a. official development assistance (ODA). These funders include the European Union, the United States, the United Kingdom, Germany, Japan, France, Sweden, Norway, the Netherlands, Canada, Australia, and (more recently) China. Their motivations for giving range from snow-white philanthropy, to incubation of new markets, and greyer geopolitical considerations. For example, in the case of China and Australia, their respective aid to the Pacific Islands (arguably) serves at least two purposes: (1) the 'official' purpose of improving the lives of local people; and (2) to influence local elites to either green-light (or to continue to block) the establishment of Chinese military bases on the Pacific atolls (Kfir, 2019; White, 2019).

Putting the motivations of funders to one side, education has been a key investment plank for both multilateral and bilateral institutions. Since at least the late 1960s, high-income nations have invested heavily in ODA to enhance education systems in low- and lower-middle-income countries. Although, the focus of this investment has changed over the decades:

Time period	Focus
1970s–mid 1980s **Infrastructure**	Much of the investment was in infrastructure projects, including the construction of schools and provision of equipment (Coombs, 1985; Tilak, 1988), with more than 80% of that expended going toward secondary and tertiary education initiatives.
Late 1980s–early 2000s **Increasing access – especially in primary education**	By the late 1980s, focus then shifted to primary education, the idea being that investment needed to start at the bottom of the 'pyramid' before fixing the top (Psacharopoulos, 1981, 1985; Psacharopoulos et al., 1986; Petrakis & Stamatakis, 2002; Psacharopoulos & Patrinos, 2004; Asiedu & Nandwa, 2007). This was reinforced in 1990 by the UNESCO 'Education for All' World Declaration and, yet again, in 2000 by the *Millennium Development Goals* (MDGs), where access to education was considered a key driver for both human capital, civil society development, and gender rights.
The contemporary era **Quality of education**	Even more recently, the focus has shifted from access to schooling to improving the quality of learning. The UN *2030 Sustainable Development Goals* (SDGs) strongly emphasize *quality education* as the core driver of ODA funding (as discussed in the section above).

Since 1994, the period from which good quality funding data is available, high-income nations have provided in excess of US$154 billion in ODA funding to their developing counterparts, at an average of US$6.4 billion per annum (OECD, 2021b). At first blush this seems like a considerable sum, but it is spread thinly across more than 180 country-level recipients and is only the equivalent of 50% of what a medium-sized middle-developing nation like Malaysia spends annually on education, or 7.7% of the UK's yearly domestic education expenditure.

Figure 2.2 illustrates the contours of this investment from 2002. Whilst real-terms funding has increased 2.6 times over 17 years, this has happened slowly in the early post-Millennium period; plateaued after 2010; and has incrementally risen again post-2016. However, more than one-third of this funding is allocated to post-secondary education, which arguably has much less return on investment than corresponding allocations to early years, primary (Basic), and Lower Secondary (Caplan, 2018). When we vector in on those Basic and Lower Secondary allocations, the 2019 funding levels only represent an increase of US$1.1 billion when compared with 2010 levels: we are still a long way from finding that extra US$39 billion++ per annum that the Education Commission and UNESCO have been calling for, let alone the US$200 billion per annum that UNESCO now believes *could* be needed for post-COVID-19 education reconstruction (UNESCO, 2020a).

There are, however, grounds for even greater pessimism. Firstly, education is losing ground to other sector areas in donor investment priorities. Back in 2003, donors pumped around 6% more into health than education, whereas by 2018 health received 60% more (UNESCO, 2020b). Secondly, the COVID-19 pandemic and associated waves of global lockdowns has significantly curtailed

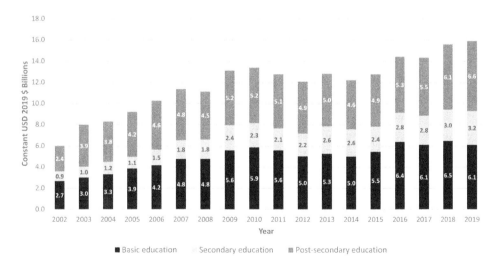

Figure 2.2 Total Aid to Education Disbursements, by Education Level, 2002–19

(OECD Statistics (2021b) – Creditor Reporting System (CRS) data)

economic productivity in high-income countries and increased the need for governments to borrow heavily to underpin their domestic economies. During 2020 and 2021, the mood music suggested that sizable reductions in ODA funding might be on the cards for the remainder of the 'roaring 20s'. Some of the early cutters included:

- **UK Foreign, Commonwealth and Development Office** – with a reduction of GBP 2.9 billion in foreign aid for 2020 (Raab, 2020), which amounted to an almost 20% cut in near-term funding. This was subsequently followed by the decision to reduce the aid budget from 0.7% to 0.5% of GNI through 2021 and beyond, with an estimated saving of GBP 4 billion+ per annum (HM Treasury, 2020).
- **European Union** – reduction in the 2021–27 foreign aid budget from a proposed EUR 88.9 billion to an agreed EUR 70.8 billion (Parandii, 2020).

Whether this is a blip that will be quickly reversed or the tip of an iceberg that will culminate in other ODA funders making similar (or even harsher cuts) remains to be seen, although UNESCO projects a cumulative 12% cut in education ODA funding across funders by 2022 (UNESCO, 2020a), and other estimates suggest that ODA funding may not return to 2018 levels until 2026 (Al-Samarrai et al., 2021).

The long-term impact of COVID-19

We can also expect COVID-19 to accelerate tendencies that were already at play in the global economy, including the rise of the robots and increased use of Artificial Intelligence (AI). As low-skilled roles become increasingly automatable and then automated, citizens with low levels of literacy and numeracy will find it increasingly difficult to transition to alternative forms of employment or to maintain self-sufficiency (Yang, 2018; Harari, 2019). To break free of this doom loop, they will need more (and more) education.

It is possible that, despite the fiscal challenges, ministries of finance in low- and lower-middle-income countries might opt to increase their level of education investment and/or international donors will come to the rescue (in spite of their growing domestic debt piles). However, even if they do, there is a second danger that they will simply be throwing good money after bad, i.e., upping their investment in the hope of getting Estonia-like student achievement returns but only ending up at the level of Malaysia; or even worse – not pushing the needle at all.

Therefore, we think it's high time to think less about the money and to instead re-focus on how we can achieve more with the same (or less). In other words, we need to get Lean. And we don't just mean this figuratively/metaphorically – we also mean it literally/methodologically. In the second part of this chapter we introduce the Lean improvement process and explain how it can be used to enhance education outcomes, even on a shoestring.

How to get Lean

When you close your eyes and visualize the state of being lean, we suspect you might be conjuring up images of thin people – like long-distance runners or gangly yoga aficionados. Or, if you are thinking of lean food, you might be imagining nutrients that are low in fat and cholesterol: perhaps salads and cottage cheese. You might also be thinking of lean as a way of acting and behaving, with a sense of speed, agility, and efficiency.

However, Lean with a capital L is a specific methodology for doing more with less. Its early origins can be traced back at least as far as the 16th century, to the *Arsenale di Venezia*; where Venetian shipwrights had perfected a continuous flow production process that enabled them to construct an entire galley ship in a single day (Davis, 2007). Whereas, in the rest of Europe – the production of a similar-sized vessel could take several months.

In the 18th century, Benjamin Franklin also established principles for managing waste and excess inventory (Franklin, 2017). But it was not until the 20th century and the arrival of Henry T. Ford that efficient continuous flow processes caught on more widely. Rather than having a group of 'Jack-of-all-trades' artisanal craftsmen that huddled together in the production of a single car, Ford introduced a systematized production line, with each worker specializing in a single specific area of expertise or input on an assembly line and with the car then moving from station to station (Wilson, 1995).

Whilst Ford's practices were widely copied, he did not systematize his thinking into a manual or production bible. For that we need to turn to post-war Japan and the work of Kiichiro Toyoda, who was the founder of the Toyota car company. As Toyoda analyzed the step-by-step activities of workers on the production floor in his automotive factories, he identified ways that processes could be simplified – increasing both the speed and quality of output. His ideas became known as the Toyota Production System (Ohno, 1988). But it took until 1989 for the framework to be translated into English, when John Krafcik, who was researching automotive production at MIT, popularized the approach, calling it Lean (Womack et al., 1990).

Lean has been defined as a way of doing more and more with less and less – i.e., less equipment, less human effort, less space, and less time – whilst inching ever closer to giving customers/service users exactly what they want/need (Womack & Jones, 2003). The five core principles of Lean are as follows.

Principle 1: Value

This is about starting with the needs of end-users and understanding what constitutes value *to them*. By understanding what customers/service users want, it's then possible to work backwards through the production chain to craft the right inputs, processes, and activities to achieve that value. In the case of education, this might include rich dialogue with children, parents, the community, and with industry to understand what they value, and then empirically investigating the degree to which (current) schooling helps to deliver this. It might also involve triangulation, by benchmarking how other systems approach the task, because service users/beneficiaries may not always have thought deeply about what value truly means to them. Or to put it in the words of a quote that is often (mis)-attributed to Henry Ford, "if I had asked people what they wanted, they would have said faster horses".

Principle 2: The value stream

Value is created for customers through the implementation of a process that contains routines and sub-routines. This is a bit like a stream – with resources and inputs flowing in at one end and valuable outputs and outcomes flowing out the other. Hence, a value stream.

However, waste often creeps into these routines and diminishes the level of value that is subsequently created. To mitigate this, the first step is to undertake *Current-state Analysis*, which involves mapping every link and activity in the current process. This is then followed by a *Future-state Analysis*, i.e., looking for waste (or *muda* in Japanese) that can be eliminated from each step. In product manufacturing contexts, *muda* comes in many forms, including:

- **Waiting**, e.g., any time that staff are idle due to unbalanced workloads or logjams in the production process
- **Excess inventory/Overproduction**, i.e., having too much of anything that is not actively used in the production process – including buildings, people, machinery, etc. – as this ties up resource that could be re-deployed on more value-creating activities
- **Excess motion**, i.e., any movement of a person's body that does not add value – including walking, bending, lifting, talking
- **Defects**, i.e., any product/outcome that does not meet the required standard that must be submitted for reprocessing or discarded
- **Over-processing**, i.e., any steps in production that do not add clear value to the end product.

Lean thinking assumes that *muda* often seeps into processes in response to problems that have a low probability of ever being experienced again. However, once a new step or sub-process becomes habitual it becomes engrained – even if no one can remember why it was inserted in the first place. And once it becomes engrained, people may simply assume that it *must* be necessary. Ergo, the production process gradually creeps toward the overelaborate, overcomplicated, and overengineered.

Now for an education example. Primary schools regularly give homework to their students. Teachers spend time designing this. Students spend time doing it. Teachers then spend more time marking it and then feeding back to the students on where to next. However, as we explore in Chapter 8, the impact of homework on primary-age student achievement seems to be negligible (see, e.g., Cooper, 1989; Hattie, 2009). Therefore, in the language of Lean, homework in primary education *could* (potentially) be considered a current-state act of 'overprocessing'. Another form of *muda* ripe for future-state elimination.

In future-state analysis, the idea is to be suspicious of every process, sub-routine, and step – to identify ALL the potential areas where *muda* can be chiseled away. According to Womak and Jones (2013), we might (over successive Lean improvement cycles) see as many as 90% of the steps in the current-state production process being rationalized in that future-state. Note, too, that value stream mapping involves the whole supply chain. In the case of car manufacturing, this means mapping and improving the production processes of *every* upstream component supplier – from the mining of iron ore to the process of converting silica into glass – so that wastage (or *muda*) is eliminated from the production, distribution, assembly, and use of each individual bolt or widget. Assuming of course that those bolts and widgets are still considered necessary after the value stream mapping process has been completed! And the mapping would also take place downstream, too: i.e., with dealerships that sell and service the assembled product; and the customers in the cars – including the ease with which they can obtain finance, maintain their vehicles, and then on-sell in the second-hand market when they eventually decide to upgrade.

In the case of education, value stream mapping would not therefore be something that starts and ends at the school gates. It, too, would involve upstream analysis of every single input that contributes to what happens *inside* the school (and ultimately inside children's heads, which is where neurons wire and fire) – including how school infrastructure is developed; how teachers are selected and trained; how curriculum materials are created, distributed, evaluated, and improved; and how children are supported outside school. And downstream analysis of the impact that school has on children's lives and life chances.

Value stream mapping also involves the creation of *Standardized Work*, i.e., consistent and replicable ways of working to reduce variation in how things are done. The assumption is that variation increases both the probability of inefficiency and of error. However, in the case of education, steps in this direction can often be perceived as reducing the professional autonomy of teachers – a subject we explore in more depth in Chapters 7 and 8.

Principle 3: Flow

This ensures that all the moving parts of the re-engineered system work, are well oiled, and still have enough in-built redundancy or slack to protect against production failure. And that nothing ever stops, and no one ever has to wait. It requires iteratively piloting, evaluating, and scaling new processes – a topic we will return to in Part 3 of the Manifesto.

Principle 4: Pull

This is about 'just-in-time' production: ensuring that resources are only procured, deployed, or 'pulled through' just before they are needed by customers – the opposite of bringing people or infrastructure online way before they are required and then being committed to pay for all, because vested interests make it difficult to dismantle. An example of Pull in action is the way that inventory is managed in modern supermarkets. A finite amount of a particular product will fit into the shelf-space. Many products also have a finite shelf-life. As goods are sold/spoiled and the space becomes empty, this acts as a signal to workers/AI to place an order to Pull additional inventory from the wholesaler on a just-in-time basis, avoiding excess stock and wastage.

Principle 5: Perfection

Perfection is achieved by repeating the steps from principles 1–4 over and over, so that the number of processes, the amount of information, and time required to service customers continually reduces. Lean improvement is a never-ending process because there is always something else to chisel away.

The guiding thread to *Perfection* is that activities and resources should only ever be added to the manufacturing process if they bring genuine additional value to the customer. Everything else is waste that should ideally be eliminated or, at the very least, reduced or simplified (Rizzardo & Brooks, 2003). The most far-reaching approach to Lean is called *kaikaku* – which roughly translates as 'radical change' or throwing out all the existing rules! This could even involve the complete reconceptualization of schooling or learning.

Lean in education

Lean thinking is not common in education improvement. A recent review led by the Carnegie Foundation for the Advancement of Teaching identified only a handful of instances where it had been systematically deployed (LeMahieu, Nordstrum, & Greco, 2017). All appeared to be efficiency drives at individual higher education institutions in high-income nations. Both they, and we, have failed to identify any instances where Lean has been explicitly used to drive K–12 system-level education improvement. Although we also note Henry Levin's excellent work on cost effectiveness in education (Levin, 2001; Levin et al., 2018) – albeit that this did not explicitly use a Lean lens.

There are likely three good reasons for why Lean thinking has not taken off more widely in our business of teaching and learning:

- It's thought of as a process for enhancing quality and efficiency in *manufactured* products, whereas education is a complex professionalized undertaking – not the production of 'widgets'.
- It is often associated with 'efficiency' (a.k.a. making staff redundant) and, quite understandably, this corporatized way of thinking does not play well in the public-service oriented (and arguably artisanal) delivery of education. Although, many developed nations are struggling with teacher retention and an often-cited reason is the unrelenting workload.
- There has been a long antipathy to Taylorism, time and motion studies, and payment by results in education that has led to some of the good ideas being ignored, which may have previously been misapplied for poor reasons.

At this stage, we don't want readers to get too hung up on the applicability of the explicit Lean processes outlined by Womack and Jones to education and whether they can truly transcend the leap from use in manufacturing products to delivering complex services.

> We just want to you to think of Lean in the leanest of senses, i.e., simply as a metaphor or shorthand way of thinking about doing more with less, or even doing better with less; for identifying Jenga blocks that could be removed, hollowed out, or not added in the first place.

In Part 3 of the Manifesto, we will go on to outline an explicit process for Improvement Science in education that builds on and re-contextualizes these Lean principles. We call this *Leaning to GOLD*.

We believe Lean thinking (potentially) has value in education – especially in low- and middle-income contexts where budgets are constrained and where funders seek the greatest leverage for their potentially stagnating investments. Our observation is that many of the education improvement initiatives in many parts of the world have sought to replicate key features of what Finnish educationalist Pasi Sahlberg (2015) calls the Global Education Reform Movement (GERM). Its key features (although arguably heavily caricatured) include those listed in Figure 2.3.

Policy	Prescription
Standardized teaching and learning	- Teacher licensing and comprehensive pre-service training - Age segregated student cohorts - National teaching standards - National curriculum - Common data standards - In-service teacher professional development workshops - Smaller school and class sizes
Market-based reforms	- School autonomies and accountability systems - School inspectorate - School league tables - Teacher performance-related pay - Parental choice/voucher systems - Public–private partnerships
Test-based accountability	- National standardized testing, linked to market-based reforms - Performance standards for teacher appraisal
Focus on literacy, numeracy, and science	- Increasing teaching hours for core subjects
Technology	- Increased use of education technology, including for monitoring and accountability
Demand-based reforms	- Cash transfers to parents - Student scholarships - Information to parents and students about returns from education - School health and feeding programs

Figure 2.3 Key Features of the Global Education Reform Movement (GERM)

(Adapted from Sahlberg, 2015)

However, many of these policies, processes, and activities are complex, costly, and time consuming. What if, for example, we were to discover through research that:

- Current initial teacher training models have limited impact on enhancing teacher expertise
- Open learning environments are no more or less effective than walled classrooms, although open can allow for a better proportion of content and deeper understanding
- Mixed-age classes result in slightly better learning outcomes than classes where students are all the same age
- Children can be effectively leveraged as 'assistant teachers', with clear two-way benefits (with often greater benefit for the student-teacher)

- Large class sizes can provide high-quality learning outcomes if teaching is organized effectively
- Equipment and resources (beyond curriculum materials) are not strongly correlated to student learning outcomes
- Many types of in-service teacher professional development have limited impact
- Esteeming expertise in how teachers think has greater payoff than merely focusing on what they do
- The number of years and number of hours per day students attend school is only weakly correlated with their future earning potential (note that Sahlberg's native Finland has one of the lowest school-hours per year in the high-income world)
- National school inspectorates are more likely to increase the stress rather than the skills of educators.

If all these things were true, then we might:

- Abandon (or significantly reduce) the licensing process for teachers. And we certainly wouldn't invest in postgraduate level qualifications for all (probably not any)
- Encourage the use of cheaper school building designs, e.g., large open barns/ hangars where interiors can be used flexibly; or even rent them on a just-in-time/by-the-hour basis
- Have mixed age groups of students collaborating rather than segregating students by age
- Worry a little less about class size and instead focus on effective instructional and school organizational strategies that enable systems to achieve far more without investing more funds
- Reduce the school year and shorten the school day – potentially doubling the number of learners each school can serve, with the same number of teachers
- Worry less about achieving universal secondary education and worry more about improving the quality of what happens in early childhood education and primary school settings first
- Close down the school inspectorates or, at the very least, refocus their energies on endeavors that awaken collaborative expertise.

Think of all the funding that could be saved by streamlining the education 'production processes'. And what if we were also able to create more 'customer value' at the same time? It would clearly be in everyone's interest to banish these over-engineered processes and get Lean. This would mean that the precious domestic education budgets, parental top-ups, and the scarce ODA investment that is allocated for early years, basic, and secondary education could be spent with more precision and generate more meaningful impact.

Conclusion

Like the game of football, this was indeed a chapter of two halves. The first half explored the thorny issue of educational finances, making the case that we both need to get used to doing more with less and embrace the fact that less really can be leveraged to achieve more (we return to this topic in Chapter 6). The second half introduced the Lean methodology as a mechanism for turning a few loaves and fishes into a feast for the five thousand.

As we described in the introduction to the Manifesto, we might think of Lean as the education reform equivalent of playing a game of Jenga. Our goal is to remove as many blocks as possible without destabilizing the tower (or at the very least, make better use of those that have already been deployed and not add more). It might also involve something that players are not allowed to do within the rules of Jenga: taking blocks out, hollowing out their centers, and putting them back in again; and/or replacing the existing wooden blocks with cheaper and more durable composite materials.

The challenge, however, is the constant danger that the whole Jenga tower collapses. In the world of the game, the consequences are negligible. But in the real world of education improvement, the ramifications are likely to be far more devastating. It's extremely risky to dismantle or hollow out infrastructure to then discover we needed it after all. When it's gone, it's gone; and it becomes fiendishly difficult to re-establish all those institutions, expertise, and workflows.

Therefore, we need an extremely robust evidence base in our pocket before we start advocating Lean, lest it turn into *Mean* education that robs children in already challenging parts of the world of any hope of a decent future. In the next chapter we explore the existing evidence base on 'what works best' in low- and middle-income countries, so that we can wiggle the Jenga blocks with greater confidence.

3

Reviewing the existing research on 'what works best' for education in developing countries

To enhance education outcomes in the low- and middle-income countries, we need access to good data about what has (and hasn't) worked previously. We can then make evidence-informed probability estimates about which Jenga blocks to add, remove, or hollow out in our quest for Lean education improvement. In this chapter we wade through the existing data trove. The first part of the chapter catalogues the research and research questions from 57 systematic reviews of circa 2,500 unique studies. Then, in the second part, we interrogate the findings for glimmers of light on 'what works best'. We conclude that the current research gives us more to go on in addressing the *easier* problem (access to education) and correspondingly less on the *hard* problem (quality of education).

A guided tour of the current research

During the last two decades, funders of official development assistance (ODA) have become ultra-focused on whether their investments are generating genuine on-the-ground impact. Back in 2000, there were only nine impact evaluations of education programs in developing contexts published that year. Now, the output is in the region of 100+ studies per year (Cameron et al., 2016; Saran et al., 2020). These have also evolved from monitoring whether agreed outputs, like school buildings or textbooks, were produced to time and budget, to whether those things have genuinely pushed the needle on enhancing children's life chances. This has resulted in many education development programs being delivered as experiments, with some settings receiving the 'medicine' and others the placebo. The idea is that funders can then compare the outcomes across both groups rather than simply measuring within-group progress, which may have happened naturally, even if the medicine had not been administered.

By our reckoning, there are now more than 80,000 research studies and reports that explore some sort of education improvement intervention within developing country contexts (which we estimate from academic database keyword searches).

DOI: 10.4324/9781003166313-5

The vast majority of these are monitoring reports, case studies, or qualitative reviews, which describe an activity/intervention and then collect perception data on whether participants *felt* that the intervention resulted in improvement. A much smaller 3% of this total is experimental or quasi-experimental in design.[1]

However, it is fiendishly difficult for Ministries of Education to locate and interpret the research. Much of the peer-reviewed content is locked behind journal publisher paywalls, and the rest – the 'grey literature' - is scattered across the disparate portals of various funders, NGOs, and research institutes, where it largely (and depressingly) languishes unread. The World Bank, for example, estimates that 87% of its public domain reports are never cited and that 31% are never downloaded (Doemeland & Trevino, 2014). Accessing the research becomes akin to wading through treacle; and, frankly, it may be too much to expect under-resourced developing country ministries of education to establish in-house teams to continuously mine and leverage the data. Thankfully, a group of researchers has been working in parallel to condense the exponentially growing body of research into more systematic reviews of 'what works', so that policymakers and intervention designers can limit themselves to leveraging these summaries.

As at mid-2021, we have identified *57 developing country systematic reviews* of high probability education interventions. Between them, these reviews draw together the findings from *3,912 individual studies*. As we illustrate in Figure 3.1, this body of research was largely non-existent at the turn of the millennium. Developing country systematic reviews only really got motoring after 2011, when there were (finally) sufficient primary studies to systematically review across a range of educational policy and practice questions.

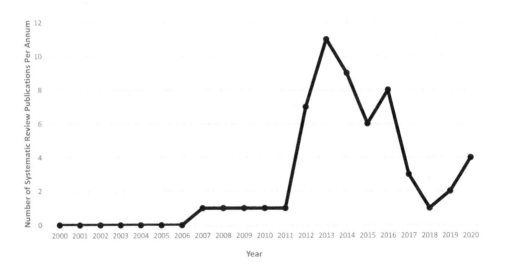

Figure 3.1 Growth in Systematic Reviews Over Time (2000–2020)

(Authors' own calculations)

As we illustrate in Figure 3.2, there is quite a bit of double/triple-counting in the studies across the systematic reviews, with c. 35% being duplicate entries. By our estimate, the number of unique studies is nearer 2,500. We are only able to estimate because many of the reviews were not very 'systematic' in delineating

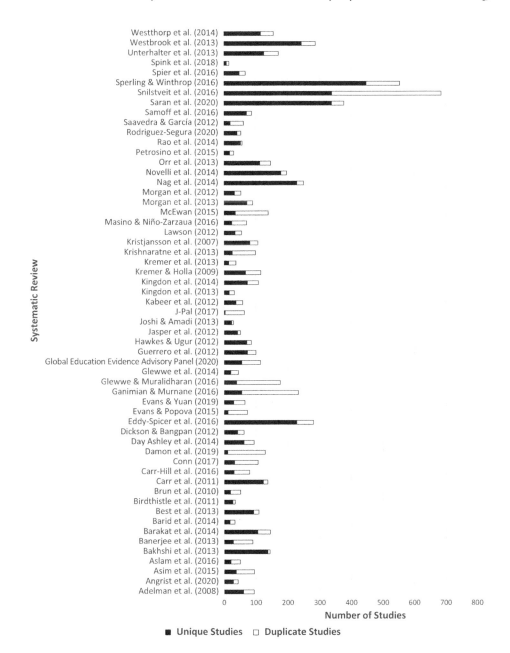

Figure 3.2 Unique vs Duplicate Studies Across 57 Systematic Reviews

(Authors' calculations)

citations that formed part of their review versus those that were merely back-ground literature. This means that whilst the 57 reviews formally declare 3,912 studies, their cumulative total citations are actually 6,925. Of this, 4,472 (or c. 65%) are unique and 2,453 (or c. 35%) are duplicates. We have deducted this latter percentage from the total number of declared studies to estimate the total number of unique studies. However, this is but an estimate.

What these systematic reviews all have in common is that they explicitly state how they selected, gathered, and synthesized the data. This means that future researchers can replicate the same steps to see if they generate the same outcomes. In addition, they have (mostly) narrowed their focus to "high quality" studies that use either experimental or quasi-experimental designs. The challenge, however, is that different systematic reviews or syntheses have used different methodologies to synthesize the data (Evans & Popova, 2015):

- **28 are narrative reviews**. These are generally written by experts in the field and they often attempt to get into the detail about the mediators and the moderators that explain why intervention X worked well in context A, was average in context B, and damaging in context C. Narrative reviews are extremely useful for helping us to understand *why* something works and how we can make it work better; and the approach has the added advantage that all relevant studies can be included – irrespective of their methodology. However, it relies on the (subjective) interpretation of the researcher to decide how to weight and make sense of the various sources of evidence. As the synthesis process is effectively qualitative, the interpretations of the reviewers are often not fully transparent.
- **9 are vote counts**. These use rubrics to count the frequency of effectiveness, e.g., a reviewer might set the bar for "highly effective" at eight or more studies that are all positive, whereas the bar for "sometimes effective" might be six or more studies where at least half have positive outcomes. An advantage of the methodology is that the synthesis process is highly transparent: it is easy to understand how the rubrics were used to interpret the data, count the votes, and come to an overall judgement about 'what works'. However, one of the drawbacks is that it ignores sample size, e.g., a small pilot study with 30 participants could be weighted equally to a large-scale intervention involving thousands.
- **20 are meta-analyses**. These convert the findings from each underlying study into a standardized statistical effect size – which is a measure of power (i.e., whether the intervention packed the punch of a mouse or Godzilla). They then weight and pool the effect sizes together to give an overarching statistical measure of power for each class of intervention. The advantage is that we get the 'power number' and that the process of aggregating individual effect sizes accounts for the sample size of each study. However, the disadvantage is that high-quality studies that do not have the right type of data to allow the calculation of an effect size have to be excluded. We will take a deeper dive into meta-analysis in the next chapter.

Between them, these 57 systematic reviews seek to answer two key questions:

1 What works best to get children to enroll in school and then to regularly attend (i.e., *access*)?
2 What works best to ensure that once children are in school, they learn (i.e., *quality*)?

Although different systematic reviews approach these core questions in different ways and with different methodologies, they each attempt to present and then test a theory of improvement, which involves the implementation of different types of interventions with different sets of stakeholders, to assess whether it either increases access to education or increases the quality of education in developing contexts.

In Figure 3.3 we provide a high-level segmentation of the key focus areas(s) for each systematic review. Sixteen of the reviews are what we term 'super-syntheses', i.e., they attempt to review all types of interventions. There are also larger pots of reviews on governance and accountability (11) and access to education (10); but surprisingly, a much smaller number focus on how to enhance the quality of provision (5). And a smaller number still (4) focus on specific regions (e.g., sub-Saharan Africa) or specific phases of education (e.g., what works for primary-school-aged children?)

In Figure 3.4 we present a smorgasbord of the key categories of intervention that have been evaluated across the systematic reviews, segmented by:

■ **Audience**, i.e., students, families, education systems (or ministries of education), schools, and individual teachers
■ **Aim**, i.e., to increase access to education (A) or quality of education (Q).

Figure 3.3 Segmentation of Systematic Reviews

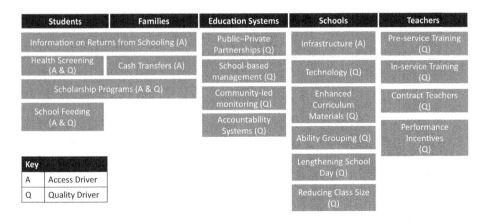

Figure 3.4 Smorgasbord of Education Intervention Categories

This figure has been shown previously in the Introduction.

If we principally seek to *enhance access* to education, then a potential theory of improvement *might* be to implement some/all the interventions listed in bullet points below. Note that whilst we provide example systematic review citations for each, this does not necessarily mean that the reviewer concluded that the approach was successful! However, the *potentially* warm leads for enhancing access include:

- **Providing information on the returns from schooling** to both children and parents so that they understand the long-term economic and health benefits associated with each additional year of schooling, so there is then an increased demand for access (Kremer & Holla, 2009); e.g., by providing parents and children with simple statistics/infographics, or through role model advocacy.
- **Screening children's health** – including the provision of deworming, anti-malaria interventions, vaccinations, and eye tests – in order to reduce the number of days that children are absent from school due to illness and to increase their concentration levels within school (Kremer et al., 2013).
- **Providing financial incentives to parents** (cash transfers) to cover the direct cost of transportation to school, uniforms, and textbooks, and to compensate for the fact that their children are unable to be economically active whilst attending school. And, perhaps also, to make these cash transfers conditional so that there are penalties/reductions for each day of non–attendance (Baird et al., 2014).
- **Providing merit–based scholarship programs** that offer children a one-time cash prize for either improving attendance or achieving grades. The idea is to directly target children and provide them with a financial incentive for them to stay in school rather than enter work (Global Education Evidence Advisory Panel, 2020).

- **Implementing school feeding programs** that provide children with a meal or snack within school that contains micronutrient fortification. The theory of improvement is that the food acts as a pull factor for parents to send their children to school and that the additional nutrients increase children's calorific intake and learning capacity (Lawson, 2012).

- **Building more schools** (a.k.a. infrastructure) so that children do not have to travel as far to access an education (Ganimian & Murnane, 2016). The assumption is that by creating provision nearer to home, this reduces enrollment friction, and also increases the time that children can devote to learning (rather than traveling to school). And, by also equipping these facilities with functioning toilets and fresh water, child absence and health complications will also be reduced.

Alternatively, if we seek to *enhance the quality of education* then we *might* implement:

- **Public–private partnerships** to 'rope in' skilled private sector organizations to directly run schools or to provide school improvement services. A potential theory of improvement is that the private sector is more nimble/efficient, less inclined to rent-seeking, and less stifled by bureaucratic logjams; and that having both public and private systems operating in parallel generates more competition and choice (Barakat et al., 2014).

- **School-based management** to give schools direct control over who they hire and how they allocate resources (Bruns et al., 2010). The assumption being that local decision-making is likely to be quicker and more responsive to on-the-ground realities than decision-taking by stakeholders hundreds or thousands of miles away.

- **Community-based monitoring** that formally co-opts parents and the local community in daily inspections of the school to check that teachers are present and in their classes teaching. The theory of improvement is that (daily) audit from local service users is an efficient way of motivating improved service delivery by teachers and school leaders (Snilstveit et al., 2015) – a.k.a. short-route accountability.

- **Accountability systems**, such as national school inspectorates and the administration and public dissemination of national testing systems (Glewwe & Muralidharan, 2016), so that schools can be publicly paraded as a positive example (or shamed into improvement).

- **Education technology**, particularly computer assisted instruction – which uses software to test children's understanding of curriculum content, and which then provides them with personalized content pathways to enhance their performance in the areas where they are weakest. The theory of improvement is that this either remediates poor teaching or amplifies the effect of effective instruction (Rodriguez-Segura, 2020).

- **Improved curriculum materials**, particularly teacher lesson plans and student resources, including textbooks. The assumption is that this will scaffold and improve both teaching and learning (Kremer et al., 2013).

- **Ability grouping**, i.e., streaming children by their current level of ability into different classes (Kremer & Holla, 2009). The assumption is that it's easier for teachers to deliver a one-pitch lesson rather than differentiate their instruction, so if all the children in the room are at roughly the same level of ability, then no one gets left behind.
- **Lengthening of the school day** so that each child receives more hours of instruction. The theory of improvement is that this increase in quantity will also result in enhanced student learning outcomes (Snilstveit et al., 2015).
- **Reduced class size** so that each teacher supports fewer students. The theory is that they will then be able to provide more individualized and higher quality instruction (Conn, 2017).
- **Pre-service and in-service training**, better equipping teachers with the pedagogic skills in high-impact instructional approaches (Muralidharan, 2017).
- **Hiring of contract teachers** who are on different employment terms and conditions and who are therefore, theoretically, not motivated by rent-seeking and not shielded by the patronage of powerful officials and unions (Angrist et al., 2020).
- **Teacher performance incentives**, such as bonuses that are awarded where teachers regularly attend school and are also visibly in their classes and teaching (Evans & Popova, 2015). These bonuses might also be linked to student examination scores.

Again, the citations for each of the above merely signpost to systematic reviews that have explored these activities and interventions. This does not necessarily mean that the reviewers concluded that these things 'work'.

So, what (actually) works?

In the previous section we catalogued the 57 'what works best' systematic reviews and presented a shopping list of (potentially) plausible high-impact interventions. Although most of these, arguably, involve adding more Jenga blocks rather than Lean-oriented 'subtraction'. So, the important question is whether any of these plausible suggestions are effective in practice.

In Figure 3.5, we provide a high-level area map that records the frequency that each key type of intervention was rated as a high probability intervention across the 57 systematic reviews. Of the 146 catalogued 'recommendations':

- **43 relate to students and families**: information on returns to schooling (10); cash transfers (17); scholarship programs (8); health screening (3); and feeding programs (5)
- **19 relate to systems**: community monitoring (4); national accountability and governance systems (9); public–private partnerships (3); school-based management (2); and national educational radio and television programs (1)

- **48 relate to schools**: ability-grouping students (4); reducing class size (2); intelligent tutoring software (8); remedial instruction (2); lengthening the school day (1); structured teaching/curriculum materials (17); building new schools (10); and Water Supply, Sanitation, and Hygiene (WASH)/sanitation infrastructure (4)
- **36 relate to teachers**: recruitment reforms (1); pre-service training (8); in-service training (12); teacher incentives (6); and contract teachers (9).

Getting students to schools, ensuring schools are built and financed, recommending methods, curriculum resources, and accountability methods all dominate. What is most lacking is how to improve the quality of teachers entering the profession; how to identify, raise, and esteem the expertise of teachers who maximize the enhanced student learning; and how to know and applaud those teachers and schools that are improving the learning lives of the students. Like policies in high-income countries, too many of the recommendations stop too far before the true source of influence – teacher expertise – is touched.

The Appendix summarizes the key recommendations from the 57 systematic reviews of 3,912 developing country studies and (for the research aficionados) it is worth quickly reviewing this before reading our interpretation of the evidence, below.

Interpreting the evidence

Getting back to some good news, when we compare the findings across these systematic reviews for what works best in terms of increasing *access* to education, we find relatively consistent conclusions. And, in the sub-sections below, we summarize these core findings.

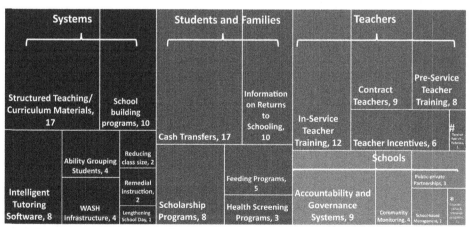

Key: # = Teacher Recruitment Reforms, 1; * = Educational Radio and Television Programs, 1
Source: Authors' calculations

Figure 3.5 Area Map of 57 Systematic Reviews

School buildings

To get children enrolled in school, the strong consensus is that we need *school buildings* (and teachers) that are situated close to the communities that they are to serve (Asim et al., 2015; Damon et al., 2019; Ganimian & Murnane, 2016; Krishnaratne et al., 2013; Petrosino et al., 2012; Snilstveit et al., 2015). The further children need to travel to school the less likely they are to go and the more fatigued they are likely to be when they get there. The provision of sanitation facilities (i.e., toilets and clean water) can also act as a pull factor for both enrollment and retention, as well as support engagement with the wider community who may also seek to use the facilities (Jasper et al., 2012). However, the data are murkier on whether toilets need to be gender segregated or simply be at an appropriate level of quantity and quality (Birdthistle et al., 2011). Buildings alone, however, are unlikely to drive up student learning outcomes; unless the infrastructure is of such high quality that it acts as a recruitment magnet to attract the best performing teachers in the locality and beyond.

We also note that the existing systematic reviews are silent on whether particular building designs are more effective than others. They do not tell us, for example, whether open space environments are more (or less) beneficial than traditional walled classrooms, or what heat/light/acoustic parameters are most conducive to learning. Although, as we shall explore in Part 2 of the Manifesto, there are other sources of data that provide extremely useful insights.

Providing information on the returns from schooling

Once schools are built, the next step is to let parents (and children) know they exist and why children should attend. One way of doing this is just to tell them, which is exactly what information provision programs seek to do – although there is variance in how these initiatives are delivered (Nguyen, 2013). Most provide information about the economic and health benefits of schooling through, for example, simple infographics. Some target the parents. Others target the children themselves. And yet others target both. The stakeholders leading this outreach activity also vary: sometimes it's government officials, other times community role models or NGO fieldworkers, and occasionally information is provided simply through leafleting.

Ten systematic reviews conclude that the provision of information is a high-impact strategy for enhancing attendance (including Angrist et al., 2020; Ganimian & Murnane, 2016; Glewwe & Muralidharan, 2016; Global Education Evidence Advisory Panel, 2020; Kremer et al., 2013; Kremer & Holla, 2009; Rao et al., 2014; Samoff et al., 2016). However, they are unable to tell us which underlying mechanisms work best – communicating with parents, vs children, vs both – or which medium of communication generates the biggest payoff. We also note that whilst none of the reviews conclude that providing information results in negative outcomes, there is skepticism about whether, once children are in school, information alone can boost learning outcomes (Snilstveit et al., 2016).

Screening children's health

School health programs vary significantly in scale and scope. In some contexts, they are limited to the provision of deworming (for intestinal worms and schistosomiasis) and/or anti-malaria medications. In other cases, they might also include the provision of macronutrient supplements, and eye tests and eyeglasses. The assumption is that to attend school and learn, children need to be in good health, and providing school-based health screening acts as a pull factor to encourage parents to enroll their children.

However, only three of the 57 catalogued systematic reviews interpreted the evidence of school screening programs as generating high impact on either access to or quality of education. One concluded that deworming was an effective intervention at extremely low cost (Kremer et al., 2013); the second drew similar conclusions about positive impact for the whole gambit of school health programs (Kremer & Holla, 2009); whilst the third was positive but circumspect about the quality of the evidence (Unterhalter et al., 2013).

The remaining reviews have been extremely lukewarm about the quality of the underlying data (e.g., Damon et al., 2019; Snilstveit et al., 2015) because the studies that they were able to identify were too diverse in terms of methodology, the outcomes being measured, and geographic contexts to provide any level of confidence about impact.

Providing financial incentives to parents

Once governments have built schools within local communities and waxed lyrical to parents and students about the benefits of schooling, the next step is to confront and remove any additional barriers and frictions that parents face in sending their children there.

Cash transfer programs seek to traverse these barriers by transferring cash either to mothers or households. The theory is that the cash will be used by recipients to remove barriers to participation – including school uniforms, textbooks, transportation, and/or loss of income from working children now being at school.

Recent World Bank estimates suggest that more than 2.5 billion people are beneficiaries of cash transfer programs (Ivaschenko et al., 2018). However, there are many differences in the sign and delivery features of these interventions – including those outlined in Figure 3.6.

A key aspect of variation is the level of conditionality. In other words, whether the cash comes with (or without) strings attached, e.g., your child must attend school at least 140 days per annum. And, in cases where there are conditions, the degree to which these are monitored and enforced.

Of the 57 systematic reviews, 17 synthesize data on cash transfer programs, and all conclude that cash transfers are effective in getting children to school. Even unconditional transfers seem to generate increased school enrollment and retention. However, greater effect sizes appear to come from attaching conditions, carefully monitoring that these are met, and penalizing any non-compliance

Feature	Examples of Variation
Recipient	• Mother • Household • Child
Level of funding	• US$10–$2,000 p.a.
Conditionality	• Strings attached (conditional cash transfer) • No strings attached (unconditional cash transfer)
Means of transfer	• Cash payments • Pre-loaded debit cards • Mobile phone credits
Frequency	• Monthly • Quarterly • Biannually
Level of enforcement for any conditionality	• Strong enforcement • Moderate enforcement • Weak enforcement

Figure 3.6 Variation in Cash Transfer Program Design Features

(Adapted from Ivaschenko et al., 2018)

(Baird et al., 2014). Alas, none of these systematic reviews was at all confident that once the children were at school the financial payments had any significant impact on their levels of achievement in standardized tests (see, for example, Asim et al., 2015; Ganimian & Murnane, 2016; Snilstveit et al., 2016).

Removal of user fees

A second approach to reduce friction on student enrollment is the *removal of user fees*. By giving additional funding to schools, the theory is it will reduce the costs they need to pass on to parents for school meals, textbooks, transportation, etc. However, we have found no strong evidence of impact across any of the 57 systematic reviews. And, perversely, in some contexts it has resulted in such an increase in student enrollments that schools became overcrowded and under-resourced (Krishnaratne et al., 2013).

Scholarship programs

Instead of (or in addition to) providing cash transfers to households, another approach is to remit funds directly to children. *Merit-based scholarships* offer either ongoing micro-payments or one-off cash prizes to students. These are usually conditional on meeting a threshold level of school attendance and/or grade achievement in standardized assessments. In some cases, these programs are collectivist (i.e., payments are contingent on *all* students cooperating to jointly meet class-level targets) and in other cases they are individualistic (i.e., payments are based solely on personal performance).

The theory is that scholarship payments are a direct incentive to children to stay in school and that they also motivate them to study harder. The evidence base is promising but is still emerging, with some of the data suggesting that collectivist programs have more impact as they incentivize high-performing students to peer tutor lower-performing students (see, for example, Conn, 2017; Damon et al., 2019; Glewwe & Muralidharan, 2016; Kremer et al., 2013; Kremer & Holla, 2009).

School feeding programs

These provide either all children or a targeted sub-group with a snack or full meal at school or, sometimes, to take home. Meals are often fortified with micronutrients to support physical development. However, evidence of impact is mixed and context specific. In low-income countries where there is food scarcity, the data suggests that feeding has a much stronger impact on both attendance and achievement; in middle-income countries, where malnutrition has already been eliminated/reduced, there is less evidence of impact (Snilstveit et al., 2016; Lawson, 2012; Adelman et al., 2008).

What works best for access to education?
As simple as 1, 2, 3 ...

If, as a local policymaker, funder, or program designer, our core aim was to increase the number of children attending school, then there are several interventions that we could select – each with fairly robust evidence of impact.

Step 1: Build local schools. From a Lean perspective we might seek to reduce costs by:

- Developing flatpack/modular school buildings that reduce cost/time of construction and provide a standardized level of quality
- Using existing local governmental/private facilities that have spare rooms that can be flexibly accessed/rented
- Providing bicycles so that children can travel further to school.

Step 2: Provide information on returns to schooling. Our understanding is that these types of programs are not (that) resource intensive. But as smartphones further penetrate even low-income countries, electronic and social media offer new and more cost-effective channels to reach parents and children with nudge messages about the returns from schooling.

Step 3: Provide cash transfers to households (e.g., conditional cash transfers) and direct to students (e.g., merit scholarships). However, from a Lean perspective we might seek to start with extremely small micro-payments and then gradually ratchet these up if the evaluation data showed limited improvements in attendance until we identify the 'Goldilocks' number. We might also seek to leverage Electronic Management Information Systems (eMIS) to automate the collection of student attendance data and to make automatic payment penalty deductions in contexts where cash transfers were conditional on a threshold level of attendance.

From a Lean perspective, we might be more circumspect about implementing school feeding programs (perhaps limiting access to high-priority groups) or school health screening initiatives – although the cost of deworming is often less than US$0.50 per child per annum and has therefore often been marketed as a 'best buy' for education development (J-PAL Policy Bulletin, 2012).

As we highlighted in Chapter 1 the global data on access to education showcases a tremendous success story. Since 1960, the trend has been up, and up, and up. Whilst there are still significant global pockets of children that don't have access to schooling, we broadly know what works best to get them that access. The further good news is that these same strategies (with a few tweaks) are also effective at getting girls into schooling (Sperling et al., 2016; Unterhalter et al., 2013).

Finally, as Kingdon et al. (2014) point out, these access–oriented interventions are also often warmly embraced by local political leaders and civil servants. Partly because of the opportunities for extraction and rent-seeking (via control of awarding infrastructure and service delivery tenders), and for patronage (through control of teacher recruitment and promotion).

And now for the less good news …

Whilst the 57 systematic reviews of c. 2,500 developing country studies provide reasonably good leads on how we can increase access to education, when we turn to good bets for improving the quality of what happens *within* schools, we are left scrabbling around in the dark.

In this section we attempt to cast some light on that darkness, although we hold back on the detail until Part 2 of the Manifesto – where we triangulate the relatively meagre developing-world research with the more gargantuan 'developed'-context evidence-base on the same types of interventions. Let's now review each intervention type, in turn.

The evidence on the effectiveness of public–private partnerships (PPP), school-based management, and accountability systems in driving up the quality of education is scant. There is moderate evidence that *PPP* can be more cost-effective than state delivery of services, but no clear evidence of difference in student learning outcomes when schooling is delivered by private actors rather than state-employed educators (Barakat et al., 2014; Day Ashley et al., 2014; Morgan et al., 2013).

The data on *school-based management*/decentralization is also inconclusive (Bruns et al., 2010; Carr-Hill et al., 2016 Snilstveit et al., 2016). Often, local educational leaders simply do not have the capability (or inclination) to embrace and leverage their new autonomies and it can take 5–8 years to build that additional capacity.

The implementation of *accountability systems* like national school inspectorates and national student testing programs do seem to influence behavioral changes in schools. However, they often prime the *wrong* kinds of behaviors, as educators spend their days searching for ingenious ways of gaming the system (Eddy-Spicer et al., 2016; Bruns et al., 2010): a.k.a. the *law of unintended consequences*.

The data on *curriculum materials* suggests that enhanced textbooks are often not effective. They are either pitched at the wrong level (i.e., to the brightest students) or they are not sufficiently localized for children to understand the examples or analogies (Damon et al., 2019). Remediating this, however, is not insurmountable if local writing teams are involved in co-development and if student voice is collected through the piloting of prototype materials (something our teams have been directly involved in with Pacific Island nations). So, curriculum and teaching materials enhancement remains a promising line of inquiry – if implemented correctly.

The research on *ability grouping* of children is mixed. On the one hand this seems to support teachers' ability to differentiate to the needs of different learners because children of roughly the same level are grouped together, which enables the teacher to deliver a one-pitch lesson (Westbrook et al., 2013). On the other hand, this stunts teacher professional development and also allows for the *Pygmalion Effect*, i.e., the labelling of children as either high or low performers, which can result in a self-fulfilling prophecy of under/over-achievement. It may be more effective to create curricula based on levels of progress rather than based on years, as then there is more guidance for teachers to advance students when they may have many levels of students within any one year group.

Whilst *lengthening the school day* can be effective, what seems to be more important is how the current, as well as those additional, minutes and hours are used. Much of the 'time and motion' research highlights that significant portions of the school day are utterly unproductive (Lavy, 2015; Aronson et al., 1998). Ergo, shortening the school day might be just as beneficial if all that time is filled with high-quality instruction!

In many developing contexts, student–teacher ratios are extremely high – sometimes with as many as 100 students being serviced by a single teacher. The assumption is that this blights the quality of instruction. However, the research on *reducing class size* is also inconclusive. Katharine Conn's (2017) systematic review of impact in sub-Saharan Africa found very limited improvement in student learning outcomes where class sizes were reduced from an average of 82 to 44. Great teaching eats class size reduction for breakfast.

There is also a tension in the research on *contract teachers* and *pre-service teacher training*. Contract teachers are untrained (or less trained) teachers who also often earn half of what their civil service tenured colleagues take home. And yet these under-trained contract hires that are pushed straight into the classroom seem to generate far stronger outcomes than their more professionally trained counterparts (Asim et al., 2015; Kremer et al., 2013; Kremer & Holla, 2009; McEwan, 2015; Spink et al., 2018). This raises serious questions about the return-on-investment from pre-service teacher training. Although we should also note that even the research on contract teachers pulls in different directions. Where the teachers are managed by a non-governmental organization (NGO) or third-party organization, they have impact. When they are managed directly by the Ministry of Education, impact becomes (more) elusive.

If our goal is to encourage educators to attend school, enter their classrooms, and teach, then the research is more promising. The evidence suggests that teacher *performance incentives* can be effective, especially if they are implemented in parallel with *community-led monitoring* (Bruns et al., 2010; Ganimian & Murnane, 2016; Glewwe et al., 2014; Guerrero et al., 2012; Kremer et al., 2013; McEwan, 2015; Snilstveit et al., 2016). This can involve teachers receiving small daily cash bonuses per day of attendance at school (this is often contractually easier to implement than deducting pay per day of non-attendance).

These performance incentives are more effective in increasing teacher attendance when it is accompanied by monitoring and enforcement (otherwise it's just a backdoor pay rise). However, monitoring and enforcement is also more likely to have an impact when undertaken independently by members of the local community (e.g., through daily parental inspections) than when it's left to the discretion of the school leadership team and/or through the use of surveillance technology, such as in-classroom video cameras. However, none of the systematic reviews found convincing evidence that teacher performance incentives and/or community-led monitoring resulted in any significant increase in student achievement. These interventions work at getting teachers to school and into class, but they do not improve what they do inside the room with the door shut (Kremer et al., 2013).

So, what (*actually*) works to increase student learning outcomes?

Across the 57 systematic reviews only two categories of intervention seem to consistently generate impact:

1 **(Some) Education technology**. The research on computer-assisted instruction showed great promise in enhancing literacy and numeracy outcomes for children. These provide students with access to an education software platform that delivers a diagnostic assessment and then uses the outcomes to provide each student with a personalized pathway through digital learning objects (Evans & Popova, 2015; Global Education Evidence Advisory Panel, 2020; Kremer et al., 2013; Rodriguez-Segura, 2020; Spink et al., 2018). The theory of improvement is that the technology bypasses/remediates poor teaching by providing children with standardized high-quality digital instruction in their specific areas of need. We will come back to this in Chapter 9, where we complement the developing-world systematic reviews with the findings from a meta-analysis of more than 200 'developed' countries involving 14,000+ individual research studies on education technology.

It is also worth noting that whilst computer-assisted instruction (a.k.a. Intelligent Tutoring Systems) has strong evidence of impact, it is not the only type of education technology intervention. Several other types have shown remarkably poor return on investment in developing contexts, for example, giving children a personal laptop device (Rodriguez-Segura, 2020; Snilstveit et al., 2016). Here the provision of the device alone does not guarantee impact, as children can equally use it to search for cat videos as to do their homework!

2   **Enhancing teacher pedagogy/structured teaching materials**. Without exception, the developing country systematic reviews tell us that to improve student learning outcomes we need to improve the quality of teacher instruction. However, there are challenges:

- Many of the reviews are not explicit in what they mean by 'high-impact pedagogies' (e.g., Evans & Popova, 2015; Ganimian & Murnane, 2016; Snilstveit et al., 2016; Spink et al., 2018 – they seem to treat pedagogy as a suitcase term but do not explicitly look inside at the contents and catalogue the high/low impact strategies and the contexts within which each approach seems to work best).

- Of the reviews that do lift the lid and look inside (Westbrook et al., 2013; Orr et al., 2013; Nag et al., 2014), we are still left with more questions than answers about what works best. Whilst, yes, they identify broad pedagogic baskets, they do not explain the stage in the learning journey or age groups that each best supports – or how we can turn these approaches into *standard work/codified approaches* (Banerjee et al., 2013). Westbrook et al. (2013) also highlight that there is still limited developing world data that specifically measures the impact of each pedagogy on student learning outcomes.

- Beyond the provision of teacher incentives (which motivate attendance rather than performance), we are left in the dark about effective strategies for enhancing instructional capability in the classroom. Orr et al. (2013) highlight that cascade training programs are ineffective, and that coaching generates impact albeit at high cost and low scalability. But we still lack detail about the different approaches to in-service and pre-service teacher training, and the relative payoffs from each.

- Perhaps the only really good lead comes from Banerjee et al.'s (2013) review of the *Teaching at the right level* (TaRL) program that involves flexibly grouping children by ability (level) rather than age/grade, adjusting pedagogy and content to the needs of each group, and regularly conducting formative assessment. We will return to this in Chapter 8 as there are many parallels to other high-impact approaches, including *explicit direct instruction* and *response to intervention* – which are being used in high-income countries and have also been heavily evaluated.

Conclusion

In this chapter, we explored 57 systematic reviews of 3,912 gross/c. 2,500 unique developing country studies about what works best for access to and quality of education. Looking at these studies from the perspective of an education minister/ministry, program designer, or school leader, we must ask:

Armed with these studies alone, would we have enough breadth and depth of datapoints and evidence of impact to design new (and Lean-oriented) interventions with confidence?

Our frank answer is NO – unless our focus was on increasing:

- **Student access to education** – where there is much research looking explicitly at how each of the various design features and setting levels can be varied in the development and implementation of cash transfers.
- **Teacher time in school** – where, again, there is a good body of data on different incentive and monitoring mechanisms, the ways that these can be iterated, and the relative payoffs from each setting change.

However, if our goal was to increase the quality of learning and the preparedness of children for life and work, we are not at all convinced that these 57 systematic reviews give us any oven-ready answers. If we are in the shoes of local (Lean) education improvement designers, we would be left with quite a quandary. Our options would be to either:

1 **Focus on the process of improvement**, i.e., using thinking tools to build a hypothesis about what needs to be improved; and identify why the problem/opportunity exists and how it could be made better. Then carefully designing an activity/intervention and a parallel evaluation framework, and running an 'experiment' to see if our design works in practice.
2 **Get better data** – which either involves (quickly) widening and deepening the pool of developing country studies so that we have more confidence about the better bets, or expanding the net and looking at data from a wider range of contexts so that we have far more datapoints for comparison.

We employ both these approaches in the remainder of the Manifesto. In the next chapter we introduce the much wider and deeper META^X dataset of 'developed' world 'what works best' studies, where we have access to 1,700+ meta-analyses of 100,000+ studies, involving 300 million+ students. In Part 2 of the Manifesto, we (carefully) interpret the relevance of 856 of these metas for Lean education improvement in developing country contexts. Then, in Part 3, we outline a specific methodology called *Leaning to GOLD*, for identifying *compelling causes* that are worth progressing and for designing and iterating high probability, and Lean-oriented, interventions that generate impact.

Note

1 We calculate this from the 3,912 gross/c. 2,500 net studies identified across the 57 systematic reviews that we explore in this chapter.

The Visible Learning META^X stop-gap

In the previous chapter we surveyed the global literature on 'what works best' for enhancing education in low- and middle-income countries. Three things of note emerged from our foray through the literature:

1   **Its scantiness.** Despite more than six decades of education improvement initiatives across low- and middle-income countries, we were only able to locate 57 (relevant) systematic reviews, which brought together the findings from a relatively slender 3,912 gross/an estimated 2,500 unique high-quality research studies.

2   **A (reasonably) consistent picture on what works for increasing access to education.** Across these 57 systematic reviews, we found strong consensus about what gets children into school – including a small mountain of research on cash transfers, health and feeding programs, and providing information to parents and children on the returns from schooling. Many of the reviews and underlying studies also get into the detail of the various design features and setting levels that can be manipulated in the implementation of these access to education initiatives. For example, in the case of cash transfers, these included the size of payments; whether they are conditional; and the degree to which any conditionality is strictly enforced (see, for example, Baird et al., 2014; Kabeer et al., 2012; Saavedra & García, 2012).

   If we were tasked with ramping up access to education in a country where relatively few children attend school, we could glean a great deal about what is likely to be effective from the existing research. No wonder, as we outline in Chapter 1, enrollment rates for schooling have been skyrocketing.

3   **A murky picture on quality of education.** There are two dimensions to this murkiness:

   (i)   That 32% of countries are not (yet) systematically collecting data on their progress toward the 2030 Sustainable Development Goals for quality of primary education – rising to 68% for secondary schooling (World Bank, 2018). There

DOI: 10.4324/9781003166313-6   73 are many black holes where we have absolutely no idea whether schooling is translating into learning. Although, as we outlined in Chapter 1, in the low- and lower-middle-income contexts where we do have data, the picture is often not pretty. And whilst it is (a bit) prettier in high-income countries, even they have not really cracked the *hard* problem of quality education.

(ii) If we were tasked with improving the quality of teaching and learning within schools, and we went back to the 57 systematic reviews for inspiration, we would be left scratching our heads. We would be confronted with a shopping list of suggestions that had been moderately effective in some contexts, neither here nor there in others, and downright harmful in yet others. And when we vector in on the small number where there is a reasonable degree of convergence and confidence in the research, we would find nowhere near the same level of data on the effectiveness of different design features or setting levels on implementation.

Take, for example, pedagogy. Whilst many of the systematic reviews suggest this is a 'good bet' for increasing student learning, it remains a blob-like suitcase term. If we were ministry officials, we would be left asking '*which* particular pedagogies'; '*when* should they be used; and '*how* do we actually enable educators to unlock these new ways?'

However, we have a wider global dataset that we think *could* be up to the task of helping ministries, funders, and deliverers identify appropriate areas to conduct Lean experiments: *Visible Learning META^X* (https://www.visiblelearningmetax.com). It synthesizes the findings from 1,700+ meta-analyses of 100,000+ research studies, involving 300million+ students. The catch is that these data are predominantly from high- and (upper) middle-income contexts. We are basically suggesting that if we cannot find a sufficient trove of good quality data from developing contexts, then why not try – at least in the short-term – leveraging the large cache of research that we do have from the so-called 'developed' world and attempt to (ultra-cautiously) interpret and apply the insights to new contexts?

The META^X, which is publicly available and open access, provides effect size data on more than 300 different influences on student achievement, ranging from school governance and accountability structures, class size, school size, grade repetition, use of ICT, and effectiveness of different curriculum models and pedagogy. It is the latest iteration of a project that John embarked on in the 1980s and which culminated in the (2009) book *Visible Learning: A Synthesis of Over 800 Meta-Analyses Relating to Achievement*.

To our knowledge, the META^X is the single largest 'what works best' database for education in the world. It is currently in beta form and we continue to enhance the data structures to increase its value to policymakers, funders, and educators. In the rest of this chapter we:

1   explain where the data has come from;
2   outline the health warnings and limitations about its applicability. Despite this, we hope you will agree that a dataset of 1,700+ meta-analyses is not to be sniffed at; and

3   outline the specific elements/categories of the META^X datasets that we have selected for Lean exploration in Part 2 of the Manifesto.

Where has the META^X data come from? The growth of education research

The story of education research in high-income countries is (arguably) almost the exact opposite of that in low- and middle-income counterparts. At risk of descending into caricature, the (recent) pattern in low-income countries is of strong interest by donors in whether their funding is generating impact, and of sizable sums being invested in large-scale randomized controlled trials that are administered by international experts in monitoring and evaluation (Cameron et al., 2016; Leão & Eyal, 2019; Riddell & Niño-Zarazúa, 2016). Whereas the (long-term) pattern in high-income countries is of governments that fund shiny (and often ideologically-driven) education improvement initiatives but that have remarkably little interest in evaluating them (Slavin, 2002; OECD, 2019a), and of burgeoning teams of academics in (local) university faculties of education conducting lots of small-scale research studies that are subsequently published in peer reviewed journals. In other words, the research on education effectiveness in low-income countries is more likely to be larger scale and centralized but with fewer research outputs, whilst the research in high-income countries is more likely to be smaller scale, decentralized but with far, far greater output of publications.

The studies are then disseminated in various ways, such as in books, peer reviewed academic journals, PhD dissertations, and working papers. Across all these distribution channels there are likely more than 2 million education research outputs. A quick search on the Education Resources Information Center (ERIC) – which is the largest education database in the world – yields 1.8 million hits. A parallel search on JSTOR generates (an overlapping) 1.3 million journal articles, 200,000+ book chapters, and almost 15,000 research reports on "education research" – sprawling all the way back to 1775. Given the pressure for academic researchers to publish, these numbers are growing by the hour. But wading through this forest and finding a pattern that can help teachers, leaders, and policymakers improve education outcomes for learners is no small task. It is further confounded by the very different research methodologies that can often result in apples with oranges comparisons.

Effect size to the rescue

Many of the quantitative studies (thankfully) have sufficient data to calculate a statistic called *effect size*. Rather than merely telling you whether there is an association between two variables (i.e., correlation), effect size quantifies on a universal numerical scale how much (or little) the intervention yields (Baugh & Thompson, 2001; Coe, 2002). In other words, does it pack the punch of a kitten, an unarmed man, or a platoon of Navy Seals? And does it do so in a positive way that improves an outcome or as a wrecking ball that damages and reverses progress?

Effect size is relatively easy to calculate. All that is needed are two sets of averages – either pre-and post-intervention with a single group, or the means from an experimental and control group – and the standard deviation across these two groups. In education research, the most common way to calculate effect size is through the use of the Cohen's d (Cohen, 1988):

$$d = \frac{\bar{x}_2 - \bar{x}_1}{SD}$$

Imagine, for example, that you have invented a new numeracy program and you want to see whether it is more effective than another approach. To find out, you might administer a numeracy test to students before you introduce the new program, and then again once the program has been implemented, to measure their level of improvement. This is called pre- and post-testing. The effect size can then be calculated by taking the mean average of the students' pre-test scores ($\bar{x}_1$) and subtracting this from the mean average of the post-test scores ($\bar{x}_2$); then dividing this number by the standard deviation (which is a measure of the level of spread or dispersion amongst the test values). This would show the *within-group pre/post* difference.

It is also possible to design research studies that show *between-group* difference. This would involve, for example, one group of students being subjected to the new numeracy program (i.e., the experimental group) and another group maintaining the status quo (i.e., the control group). Here, the effect size is calculated by taking the mean average of the control group's post-test scores ($\bar{x}_1$) and subtracting this from the mean average of the experimental group's post-test scores ($\bar{x}_2$); then dividing this number by the (pooled) standard deviation. It is noted that these two methods (comparing groups and comparing over time) can lead to different interpretations, and in more recent versions of META^X we identify which method was used.

The output of the effect size calculation is a numerical value that shows the gain (or decline) in performance from the intervention as a proportion of a standard deviation. In other words, an effect size of $d = 0.35$ means that the second basket of scores was 35% of one standard deviation higher than the first set of scores. And a minus effect size score of say $d = -0.23$ would mean that students declined in performance by an average of 23% of a standard deviation after receiving the treatment.

The benefit of effect size is that it is a form of universal translator. Irrespective of the testing/assessment instrument used by a researcher, as long as there are sufficient data (i.e., the means of two different sets of scores and the standard deviation) we have all that is required to make the calculation. But once we have the effect size score, we then need to interpret whether the number represents the punch of that kitten or the firepower of those Navy Seals.

Jacob Cohen (1988) developed a scoring table to support that interpretative process, which was later revised and updated by Shlomo Sawilowsky (2009). In our own work we generally regard an effect size of less than $d = 0.20$ as being 'small'; and anything over $d = 0.60$ as being 'high' (Hattie, 2016) —we will explain why later in this chapter. But there are caveats. What is 'small' may be life-saving: the effect of taking aspirin to reduce myocardial infarction (a.k.a. heart attacks) is exceedingly small (Guirguis-Blake et al., 2015). But so is the cost and the risks, and it could be the difference between life and death in the right context. Further, some of the 'small' effects should worry us and demand that we investigate the possible reasons why they are so low, with the aim of enhancing them. When we work with schools, we assist them to build their own interpretations, often using their school average as a pivot point to then see who is making greater compared to lesser growth.

From the early 1980s, many quantitative education researchers in high- and upper-middle-income countries have included effect size scores in their research outputs. This means that we currently have access to effect size data from more than 100,000 studies, involving more than 300 million students (Visible Learning META^X, 2021) – or we have sufficient data (the means and standard deviation) to calculate them ourselves. But we need some way of consolidating all these data so that we can see the big picture or what works best overall; this is where meta-analysis comes in.

From effect size to meta-analysis

With 100,000 studies to hand, we need a way to synthesize the findings from disparate research projects that address similar research questions into an overarching meta-analysis or study of studies. Karl Pearson, who founded the world's first university statistics department at University College London, was also the first to combine observations from different clinical studies. In this case, comparing infection and mortality rates amongst soldiers who had been inoculated for typhoid and those that had not (Pearson, 1904). A little later, Ronald Fisher – the noted statistician and biologist – pioneered similar approaches to synthesize multiple studies in agriculture (Fisher, 1971 [1935]); and in a similar vein, Joseph Pratt et al. (1940) aggregated the (now discredited) findings from 60+ years of research into extra sensory perception (ESP). Their methods form the basis of what we now call meta-analysis.

It took until 1976 for Gene Glass to coin the actual term 'meta-analysis' to refer to "the statistical analysis of a large collection of analysis results from individual studies for the purpose of integrating the findings" (Glass, 1976, p. 3). Many wrongly suppose that meta-analysis was invented in medicine and then later applied to education, but this is a case of the reverse: Glass was an educational psychologist.

John was in the audience on the day of Glass's presidential speech to the American Educational Research Association when 'meta-analysis' was born; the excitement was palpable as many in the room recognized that the world of literature reviewing and data synthesis was about to change. Soon after, to better understand how to do meta-analysis, John and his colleague Brian Hansford completed one of the early meta-analyses, on the relationship between self-concept and learner achievement (Hansford & Hattie, 1982).

One of the reasons for the invention of meta-analysis was the perceived deficiencies of other approaches to systematic review (Borenstein et al., 2011; Evans & Popova, 2015). As we outlined in Chapter 3, narrative reviews are prone to unconscious bias, as researchers are (potentially) more likely to weight and interpret findings that agree with their pet-beliefs more favorably than those that do not. And vote counting, whilst an improvement, is still arguably a blunt instrument as it awards the same point score to big positive effect from a small pilot study as it does a large negative effect from a large study. You will remember that in Chapter 3, the vast majority of the 57 low- and lower-middle-income country systematic reviews we identified were narrative reviews (28) or vote count (9), with 20 being meta-analyses.

The first step in meta-analysis is to formulate the research question, such as whether school class size affects student achievement. The second and third steps are to search all the literature and then to select studies based on explicitly articulated inclusion criteria (Hedges & Olkin, 1985). These initial steps are not terribly different to the more traditional approach to (re)search that might be undertaken using a narrative review or vote count methodology. However, the selection is limited to studies that contain numerical data, that use experimental/quasi-experimental methods, and that can report effect size.

The true beauty of meta-analysis is that is uses statistics such as effect size to develop a pooled estimate of the size of the effect. Meta-analysis starts by identifying a research question, like, does pre-service teacher training increase student achievement (e.g., Whitford et al., 2018), or, are open-space learning environments more conducive to learning than traditional walled classrooms (e.g., Giaconia & Hedges, 1982)? The researcher then trawls ALL the available literature they can find on, say, pre-service teacher training, by identifying and reviewing every available peer reviewed article, conference paper, PhD thesis, and action research project summary.

With the literature gathered, the researcher then sifts and sorts it to identify the individual studies that are worthy of inclusion in the meta-analysis. The selection process involves the researcher making, explaining, and justifying a judgment call about the types of studies that will make it to the final cut, including:

- Are correlational and/or pre/post-test studies acceptable or only randomized control trials (RCTs) involving matched pairs?
- Does it matter whether the original research was published in a reputable peer reviewed journal?
- Can studies from any geography be included or only specific ones?

Once the researcher has decided which studies are to be included, the next step is to start packing them together. The process is technical and complex, but it basically involves taking and weighting the effect size data from each individual research study and averaging this to calculate a pooled average. Meta-analysis enables researchers to combine the findings together from hundreds of studies that asked the same or similar research questions. And as well as helping us to see underlying patterns across the various studies, it also helps us to vector in on major disagreements between the studies and to unpick the potential causes of those contradictory findings.

A most exciting option then opens up. Any overall effect size might be different for younger compared to older students, for students in single-sex compared to co-ed schools, and so on. These moderators become most important in the interpretations that can be made via the meta-analyses methods. The search for these moderators has long been a pursuit of educationalists, and that so few were found in the Visible Learning work does not mean we should not keep looking for them. That there were so few means that what works best for younger is similar to what works best for older students, and so on. Some find this hard to swallow as they have an intrinsic belief in 'individual differences'. But they are mixing messages – that there seem so few does not mean every child is not unique, of course they are. Rather, it means that what works best is less related to attributes of the students (and more to the quality of teaching by the educators). Again, this can be hard to hear as it can, sadly, lead to beating up teachers – saying they are doing a bad job. In contrast, the message is the opposite – what drives success for students is a function of educator expertise, and the evidence in the Global North is that there is so much evidence of excellence, of educators leading their students to have at least a year's worth of achievement growth for a year's input. We will come back to this message for the Global South in Part 2 of the Manifesto.

From meta-analysis to meta meta-analysis

With so many meta-analyses at hand on what works best to improve student learning outcomes, we need some way to build these into a super-synthesis, or what John calls meta meta-analysis, so that we can all make even better sense of the data. John's (2009) book, *Visible Learning: A Synthesis of Over 800 Meta-Analysis Relating to Achievement*, represented an early (but not the first attempt) at this type of mega-synthesis. What it does is double-distill the data. It does this, firstly, by building a map of all the research questions that the 1,700 (and growing) meta-analyses are attempting to answer. We illustrate this in Figures 4.1 and 4.2.

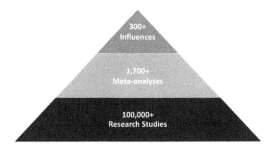

Figure 4.1 From Meta- to Meta Meta-Analysis

Student	Home	School
Factors relating to the background, beliefs, and physical influences on student achievement	Factors relating to the family resources, structure, and environment	Factors relating to the school type, composition, and leadership
Classroom	**Teacher**	**Curricular**
Factors relating to the classroom composition and classroom influences	Factors relating to teacher attributes, teacher–student interactions, and teacher education	Factors relating to various curriculum programs
Student Learning Strategies	**Teaching Strategies**	**Technology, School, and Out-of-School Strategies**
Factors relating to self-regulation, student perspectives, and learning strategies	Factors relating to learning intentions, success criteria, feedback, and teaching strategies	Factors relating to technology, school-wide methods, and out-of-school learning

Figure 4.2 The Visible Learning META^X Domains of Influence

(Adapted from Visible Learning META^X)

At its highest level, this map comprises the nine domains of influence outlined in Figure 4.2.

Under each domain it then, secondly, provides a list of *influences*. The reason that we do not use the terms 'intervention', 'program', or 'approach' is that whilst some of these influences are explicitly designed interventions (like giving children their own personal laptop or introducing charter schools), others are beyond the direct control of the school system (e.g., the social background of the learner, family composition, whether the child was adopted, etc.). Hence, we refer to them collectively as influences on student achievement. But, yes, some influences are also interventions.

Under, for example, the Student domain, a range of individual influences are catalogued, including student personality, self-efficacy, motivation, lack of sleep, gender, prior achievement, and their birth weight. And for each influence, the META^X lists in table form all the relevant meta-analyses and their respective reported effect sizes.

In Figure 4.3, we provide a snapshot of the META^X data on the relationship between birth weight and student outcomes. This is not the full dataset for this influence. The full table lists the effect size data for 10 meta-analyses of 226 studies, involving 61,508 study participants.

For each influence, the META^X reports both the individual effect sizes from each relevant meta-analysis and the mean average effect size across all the metas. Sticking with our birth weight example, across the 10 metas the lowest effect size reported is $d = 0.34$, the highest is $d = 0.75$, and the mean average is $d = 0.57$.

Author	Journal Title	Year	Variable	No. Studies	No. Students	No. Effects	Effect Size
Brydges, Landes, Reid, Campbell, French, & Anderson	Cognitive outcomes in children and adolescents born very preterm: a meta-analysis	2018	Full vs pre-term on intelligence, executive functioning & processing speed	44	10,734	44	0.61
Twilhaar, de Kieviet, Aarnoudse-Moens, van Elburg, & Oosterlaan	Cognitive outcome of children born extremely or very preterm since 1990s and associated risk factors: a meta-analysis and meta-regression	2018	Full vs pre-term birth weight	17	3,939	17	0.56

Figure 4.3 Snapshot of META^X Influence Data

(Visible Learning META^X, 2021)

This suggests that children that are born after a normal nine-month gestation period perform (on average) 57% of one standard deviation higher on cognitive and academic achievement tests than children born prematurely. Obviously, there is nothing that a school system can do to undo premature birth, but it can provide differentiated support to help *each* child gain at least a year's achievement growth for a year's input!

Meta and meta meta-analysis health warnings

Winston Churchill once said that "democracy is the worst form of Government except for all those other forms that have been tried from time to time" (Hansard, 1947, col. 208). The same goes for both meta and meta meta-analysis. Whilst they offer significant improvements on narrative review and vote counting methodologies, they do not offer us omniscience. As we have reported elsewhere (Hattie & Hamilton, 2020), some of the key META^X caveats include:

■ **The data aggregation process** – the effect sizes for each influence in the database are the combined mean average effect size of all meta-analyses conducted in the specific review area, e.g., there are currently eight meta-analyses on reducing class size and our database reports the mean average effect size of those eight, which is $d = 0.15$ (although the spread of effect sizes ranges from $d = -0.10$ to $+0.34$). Use of the data still requires careful interpretation to understand the different mediators and moderators that resulted in varied outcomes. This means that we should treat the data as a kind of heatmap. Within the 'red zones', if we zoom in close enough, we will still find bright pockets of 'green' and vice versa. Therefore, in addition to reporting the mean average effect size for each influence, in Part 2 of the Manifesto we also signpost instances of significant spread and encourage you to explore the base data within the META^X.

- **What best worked vs what works best** – as Frederick Nietzsche (2008 [1896]) proclaimed, there is no such thing as immaculate perception. The META^X can only tell us, on average, which approaches *have* been effective when implemented previously. There are no guarantees the same approaches will work again in similar (let alone different) contexts. The data gives us mere probabilities, i.e., a sense of the 'good' and 'bad' bets to enhance student learning. Therefore, in Part 3 of the Manifesto, we outline explicit processes for leveraging the data (alongside local practice-based research) to discover, design, deliver, and evaluate Lean-oriented improvement initiatives that are explicitly focused on addressing local priorities. This includes explicitly mapping the design features and setting levels that are more likely to generate impact, carefully evaluating and iterating to further enhance that impact, and/ or to agreeing to stop where the effect simply does not translate to the new context.

- **Sources of the underlying data** – we have taken a catch-all approach. For metas to be included they need to have effect size data (or allow for this to be derived from other included quantitative data), but beyond this we have no other restrictions. Some of the underlying data within the individual metas are from randomized controlled trials (RCTs), some from pre-/post-testing without controls, some used standardized assessment tools, and others use localized instruments. This has been criticized for aggregating data from studies with different methodologies (Snook et al., 2009). However, we have taken this approach because by narrowing down to the circa 200 'gold standard' RCTs we would have much less to say than we do by pooling and then very carefully interpreting the findings of a further 1,500 metas, which we would otherwise have to have discarded simply because they contained no control group.

- **High-income country bias** – many of the meta-analyses do not explicitly state the geographies that the original research studies were conducted in, and the ones that do often have a high- and upper-middle-income country bias. In some domains we are not convinced this really matters. As we have already argued, the biological structure of the human brain is no different in high- and low-income country contexts. So, the research that draws on insights from cognitive psychology related to attention, information processing, memory, retrieval, cognitive load, etc., and the linkages to appropriate pedagogies, is likely to be equally applicable everywhere. Where we need to take (far) more care is in the interpretation of the effectiveness of structural and policy drivers – where ecosystem dynamics mean that what's good for the goose may be highly poisonous to the gander.

Therefore, we do not advocate making policy, practice, and investment decisions purely by looking at the numbers within the META^X, but we think it could be an extremely good place to start (a better place would be a meta meta-analysis of low- and lower-middle-income contexts, but as we have already demonstrated, this dataset is still frustratingly small). And, of course, all these data need to be combined with practice-based insights within the local context, as stakeholders can only implement initiatives/activities that are locally feasible and that leverage locally latent capabilities.

Using the META^X to get Lean

In this preliminary application of the META^X data to Lean education improvement, we have limited our selection to 107 of the 314 influences on student achievement recorded within the database (which amounts to 856 metas of 50,719 studies, or 913 systematic reviews of 53,219 studies when the developing country research explored in Chapter 3 is also blended in). Our selection is primarily made up of:

- **High cost/resource intensive interventions that have relatively low effect sizes** (i.e., Jenga blocks that are potential candidates for removal, hollowing out, or at least not adding in the first place)
- **Low(er) cost/less resource intensive interventions that have above average effect sizes** (i.e., Jenga blocks that are *potentially* worth inserting).

We also acknowledge that our dataset does not yet publicly list the average/estimated USD purchasing power parity cost per student for each intervention – this is a work in progress. However, we urge you to review the full database of 314 influences to identify other Jenga blocks that are more relevant to the local contexts where you are/plan to be undertaking an education improvement activity at scale, and then to run the numbers yourself in your own local context.

Five categories of influence

In addition to selecting 107 of the most provocative influences on student outcomes, we have further segmented these into five baskets of categories of intervention, which we explore across Chapters 5–9. These are summarized in Figure 4.4.

Although the META^X contains strong data on the characteristics of learners and on family composition and health related variables, we have decided to exclude these from our preliminary Lean analysis because we are (even) less convinced that

Cat 1: Teacher Enhancement *(Chapter 5)*	Cat 2: Structural Enhancements *(Chapter 6)*	Cat 3: Accountability and Motivation Enhancements *(Chapter 7)*	Cat 4: Pedagogy and Integrated Program Enhancements *(Chapter 8)*	Cat 5: Education Technology *(Chapter 9)*
This is about how: teachers are selected, trained, and continuously supported to undertake their role — *Assumed mechanisms of improvement:* as a result of training, teachers have increased skill/ professional competence, which results in stronger student learning outcomes	*This is about how:* the school operates, e.g., its size, finances, building design, hours, and months of operation, etc. — *Assumed mechanisms of improvement:* better resources and facilities amplify the efforts of teachers and motivate students to attend and participate in learning	*This is about how:* school leadership and governance processes, school accountability drivers, parental choice, performance-related pay, and use of public–private partnerships impact on student achievement — *Assumed mechanisms of improvement:* accountability drivers and incentives encourage 'cruising' educators to up their game via a combination of 'carrot and stick'	*This is about how:* individual pedagogies can enhance student learning, and how these approaches can be combined into integrated programs for effective teaching and learning — *Assumed mechanisms of improvement:* utilization of evidence-based pedagogies for teaching and learning (which fully align with what is known about memory, attention, and transfer) will result in stronger learning outcomes for students	*This is about how:* teachers and students can leverage digital technologies to improve the quality of both teaching and learning — *Assumed mechanisms of improvement:* technology acts as a scaffold to teachers and enhances/ amplifies their use of effective pedagogical approaches AND/OR technology bypasses ineffective teaching and allows students to learn more effectively on their own

Figure 4.4 The Five Categories of Influence Explored in Part 2 of the Manifesto

the research for these areas transports effectively from high- and upper-middle-income countries to their low- and lower-middle-income counterparts.

In Part 2 of the Manifesto, we introduce the five categories of enhancement and the assumed theory of improvement. We then provide an overview of the relevant data from the META^X in tabular form. The first column of each table lists what we call the *influence* (on student achievement), i.e., the intervention type. The second column lists the number of meta-analyses that have been conducted; the third and

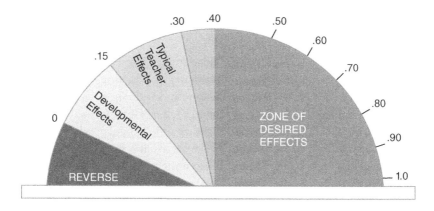

Figure 4.5 The Visible Learning Barometer of Influence

fourth aggregate the total number of studies that these meta-analyses involve and the number of participating students. The final column in the table aggregates the effect size from the various meta-analyses, i.e., the power of the intervention.

However, it is worth noting that across the 314 influences in the full Visible Learning META^X, the mean average effect size is $d = 0.40$. John has used this to build a barometer of influence (Hattie, 2009), which is illustrated in Figure 4.5.

This interprets the effect size data as follows:

- Any influence/intervention that achieves an **effect size greater than the mean average of $d = 0.40$** is more likely to be worth our collective time, effort, and investment (subject to the costs and anticipated ease/difficulty of implementation). We call this the Hinge Point.
- **Effect sizes of $d = 0.16$ to $d = 0.40$** are what we would expect the typical teacher to achieve without any additional support, training, or resources, i.e., just the execution of their day job and gradual improvement by osmosis.
- **Effect sizes of $d = 0.15$** or lower are what we would expect students to achieve through independent, peer, and community learning, i.e., the way that hunting and farming skills were passed down from generation to generation before the relatively recent invention of mass schooling. Learning still happens – just at a much slower rate.
- **Negative effect sizes** are influences or interventions that harm or reverse learning. The good news is that within the full META^X database, there are less than a handful that fall into this category and few (apart from teacher bullying and corporal punishment) relate to interactions between teachers and learners inside school. Most things that teachers do in classrooms 'sorta' work – it's 'just' that some of the interventions they (and their system leaders) could undertake have the potential to enhance student learning gains 4–5 times over, versus very marginal gains from some of the others.

Conclusion

In this chapter we explored how decentralized researchers in high- and upper-middle-income countries have been busily conducting small-scale evaluations of a wide range of education interventions and influences over the last six decades. We then explained how later pioneers, such as Gene Glass, devised meta-analysis as a mechanism to aggregate these studies into a bigger 'what works best' picture. Finally, we introduced the META^X, which harvests and aggregates the 1,700+ meta-analyses of 100,000+ studies into a meta-of-metas, or a super synthesis. We also outlined some of the key health warnings related to the use and interpretation of this data, the biggest of which is that much of the data comes from the Global North.

You have now reached the end of Part 1 of the Manifesto. In Part 2 we make a range of (deliberate) provocations about how the research findings from each of these META^X influences *could* be leveraged for Lean improvement. In other words, we explore the Jenga blocks that could potentially be entirely removed, hollowed out, more efficiently re-designed, or judiciously added, so that education systems can do more with the same (or less) resource. For clarity, we do not advocate blind adoption of any of these provocations, we merely present them as potential options. And this is why, in Part 3, we also then go on to outline clear processes to help discover, design, deliver, evaluate, iterate, and then scale Lean-oriented education improvement. However, in the immediate next chapter we start the whole process by exploring the implications of the META^X data for how we recruit, train, and support teachers.

Warm leads and blind alleys

5

Returns from teacher selection and training

Welcome to Part 2 of the Manifesto, which is the 'meat' of our endeavor. Over the next five chapters, we blend the insights from the 57 developing country systematic reviews with 856 META^X meta-analyses from high- and upper-middle-income countries. That's 53,219 studies worth of joy juice. In this first chapter, we ease you in gently. Not in terms of the level of provocation or controversy but in terms of length. We start out with a gentle jog, limbering you up for successively longer cantors, and then mini marathons as we progress. So, let's get on with our search for Jenga blocks for removal, hollowing out, not for adding, and (very) occasionally for fresh insertion.

To support children's learning, governments collectively employ and deploy a global army of 84 million teachers (World Bank EdStats, 2021a). They do this because policymakers, rightly, assume that school buildings alone are not enough. Once children are sitting in classrooms, they need support from teachers that understand how to deliver high-quality instruction, know the curriculum content, know how to evaluate their impact on student learning, and how to teach students strategies of learning. It also helps greatly if those teachers have the deep motivational dispositions to turn up each day to do their very best and the drive to continuously get better. So how those teachers are recruited, prepared, and nurtured is, therefore, extremely important. But can we do all this more efficiently?

Overview

In this chapter we explore the Lean implications of the META^X and wider data about *how teachers are selected, trained, and supported to undertake their role*. A potential theory of change, which we will go on to stress test, is as follows:

DOI: 10.4324/9781003166313-8

Theory of change

Assumptions:

1   Student success is influenced by a wider range of variables than simply their own individual characteristics and socio-economic status
2   In particular, the quality of teaching that students receive has a *significant* impact on accelerating their learning outcomes
3   The quality of initial training and ongoing professional development activities that teachers undertake also has a strong impact on their performance in the classroom (i.e., in unlocking point 2).

Therefore, invest in the following **inputs**:

1   High-quality **initial teacher education programs/licensure** that equip teachers with knowledge and skills in high-impact instructional approaches (i.e., unlocking effective pedagogy)
2   **Degree-level training and qualifications** in the subject(s) that educators will teach (i.e., developing expert-level curriculum content knowledge)
3   Ongoing pathways for **in-service teacher professional development** to enhance both pedagogy and subject matter knowledge.

The **outcome** of this investment will be:

1   Enhanced teaching quality
2   Enhanced learning outcomes for students.

One of the dirty secrets of our business of education is that individual characteristics – like intelligence and personal dispositions – are highly heritable; and that socio-economic status (SES), which is also strongly correlated with student achievement, is of course a function of our parents (Ciftci & Cin, 2017; Kim et al., 2019; Roth et al., 2015; Sirin, 2005). By our estimate, what learners bring to the table in terms of their biological endowments, prior achievement, their home environments, and the catalyst of SES accounts for approximately half, if not more, of the difference in learner outcomes (Hattie, 2009). We know that students do not leave poverty, poor attitudes to schooling, and inability to work with others at the school gate.

Thankfully, the research findings also strongly suggest that some teachers and some schools (even when they are endowed with the same resources) are *significantly* more effective than others in enhancing student learning outcomes. This holds true even when SES and other background variables of the students are filtered/controlled for. The assumption is that this is the result of greater skill in the planning, execution, and evaluation of the teaching and learning process; and this is largely supported by the evidence (Barber & Mourshed, 2007; Darling-Hammond & Youngs, 2002; Sanders & Rivers, 1996; Staiger & Rockoff, 2010; Stronge et al., 2007).

Therefore, in principle, we (warmly) accept assumptions 1 and 2, although we recognize that at the individual teacher-level, it is extremely difficult (but not impossible) to identify which educators are more effective or what it is about their specific tradecraft that consistently results in enhanced outcomes. By our estimates, educators provide approximately one-quarter to one-third of the inputs that contribute to student learning outcomes, and this is the only piece of the pie that education systems have the potential for any direct control over (Hattie, 2003). So, onto the remainder of the theory of change – which is the 'meat' of this chapter.

Recognizing that teachers make the difference, many education systems make a considerable investment in enhancing the skills of educators. This includes:

- **Dimension 1: Mandatory initial teacher training programs** – these generally focus on pedagogy and culminate in a professional license to practice. In many jurisdictions, practicing without this license is a serious regulatory breach.
- **Dimension 2: Recruitment of educators that have a degree-level qualification in the subject that they teach** – e.g., a math teacher has at least a mathematics bachelor's degree or equivalent; and in some countries, like Finland, the requirement that teachers have a master's degree before stepping into the classroom.
- **Dimension 3: Ongoing in-service professional development programs** – to build on and enhance skills developed during the pre-service training. Many systems mandate a certain number of hours of professional development per annum, which must be officially logged to retain a teaching license.

Global data on the percentage of teachers in each country that have received pre-service pedagogical training and licensure are, however, patchy. Only around 75 countries report these statistics (World Bank Edstats, 2021c), and the picture that emerges for low- and lower-middle-income countries is not pretty. In Suriname, Madagascar, South Sudan, Guinea-Bissau, and Angola, for example, fewer than 50% of new entrants to primary teaching have undertaken pre-service teacher pedagogical training. For a further 20 sub-Saharan African, Caribbean, and Pacific Island nations the figures are slightly better but still underwhelming, with less than 65% of primary teachers walking into their classrooms on their first day with pre-service training.

The picture becomes more depressing when we recognize that the reported data is not against an international minimum standard but merely against whether new teachers in country X or Y have received training that complies with their country-specific licensing requirements. The quantity and quality of training required to meet national teacher licensing requirements can vary significantly across countries, from several years to a few weeks.

The second dimension is whether teachers have an advanced qualification in the subject they teach. If they teach (say) science, do they hold a relevant degree or diploma that equips them with expert content knowledge? Yet again, the global data is sparse and reports against country-level academic qualification standards rather than any internationally agreed thresholds. However, in Cameroon, Ghana, Ethiopia, Sierra Leone, Nauru, Palestine, and Belize, for example, we find that fewer than 60% of teachers have an academic qualification in the subject that they teach (World Bank EdStats, 2021c).

Whilst most countries that report either high or low percentages on one of these dimensions also tend to have correspondingly similar levels for the other (i.e., high percentage of teachers licensed PLUS high percentage with academic qualification in the subject that they teach – or vice versa), there are other countries like Madagascar, Niger, and Serbia that do extremely well on one axis (an advanced qualification in the relevant curriculum area) and equally badly on the other (pedagogical training).

Data on the third dimension – ongoing professional development programs for teachers – is even more challenging to locate in a globally standardized manner. The most recent statistics come from the OECD Teaching and Learning International Survey 2018 (OECD, 2020b). This only covers high- and upper-middle-income countries. Here, 90% of surveyed teachers reported participating in at least one professional development activity in the preceding year. However, even across these prosperous nations, 45% of teachers indicate that professional development opportunities are too expensive and 32% state that there is a lack of employer support/funding (OECD, 2019b).

From our own work in the Pacific Islands, we know anecdotally of several nations (including Kiribati and the Solomon Islands) where in-service professional development for teachers has only been systematically activated in recent years, and where it still only amounts to a few workshops or radio broadcasts. We are also aware of other contexts in South East Asia where teachers are sometimes expected to fund their own travel and subsistence to participate in workshops during their weekends, and in sub-Saharan Africa where in-service training is often made conspicuous by its absence.

Therefore, it rather looks as though we might need to throw more money, more people, and more time at the preparedness of teachers – particularly in those countries where few teachers are licensed/qualified. This would not, however, be terribly Lean; so, we need to explore the META^X with great care to double confirm that investing in these three dimensions results in significantly enhanced student learning outcomes.

What does the META^X reveal?

In Figure 5.1, we present relevant data from 51 meta-analyses of 2,240 studies within the META^X. The (good) counterintuitive news is that these data do not

Influence	No. of Metas	No. of Studies	No. of Effects	Aggregate Effect Size d.=
Pre-service initial teacher education programs	4	93	509	0.10
Teacher expert subject matter knowledge	4	136	470	0.19
Teacher personality	5	72	251	0.24
Teacher verbal ability	1	21	58	0.22
In-service teacher professional devel-opment programs	23	1,255	3,205	0.37
Teacher coaching programs	3	88	149	0.18
Whole school improvement programs	4	88	770	0.28
Micro-teaching/ video lesson review	4	402	439	0.88
Collective teacher efficacy	3	85	85	1.36
Totals	**51**	**2,240**	**5,963**	**N/A**

Figure 5.1 Teacher Enhancement Influences

(Visible Learning META^X, 2021)

strongly support all the assumptions or mechanisms outlined in points 3–5 of the theory of change we introduced at the very start of this chapter. Instead, they point to several Jenga blocks that can be hollowed out or potentially removed, or at least not added in, as well as to one that very much should be inserted and even fortified.

The key column in the table above is the aggregate effect size, which is reported in the right-hand column. You will remember from Chapter 4 that effect size is a statistical measure of power, i.e., whether an intervention packs the punch of a mouse, of you or us, or of Godzilla. You will also remember that across all the META^X influences the mean average effect size was $d = 0.40$. So, by implication, anything lower than this is "below average".

In the sub-sections that follow, we unpack what each of these META^X findings mean and how they might help us to do more with the same or less.

Pre-service initial teacher education programs

We have identified four meta-analyses that systematically review the impact of initial teacher education and licensing on student learning outcomes (Kelley & Camilli, 2007; Qu & Becker, 2003; Sparks, 2005; Whitford et al., 2018). These collate the findings from 93 individual studies – involving more than 100,000 study participants (trainee and newly qualified teachers). The mean average effect size across these four meta-studies is $d = 0.10$, which is exceedingly low. We also note that there is very little spread, with the upper and lower effect sizes being $d = 0.15$ and $d = 0.03$ respectively.

The first thing we should therefore notice is the poverty of evidence for the impact of pre-service initial teacher training – despite the protestations and many claims by the vested interests that they have so much evidence for its impact. Indeed, the consistent (and disheartening) finding is that when we compare teachers who are thrust into the classroom with close to zero pre-service training with those that have had a comprehensive package of support (usually culminating in either a Bachelor of Education qualification or a postgraduate certificate in education), there is scant difference in student outcomes on standardized assessments between either category of teacher at the end of their first year on the job. There is also no trendline suggesting that those that receive initial teacher training become more effective than their untrained colleagues in years 2–5, either.

Added to this, when we track expertise as a teacher, most learn half of their knowledge and skills in the first year, half as much again in the second, and it often plateaus after this (see, for example Papay & Kraft, 2015; Rice, 2013). Not much can be attributed to the pre-training, and heaven help those who do not learn in the first two years of actual teaching. Perhaps it is, thus, not surprising that some studies have suggested that IQ (or at least working memory) is one of the better predictors of initial success in teaching in the first few years on the job – those teachers who can adeptly adjust to the environment of the first two years, who know how to seek help and skill building, and who can cope with the busy, buzzy, and sometimes fuzzy first years, seem to perform best (Hanushek, 1971; Slater et al., 2012; Wiliam, 2014). For balance, we should note that these IQ and working memory-related findings are not cast iron (see, for example, Bardach & Klassen, 2020; Harris & Sass, 2011), although the literature on IQ and workplace performance is *reasonably* robust in the wider economy (Bertua et al., 2005; Ones et al., 2012; Schmidt, 2015).

Astute readers will of course notice that these META[X] research findings come from high-income countries. However, there is also a growing body of research from low-income contexts on deployment of contract teachers (also known as para-teachers) that also seems to support our tentative conclusions (see Asim et al., 2015; Kingdon et al., 2013; Kremer et al., 2013; Kremer & Holla, 2009; McEwan, 2015). This research, which explores the utilization of minimally qualified teachers in Africa, South Asia, and Latin America, finds that contract teachers can generate at least the same (and often better) student learning outcomes than their tenured counterparts, who had undergone more lengthy pre-service pedagogical training.

Bizarrely, one of the key variables that determined (or at least predicted) whether contract teachers were more likely to be successful was the nature of their employment contract. The more precarious their contractual terms, the more effort they seemed to put into their teaching – even where they were paid as much as two-thirds *less* than regular teachers. In fact, their level of personal motivation seemed to be a more significant driver of student learning than whether they had received pre-service training. However, where contract teachers' employment terms were regularized and they became tenured, their impact on student learning often subsequently declined (Bold et al., 2018).

The research on contract/para-teachers highlights the importance of account-ability and motivational drivers that we will return to in Chapter 7. It also under-scores the (arguably) more limited importance of pre-service initial teacher training in unlocking student learning: research from both high- and low-income coun-tries finds remarkably limited return on investment from training (and licensing) teachers in pedagogy *before* they enter the classroom.

In high-income country contexts, where there is arguably a strong vested inter-est in keeping institutes of education open, the response to this research is often to say that we need to double-down and identify ways of enhancing initial teacher training so that it is far more effective. But in low-income country contexts, and particularly with our Lean lens, we are tempted to speak sacrilege: maybe elongated initial teacher training is a frivolous expense with limited evidence of payback?

We would not necessarily advocate dismantling the whole enterprise, but it might be possible (or even desirable?) to reduce the quantity of initial pre-service training down to a handful of weeks and then spend more time and resources on training in situ. This is the approach that the *Teach for All* network adopts, with an initial 5-week+ institute followed by support from peripatetic coaches once program participants are active in classrooms. And it is a model that is generally rolled out across *Teach for All*'s high-, middle- and low-income country network partners. There is also tentative evidence suggesting that *Teach for All* teachers can generate better learning outcomes in reading and mathematics than their tradi-tionally trained colleagues (Clark et al., 2017), although this data comes from the United States and from entrants to the teaching profession from Ivy League uni-versities with high GPAs: it may, therefore, be that only extremely clever initiates to teaching can master the ropes this quickly. It may also be the case that the *Teach for All* selection processes – which vector in on high-performing graduates with high verbal-linguistic abilities – are a sort of proxy working memory/IQ-cum-psychometric test.

It *might*, therefore, also be feasible to administer cost-effective standardized psy-chometric, working memory, and/or IQ tests in low-income contexts – which could be a reasonable proxy for some of the characteristics that *Teach for All* screens for. Although as Bardach and Klassen (2020) highlight, the global dataset of teacher working memory and IQ test results is small and most of the inferences on the strong relationship between working memory, IQ, and job performance come from studies conducted outside teaching. So, we must tread with GREAT care.

Teachers having advanced subject matter knowledge (e.g., degree-level qualifications)

The META[X] research on the benefits of teachers having university degree-level subject matter knowledge is almost as equally uninspiring as that for pre-service initial teacher training. The four meta-analyses, pooling the findings from 136 studies, generate a cumulative effect size of $d = 0.19$ (Ahn & Choi, 2004; Druva & Anderson, 1983; Kelley & Camilli, 2007; Manning et al., 2017). There is, however, more spread in the individual effect sizes for these metas than there was for initial teacher training, with the highest and lowest being $d = 0.41$ and $d = 0.06$ respectively. More recent meta-analyses show similar results for special education and early childhood: having specialized/advanced knowledge does not seem to make much difference to the learning of students.

What the research tentatively suggests is that there is no strong value added from having a degree-level qualification in a subject that you teach at school level. Indeed, the more expert you are the more likely that you will suffer from the *Expert Blind Spot Effect* (a.k.a. 'the curse of knowledge'). When you have deep knowledge of a subject you tend to forget how difficult it was to acquire initial understanding or what the steps were that you undertook to develop this knowledge in the first place (Nathan & Petrosino, 2003).

It may even be the case that students, who have recently stumbled and then successfully traversed the same learning episode, might be more effective activators of learning in their peers than credentialled subject matter experts. This is because those learners still vividly remember the explicit steps and strategies that they used to generate their recent successes. For example, Graham Nuttall's (2007) research suggested that significant gains in student literacy could be achieved in contexts where the tutor's subject matter knowledge was only 6 months ahead of those they were tutoring. The tutor arguably unlocks these gains because they are teaching something that they have only just mastered themselves!

Educators do not, therefore, need to be trained scientists or mathematicians – they may merely need the exact same subject knowledge as is required by their oldest learners. *Instead, their pedagogical content knowledge is far more important than expert subject knowledge.* By this we mean their understanding of the areas where students commonly stumble when learning school-level subject content, and the most suitable approaches for helping learners to overcome these hurdles.

We are finding that if teachers teach in a way where they merely need to be one page ahead of the students, if they dominate the class with their talk, if they ask lots of content/fact-based questions, then there seems little reason to have the deeper knowledge and understanding. But if there is a more balanced proportion of surface facts and content along with deeper relational understanding, if there is greater quantity of student talk and questions, then maybe greater teacher content knowledge is not only worthwhile but necessary. So, initially subject matter knowledge may not be so critical, but as students move to more deeper understandings then there may be a need to enhance the levels of content knowledge.

However, through our Lean lens, we *might* argue that there is limited value in recruiting trained scientists, mathematicians, etc. into education and/or paying a premium to attract them or to fund their initial studies. It *might* even be argued that teachers require no university-level training at all.[1] In fact, prior to the 1970s, remarkably few educators in high-income countries held degree-level qualifications (Pritchett, 2013). And when we explore international comparative data on student achievement from the 1970s onwards (see Altinok et al., 2018 dataset), we can see no remarkable improvement in student learning outcomes after high-income nations implemented the requirement for degree-level subject matter knowledge. Across many of the high-income nations in this dataset, student learning outcomes had arguably already near-peaked by 1970, with only a modest further uplift thereafter. So, there is an (extremely controversial) argument that the investment in degree-level subject knowledge for teachers generates more returns for (their) social and professional status than for improved student learning outcomes. Although there is a stronger case that teachers in upper-secondary/high school would benefit from more advanced subject knowledge training, e.g., something equivalent to a 1-year undergraduate diploma.

Therefore, in developing country contexts, if budgets are constrained, teachers having degrees (or even diplomas) in the subject they teach is perhaps one of the Jenga blocks that could be removed, hollowed out, or not added in the first place. Generalist teachers would, however, strongly benefit from ongoing support to enhance their pedagogical content knowledge, either through subject specialist support networks or simply by ensuring the curriculum materials are sufficiently scaffolded (or even scripted) to provide generalist educators with the supports they need. They can be offered this enhanced learning while on the job.

Teacher dispositions

One area that generates moderately higher effect sizes than either pre-service initial teacher training programs or teacher subject knowledge is the personal characteristics/dispositions of those that are selected to enter the teaching profession in the first place.

Here, the research suggests that teachers' personality and dispositions have *some* impact on student learning outcomes. Some of the meta-analyses explicitly explore the relationship between teacher self-efficacy – which is an educator's level of confidence in being able to execute their role effectively and generate impact – and student academic achievement (e.g., Kim & Seo, 2018).

Other meta-analyses within the basket of teacher dispositions may be of more relevance. These explore the relationship between educators' Big 5 personality profiles (i.e., their level of openness, conscientiousness, extroversion, agreeableness, and neuroticism on standardized personality questionnaires) and student learning outcomes. The findings suggest that educators' personality profiles are modestly but significantly associated with both student learning outcomes and independent evaluations of their teaching performance. The highest (but still quite low correlates) include personal confidence in oneself as a teacher, demonstrating enthusiasm for the job, and those who prefer a more structured and decided lifestyle vs a more flexible and adaptable lifestyle.

The research suggests that educators with certain personality profiles are likely to be more effective and that others are more likely to be candidates for burnout (Klassen & Tze, 2014). There are similar findings for educators' verbal-linguistic abilities (Abrami et al., 1982; Aloe & Becker, 2009). Better talkers and better listeners are better teachers. We also see similar findings for teachers that score higher on empathy constructs in psychometric surveys. The proficiency to stand in the shoes of others and appreciate their world view and ways of thinking can make a great teacher. Where students feel their teachers genuinely care about them, and understand and listen to them and their progress, positive things happen.

From a Lean perspective there are interesting applications. The cost of administering psychometrics to potential entrants to the teaching profession is relatively low. These assessments could potentially be used to screen for applicants with higher empathy, stronger verbal-linguistic ability, and the 'right' Big 5 personality profiles to be effective. They *might* also be used to screen for working memory and/or IQ, as we previously suggested. There are, of course, potential side effects. Those hellbent on entering the teaching profession might bone up on what the tests measure, how they are scored, and what multiple choice options they should be ticking to guarantee the 'right' outcome.[2] This highlights the law of unintended consequences and the need to think five or six steps ahead to anticipate the cycle of measures and countermeasures and whether, after implementing these, the "cheap, simple, and effective" solution remains so. However, at minimum, these constructs need to be part of screening in the profession, to maximize the chance of identifying the highest impact teachers (at least in the first few years on the job).

In-service teacher professional development programs

We noted in the sub-section on initial teacher training the importance of teacher learning on and from the job in the first few years, and that continued improvements are not so steep after this initial burst of learning. The research on in-service professional development begins to offer us more viable pathways for impact than what is likely to be achieved from either investing in pre-service training or enhancing teachers' subject matter knowledge to advanced/degree-level.

We know that teachers do most of their professional learning on the job, often through trial and error. The research also tells us that this principally happens during the first three years – after which educators often enter what psychologists call arrested development (yes, an unfortunate term). The *right* kinds of professional development and collaboration opportunities can reverse this arrest.

The 23 meta-analyses of teacher professional development, involving 1,255 research studies and more than 2 million study participants, generate an aggregated effect size of $d = 0.37$ (e.g., Curlette et al., 2014; Haystead, 2009; Markussen-Brown et al., 2017; Salinas, 2010; Timperley et al., 2007; Yoon et al., 2008). Yes, it is worth having, however, the headline research hides considerable heterogeneity within the findings:

- Professional development for educators in the form of **conferences and workshops** that introduce tips, tricks, and theories has (almost) zero impact. The research suggests that educators remember less than 10% of what they have been trained in on these workshop days, and put almost none of this into practice – at least not in the way intended (Joyce & Showers, 2002).
- **Cascade programs**, where a small group of educators receive initial training and are then expected to replicate this experience with colleagues locally, also show similarly low levels of impact. It ends up being a photocopy of a photocopy (Elmore, 1996).
- However, **carefully designed professional development** that is spaced over time and that involves theory, demonstration, modelling, practice, collaborative review, exploration of how the new approach aligns within or contradicts existing teacher beliefs, and expert in-school coaching are more likely to generate effect sizes above the $d = 0.40$ hinge point (Timperley et al., 2007). It is the focus on how the teachers are thinking and evaluating the impact of their teaching, as they teach, that needs development much more than providing resources, tips, or tricks. Where this training is combined with highly scaffolded or even scripted curriculum materials, we would expect even higher impact in developing country contexts.

There are other interesting findings buried within these meta-analyses on in-service teacher professional development:

- **Teacher coaching programs** generate a relatively modest effect size of $d = 0.18$ but with spread/divergence across the three metas (Batts, 2010; Dietrichson et al., 2017; Kraft et al., 2018). Our interpretation of this is NOT that coaching is ineffective. Instead, these findings demonstrate the importance of deploying skilled and trained coaches rather than individuals that have been provided with a few days of workshops before being let loose. The challenge with coaching is how difficult it is to scale fast. Coaching also seems to be more effective when it is deployed as part of a wider teacher professional development initiative that involves other modalities of support closest to the teachers thinking and performance in the class, than as a standalone intervention.
- **Whole school professional development programs** – including professional learning communities – also show the potential for impact (Lomos et al., 2011). These are more likely to be successful when they focus on *compelling*

causes that are relevant to the school; are multi-component (e.g., engage with district leaders, school leaders, educators, parents, students, etc.); are multi-year; and where they contain rigorous formative evaluation processes, which are used by all parties to iteratively ask, "how has it gone and where to next?"

- **Videoing lessons (a.k.a. microteaching)** and undertaking systematic reviews with school-based colleagues has very strong potential to improve teaching and enhance student learning outcomes, with an aggregate effect size $d = 0.88$ (see, for example, Metcalf, 1993; Yeany & Padilla, 1986). However, this requires access to technology – which is arguably easier now, even in contexts like sub-Saharan Africa where a growing base of mobile phone users have a device equipped with video recording technology (GSMA, 2020). It may be more feasible to think how using such mobile technologies may lead to better training, coaching, and professional learning, as well as enabling communities of teachers across sites to work together to improve their impact on students. Beyond the technology, educators require access to suitable rubrics to facilitate collaborative lesson review and support/training to build the trust to share their classroom videos with one another. We return to the topic of videoing lessons in Chapter 9.

Collective teacher efficacy

Finally, there is extremely interesting research emerging on a psychological construct called Collective teacher efficacy (Çoğaltay & Karadağ, 2017; Donohoo, 2016; Eells, 2011). This refers to the presence (or absence) of a *collective belief* amongst a group of educators that (a) their combined efforts have the biggest impact on student learning and (b) that they have the skills and access to appropriate evaluative enquiry processes to collaboratively enhance their outcomes.

The aggregated data for collective teacher efficacy show an effect size of $d = 1.36$, which is extremely high. In other words, when teachers report that they *believe* their collective efforts are the prime driver of student achievement, they are. However, when teachers deficit theorize and explain (away) differences in student learning as a consequence of student motivation, IQ, or socio-economic status – rather than it being about the quality of the teaching – student achievement tends to be far lower. According to Donohoo (2016), some of the enabling conditions for the emergence of collective teacher efficacy include:

- **Advanced teacher influence** – the degree to which they can collectively participate in and influence school decision-making
- **Goal consensus** – the degree to which teachers share the same goals about what needs to be improved
- **Teacher collaboration** – including having knowledge of the professional practices of their colleagues and being able to discuss this and learn from one another
- **Responsive leadership** – that reinforces the message that teachers are key change agents and that supports educators' collective focus on collaborative improvement in teaching and learning.

All of this relates to teacher beliefs and motivations, which we will return to in Chapter 7. However, much more work needs to be done to unpick whether reverse causality is at play (i.e., teachers that work in a good school with bright learners might become more optimistic about their collective agency and its impact on learning). We also need to be careful that collective efficacy does not become the next fad, as it is more than feeling good together, and needs a laser focus on the impact of all the teachers in a school on the learning lives of students. We have seen sessions on collective efficacy in curriculum and in managing school bus timetables, and these will dramatically dilute the effect. We also need to learn much more about the explicit strategies that enhance collective teacher efficacy, fed with the evidence of impact. This is an emerging but very exciting research area; we come back to it in Chapter 7.

Conclusion

In this chapter we explored the global research on how we best select, train, and support teachers to undertake their role. From a Lean perspective, where our focus is on identifying which pieces of the Jenga Tower can be removed, hollowed out, or not inserted in the first place, we might draw the following tentative conclusions (with attendant health warnings) from the META^X and wider research:

Tentative Lean Conclusions	Health Warnings/Side Effects
• Initial teacher training programs could *possibly* be reduced in length and intensity without serious implications for student learning outcomes • These shorter programs could focus on pedagogic content knowledge and could likely be undertaken on the job	• May reduce the status of the teaching profession and reduce interest from high-quality applicants • May result in the decimation of university faculties of education. Implementers would therefore need to explore carefully how to refocus the energies and expertise of universities into more appropriate in-service professional development for teachers already in the classroom, and school-based action research partnerships
• Teachers do not *necessarily* require deep subject matter expertise in the curriculum areas they teach, nor a graduate-level qualification. Instead, pedagogic content knowledge is far more important – and this can be learnt on the job	• May result in significantly reduced student demand for higher education as teaching would no longer provide an alternative safe route of employment for those that cannot obtain employment in industry • Education systems may need to be more concerned with supporting teachers to develop deeper subject matter knowledge after the first few years of becoming a teacher • May not be as viable for upper secondary/high school, where teachers still need more advanced subject matter knowledge to be effective in their role

(Continued)

Tentative Lean Conclusions	Health Warnings/Side Effects
• Psychometric tools, working memory, and/ or IQ testing *might* be cheap, useful, and valid tools for the initial screening of suitable candidates for the teaching profession	• Candidates for entry to teaching may look for ways to (successfully) game the assessments • The use of IQ tests for candidate selection is illegal in some country contexts – mainly because it has had some dirty history of mis-use. And whilst there is data on the correlation between IQ and job performance outside the education sector, the dataset within the sector is currently weak • The 'optimal' personality characteristics of educa-tors may vary significantly across cultures. Most of the META[X] data comes from Western contexts that are, for example, more individualistic and have lower power-distance relationships; and there are cross-cultural differences in personality construct validity
• Integrated professional development programs for in-service teachers (which combine spaced-learning, presentation of theory, modelling, practice, coaching, and peer collaboration, e.g., through professional learning communities) are likely to significantly enhance teacher per-formance and student learning outcomes	• This type of professional development is more expensive than (ineffective) workshops and con-ferences, and takes a longer time to scale. How-ever, it is possible that the budget savings from initial teacher training could be re-appropriated for in-service professional development

Given the health warnings, our message is start small and evaluate carefully before embarking on system-wide implementation that is subsequently difficult to reverse. And a good Jenga block to add is high-quality in-service teacher pro-fessional development that unlocks expertise in the high-impact instructional approaches we will discuss in Chapter 8.

Notes

1 Some care is needed here – the advantage of having an experienced scientist retrain as a teacher is that they bring the 'world of work' into the classroom, they can make the direct link to real life explicit, and they give the students access to the cultural capital to gain a placement in the world of work if the teacher identifies them as a suitable candidate. This is provided they teach in a way that values deeper as well as content-based knowledge, and that they actively promote links to students' past experiences and highlight the value to real life contexts. There is also some debate about the value of advanced subject knowledge in upper-secondary/high school

contexts. This is an example of a "hollowed out Jenga block" possibly losing its strength and integrity after being hollowed out, but it is still worthy of investigation and piloting given the high costs of advanced subject matter training.

2 However, in our national work on teacher selection in England and Australia we utilize online psychometric tools that are extremely difficult to game or to prepare for, although we recognize that there are both cross-cultural differences in personality construct validity and challenges with utilization of online testing in many developing contexts.

Returns from structural enhancements to school systems

In Chapter 5, we explored the crucial role of teachers in the learning lives of children. We also made some (tentative) Lean recommendations about how we can select educators more effectively and train them more efficiently to unleash success at reduced cost.

However, unlike the Roman or Medieval days, contemporary teachers tend not to be employed individually by great houses to provide one-on-one tuition to heirs and spares. Instead, governments have opted to raise funds to recruit educators *en masse* and to deploy them within schools constructed and operated by the state. This involves ministries and departments of education making resourcing or structural decisions, including how much funding to allocate; the size, shape, and location of school buildings; class size; the length of the school day and year; and whether students that are unsuccessful should repeat the whole year over again. Each of these structural decisions represents a trade-off between financial costs on the one hand and expected returns to student access and learning on the other.

Overview

Teachers are agents that operate within structures and the assumption is that the structures themselves can have enabling or disabling features. In this chapter, we explore the Lean implications of the META^X and wider data about these structural dimensions. We are especially interested in identifying Jenga blocks for hollowing out, removing, or just not adding, where we can show that they are overengineered and have limited impact on improving student learning.

As with the previous chapter, we start by outlining a (potential) theory of improvement and then move on to consider this in the light of the META^X data, although the first two assumptions in this theory of change have been greyed out

DOI: 10.4324/9781003166313-9

because we have already discussed them (and found them to be largely true) in Chapter 5.

Theory of change

Assumptions:

1 Student success is influenced by a wider range of variables than simply their own individual characteristics and socio-economic status
2 In particular, the quality of teaching that students receive has a *significant* impact on accelerating their learning outcomes
3 Increased investment in structural features, like increased per-pupil funding, school buildings, and reducing the ratio of teachers to students, will increase the quality of both teaching and learning because each teacher's effort will be amplified by the supporting structures they operate within.

Therefore, invest in the following structural **inputs**:

1 Increased per-pupil funding
2 Better quality school buildings
3 Smaller schools
4 Smaller class sizes
5 Same-age classes
6 Longer school years and school days
7 Allowing unsuccessful students to repeat the school year.

The **outcome** of this investment will be:

1 Increased quality of teaching
2 Enhanced learning outcomes for students.

In Figure 6.1, we present relevant data from the Visible Learning META^X.

As per Chapter 5, the key column in the table above is the aggregate effect size –reported in the right-hand column. You will remember from our previous discussion that effect size is a statistical measure of power, and that across all the META^X influences the mean average effect size was $d = 0.40$. So, by implication, anything lower than this is "below average".

Influence	No. of Metas	No. of Studies	No. of Effects	Aggregate Effect Size $d =$
School finance	6	228	1,048	**0.21**
Building quality	1	594	594	**0.24**
School size	1	21	120	**0.43**
Single sex schools	1	184	114	**0.08**
Consolidation/merging schools	1	12	12	**0.00**
Open vs traditional classrooms	4	315	333	**0.01**
Multi-grade/age classrooms	3	94	72	**0.04**
Tracking/streaming	13	459	1,328	**0.12**
De-tracking	1	15	22	**0.09**
Grade repetition	9	255	3,127	**−0.32**
Reducing class size	8	176	1,158	**0.15**
Summer vacation length	2	78	711	**−0.01**
Modifying school calendar/ timetable	3	124	1,318	**0.10**
Summer schools for disadvantaged students	4	127	626	**0.19**
Totals	**57**	**2,682**	**10,583**	**N/A**

Figure 6.1 Structural Enhancements

(Visible Learning META[X], 2021)

Interpreting the META[X] data

The challenge, yet again, is that the data in the META[X] do not support all the central assumptions of the theory of change outlined at the start of the chapter; and thankfully so – because implementation would require the insertion of more Jenga blocks (i.e., more funding) rather than present opportunities for Lean improvement. In the sub-sections below, we unpack the research findings and Lean implications for each of the key areas.

School finance

We have already discussed the impact of financial resources in Chapter 2. However, the data in these additional META[X] systematic reviews provide a deeper window. From six meta-analyses of 228 studies, involving 2.27 million participants, we see an aggregate effect size of $d = 0.21$ (Childs & Shakeshaft, 1986; Davis-Beggs,

2013; Hedges et al., 1994; Murdock, 1987; Shakeel et al., 2021). This is positive but well below our suggested $d = 0.40$ hinge point.

We need to flag at the outset that all this research was conducted in the US, and we need to be *extremely* cautious about generalizing from high-income contexts (that are already well-funded and then receive yet more money) to middle or low-income terrains. The research is also unequivocal about the fact that schools/systems need funds to hire teachers and to pay for infrastructure, teaching and learning resources, and teacher professional development – amongst other things. But there is a 'sweet spot', beyond which, each additional dollar invested suffers disproportionately from the law of diminishing returns.

Much of the required core investment is for teacher salary and pension costs – ensuring that teacher salaries are sufficiently rewarding to entice talented candidates to the profession and to cover their full living costs, without them having to resort to private tutoring, taxi driving, farming, fishing, or tour guiding on the side. What this number is will depend on the labor market economics in each country. However, significant enhancements in teacher salaries – on their own – are extremely unlikely to generate better teaching performance. A recent Indonesian study that experimentally doubled teachers' salaries on a permanent basis resulted in exactly zero improvement in student learning outcomes (de Ree, et al., 2018). In many low-income contexts, there is little evidence to suggest that teachers are underpaid relative to local salary norms (provided they are actually paid regularly). For example, Evans et al. (2020), in their review of teacher salaries across 15 African countries, found that teacher annual wages were already higher than those of workers in other sectors that had commensurate experience and qualifications. This ranged from teacher pay of 1.5 times the GDP per capita in the Democratic Republic of Congo to 5.1 times in Zambia.

Aside from this large chunk of teacher salary operating expenditure (Opex), the second largest budget line is often infrastructure related: building and maintaining schools, and the associated costs around keeping the (metaphorical) lights on (Capex). However, as we discuss in the next sub-section, this needn't cost the earth. And enhancing spending beyond these two key areas results in ever-diminishing returns (Hanushek & Wößmann, 2006).

In Chapter 2 we presented data cross-tabulating cumulative spending per student with average national performance in the 2018 PISA assessments. Yes, there were differences in student outcomes between well-funded and poorly funded systems. However, this plateaus after nations surpassed a certain funding envelope. As discussed in Chapter 2, Vegas and Coffin (2015) plotted the tipping point as (tentatively) being US$8,000 per student per annum – in purchasing power parity (PPP) terms – across low-, middle-, and high-income nations.

And, yes, this 'tipping point' sum is still well out of the reach of low-income nations, particularly those that are still struggling with access to education because of shortages of school buildings and teachers: these systems really do need more funds. But when we vector in on countries in the bottom quartile of per student funding that have met these basic investments in facilities and teachers, there is massive heterogeneity of outcomes. We see, for example, lower-middle-income Indonesia and Ukraine investing at similar levels but with a near 100-point difference in student outcomes on PISA assessments. And, no, these are not single anomalies within the data. There are many other examples of countries with similar levels of per student funding generating wildly different student learning returns – including upper-middle-income Malaysia and high-income Estonia with a 108-point difference in average PISA scores. We note, too, that the World Bank has also failed to identify a definitive causal relationship between increased spending and student outcomes (World Bank, 2003, 2018). More recent econometric research suggests that each 10% increase in education expenditure translates into a modest 0.8% growth in student learning outcomes (Al-Samarrai et al., 2019). And Eric Hanushek's (2020) review was also highly skeptical of the student learning returns from increased funding. Ouch.

So, how should we interpret these findings? When middle- and high-income country system leaders and educators (who have already cracked the access challenge) explain low levels of student achievement in terms of (lack of) funding, and where they say, "things would be better if only we had the money", our first reaction should be one of great suspicion – because there is a reasonable likelihood that their focus is on the wrong drivers. Although, when low-income nations say that they literally do not have enough funds to pay teacher salary costs – assuming all the teachers are genuinely needed and are operating at optimal utilization rates – then money clearly does make a difference. And, as we have noted in Chapters 2 and 5, whilst only a slender sliver is invested in teacher professional development (and whilst the evidence also shows high variability in the impact of this training), there are very good arguments for further investing in enhancing the in-service professional competency of educators.

School buildings

As with school finances, education systems (currently) continue to need buildings, as these play a critical convening role for teaching and learning. One of the few areas of agreement amongst the systematic reviews we surveyed in Chapter 3 is that the presence of school buildings nearer to where children live (and/or bicycles to help them travel further) is a significant catalyst for school enrollment in low-income countries that are grappling with access challenges (Asim et al., 2015; Damon et al., 2019; Ganimian & Murnane, 2016; Krishnaratne et al., 2013; Petrosino et al., 2012; Snilstveit et al., 2015). There is also evidence that provision of water, sanitation and hygiene (WASH) facilities acts as a pull factor for both enrollment of children and engagement with parents and the wider community (Birdthistle et al., 2011; Jasper et al., 2012). But the key question is whether, once these basics are met, we need 'architectural delights' or just a roof with walls and plumbed in utilities?

The META[X] evidence-base on school building design is still relatively under-developed. We have identified a single meta-analysis that directly explores the relationship between buildings and learning (Gunter & Shao, 2016), which aggregates data from 594 high-income country studies – generating an effect size of $d = 0.21$. Again, this is positive but well below our $d = 0.40$ hinge point.

Broadly, the research tells us that *all* we need to ensure is that school buildings have an appropriate level of shelter, heating/cooling, lighting, acoustic suppression, and that they are safe/secure (Clark, 2002; Fisher, 2001; Schneider, 2002; Weinstein, 1979; Woolner et al., 2007). Predictably, students do not learn well in extremely hot/cold, loud, or dark environments. The research also highlights the importance of having functioning toilets that are clean and safe; and hygienic facilities for food preparation and consumption. However, beyond this there is extremely limited additional value generated from each dollar of enhanced expenditure.

From our own work in the Pacific region, we are aware that some donors have invested in innovative modular classrooms that have been transported to the islands and assembled by local craftspeople. These shiny new schools can be a great source of pride for local communities, and they can also pump-prime the local construction industry. But they can also lead to overcrowding and over-enrollment as parents vie to register their children at these newer facilities. And as we review the evaluation data for micro-nations like Kiribati, we see no significant difference in student learning outcomes for children that have attended these modern modular Kitset schools versus those that attend more traditionally built schools (Smith & McNaughton, 2018). But what we do see is the Ministries of Education potentially saddled with additional maintenance costs for this imported infrastructure that they may subsequently struggle to budget for.

The research also suggests that:

- Whilst **smaller schools** that provide a more family-like culture correlate with higher levels of student achievement for marginalized students (Leithwood & Jantzi, 2009),[1] larger schools can achieve a similar effect by implementing, for example, a 'house' system that allows students and staff to form sub-units that build those family-like bonds or through the implementation of a relationships-based learning approach (see Bishop et al., 2012 for an overview of the relationships-based learning literature).
- It may not really matter whether schools are **single gender or mixed gender** (see Pahlke et al., 2014 for an overview of the literature). Mixed gender schools are also likely to be more economically efficient, e.g., one school in a rural community serving both boys and girls requires less capital expenditure than two separate schools serving the same number of learners. And if there are local socio-cultural reasons for enforcing segregation, this can (often) be implemented within a single facility with different entrances and clearly delineated zones.
- The **consolidation or merging of schools** likely has zero long-term negative impact on student achievement. However, this inference comes from a single meta-analysis of 12 research studies (Hall, 2019). We suspect that there

may be more potential for harm to learning for students who are in their final (examination) year and those who live far away from the new school location. The increased time and cost of travel may add friction that reduces access and participation to learning.

■ The **more efficient use of school buildings through multi-session/'hot seating' arrangements** likely has zero (to low negative) impact on student achievement (Bray, 2008; Carrell et al., 2011; Hinrichs, 2011; Lusher & Yasenov, 2016). This research explores the impact of running two (or even three) schools under the same roof with different sets of teachers and students in the morning, afternoon, and night shifts, and/or varying the start time of single shift schools. Whilst the evidence base is still emerging and the datapoints pull (mildly) in different directions, multi-session schools represent a more cost-effective use of infrastructure and with minimal difference in the quality of student learning outcomes, providing that each session is delivered by different teachers. In the Punjab, for example, the government saved an estimated 16 billion rupees by simply using the existing school infrastructure and introducing evening shifts. This enabled schools to serve to an additional 100,000 previously out-of-school children (Raas & Riaz, 2021).

The one area where double/triple-shift schools does, admittedly, have a negative impact is on extra-curricular activities, which often have to be curtailed to make way for the arrival of the next shift. However, our Lean message to systems that currently run double or triple session schools and that are considering the move to a single session model is (unless you are awash with money) don't bother. The cost of constructing and maintaining extra buildings is extremely unlikely to push the needle on student achievement – unless children are currently traveling vast distances to get to school and you are going to build the new schools much nearer to their homes.

However, the META^X research tells us nothing about contexts where there are no dedicated school buildings and individual rooms are rented by the hour or day. Although we see no reason why – if heating, lighting, acoustics, and security are at appropriate settings – this should be any less effective than operating out of dedicated school buildings. We are aware of some school operators in South Asia – like BRAC – that have rented individual school rooms rather than incurring the expense of building full school compounds and that even deploy school boats to get to hard-to-reach locations (Chabbott & Chowdhury, 2015).

The research also tells us nothing about contexts where there are no school buildings at all and where learning takes place under a large central tree in the village on days when it is not raining. Our best guess is that high-quality teaching and learning *could* still take place. But with flies buzzing around children's heads and the occasional caterwaul of animals and even villagers, we would expect student achievement to be significantly lower.

The structure of the classroom

The META^X data also highlights several aspects related to how classrooms within schools are organized that have relevance to a Lean agenda.

Open vs tradition classrooms

This research explores whether open-plan learning environments have greater impact than traditional walled-in classrooms. The 315 studies and four meta-analyses evaluating both intervention types show no strong improvement in learner outcomes on standardized student assessments either way (Giaconia & Hedges, 1982; Hetzel et al., 1980; Madamba, 1981 Peterson, 1980). If you have an open space, it generally works. If you have a traditional closed classroom, it also generally works. In terms of student achievement, whether you have walls or not matters far less than what teachers and students are doing, in whatever space they have, to make learning happen. Indeed, the research seems to point ever so slightly toward open spaces generating a higher level of student achievement.

The more flexible and open the space, the greater the chance of more teachers in one room critiquing, sharing their strengths, and feeding off each other, and much more student-to-student learning. But it requires high levels of social sensitivity, and high levels of joint planning by the teachers – perhaps not the best place to start, but it can be powerful to fast track newer teachers. From a Lean perspective, it is also (likely) cheaper to build large barn/aircraft hangar-type spaces that can be used flexibly than to construct walled classrooms that provide considerably less space-usage options. As has happened so often in these more open innovative spaces, it forces teachers to work collectively, it offers opportunities to group students in many ways (and not necessarily just by age), and it demands teaching students skills of self-regulation to work effectively by themselves, with others, and outside the teachers' direct involvement – all worthwhile.

Multi-grade/age classrooms

In high-income countries, most education systems operate a grade/year system that segregates students by age. Our understanding is that many developing countries either emulate or seek to emulate this approach to schooling. However, the META^X data on multi-grade/age classrooms strongly suggests there are limited benefits to this form of age segregation (Kim, 1996; Veenman, 1995, 1996). If anything, learning outcomes appear to be slightly higher where children, whose ages span a 2 or 3-year gap, learn together. This may be for similar reasons to those discussed under the category of teacher subject matter knowledge.

There is no logic in assuming that all students the same age are at the same level of learning, development, and understanding. More advanced learners (whether they be older/younger/the same age) who have only recently mastered a topic or curriculum area can still remember the pitfalls and hurdles that they faced and can, therefore, coach their less advanced colleagues through those steps. The aligned research on *peer tutoring* also suggests a strong positive washback to the more advanced learners, whose own understanding of the content is reinforced and deepened through the act of providing support (see the Chapter 8 data tables for the effect size data related to the two-way benefits to the tutor and tutee. In both cases this is significantly above the $d = 0.40$ hinge point).

Tracking

Tracking/streaming/ability grouping is a school-wide approach where children are sorted into different groups or classes based on their prior academic performance. It is a common structural approach to the organization of secondary schooling, particularly in low- and middle-income countries (Arteaga & Glewwe, 2014; Banerjee & Duflo, 2011; Glewwe et al., 2014; Hanushek & Wößmann, 2006). The argument deployed in favor of tracking is that it is less pedagogically taxing for lower skilled teachers – who only have to deliver a one-pitch lesson rather than having to differentiate to the various learning needs of a mixed ability classroom (Booij et al., 2017; Duflo et al., 2012).

The predictable argument against tracking is that it leads to labelling and self-fulfilling prophecy, with lower tracked students being inhibited from upward social mobility in adulthood and stigmatized during childhood (Hanushek & Wößmann, 2006). The META^X contains 13 meta-analyses on implementing tracking, with an aggregate effect size of $d = 0.12$ (e.g., Mosteller et al., 1996; Neber et al., 2001; Slavin, 1987); and one on its removal (de-tracking), with an effect size of $d = 0.09$ (Rui, 2009. Our preliminary interpretation is that the positive impact of both implementing OR rolling back tracking are incredibly low.

However, there is one massive disadvantage of tracking. It sets expectations for performance levels for students, and if any become fascinated with in-depth learning they often can't (i.e., are not allowed to) continue with their learning at the more advanced level. Ergo, so much talent can be wasted. Too often lower tracks have more students from lower home resources, again, locking in inequities that schools were supposedly set up to overcome. Thus, where there is a choice, do not track, no matter how much teachers might like teaching a narrower range of students.

We also note that in many contexts that implement tracking, children in the 'top set' are often assigned the better teachers and better resources. Whereas (perhaps) it should be the other way around – with 'bottom set' children being allocated the ace teachers, extra 1:1 tuition, and the best equipment; and the more novice teachers, instead, being assigned to the highest performing students. This really would support equitable leveling-up!

Grade repetition

The META^X research findings on grade repetition/student retention is clearer cut. Nine meta-analyses of a combined 255 studies (all from the US) explore the relationship between making underperforming students repeat the whole school year before being promoted to the next school grade. The alleged theory of 'improvement' is that if at first you don't succeed, try, try again. However, the aggregated effect size of retaking the whole school year again is $d = -0.34$ and, yes, this is a negative effect. Whilst there is some spread between the metas, with the lowest reporting $d = -0.66$ (Drany & Wilson, 1992) and the highest reporting $d = 0.04$ (Allen et al., 2009), eight out of the nine report negative values. In low-income contexts, the data suggests that it is poor children who are both more likely to repeat and more likely to subsequently drop out from being held back, with significant (negative) impact on their self-efficacy (UNESCO, 2012; UNESCO UIS, 2020). A clear potential consequence of grade repetition is overcrowded classrooms with age distortions, which is also arguably anti-Lean!

However, we also note that the alternative social promotion system, which automatically advances children to the next grade/year even if they have NOT learned/mastered the curriculum from the current grade/year, also has a built-in failure mechanism. It assumes that all 7-year-olds are working at the 7-year-old curriculum level, and so on up the ages. This is patent nonsense. A worthwhile alternative is to structure curricula by levels of complexity (and not age-based) and evaluate where each student is, how they are progressing, and what level they end up at – and it will soon be clear that these levels are related but not the same as age groupings. Open classes, multi-age groupings, and peer tutoring are more likely to promote students, regardless of age, up the levels. And then there is less need for the nasty effects of retention or holding a child back from his (a disproportionate percentage of those retained are males) age peers. Indeed, there is highly promising research from Ghana, India, and Zambia, where children are either grouped together for part of the day by level (i.e., what they currently know and can do, irrespective of their age) or where they follow individualized curriculum activity worksheets, which they work through at their own pace (Banerjee et al., 2017; Global Education Evidence Advisory Panel, 2020). We come back to this in Chapter 8.

—

The research on *open space schools, multi-age/grade teaching and learning, and teaching by level rather than grade* has Lean implications. It suggests the potential for reducing school construction costs by using open-space designs, for having mixed age groups learning together, and for keeping teacher headcount down by using other students as 'assistant teachers'. Most teachers would acknowledge that they learn more when they are asked to plan to teach something that they do not (yet) know much about than when sitting in a room listening to someone talk to them about it. It is the same with students: inviting and teaching them to become teachers has a marked positive impact on these students, and then when they teach it to others the effects are positively compounded. If lifelong learning means we equip students with the skills of knowing what to do when they do not know what to do, this is akin to inviting them, while still at school, to learn to become teachers of themselves and others.

Of course, many low-income systems already leverage peer tutoring, but they may be inclined to see this as a deficiency in their education delivery model and something that budget should be set aside to stop. Our Lean message, however, is that leveraging students to become teachers is a wondrous virtue, not a vice.

Does class size matter?

A (controversial) parallel question: if we want to be Lean, could we literally *increase class size* without it hampering student learning outcomes? The META^X data do not directly tackle this question, although they do explore consequences for student learning outcomes of *reducing* class size. The eight meta-analyses of 176 studies, involving almost 1.5 million students, report an aggregated effect size of $d = 0.15$ (see e.g., Brunsek et al., 2017; Filges et al., 2018; Leuven & Oosterbeek, 2017). This is positive but not sufficiently positive considering the significant extra cost of building classrooms and hiring teachers that is required to implement the reduced size of classes. However, these data principally tell us about the impact of reducing class size from 30 down to 25–15. They tell us little about the impact of reducing from much higher numbers.

However, we do know from both Hong Kong and China that there was only a very modest improvement in student learning outcomes when class sizes were reduced from 60 to 30 (Galton & Pell, 2012). And, yes, these are two very specific and well-resourced contexts with Confucian values that might be more supportive of larger numbers. However, Conn's (2017) systematic review of impact in sub-Saharan Africa also found very limited improvement in student learning outcomes where class sizes were reduced from an average of 82 to 44.

The big question is WHY don't we see a quantum leap in student learning outcomes after class size is reduced? Across the data a common theme emerges. Teachers typically teach in the same way regardless of class size, so no surprise there is little effect. Indeed, teachers often tend to do 'more' of what they did in larger classes when moving to smaller size classes – talk a lot, ask many content-based questions requiring less than 3-word responses from the students, and an overemphasis on facts (Hattie, 2006). Our interpretation is that it would be a better use of resource to equip teachers with the skills to work effectively in larger classes than to invest heavily in hiring more teachers and building more classrooms to allow ratios to be cut, and then seeing no positive outcome.

However, we prefer to be *ultra-conservative* in making Lean recommendations about actively and deliberately *increasing* class size. There is probably no reason to increase class size (unless finances are extremely constrained), but reducing it may equally not be the place to start to make major progress for a low- or middle-income nation (and the same goes for high-income). With the right use of space, appropriate curriculum/teaching and learning materials, and educator professional development, it *might* be feasible to deliver quality education in explicitly larger class sizes. Even more so if students are leveraged as 'assistant teachers' as we discussed above. But it requires very careful exploration and piloting before system leaders agree to remove this particular Jenga block: a less contentious and more sensible approach would simply be to look at ways of enhancing learner outcomes with existing class sizes, whatever they may currently be.

The quantity of schooling

In high-income country contexts the common model of schooling is one that offers 4–6 hours per day of instruction x 170–220 days per annum x an average of 12 years (Hincapie, 2016). From our Lean perspective, an obvious question is whether this is overkill? What if, for example, we could reduce schooling down to 3-hours a day x 100 (spaced) days x an average of 8 years without any noticeable impact on literacy, numeracy, and 'human capital development'? This would enable education systems to either reduce the number of teachers or to reduce class sizes, i.e., less frequency but higher intensity of engagement, and/or allow teachers more time for collaborative professional development – thereby increasing the impact of each (reduced) hour of contact with students.

META^X data give us some tangential insights. It tells us that during the long school vacation there is a decline in learning retention ($d = -0.01$) and that significantly increasing the length of the school day/year results in an (aggregate $d = 0.10$) increase in student achievement (see for example, Cooper et al., 2003; Kim, 2002; Lauer et al., 2004). At first blush, this seems to support the notion of schooling longer, but the summer decline in learning is arguably modest, as is the gain from significantly ramping up the quantity of instruction – although this gain appears to be larger for students from more disadvantaged backgrounds, where four metas of 127 summer school catchup program studies generated an aggregate effect size of $d = 0.19$.

Some of the findings from the wider literature include:

- The importance of distinguishing between Time at School (TaS) and Productive Learning Time (PLT); and the fact that school and system leaders should work to maximize use of the existing TaS to increase the proportion that is PLT before even considering increasing the length of the school day (Aronson et al., 1998; Fryer & Dobbie, 2011).
- Lavy (2015) explored the relationship between instruction time and the PISA 2006 rankings. Although he found a positive relationship between extending school hours and PISA scores, this was not uniform and depended on the presence or absence of a range of other school-based factors. For example, schools that streamed/tracked students saw limited improvement in student achievement when operating longer school days and years.
- Longitudinal studies looking beyond immediate student achievement in exams, to the longer-term economic impact and retained learning in adulthood, have shown very weak (i.e., non-statistically significant) associations between the length of the school day and year and these wider outcomes (see e.g., Grogger, 1996; Pischke, 2007).
- Patall et al. (2010) do, however, find that extending the school day can generate positive outcomes for marginalized groups who are most at risk of

school failure. Although, we wonder whether this needs to be focused on teacher-directed PLT or the degree to which the same can be accomplished via youth clubs and extra-curricular activities that take place inside the school compound, keeping children on site and engaged in fun activities but without increasing the risk of teacher burnout. This would provide a few core hours of structured PLT per day, with the remaining time being allocated to student-selected/led co-curricular projects. Peter Gray (2013), in his excellent review of the Sudbury Valley School Model, provides some good leads on how this could be implemented, with self-selecting mixed-age groups of students working together on self-directed passion projects and calling on the teacher as a source of help when they get stuck.

The most recent PISA assessment (OECD, 2020c) also cross-tabulated the relationship between official hours per subject area and student performance in the international assessments. This pointed to a "hump-shaped" association. In broad brush terms, more instruction time resulted in enhanced student achievement where hours of instruction in a curriculum area were increased from one to two or three hours a week. However, the impact of additional instruction then plateaued between three and four hours per week; and then declined from five hours and beyond.

Bryan Caplan's highly controversial (2018) work also offers food for thought. After exploring the level of school-based learning retained and used by US students in adulthood, he concluded that only literacy and numeracy skills have universal value for life and work; and that these can be learned to a largely satisfactory level by the end of primary school education (i.e., age 11 or 12). Beyond this, he argues that much schooling and curriculum content is effectively 'padding' that confers no additional added value/human capital development – because of the largely irrelevant academic focus. If we follow Caplan's logic, the push by middle- and low-income countries to universalize secondary education and to increase the duration of schooling to 12 years is neither an efficient nor effective use of resource. Indeed, Caplan's argument is that high-income nations also need to scale back on their over-engineered school systems.

Controversy aside, the major theme across many of the studies on the quantity of education is that the amount of instructional time is less important than how that time is utilized. Therefore, from a Lean perspective, we need to focus relentlessly on how we can increase Productive Learning Time without increasing Time at School.

Conclusion

Recognizing that teachers are agents that work within structures, this chapter has explored some of the key structural features that potentially impact on student learning outcomes. These include the level of education funding; the size, shape, and location of school buildings; class age groupings; tracking/streaming of students; grade repetition; class size; and the length of the school day and year.

Through a Lean lens, we draw a range of tentative conclusions (with attendant health warnings) from the META^X and wider research – as summarized in the table below. *But most of all, we urge you to start slowly and tread carefully, lest you bring the tower crashing down.*

Tentative Lean Conclusions	Health Warnings/Side effects
• Money makes the difference only to a point: system leaders and school leaders should be discouraged from thinking that enhanced financial resources are the *key driver* to enhanced student learning outcomes. The real key is their collective teacher efficacy and their commitment to continuously evaluating their impact (although this also costs in time and resources for professional development – and funding is better spent here than on other enhancements)	• Changing this belief is hard and requires perseverance. Consider leveraging the successful parent and student information-giving strategies and applying them to teachers, so that they fully understand the contribution of teacher beliefs to student learning returns — *N.B.* teachers still need to be paid a fair living wage, and this needs to be remitted at predictable/frequent intervals so that they have the economic resources to focus 100% on their role
• New-build schools should probably only be considered where the geographic distances are too great for existing service users and where more economical options, such as renting individual classrooms, are not viable • Where new-build schools are required, consideration could be given to more efficient designs that are open-space 'barns', with multi-age/grade learners and higher student–teacher ratios that may allow more cost-effective schooling and potentially also contribute to enhanced student learning outcomes via opportunities for peer tutoring • School building upgrades should only be considered where there is clear evidence that the level of heating/lighting/acoustics/ shelter/sanitation within the existing infrastructure is harmful to learning outcomes	• There might be other non-education reasons that warrant investment in school infrastructure upgrades, e.g., economic stimulus/unlocking the fiscal multiplier effect during economic downturns • Requires extremely careful piloting and extensive evaluation to ensure Lean does not become Mean • Can be difficult for service users to accept that the surface appearance of the infrastructure does not affect the quality of education outcomes

(Continued)

Tentative Lean Conclusions	Health Warnings/Side effects
• Implementing (or maintaining) double or even triple-shift schools maximizes use of existing infrastructure, with minimal negative impact on student learning outcomes	• Requires extensive information-giving sessions to all stakeholders so that they understand that more intensive use of school buildings is – overall – a net positive • Although the evidence is mixed, it is likely better to schedule younger learners in the morning and older learners in the afternoon and evening • Intensive facilities use makes it difficult to undertake extra-curricular activities within the school compound, as the next shift of learners will already have arrived
• Reducing class size is an expensive intervention that rarely generates significantly improved learning outcomes. Only go here once you have exhausted ALL other avenues for enhancing the quality of learning, and provide teachers with comprehensive professional development on how to effectively teach smaller groups alongside this	• Teacher professional development alone is more likely to enhance student learning outcomes. Consider prioritizing this way above the bigger ticket costs of hiring additional teachers and building extra classrooms
• Reduced hours, weeks, and/or years of schooling may have no/limited negative impact on long-term human capital development • Timetable reductions can be used to give teachers more time for professional development and/or enable the school to support a larger number of students	• There are limits, below which reductions in hours are likely to be extremely harmful. A reasonable rule of thumb is to allocate a minimum bedrock of 3–4 hours per core subject, per week (but pilot any changes *carefully* with consideration of age of students and other locally relevant background variables) • There are non-academic benefits to students being in school longer, even if they are not learning, e.g., reduced crime rate, and fewer early marriages and teenage pregnancies (Duflo et al., 2019). Be careful to ensure that these benefits are not lost • It is extremely challenging to convince service users that less inputs can achieve the same (or sometimes even better) outcomes

Tentative Lean Conclusions	Health Warnings/Side effects
• Grade repetition increases the cost of schooling without increasing completion rates. Do not hold children back!	• Automatic (social) promotion to the next grade also has bult-in failure mechanisms for children that have fallen behind – unless they are provided with opportunities for additional targeted support
• Schools that operate on the basis of levels rather than grades can be highly effective at flexibly leveraging space and schooling hours, enabling children from different ages to work together and peer tutor one another and removing the concepts of grade repetition and streaming from the schooling lexicon	• Avoid the temptation of 'plug in and play'. Instead, draw on inspiration from other systems but build from the ground up to better fit the local context. Start small, pilot, iterate, and then grow. The Escuela Nueva, which originated in Columbia, is one suggested source of inspiration for this type of approach

Note

1 We note, too, the paradox that smaller schools seem to generate greater impact than smaller class sizes within schools. However, with only a single meta on school size versus eight on class size, we have greater confidence in the latter findings.

Returns from teacher accountability and motivation enhancement

Once a system has sufficient teachers and an adequate supply of school buildings, the next challenge is in motivating every educator to do their absolute best. And for them to continuously strive to get even better. From the research on elite performance, we know that achieving world class performance in fields as diverse as chess, violin playing, and athletics requires an average of 10,000 hours or 10 years of *deliberate* and *effortful* practice (see, for example, Ericsson et al., 2018; Ericson & Pool, 2016).

This deliberate practice is very different to the automatic, reflexive, and effortless execution of a skill you have already mastered. It involves careful, critical, and ongoing self-review of your prior performance to identify priority areas for improvement. It then requires you to doggedly implement and carefully evaluate your selected performance enhancements, over and over. But it is cognitively taxing to do this your whole career. It demands immense self-discipline, continued commitment to the mission, and ongoing self-belief in self-improvement. Which is probably why there are so few chess grand masters or Olympic contenders.

From the parallel research on teacher expertise, we know that many educators only engage in deliberate and effortful practice during their initial 3 years on the job; after which they often enter 'arrested development', having already learned sufficient tradecraft to get by (see Papay & Kraft, 2015 for overview of the literature). So, the important question is how do we keep teachers motivated to improve continuously, deliberately, and effortfully? And at an even more basic level, how do we motivate them simply to turn up at work each day, to enter their classroom, and to take a genuine interest in the learning lives of their students?

Overview

Many industries have attempted to enhance employee productivity through a range of incentive structures that wield the 'stick' at undesirable behavior, and reward

DOI: 10.4324/9781003166313-10

or incentivize positive actions with 'carrot'. In this chapter we explore the various drivers that have been used in education settings to unleash the better angels of teachers' natures. From our Lean perspective, we are clearly most interested in approaches that generate the greatest efficiency of impact. A potential theory of change, which we shall test, is as follows:

Theory of change

Assumptions:

1 Student success is influenced by a wider range of variables than simply their own individual characteristics and socio-economic status
2 In particular, the quality of teaching that students receive has a *significant* impact on accelerating their learning outcomes
3 Not all teachers have an equal level of motivation to improve and extend their impact: some plateau/cruise and others are 'bad actors'
4 It is hard to weed out 'bad actors', so we need a range of carrot and stick measures to get them back on track (and also to re-motivate the cruisers).

Therefore, invest in the following **inputs**:

1 Enhanced **school leadership skills** to nurture enhanced quality of teaching and learning
2 **Teacher performance-related pay** to provide 'carrots' that incentivize improved educator performance
3 **External accountability drivers**, e.g., national standards for school leadership and teaching, national student exams, school league tables, and national school inspectorates – which provide the 'stick' of accountability
4 Use of **public–private partnerships** to bring corporatized thinking to education – including market efficiency, competition, and choice.

The **outcome** of this investment will be:

1 Enhanced teacher performance
2 Enhanced learning outcomes for students.

In Chapter 5 we reviewed the evidence on assumptions 1 and 2 of the theory of change presented above, concluding that the research findings were broadly supportive: so, onto assumption 3. Overall, in high-income country contexts, (most) teachers turn up to school every day. And whilst they are at school, they generally undertake the teaching duties that have been allotted to them by school leadership. We do not know many teachers who come to school either wanting to or planning to do a poor job, but some do not invest in the *right* job (i.e., having a profound impact on the learning lives of students).

Therefore, in high-income contexts, when we think about accountability drivers it is generally to enhance the performance of 'cruising' teachers, who have lost motivation, who are going through the motions, and who are no longer systematically evaluating their own impact. Children taught by such teachers will still be learning. It's just that the amount of growth they will experience will likely be lower than what it would be with more motivated colleagues who engage in self and peer evaluation and collaborative continuous improvement. And in contexts like the US, the UK, and New Zealand, governments are also grappling with high teacher turnover – with more than 50% exiting the profession by their fifth year – and a seemingly endless requirement to recruit and train replacements (See & Gorard, 2020; Sutcher et al., 2016). Along with stress and workload, one of the reasons for this exodus is that perhaps some of these teachers have lost interest and enthusiasm in their roles. They have lost their mojo.

However, in some low- and middle-income contexts the challenges are far more profound. System leaders are often confronted with the following four 'bottlenecks' (Guerrero et al., 2012, 2013):

- **Bottleneck 1: teachers (and principals) might not turn up to school at all.** In sub-Saharan Africa, on any given day, approximately one in five teachers are estimated as missing from school (Bold et al., 2017). In India, the national mean average absentee rate is similar, but with rates of abscondence reaching 50% in the poorest performing state (Kremer et al., 2005; Muralidharan et al., 2017); these absences are estimated to cost the Indian government US$1.5 billion per annum in teacher salary payments for days that have not actually been worked (Muralidharan et al., 2017). And from the direct work of our teams, we know that similar challenges exist across many of the education systems in the Pacific.
- **Bottleneck 2: teachers who are at school might not go into classrooms for their allotted periods or may only do so sporadically.** As we highlighted in Chapter 1, in many countries there is a serious discrepancy between the 'official' duration of the school day and the number of minutes teachers are physically in their classrooms. Recent data suggests that in Kenya, Mozambique, Uganda, and Ghana, teachers are in their classrooms for less than 50% of the time they are supposed to be (World Bank, 2018). Instead they might be found in the staffroom, drinking tea with their colleagues, as the students work independently on their assignments (or not).
- **Bottleneck 3: teachers that are in their classroom might not do any actual teaching!** They might, for example, deliberately withhold their services to extract additional fees from parents for afterschool extra-tuition in curriculum areas that should have been taught during the standard school day; stoking demand for their 'extra' services by carefully slowing down the pace of

learning or by intentionally withholding instruction on key concepts (see, for example, Bray & Lykins, 2012; Liu & Bray, 2020).

■ **Bottleneck 4: teachers are teaching but they are using sub-optimal pedagogy, which reduces the rate of student learning and learning retention.** We will come back to this in the next chapter, where we explore high-impact instructional approaches, pedagogy, and curriculum enhancements.

There are also, sometimes, wider challenges linked to the political economy of education (Kingdon et al., 2014). This includes the use of the education system by political/bureaucratic elites to pursue the 'dark drivers' we discussed in Chapter 1, i.e., rent-seeking, patronage, and kickbacks. This can encourage elites to continue focusing on big-ticket items like building schools, hiring more teachers, reducing class size, and rolling out EdTech, rather than on attempting to increase efficiency of outcomes (Béteille, 2009; Gupta et al., 2000; Kingdon & Muzammil, 2013), as the challenge with efficiency is that it reduces the potential for all those illicit out-flows. This can mean that policymakers become locked into interventions that are good for enhancing access to schooling (the *easy* problem) but which have limited impact on improving student learning (the *hard* problem).

The META^X data

In Figure 7.1, we present relevant data from the Visible Learning META^X about the various 'sticks' and 'carrots' that might enhance the collective performance of teachers. The influences shaded in grey all relate to system, process, and funding-oriented interventions; the ones shaded in white relate to the motivation of hearts and minds to unleash our better angels.

You will remember from our previous discussion that effect size is a statistical measure of power, and that across all the META^X influences the mean average effect size was $d = 0.40$. So, by implication, anything lower than this is "below average".

Given this vast difference in context, we must be *especially* careful about the Lean inferences we make from applying META^X data generated from high-income to middle- and low-income contexts. But, in the remainder of this chapter, we (cautiously) attempt the task. Spoiler alert: we question the efficacy of many of the inputs outlined in the theory of change at the beginning of the chapter.

School leadership

Do leaders make the difference? The findings from 19 meta-analyses of 693 studies, involving more than a million participants, generate an aggregate effect size of $d = 0.34$. This seems low when compared to the effect sizes we will see in the next chapter related to very simple pedagogical interventions that achieve effect sizes in the $d = 0.50$ to 1.20 range. However, as ever, the devil is in the detail. When we

Influence	No. of Metas	No. of Studies	No. of Effects	Aggregate Effect Size d =
School leadership	19	693	2,100	**0.34**
Performance-related pay for teachers	1	40	40	**0.05**
Accountability systems/school-based management	2	83	83	**0.20**
Charter schools/ public–private partnerships (PPP)	6	347	780	**0.04**
School choice programs/school vouchers	1	22	28	**0.02**
Teacher collective efficacy	3	85	85	**1.36**
Teacher expectations	8	674	784	**0.43**
Teachers not labelling students	1	79	79	**0.61**
Teacher–student relationships	3	351	1,641	**0.48**
Totals	**44**	**2,374**	**5,620**	**N/A**

Figure 7.1 Accountability and Motivation Enhancements

(Visible Learning META^x, 2021)

Basket 1: Transformational Leadership	Basket 2: Instructional Leadership about Impact
School and system leaders who set challenging goals, and a vision and moral purpose, to generate collective energy and enthusiasm to encourage staff to work collaboratively in the achievement of said goals; and who establish clear performance targets, monitor progress, and ensure compliance	*Leaders who focus their energies on the teaching and learning that takes place within the classrooms of their school. This includes collaborative and trust-based lesson observations; review of student achievement data; collection of student voice; and establishment of teacher professional learning communities for the purpose of collective impact evaluation and improvement*
Effect size d = 0.11	***Effect size d = 0.42***
Better for teacher attendance, discipline, and compliance	***Better for deliberate practice and quality improvement***

Figure 7.2 Transformational Leadership vs Instructional Leadership about Impact

(Adapted from Robinson et al., 2008)

unpick the research, we find massive heterogeneity in the data. The lowest effect size is $d = -0.26$ (Wiseman, 2002) and the highest is $d = 1.12$ (Chin, 2007) – with the remaining 17 metas dispersed between. There is also significant heterogeneity in the types of leadership approaches that these studies catalogue, although many of the researchers distinguish between two broad (but overlapping) baskets of leadership profiles, which we summarize in Figure 7.2.

Transformational leadership is akin to the approaches used in the corporate world, where the leader sets 'big hairy and audacious goals' and galvanizes the workforce into energetic action through carrot and stick – including formalized goal setting, performance review, and bonus payments or sanctions. However, we should stress that the $d = 0.11$ reported aggregate effect size relates to the impact of this leadership approach on student achievement in standardized assessments. The META[X] research does not directly evaluate its impact on corralling teachers and ensuring they enter their classrooms and engage in some form of performative activity. So, if this is your main goal, having the leadership walk round the village and school waving a big stick/grin and demanding/encouraging compliance might well do the trick (particularly, as we discuss below, if it is supported by community monitoring).

However, the challenge with transformational leadership is that it tends to treat what goes on in the classroom as a black box; instead privileging administrative processes, resource management, monitoring, and compliance, without drinking deep on teacher pedagogy and how to enhance it. This means that school improvement often stops at the classroom door, with school leaders that are uncomfortable crossing the threshold to the private inner sanctums of teachers and/or with teachers that metaphorically barricade themselves within.

Instructional leadership about impact, by contrast, focuses more explicitly on the impact *within* the black box of the classroom. The assumption is that most of the important things that happen in a school have little to do with the budget, the timetabling, the curriculum standards, or any of the structural dimensions we discussed in the last chapter. Instead, what matters most is the moment-by-moment interactions between teachers and students in the classroom. This can't be influenced from afar in the principal's office. Instead, it needs the school leadership to get down and dirty in the classrooms, collaborating with teachers to collectively enhance student learning.

The idea is to make the black box disappear and to get everyone focused on understanding their current impact on student learning, and to continually run action research experiments/inquires to improve it. Key elements include building a culture of trust; collectively reviewing student achievement data to identify priority initiatives; collaborative implementation, including peer lesson observation; and ongoing formative evaluation to decide "where to next?".

Although there are pockets of disagreement within the research, the findings point to instructional leadership about impact having the biggest payoff for bottleneck 4 – i.e., focusing on and enhancing the impact of classroom pedagogy (by teachers) has the biggest return for student achievement. We unpack what those higher impact instructional approaches are in the next chapter. Admittedly, instructional leadership about impact is also culturally a "Western" approach to leadership that might not transfer well to other global contexts, although we note promising case studies in a diverse range of education systems spanning Malaysia (Harris et al., 2017), Iran (Hallinger et al., 2018), China (Qian et al., 2017), Vietnam (Hallinger et al., 2017), and Kiribati (Owen, 2020).

However, the instructional leadership about impact research does not provide explicit low- and middle-income country approaches for how we overcome bottlenecks 1–3 (i.e., getting teachers to turn up at school and actually set foot in their classes); whereas, alongside transformational leadership, the 'carrot and stick'-oriented interventions we go on to discuss below do attempt to do so.

Performance-related pay for teachers (a.k.a. a slice of carrot cake)

The assumption behind performance-related pay is that enabling educators to access a cash bonus – if they meet certain pre-conditions or targets – will incentivize them to perform their role to a higher standard. META^X evidence on the impact of cash bonuses is relatively modest, comprising a single meta-analysis of 40 studies with an overall (minuscule) effect size of $d = 0.05$ (Pham et al., 2017). However, the emerging consensus amongst researchers is that (in high-income contexts) performance-related pay is, at best, a waste of money, but at worst, it may be a malignant form of intervention. Some of the arguments commonly deployed, include:

- That it is extremely difficult to unpick the precise contribution of individual teachers to student learning outcomes: the legacy effect of high-quality teaching can last up to 3–5 years (Konstantopoulos, 2007). Therefore, we may be awarding this year's teacher for positive legacy of the previous teacher's good work (and vice versa).
- Many performance-related pay systems tend to encourage competitive rather than cooperative behavior – more so when there are quotas that restrict bonus payments to the highest performers. This arguably encourages educators to compete rather than collaborate, whereas the research tells us that collective teacher efficacy generates the highest effect size for student learning gains – and this is a highly collaborative undertaking (Donohoo, 2016; Eells, 2011).
- Performance-related pay can also encourage extrinsic rather than intrinsic motivation (Bénabou & Tirole, 2003). People act and perform to get their cash prize rather than for the intrinsic motivation of doing a good job for its own sake.
- There is also evidence from lab-based cognitive psychology studies suggesting that where people are motivated to perform complex tasks for monetary reward, the financial element often seems to crowd out their working memory and their critical thinking ability (Bonner & Sprinkle, 2002). It seems that whilst paying bonuses to people undertaking routine work enhances their rate of production, the opposite is the case for complex professional undertakings like teaching.

As we highlighted in Chapter 3, performance-related pay in low- and middle-income contexts can be effective in getting teachers to turn up to work (Evans & Popova, 2015; Guerrero et al., 2012, 2013), enter their classrooms, and possibly also to do something that looks a bit like teaching (i.e., bottlenecks 1–3)

(Ganimian & Murnane, 2016). But we are not at all convinced that it is a useful 'carrot' for unlocking the kinds of collaborative expertise, which we will discuss in Chapter 8, that are essential for overcoming bottleneck 4.

Indeed, the research suggests that performance payments do not result in any change in pedagogy, except in relation to running more exam preparatory sessions in contexts where the exam scores determine the level of teacher payments (Duflo et al., 2012)! We also note similar findings in contexts where CCTV-type teacher surveillance systems have been deployed (e.g., Kremer et al., 2013), i.e., the panopticon effect boosts teacher attendance but not teaching performance.

This is perhaps why some education systems have implemented community-based monitoring approaches – where the parent body systematically inspects or audits the school, making sure that teachers are present and teaching (Westhorp et al., 2014). Developing country research (e.g., in Brazil, Chile, Kenya, Madagascar, Pakistan, and Uganda) suggests that community monitoring is more cost-effective and has greater potential for impact than teacher bonuses (Snilstveit et al., 2016; Sperling et al., 2016). However, the potential for parent and community groups to enhance pedagogy, through this monitoring, is extremely limited. We still need good old instructional leadership about impact alongside this that is focused on high-impact instructional approaches.

The obvious implication from a Lean perspective is not to waste money on teacher performance-related bonuses. We might even argue that the types of educators that require additional payments to motivate them to attend work are perhaps not the kinds of candidates we want in teaching in the first place. Of course, this presumes teachers receive their salary in a timely way so they are not forced to choose to feed their family through other outside employment.

Accountability systems and school-based management (a.k.a. a bag of sticks and half a carrot)

Education systems deploy a range of accountability-based systems that are designed (or at least intended) to enhance teacher performance and, ultimately, student achievement. These include (Bruns et al., 2010; Eddy-Spicer et al., 2016; Sahlberg, 2015):

- **National standards for school leadership and teaching**, i.e., set of competency rubrics or scales. The idea is that educators collect evidence to exemplify their current level of personal development on this continuum, which is then independently assessed and validated.
- ○ *The theory*: it stops arrested development – keeping educators motivated to continuously improve and demonstrate their progress along the continuum.
- **National school inspections**, i.e., the school-level equivalent of leadership/teaching standards and the deploying of teams of government-funded inspectors to visit schools, sample evidence, observe lessons, and rate the school against the rubrics.

- ○ *The theory:* it unlocks the *Panopticon Effect* (i.e., you never know when the inspectors will turn up), keeping schools focused on improvement.
- ■ **National testing**, i.e., conducting regular standardized national assessments to provide comparative snapshots of the performance of different schools and of different teachers within individual schools.
- ○ *The theory:* it provides a measure of progress and motivates teachers to incrementally improve the test scores for their learners.
- ■ **National league tables**, i.e., taking the data from some/all the accountability instruments described above and using these to publicly rank schools.
- ○ *The theory:* it 'names and shames' poor performers into improving.
- ■ **School-based management**, i.e., giving partial or total control to the school for budget, teacher hiring (and firing), and for the end-to-end management and operation of the school.
- ○ *The theory:* by giving autonomy to the school, principals have no one to blame but themselves for poor learner outcomes and therefore will get busy at getting better. They also know best what is needed locally and will have all the autonomies they need to make it happen.

Let's now review the evidence for each of these claims.

National teaching and leadership standards

Systematic evidence on the impact of national teaching and leadership standards is slim, although their use is relatively widespread (Call, 2018; OECD, 2013a). Such standards without associated measures that enhance teachers moving up the levels of standards are mere papers in the wind. Both are needed, as well as the focus and resources to show that implementing the standards leads to greater unity among the profession and enhancements in student learning. We note that in some contexts the standards are weighted more to measuring/validating the successful performance of administrative activities than to teaching and learning. Therefore, our recommendation is that where standards are used, these focus exclusively on instructional leadership about impact and on classroom pedagogy enhancement, i.e., activities that *directly* result in enhanced student learning outcomes. Otherwise, we might be incentivizing educators to fetishize about things that have zero relationship with learner outcomes.

School inspections

There is a similar lack of systematic evidence on the impact of school inspections. Whilst many systems have national or regional school inspectorates, e.g., the United Kingdom; Singapore; Hong Kong; New Zealand; Malaysia; and Korea, many others do not, e.g., Finland; Japan; Luxemburg; Mexico; Italy; Australia; and Hungary (OECD, 2013b). There are countries in both categories that are highly (and lowly) ranked in the international PISA assessments and that argue that the presence/absence of national inspections is a key driver for the success of their national education system. Care is needed to make sure, where inspection systems exist, they are constructively aligned with other policies, or they can be a negative disruptive effect.

And it is important that if schools are not markedly improving then these inspectors should be changed or removed. It is, of course, very hard to remove/dismantle inspection once it starts. There is also emerging comparative evidence about the tendency for inspections to generate perverse incentives (Jones et al., 2017).

Through data we can verify that establishing and operating inspection systems costs money, but we cannot (yet) verify whether that expenditure generates improved quality of education or whether inspection systems have more impact within certain types of schooling/cultural ecosystems than others. Our best guess (and it is a guess), is that inspectorates *might* support remediation of bottleneck 1. In other words, the fear of inspection *might* encourage teachers and leaders to be present within the school compound. But unless the inspections are a near-daily occurrence, we cannot see how they would motivate malfeasant teachers to enter their classrooms and engage in performative activity (bottlenecks 2 and 3). Instead, grass roots community-based monitoring, with daily/twice-daily inspections by parents, is more likely to be effective – and at significantly lower cost than what would be incurred by setting up a national brigade of school inspectors.

We are also not (yet) convinced that accountability-oriented inspections are the best mechanism for unlocking bottleneck 4 – the quality of teaching and learning. The first challenge is in equipping inspectors with the skills to 'see' good teaching and learning, and there are major methodological and inter-rater reliability challenges with this – to which there are (currently) no full proof answers (Cohen & Goldhaber, 2016). Different inspectors/observers 'see' different things when they look at the same classroom phenomena and therefore observer ratings/judgments can be wildly different (Kane & Staiger, 2012).

Yes, inspectors can be trained with rubrics and, yes, more lesson observations of the same teachers by different inspectors can increase the consistency of their judgments. But there is still the hanging question of whether accountability-oriented inspections and faultfinding enhance quality or whether the real value comes from collaborative (trust-based) coaching conversations that identify and leverage teachers' strengths.

National testing

The only area where the META^X provides some systematic insight is in relation to national testing (Hendriks et al., 2014; Lee, 2008). Both these studies suggest that there is *some* beneficial impact to regular national testing, but their effect sizes ($d = 0.31$ and $d = 0.11$ respectively) both fall below the $d = 0.40$ hinge point. However, we note that these two meta-studies only synthesize the findings from 83 studies, which were principally conducted in the US and the Netherlands. Therefore, our confidence level is not high. It is likely that national assessment may help to move the bottom to the middle, but may not assist, and can even stifle, schools moving from the middle to the top of the success ladder. This is because these systems often incentivize performance goals (a.k.a. gaming the grades) rather than mastery goals: the relentless pursuit of excellence for its own sake.

We note, too, that rolling out standardized national assessments is not an inexpensive endeavor. There is evidence from many of these systems that they can raise schools below average but have little, indeed often perverse, effects on schools above average. There are models which are welcomed by teachers and can provide systems with great information on the performance of the system (e.g., the one we developed in New Zealand, https://e-asttle.tki.org.nz/). And there are many advantages in stratified and not population sampling, and the worthwhileness is a function of how it helps educators improve the quality of education – but there are too few examples of this. Therefore, our Lean advice to developing countries would be to pilot and evaluate the impact and potential for perverse incentives carefully before rolling out a national testing regime.

The Eddy-Spicer et al. (2016) narrative review of 68 low- and middle-income studies in relation to the impact of high-stakes testing, monitoring, and school inspections draws similar conclusions. It found limited evidence of improved service delivery, system efficiency, or student learning outcomes through implementation of any of these measures. In fact, in many cases, implementation seemed to result in unintended consequences, as local actors simply looked for ways to game the system.

School-based management

Many of the arguments and evidence for school-based management overlap with the research on public–private partnerships and charter schools, so we discuss these below. At the same time, it's worth remembering the research on school leadership – which we have already reviewed. This finds that the motherlode is in instructional leadership about impact. Giving principals responsibility for fixing the roof, managing the payroll, tendering for the gardening contractor, etc., keeps them firmly locked in their office, eroding their instructional leadership capacity to get into the classrooms to collaborate with the teachers!

Yes, leaders need to master sufficient skills in management to make the school run smoothly, but this is the pedestal on which to stand to then be an instructional leader and really make the difference to the learning lives of teachers and students. This is arguably why both New Zealand and New South Wales (who were previously enthusiastic adopters of school autonomies and decentralization) have both attempted to reduce school-based management of these non–education inputs – to get principals to stick closely to the instructional leadership about impact knitting.

We note, too, the findings of the Carr-Hill et al. (2016) systematic review of 35 studies exploring the impact of decentralization in developing countries. This concluded that decentralized budget management, school administration, and pedagogic decision-making had limited impact in increasing teacher attendance, the quality of instruction, or student learning outcomes – in low-income countries. However, it suggests that decentralization *might* generate greater impact in middle-income countries – where school leaders and teachers have the professional skills and confidence to effectively leverage their new autonomies. Although, again, our interpretation is that it is instructional leadership for impact *within and between* classrooms (or what Carr-Hill et al. call pedagogic decision-making) where the real gains are to be made – rather than in the wider corporatized autonomies.

Public–private partnerships and voucher systems

Two other areas where there is some data within the META^X to make Lean interpretations are public–private partnerships and school voucher programs.

Public–private partnerships (PPP)

There are many varieties of PPP, ranging from (LaRocque, 2008; Patrinos et al., 2009):

- **Private finance initiatives**, i.e., getting the private sector to fund and build infrastructure, with the state paying down these (interest bearing) loans over time
- **Outsourcing non-educational services**, i.e., building management, ICT, school canteens, etc.
- **Outsourcing 'peripheral' education services**, i.e., school inspections, teacher training and teacher professional development, staff recruitment, curriculum and materials/textbook development, and delivering national student assessments
- **Outsourcing 'core' education services**, i.e., management and operation of schools (ranging from hybrid approaches where school leadership is outsourced to full private management where even the teachers are privately contracted).

When governments seek to inject private sector operators into the educational ecosystem it can be for a variety of reasons, including access to finance (buy now – pay later, with interest), risk sharing, depoliticization (a.k.a. having someone else to blame for poor performance), cost reduction, and of course improving education outcomes.

The META^X does not help us systematically answer whether there are genuine financial efficiency gains from PPP – but from a Lean perspective it is an interesting question. It does, however, provide insight into the student outcome returns from outsourcing core education services via implementation of the *charter school* model, which involves private sector operators hiring the teachers, managing the school, and being paid by the government/state for each student 'bum-on-seat'. It also offers insights on *school voucher* systems. We discuss both these areas below.

Charter schools

The theory of change behind charter schools is that private sector operators become unshackled from unwieldy public sector bureaucracy and can use their professional expertise to run schools how they see fit. The idea is that, in turn, they are held accountable by the commercial imperative to make a profit. As they get paid per bum-on-seat, they need to make sure the school delivers a high-quality education to encourage parents to enroll their children and to ensure that the government allows them to maintain their operating concession.

The META^X houses six systematic reviews, which aggregate the findings from 347 (mainly US studies) into the educational impact of charter schools (Betts & Tang, 2011; Cheng et al., 2017; Erickson, 2013; Jeynes, 2012; Krowka et al.,

2017; Miron & Nelson, 2001). There is considerable heterogeneity in the data, with the lowest effect size being $d = -0.27$ and the highest being $d = 0.20$. The aggregated effect size for all six metas is $d = 0.04$ – which is extremely small. This means that for every charter that is wonderful there must be one that is woeful. This is what an average close to zero means.

The challenges that we note are:

- Charter schools are accessing the same pool of teachers as their public sector counterparts. There is no 'magic waiting room' filled with higher quality teachers that only the private sector is allowed select from.
- Many of the corporatized drivers that the model emphasizes (performance objectives, bonuses, accountability) come from the same basket that the research already concludes do not work particularly well in education (i.e., transformational leadership and teacher incentives/performance-related pay).
- Whilst some charter/PPP operators have genuinely good operating models, they struggle to scale these as they open or convert more and more schools whilst maintaining high-quality standards (i.e., no different to the pockets of excellence within their state sector counterparts, which ministries of education also struggle to scale up).
- There needs to be provision for the state to take back charters that do not make the difference. Too often, when this happens charters scream for more money to be left alone, and often continue the cycle of low impact.
- There is a hard, cold reality: within 6 months of setting up a charter school, most realize they are "running a school" with all the usual pressures, and with all the research influences pertaining to them just the same.

We have no particular axe to grind against charter schools and like the quote attributed to Deng Xiaoping: "it doesn't matter whether a cat is black or white, as long as it catches mice." Both public and privately operated education systems seem to "catch mice" at around the same rate. So, the appropriate approach might be to just stick with whichever modality you currently have, as the investment required to either roll out charter schools or to roll them back in is unlikely to reap a particularly large dividend.

This conclusion is largely supported by the Day Ashley et al. (2014) systematic review of 59 studies on the returns from low-cost private schooling in low- and middle-income contexts. Whilst this found that privately operated schools generated better *top-line* student learning outcomes than state operated counterparts, once student background/socio-economic status is filtered/accounted for, the *bottom-line* outcome is much less marked. Although it did find evidence of more efficient use of resource – particularly where school operators worked within commercial imperatives. Romero and Sandefur's (2019) review of outsourced school management in Liberia also found only modest improvements in student learning outcomes, but with some private contractors achieving this through mass student expulsions to game the system. Therefore, who the contractor is matters – as does the nature of the monitoring and contractual/incentivization processes enacted by state actors.

In contexts where government provision is suffering from complete service delivery failure (e.g., teachers are not being paid/not turning up, equipment is being filleted, and where the 'real' purpose of the education system is patronage and rent-seeking) we can understand why it can sometimes be tempting to conclude that it is just too difficult to fix the existing system and so the only path to improvement is to work outside the straitjacket. As private chains scale up though, they quickly create the potential for new straitjackets of their own.

School choice/voucher systems

A policy which is often implemented in tandem to charter schools (but which can be implemented solo) is school choice/voucher systems. This is sometimes traced to an argument made by Milton Friedman (1955), where he suggested that parents should have control over the kind of school their children attend. Where this approach has been implemented it has sometimes been in the form of a "voucher" (in the form of standardized per pupil funding) – with the level of school funding being a function of the total number of students they are able to enroll in a given year (i.e., the number of "vouchers" they are able to collect). The assumption is that the risk of losing funding will incentivize schools to up their game and deliver a higher quality of "service" to attract new students and retain the existing school roll.

Systematic evidence for the benefits of school choice/voucher systems is scant. The META[X] contains a single meta-analysis of 22 studies, generating an overall effect size of $d = 0.02$ (Jabbar et al., 2017). This is extremely low given the administrative overhead in managing the financial transfers and the time that school leadership teams undoubtedly need to spend in 'marketing' their schools to prospective parents (and that marketing time means less remaining energy for instructional leadership). We note, however, that the Morgan et al. (2013) narrative review of voucher programs in Colombia and Pakistan concluded that student enrollments increased and there was lower cost of service delivery, although its evidence base of two studies is (arguably) far too small to generalize from.

The voucher model also assumes informed parents who are getting optimal information from schools (about magnitude of learner progress), which is very, very difficult. Given that even 'experts' find it extremely challenging to tell the difference between good and average lessons via visual observation (Wiliam, 2018), there is strong likelihood that parents will be hoodwinked by the wrong visual proxies. So, from a Lean perspective, we do not (currently) believe that school choice/voucher systems have sufficient supporting evidence to warrant immediate mass adoption by any education systems.

The better angels of teachers' nature

In Chapter 1, we discussed Sabarwal and Abu-Jawdeh's (2018) survey of 16,028 teachers' beliefs, across eight low- and middle-income countries. This demonstrates that in some contexts, teachers simply do not *believe* that additional time, effort, or changes to their instructional approach will make the slightest difference to the learning lives of their students. In Pakistan, for example, more than 60% of surveyed teachers agreed that there was little they could do to improve learning outcomes for children from poor backgrounds, and more than 50% agreed that they could not improve outcomes for children who had already fallen behind. Teachers reported these perceptions at similar levels in Senegal, Zanzibar, and Uganda.

The strong possibility is that these mental models or mind frames are driving teacher actions. After all, if you believe that children from poor families, or those that have already fallen behind in their learning, are 'fated' to failure, why bother helping them? And if your school is full of children from low-SES backgrounds, you might conclude that there is no point in even turning up to teach them because nothing you do will make one iota of difference. And if you do turn up, these beliefs may make you feel accountable for delivering the agreed curriculum by the agreed deadlines but not for whether students learned anything (Banerji, 2000; Beatty & Pritchett, 2012).

In other words, you might see yourself as being responsible for getting horses to water but might not hold yourself accountable for whether they do any drinking. The Sabarwal and Abu-Jawdeh (2018) survey also suggests that, in some contexts, teachers believe that it is their role to help only the students that come pre-primed with the correct foundational learning from the previous grades. In other words, focus on the horses that are already drinking and hydrate them yet further!

Whilst, yes, intelligence is heritable and whilst, unfortunately, socio-economic status is strongly correlated with student achievement (Ciftci & Cin, 2017; Roth et al., 2015; Sirin, 2005), teachers can and do make a profound difference to the learning lives of all children (Barber & Mourshed, 2007; Darling-Hammond & Youngs, 2002; Sanders & Rivers, 1996; Staiger & Rockoff, 2010). In Chapter 5, we reviewed the research on *teacher collective efficacy*. This refers to a *collective belief* amongst a group of educators that (a) their combined efforts have the biggest impact on student learning and (b) that they have the skills and access to appropriate evaluative enquiry processes to collaboratively enhance their outcomes. Where both these factors are present and where teachers leverage their shared belief to develop, implement, and evaluate improvement-oriented plans, the research shows an aggregate effect size of $d = 1.36$ (Çoğaltay & Karadağ, 2017; Donohoo, 2016; Eells, 2011). This is extremely high.

We also see (reasonably) high effect sizes for other teacher belief-oriented influences within the META[X], including:

- **Teacher expectations.** This refers to the relationship between teachers' beliefs about specific learners and the impact that this has on their subsequent level of student achievement. Teachers often espouse those beliefs directly to students ("the world is your oyster" or "you're only good for milking the goats") or indirectly through body language or subliminal cues. The research suggests that teacher expectations influence student learning and effort, creating a self-fulfilling prophecy. The eight meta-analyses catalogued in the META^X aggregate the findings from 674 studies – generating a mean effect size of $d = 0.43$. However, this headline number hides significant heterogeneity in both the focus areas of the metas and their respective effect sizes. The ones focused on interpersonal expectancies (i.e., where the student gets the result you expected them to get) generated by far the highest effects (e.g., Rosenthal & Rubin (1978) $d = 0.70$; Smith (1980) $d = 0.82$). Rubie-Davies (2018) has demonstrated that teachers who have high expectations tend to have them for all students and, similarly, those with low have them (sadly) for all students. How teachers think *really* matters.

■ **Teachers not labelling students.** This single meta of 79 studies (Fuchs et al., 2002) focuses on the impact of applying a medical label and diagnosis (e.g., learning disabled) to some students that had fallen behind in reading and not to others. The children that did not receive the label performed $d = 0.61$ of a standard deviation higher than the children that were given a medical explanation for their lower performance. Our interpretation is that the label potentially becomes a justification to the child that it is OK to stop trying; it sets low expectation and, sadly, these are more than realized; and it is not much of a leap to suppose that non-medical pejorative labels like "stupid", "slow", or "lazy" are likely to be equally damaging to any child's confidence and learning progress.

■ **Teacher–student relationships.** These three meta-analyses of 351 studies, involving 541,157 participants, explore the interpersonal relationships between teachers and students, and the subsequent impact on student achievement. In many cases it is the teacher that takes the lead for establishing relationships and setting the tone and power dynamic of the classroom. One of these metas, Cornelius-White (2007), found that when children in high-income countries dislike school it's primarily because they don't like their teacher! Conversely, where teachers display high levels of empathy, warmth, and encourage all students to learn, the three metas record an aggregate effect size of $d = 0.48$. This is an impressive return on investment from simply being nice and developing a caring relationship in the classroom. And all the more amazing when these improvements in student learning outcomes occurred without any changes to the teachers' pedagogical approach!

What strikes us most from all this research is just how important beliefs are for driving action and enhancing student learning outcomes. Yes, we can monitor teachers' attendance with CCTV or GPS and, yes, we can pay them small bonuses for each day they show up. We can also introduce accountability systems like national testing and school inspections. And, yes, these approaches are effective at getting unmotivated teachers to attend and share tips on the best ways to game the accountability systems. But we see no subsequent impact on what these teachers then do to enhance the learning lives of the children in their classrooms. Instead, we are more likely to generate impact by influencing teachers' collective beliefs and leveraging these into enthusiastic and beneficial action, i.e., by unlocking ollective teacher efficacy, as we discussed in Chapter 5.

In our work we have been promoting a set of evidence-informed teacher mind frames that explicitly include beliefs and actions (Hattie & Zierer, 2018):

1 I am an evaluator of my impact on student learning
2 I see assessment as informing my impact
3 I collaborate with all about my conceptions of progress and impact
4 I am a change agent and believe all students can improve
5 I strive for challenge and not merely "doing your best"
6 I give feedback and act on feedback given to me
7 I engage as much in dialogue as monologue
8 I inform students of what successful impact looks like
9 I build relationships and trust
10 I focus on learning and the language of learning.

This Visible Learning equivalent of the Nicene Creed contains a mixture of practical actions (like constantly evaluating one's own impact and using assessment data to inform how to enhance that impact) and belief-oriented statements, like, "I am a change agent and believe all students can improve". Of course, in this case, the belief is buttressed by strong empirical data. And the idea is that the enhanced self- and collective teacher efficacy that emerges snowballs into a bountiful dividend for student learning and achievement, generating wave upon wave of positive feedback loops.

At a seeming tangent, we also note that several high-income nation education systems have significantly upped their education research popularization and dissemination wings in recent years, with, for example, the What Works Clearing House (the US), Education Endowment Foundation (England), and the Australian Education Research Organisation turning the global what works best research into plain language digests that can be easily understood, and then engaging in national dissemination campaigns to spread the word and virally to influence teacher beliefs. These approaches are similar to those employed in developing countries to provide information to parents and students on the benefits of school, but, this time, with a core focus on evangelizing the benefits of growing teacher impact. Evidence of impact (on the returns from disseminating evidence of impact) is still a work in progress. But reorienting teacher beliefs so that they embrace the fact that ALL children can learn; that teachers make the BIGGEST difference; and that all teachers must know and grow their IMPACT is profoundly important, and it is at the beating heart of the Visible Learning agenda.

Conclusion

In this chapter we explored the global evidence on how to best motivate teachers to attend school (bottleneck 1); enter their classes (bottleneck 2); deliver the curriculum (bottleneck 3); and strive for professional excellence (bottleneck 4). Through a Lean lens, we might draw the following tentative conclusions (with attendant health warnings) from the META^X research on teacher accountability enhancements:

Tentative Lean Conclusions	Health Warnings/Side Effects
• Training and support for school and system leaders should be oriented to equip them with skills in instructional leadership for impact, so that they can better unlock the high-impact instructional approaches we outline in the next chapter	• Requires comprehensive in-service training and support to leaders – including coaching. But this can be difficult to scale up with fidelity. It can also be an extremely costly intervention
• Performance-related pay increases the cost of education service delivery without increasing the quality of student learning outcomes: there are likely very few circumstances where implementation in education settings will be beneficial	• Can be challenging to reverse performance-related pay in contexts where it has already been embedded — N.B. teacher base-level pay needs to be sufficiently enticing (within local labor market norms) to attract and retain good quality entrants to the profession, and it needs to be remitted
• Given the lack of robust findings about the various accountability-based drivers, each should be piloted and independently evaluated in the local context before any consideration is given to regional/national scaling up. Account for the Hawthorne Effect (i.e., that people behave differently when they are being observed by inspectors or researchers) during the trial process. And assume that the impact will be significantly less during mass-rollout and that it will suffer from the law of unintended consequences/perverse incentives	• Stakeholders may be impatient that 'obvious' interventions are not being implemented. But it is better to delay and fully explore what has a high probability of impact locally than to implement systems that result in perverse incentives, that are difficult to reverse, and that potentially undermine student learning outcomes for decades to come
• Public and privately delivered education are likely to achieve similar levels of student learning outcomes. Therefore, in many contexts it is likely to be a waste of time to either undertake privatization or nationalization as the principal policy driver for education improvement. Just stick with whichever delivery type you already have in place and focus energy on enhancing quality *within* that system	• Debates around the benefits of public–private partnerships can be ideologically tinged, as opposed to focused on hard evidence • There *might* be a narrow range of circumstances where government education provision is suffering from catastrophic and seemingly irreversible delivery failure and/or where private provision complements and extends state capacity

(Continued)

137

Tentative Lean Conclusions	Health Warnings/Side Effects
• Re-orienting teacher beliefs about their role in student learning may have considerably more impact than leveraging performance incentives, accountability drivers, and public–private partnership	• This is easier said than done. There are many promising approaches but no surefire results, so pilot and iterate with great care. The collective teacher efficacy and Visible Learning Mindframes research is a good place to start
• Across many studies we confront the 'replication crisis', i.e., small-scale studies run by non-governmental actors show great promise but then fail to scale-up when delivered by government agencies on a regional/national basis (Mbiti, 2016)	• Always work on the assumption that whatever you are doing will not easily scale. Be pessimistic to enhance your long-term impact! But not so pessimistic you do nothing

As ever, tread carefully to grow your tower.

8

Returns from high-impact teaching and learning approaches

Back in Chapter 5, we started our Lean foray by exploring the global evidence on how best to select and train teachers. What was conspicuously absent from our discussion is what that training should be *in*, *for*, and *about*. In other words, once we have corralled teachers into workshops, arranged for subsequent in-school coaching and the activation of school-based professional learning communities, what is it (exactly) that we expect them to be able to do back at school?

We now close the circle by reviewing how individual pedagogies can be used by teachers to enhance student learning, and by exploring how the most effective approaches can be woven together into integrated programs for highly effective teaching and learning. We suspect this chapter will divide readers, although not because of controversy.

For some the reaction will be: "*At last!* We're finally getting into the detail of the important stuff that actually works for enhancing quality rather than the weeds of school voucher programs, accountability systems, and governance frameworks". Whereas, for others, the counterreaction might be: "Pedagogy is about as interesting as watching paint dry. And surely the best way to unlock great teaching is *through* voucher programs, accountability initiatives, and governance frameworks that influence what teachers do in their classrooms".

Whilst, yes, we agree that the various structural drivers can have a *nudging* influence on what happens in classrooms with the doors shut, perhaps nudging isn't enough. In fact, maybe (mere) nudging is the weakest and least effective thing we could be doing to enhance the quality of student learning. A potentially stronger theory of change is as follows:

Theory of change

Assumptions:

1 Student success is influenced by a wider range of variables than simply their own individual characteristics and socio-economic status
2 In particular, the quality of teaching that students receive has a *significant* impact on accelerating their learning outcomes
3 The quality of teaching is largely determined by the pedagogical approach that teachers use and its fit with the specific subject matter (i.e., approaches that align with what is known about human memory, attention, and learning transfer).

Therefore, invest in the following **inputs**:

1 **Training teachers in *high-impact* instructional approaches** (covered in the first part of this chapter)
2 **Developing and deploying integrated, localized, and scripted/ scaffolded teaching, learning, and formative assessment materials/programs**, which are built from the evidence about the instructional approaches that work best (covered in the second part of this chapter).

The **outcome** of this investment will be:

1 Enhanced teacher performance
2 Enhanced learning outcomes for students.

As with previous chapters, we have greyed out assumptions 1 and 2 as we covered (and confirmed) the evidence base related to these claims back in Chapter 5. We will address claim 3 – that the quality of teaching is largely determined by the instructional approach used by the teacher – throughout this chapter.

In each of the preceding chapters you may also have noticed a theme emerging. We started by presenting what, on the surface, looked like a plausible theory of change and then displayed an array of META^X data that completely contradicted it. This time it's different. If you flick forward to the various tables nestled within this chapter you will notice two things:

1 There are a LOT more interventions listed – more than across the preceding four chapters
2 ALL the teaching and learning-related enhancements we have selected generate an effect size greater than the $d = 0.40$ hinge point. Several are even double or treble this value.

When we first drafted this chapter, our initial aim was just to tantalize and titillate. In our opening cut, we simply plucked the top-20 teaching and learning strategies from the META^X and listed them. Our message was going to be, "look at these shiny things that generate so much impact and which can be unlocked by training teachers – step by step – in how to follow the cooking recipe". And our hope was that this would encourage policymakers, ministries, deliverers, and funders to conclude that they had been looking for solutions to the *hard problem* of education in all the wrong places.

However, simply listing the high-impact teaching and learning approaches like some sort of book publisher's bestseller list is too simplistic. Whilst all the practices we have identified "work", you need to know *when* and *how* to use them, and *who* to use them with (Hattie & Donoghue, 2016). Some of the approaches work better at the start of a lesson or inquiry cycle; others are more effective at helping students with surface learning; others are best for deep learning; and (yet) others for transfer, i.e., applying what has been learned to new contexts that look quite different.

None of the approaches we have catalogued work as a solo strategy. So, for example, whilst use of success criteria generates an average effect size of $d = 0.88$, you wouldn't get very far if you spent every minute of every day telling children what they were going to learn and what success in their learning looks like without then providing any subsequent instruction. Instead, you need to *start* with success criteria and *then* dance and weave with other strategies as the learning unfolds (Marzano et al., 2001).

High-impact teaching and learning approaches

Bearing in mind what we have said about high-impact approaches having different levels of utility at different stages of the learning process, we thought it would be useful to spell this out. So, in this first part of the chapter, we explore effective approaches related to:

1 **Starting a lesson, topic, or inquiry cycle**
2 **Activating surface learning**, including:
   o *Acquiring surface learning*, i.e., the initial storage of new information in the brain
   o *Consolidating surface learning*, i.e., enhancing the durability and long-term retrieval capability of stored memories.
3 **Moving to deep learning**, including:
   o *Acquiring deep learning*, i.e., strategies that support learners to understand the relationships, interconnections, and applications of their initial surface learning
   o *Consolidating deep learning*, i.e., enhancing and strengthening the durability, so that the new knowledge, understanding, and skills can be drawn on automatically and effortlessly.
4 **Achieving transfer** (a.k.a. transferable skills) that enable learning from one domain to be applied to another
5 **Cross-cutting approaches** that work across all stages.

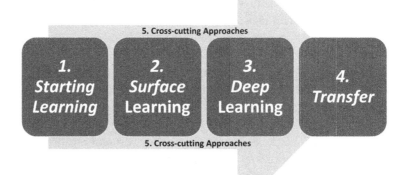

Figure 8.1 Overview of the High-Impact Teaching and Learning Approaches

(Authors' illustration)

You will also notice that for the META^X data tables this chapter we have inserted an additional "description" column that briefly explains the core features of each approach. We have included this because, unlike previous chapters, we cannot unpack and discuss each approach without turning the chapter into a book. For the book(s) see Hattie (2009, 2012).

Approaches related to starting a lesson, topic, or inquiry cycle (starting learning)

Figure 8.2 summarizes high-impact teaching and learning approaches that work best at the start of a lesson, topic, or inquiry cycle.

All the "stuff" on the table above is about making sure that the learning process isn't a magical mystery tour. It's about ensuring that when learners come to class, they know what it is they are supposed to be doing and why they are doing it. And that *why* is, of course, much wider than "because it's on the exam".

The meta-analyses in this 'starting' category tell us that students are more likely to be successful in their learning when they can see how it links to the bigger picture; when they understand what success looks like; when they are given explicit targets or goals; where those goals are realistic and build from their current knowledge, understanding, and skills; where the learning is connected or situated within the context of what they already know and can do; and when they are given worked examples that model success.

Influence	Description	No. of Metas	No. of Studies	No. of Students	No. of Effects	Aggregate Effect Size
Approaches Related to Starting a Lesson, Topic, or Inquiry Cycle						
Success criteria	A (concise) description outlining what will be taught/learnt and what the expected learning outcomes are. Often co-constructed with students and returned to regularly during transition from surface, to deep, to transfer of learning	2	163		163	**0.88**
Planning and prediction	Strategy used by both teachers and learners to prioritize how time will be allocated during and across lessons, to then plan, evaluate, and adjust	4	399		420	**0.75**
Goal difficulty/ Appropriately challenging goals	Where teachers ensure that student outcome goals are set at a sufficiently challenging level (i.e., not too hard, not too easy, just right)	6	375	23,886	473	**0.59**
Goal intentions	Students developing their own outcome goals for the level of progress/competency/mastery they wish to achieve. This aligns with goal difficulty and the role of the teacher in encouraging 'stretch targets'	7	504	76,287	613	**0.51**
Concept mapping	Creating graphic representations of topic material, and the interrelationships and hierarchies, so that learners can see the connections	11	1,232	26,374	1,324	**0.64**
Behavioral-advanced organizers	Framework that demonstrates to learners how their prior learning links to their new learning goals. Enables them to make connections and reduces stress	12	935	3,905	2,291	**0.42**
Scaffolding and situated learning	Connecting learning to students' prior knowledge so that students can see the relationships and connections to what they already know. It also involves contextualizing/localizing the examples so they relate to students' lived experiences. Scaffolding is gradually removed during the learning process	4	192	5,326	431	**0.58**
Worked examples	Providing students with partially completed exemplars so that they have greater understanding of the task requirements	2	83	3,324	179	**0.37**

Figure 8.2 Approaches Related to Starting a Lesson, Topic, or Inquiry Cycle (Starting Learning)

(Adapted from Visible Learning META^X, 2021)

All these activities are about providing students with a "a 'coat hanger' on which surface-level knowledge can be organized" (Hattie & Donoghue, 2016, p. 6). However, how these strategies are implemented also matters. Take concepts maps as an example. When the teacher says, "Voilà! Here's a concept map that links current learning to past learning and that shows the relationships and hierarchies between the new things we are going to learn", the impact is fairly muted. But where the teachers and learners collaborate to collectively craft that concept map, the subsequent impact on student achievement is far greater (see, e.g., Schroeder et al., 2018).

Approaches related to surface learning (acquisition and consolidation)

Acquisition of surface learning

Once students know where they are going and what success looks like, the next step is to start learning. The meta-analyses that we detail in the tables below relate to how students can learn new things (Figure 8.3) and then consolidate that learning (Figure 8.4).

In our work with ministries of education we often hear things like, "the problem with our education system is that it's all drill and kill. We need to stop rote learning and move to more authentic, fun, and project-based approaches". However, what you will notice as you scan the data tables is that some of the highly effective strategies for *this* phase of the learning cycle include mnemonics, rehearsal and memorization, re-reading, and testing – just the sorts of things that many people seem to complain (to us) that teachers shouldn't be doing at all! However, we need to do it for the reasons we explain below.

From longstanding cognitive psychology research, we know that human working memory is hideously under-powered (Miller, 1956; Robertson et al., 2004). On average we can hold seven (plus or minus two) chunks of information within it, simultaneously. This is considerably worse than the storage capacity of a solar powered pocket calculator that you can buy for a few dollars. And, if you've ever tried to hold an unfamiliar phone number, postal address, or set of facts in your head and then had someone start talking to you or asking you a question, then you know how quickly the data evaporates from your mind.

When you learn something new, the idea is to get it to move from working memory to long-term memory so that you can later draw it back down and do something useful with it. But to store it in the first place, it helps considerably if there is an explicit instructional strategy to integrate with prior knowledge ($d = 0.93$, see, e.g., Marzano, 1998). Things that you know already are like pre-existing 'files' in your mental filing cabinet. If the learning can be explicitly mapped and tagged to one of these, then you already have a relevant data compartment you can store it in or connect it to.

Influence	Description	No. of Metas	No. of Studies	No. of Students	No. of Effects	Aggregate Effect Size
Approaches Related to Surface Learning Acquisition						
Strategy to integrate with prior knowledge	Interlocking new learning with prior knowledge so that students can situate their learning within an existing conceptual framework. This speeds the transition of learning from working memory to long-term memory	1	10		12	**0.93**
Mnemonics	Technique for encoding information to long-term memory through storage and retrieval cues (e.g., use of mental images or acronyms linked to lists of words/concepts)	4	166	4,278	191	**0.80**
Working memory training	Techniques used to enhance the number of items learners can hold in working memory at the same time. May involve nested concepts, mnemonics, and checklists	8	232	14,596	1,126	**0.49**
Outlining and summarization	Student-led strategy focused on taking the main ideas from source material and putting them in your own words	3	384	1,914	384	**0.74**
Underlining and highlighting	Using pencil/pen or marker to highlight key facts and concepts in a printed text	1	56	2,070	56	**0.44**
Note taking	Taking notes during class to record key concepts, ideas, and learning, and doing so in a systematic and structured manner (i.e., via prior study skills training)	6	155	6,476	266	**0.51**
Imagery	Use of images (e.g., displayed by a projector or within a textbook) to reinforce learning (i.e., a picture speaks a thousand words)	2	147	2,043	194	**0.51**
Receiving peer tutoring	Receiving guided support from another student who has already progressed to the deep or transfer learning stage	3	113		127	**0.54**

Figure 8.3 Approaches Related to Surface Learning Acquisition

(Adapted from Visible Learning META^X, 2021)

145

Influence	Description	No. of Metas	No. of Studies	No. of Students	No. of Effects	Aggregate Effect Size
Approaches Related to Consolidation of Surface Learning						
Deliberate practice	Challenging, deliberate, and effortful practice for the explicit purpose of improvement. This is cognitively demanding and can usually only be undertaken in short bursts	3	161	13,689	316	**0.79**
Effort management	Techniques used by learners to maintain effort, persistence, and focus (e.g., self-reward for achieving goals)	1	15		15	**0.77**
Rehearsal and memorization	Techniques for repeating information over and over until it is memorized (e.g., use of flash cards that are shuffled and reviewed)	3	132		132	**0.73**
Re-reading	Transferring information to long-term memory by re-reading. Linked to rehearsal and memorization	2	159	1,529	159	**0.53**
Feedback	Two-way feedback between teachers and learners that enhance the learning process	26	1,201	45,800	1,606	**0.64**
Spaced (vs massed) practice	Placing a time gap (space) between deliberate practice/ rehearsal and memorization repetition cycles – rather than cramming in during a short interval	5	510	167,763	1,115	**0.65**
Interleaving	Involves the teacher spacing coverage of a topic over several weeks and alternating between one topic and another. It is a teacher-led/classroom version of spaced practice	1	104	972	104	**0.47**
Time on task	The total amount of time devoted to a specific learning episode/ concept/topic	11	326	28,034	445	**0.44**
Effects of testing	The effect of undertaking standardized testing on the consolidation/reinforcement of student learning	4	335	7,011,700	1,052	**0.59**

Figure 8.4 Approaches Related to Consolidation of Surface Learning

(Adapted from Visible Learning META[x], 2021)

To speed initial transfer from short-term to long-term memory, approaches like mnemonics ($d = 0.80$) work well (Kim et al., 2008; Mastropieri & Scruggs, 1989). Other effective strategies include underlining and highlighting ($d = 0.44$, see Donoghue & Hattie, 2016) and – even better – writing down short summaries of the main facts, concepts, or ideas in your own words ($d = 0.74$, see for example Dignath et al., 2008). Some interesting adult education research, exploring knowledge retention rates between students that made their notes via laptop vs those that wrote them down by hand, illustrates this (Mueller & Oppenheimer, 2014). Most of us cannot write as fast as a teacher speaks so we are forced to mentally interpret the key points and summarize them in a few bullets. Whereas many of us can type at speaking speed. The research found that where students typed their notes, they were not really engaging with the content, chunking/summarizing it, or linking it to their prior learning. Ergo, it didn't travel from short-term to long-term memory. But where they took notes (more slowly) by hand in summary form, they remembered far more.

Yet other approaches, like receiving peer tutoring ($d = 0.54$) and pairing appropriate images with specific concepts ($d = 0.51$), are also effective (see, e.g., Lavery, 2008; Zeneli et al., 2016). We discussed peer tutoring in Chapter 6, suggesting that this was likely to be both more cost-effective (or Lean) and generate more impact than reducing class size. The benefits from peer tutoring to the tutee are that the more advanced student was themselves struggling with the topic, concept, or idea only weeks or months prior. So they understand what their fellow student is going through more than the teacher, whose own similar struggle may have been decades ago.

During COVID teaching we introduced a notion based on peer tutoring but without the assumption that the more able or older student become the tutor – recalling that the greatest impact in peer tutoring is on the teacher/tutor. *Teach-Back* invites student to learn material (from the teacher) with the aim that they then need to devise and execute a lesson for fellow students, teachers, and/or parents. From listening to the teaching, the teacher can 'hear' the student's thinking, and see the strengths and gaps, and the knowledge and understanding is more likely to move to long-term memory.

Finally, a comment on working memory training ($d = 0.49$). There are several exercises and apps that are designed to increase the number of bits of information that we can hold in our working memory at the same time. Whilst these show that people get better at retaining data in the context of the exercise or app, subsequent ability to transfer this 'skill' or enhanced 'memory muscle' to other activities is currently near zero (Alloway, 2006; Melby-Lervåg & Hulme, 2013). Instead, it is likely better to reduce the demands on children's working memory in the classroom through cognitive task analysis, which we will come onto shortly.

Consolidation of surface learning

Once, through effective teaching and learning approaches, students have successfully transferred new information from their working memory to long-term memory, then the next challenge is keeping it there without degradation and fading. If you cast your mind back to your own student days, you may remember cramming for exams through the use of some of the strategies outlined in the *acquisition of surface learning* section. These strategies were likely good enough for you to remember the facts, concepts, and ideas long enough to pass the exam. But it's likely that a few weeks later, all that learning would have become hazy and evaporated.

Bryan Caplan (2018) presents longitudinal analysis of how much students remember from their high school civics classes in the US, where students spent several hours a week (for several years) learning about the history and political institutions of their nation. When those students were followed up – over a decade later – remarkably few could remember the dates of the founding of the nation, the civil war, or the constitutional principles related to the separation of powers. Their learning had faded away.

To reduce the probability that surface learning evaporates, students need to be primed and supported to consolidate it, which involves regularly drawing it back up and manipulating it in working memory (Robertson et al., 2004). Figure 8.4 highlights the high-impact approaches that support this phase of the learning journey. Again, you will see that many of them come from the rote, drill, and testing playbook. To us, this highlights that these 'traditionalist' strategies have their time and place. Irradicating them completely from the classroom is likely to be counterproductive. But being a pedagogic one-trick pony and *only* using these approaches is equally problematic because they do not support children to apply their learning to new problems and situations: surely the whole purpose of investing in schooling. So, we need to get to deep learning (covered in the next section and Figure 8.5).

Approaches related to deep learning (acquisition and consolidation)

Whilst the surface learning phase is more about content and skills, deep learning is about understanding the relationships, interconnections, and applications of that initial surface learning (i.e., moving from one 'thing', to multiple 'things', to the relationship between the 'things'). During the acquisition stage of deep learning, high-impact approaches include elaboration and organization ($d = 0.75$, see Donker et al., 2014), which involves teachers supporting students to make their own connections and linkages between content (micro), topics (meso), and areas (macro); and meta-cognitive and self-regulation strategies ($d = 0.58$ and $d = 0.52$), which are about supporting students to think about how they learn and to think about how they can motivate themselves to maintain greater task focus (see, for example, Sitzmann & Ely, 2011; Yildirim et al., 2019).

Consolidation of deep learning

There are also a wide range of effective approaches for consolidation of deep learning. Many of these leverage students to teach one another, for example, the

Influence	Description	No. of Metas	No. of Studies	No. of Students	No. of Effects	Aggregate Effect Size
Approaches Related to Acquiring Deep Learning						
Elaboration and organization	Student learning strategies for making connections and linking concepts and knowledge together	1	50		50	**0.75**
Meta-cognitive strategies	Literally thinking about thinking (i.e., supporting students to understand their own learning patterns and to develop their own learning strategies)	10	637	1,278,311	1,665	**0.58**
Self-regulation	Combination of effort management (to have willpower to undertake the task), deliberate practice (to execute) and meta-cognitive strategies (to evaluate self-performance)	11	1,109	323,497	2,087	**0.52**
Elaborative interrogation	Critical thinking technique focused on asking successive 'why?' questions	1	254	2,138	254	**0.56**
Inductive teaching	Teaching technique that starts with case studies/observations/data and asks students to derive general principles from the data	3	206	8,263	212	**0.44**

Figure 8.5 Approaches Related to Acquiring Deep Learning

(Adapted from Visible Learning META[X], 2021)

Influence	Description	No. of Metas	No. of Studies	No. of Students	No. of Effects	Aggregate Effect Size
Approaches Related to Consolidating Deep Learning						
Questioning	Involves the teacher posing questions to the class for them to respond to	8	241		301	**0.48**
Classroom discussion	Wider than teacher questioning, this involves rich and fluid whole-group or break-out group discussions	1	42		42	**0.82**
Problem-solving teaching	Providing students with specific rubrics or quick sheets to help them solve specific kinds of problems	12	714	17,656	1,854	**0.67**
Giving peer tutoring	Providing tuition to another student that is at an earlier stage in their learning journey. The act of teaching consolidates the understanding of the peer tutor	3	113		100	**0.48**
Self-judgment and reflection	Teaching students to evaluate their own work against the assessment criteria/mark scheme and to identify improvements	1	54		54	**0.75**
Self-verbalizing the next steps	Literally talking to yourself about a difficult task – this can be scaffolded by providing students with task-specific questions	11	521	10,352	1,624	**0.59**
Coopera- tive learning strategies	Strategy where two or more learners hold responsibility for a shared goal/project/inquiry, requiring students to cooperate as a team. Often used for more complex projects that individual students might struggle to undertake alone	23	630	34,127	1,191	**0.40**
Reciprocal teaching	Two-way tutoring where student and teacher take turns lead- ing dialogue through a four-step process; can also involve more advanced students	2	38	677	53	**0.74**
Inquiry-based teaching	Students are asked to undertake a small-scale project/investiga- tion or inquiry using, for example, the scientific method	8	353	15,728	553	**0.46**
Problem-solving teaching	Involves teachers posing a problem and equipping students with the tools to solve it themselves. The tools are often extracted from prior learning	12	714	17,656	1,854	**0.67**
Jigsaw method	Students are divided into groups that are each tasked with becoming experts on a specific concept or content area. Each group then teaches the other groups what they have learned	1	37		37	**1.20**

Figure 8.6 Approaches Related to Consolidating Deep Learning

jigsaw method ($d = 1.20$; e.g., Batdi, 2014); reciprocal teaching ($d= .74$; e.g., Galloway, 2003); giving peer tutoring ($d = 0.48$; e.g., Zeneli et al., 2016); and cooperative learning ($d = 0.40$; e.g., Tuncer & Dikmen, 2017). And it helps considerably when the focus is on the ambiguity and applications of the learning, for example, via questioning ($d = 0.48$; e.g., Gayle et al., 2006); classroom discussion ($d = 0.82$; e.g., Murphy et al., 2009); and problem-solving teaching ($d = 0.67$; e.g., Liao & Chen, 2018).

Approaches related to transfer and cross-cutting strategies

Transfer

Next, comes transfer. This is arguably the 'holy grail' of education. Many, many governmental reports have been written and inter-governmental symposia organized on 'transferable skills'. This is about how children (and for that matter adults) can develop the ability to apply their deep learning from one context and use it successfully in another.

We should start our exploration of this holy grail with the negatives. Much of the research into transfer concludes that it is extremely hard to do (Gilbert et al., 2011; Willingham, 2007). This seems to be because when we encode information to long-term memory it gets stored in domain-specific silos. If the new context that you are trying to transfer to is similar to the existing context that you already have deep knowledge of, then transfer is easier. So, transferring your knowledge of driving a red car to driving a near-identical blue car is extremely easy. Transfer from driving a red car to small van is marginally harder, but doable; and from a car to articulated lorry or bicycle, extremely challenging. Yes, all your knowledge about the rules of the road and prediction of traffic flow will still be useful but you are sitting at a different height, using different implements (more so for the bicycle), and in control of a vehicle with a different weight distribution and turning angle.

Some of the key principles from the research are that transfer is easier if: (1) the new context is similar to the existing one – this is the *theory of identical elements* and where students are explicitly shown what those elements are (Schunk, 2004); (2) where the number of overlapping elements is higher (Marton, 2006); (3) it is accompanied with *hugging* (guiding learners to understand and operate at the required performance level in the transfer area) and *bridging* (using more abstract thought as an analogy to look for similarities between two seemingly different contexts). A key skill in transfer is detecting similarities and differences between the old and new problem or situation, and such pattern recognition can be taught to enhance the skills of transfer.

Whilst the META[X] reports an effect size of $d = 0.86$ for transfer strategies, this is aggregated from 211 studies involving 7,315 students. This is too small for us (yet) to have confidence about the best ways to operationalize these approaches across different ages and curriculum areas. But given the growing speed of the

Influence	Description	No. of Metas	No. of Studies	No. of Students	No. of Effects	Aggregate Effect Size
Approaches Related to Transfer						
Transfer strate-gies	Approaches for making current learning relevant to new topics, contexts, and domains. Often involves supporting students to distinguish between the surface features vs deep structure (and similarities) in seemingly different contexts	5	211	7,315	234	**0.86**

Figure 8.7 Approaches to Transfer

(Adapted from Visible Learning META^X, 2021)

global economy in both the creation and destruction of job roles, transferable skills will become even more important as adults will increasingly need to reinvent themselves.

Cross-cutting approaches

Finally, some of the approaches catalogued within the META^X are cross-cutting (as outlined in Figure 8.8). By this we mean they can be used throughout the learning journey – from starting a lesson, to surface learning, then onto deep learning, and finally, in the holy grail of transfer.

Cognitive task analysis ($d = 1.29$), for example, is a teacher evaluative process. Building on what we know from cognitive psychology about the limitations (and fragility) of working memory, it centers on analysis of each proposed lesson activity to count how many new items, chunks, or concepts students will have to juggle in their working memory simultaneously (Tofel-Grehl & Feldon, 2013). Given the limits of working memory, we don't really want learners to be juggling any more than five items at once – through any type of learning (i.e., starting, surface, deep, or transfer). Otherwise, we overburden their cognitive load.

A second cross-cutting approach is differentiation ($d = 0.68$), which involves developing activities at different levels of difficulty – so that whilst students are working on the same topic area, they are divided into within-class groups that explore these at varying levels of challenge (Kim, 2015). Another form of differentiation involves students undertaking individualized learning pathways – working independently through activities at their own pace. Kumon and computer-assisted instructions programs are examples of these that we will return to in the next chapter.

Testing ($d = 1.07$) is also a cross-cutting approach that can be used at all stages of the learning cycle (Fuchs & Fuchs, 1986; Reschly et al., 2009). It comes down to the assessment questions and whether they are asking you to *describe* (surface level), *explain* (surface to deep), *analyze* and *evaluate* (deep), or *compare* and *apply* (transfer). This, of course, also links to learning hierarchy taxonomies like Bloom's and SOLO. And testing is nothing without feedback to signal where to next. It is the use of testing in the teaching cycle that helps, not merely testing at the end for accountability reasons.

Finally, homework ($d = 0.28$; e.g., Fan et al., 2017; Hendriks et al., 2014). This seems an exceedingly low effect size return from an extremely common cross-cutting practice and it is the only influence we have included that falls below the 0.40 threshold. However, there is *much* heterogeneity of impact across different age groups. Cooper (1989) finds that homework generates double the impact for upper-secondary/high school students than it does for lower-secondary/

Influence	Description	No. of Metas	No. of Studies	No. of Students	No. of Effects	Aggregate Effect Size
Cross-Cutting Approaches						
Cogni-tive task analysis	Teacher analysis of the likely student cogni-tive load related to each aspect of the lesson. This is a teacher meta-cognitive strategy focused on reducing working memory burdens on stu-dents during learning	2	27		95	**1.29**
Differen-tiation	Providing content/tasks at different levels of difficulty to cater to students of dif-ferent ability levels	1	49		80	**0.68**
Testing	Impact of testing on stu-dents' subsequent level of student achievement. Works across all levels as tests can assess across surface, deep, and trans-fer learning	2	63	1,489	323	**1.07**
Homework	Providing students with assignments to undertake outside class time, usually at home	8	217	106,144	386	**0.28**

Figure 8.8 Cross-Cutting Approaches

(Adapted from Visible Learning META[x], 2021)

junior-high school; and double again from lower-secondary to primary/elementary level. To put this into effect size terms, the impact of homework on primary-level students is $d = 0.15$ and on secondary level learners is $d = 0.64$. The key seems to be prescribing homework to provide an opportunity to practice that which has already been taught in school, and resisting assigning homework that requires students to generate new information or do tasks that they have yet to be exposed to in class. From a Lean (time management) perspective, reducing the amount of homework at primary to fewer, shorter, sweeter surface-level learning consolidation activities is probably a good bet. But at secondary/high-school level, homework is an extremely important cross-cutting strategy.

Bringing it all together

Let's start with the good news. Out of all the categories of intervention that we have reviewed in Part 2 of the Manifesto, we have the greatest degree of confidence about the potential for high-impact instructional approaches to positively impact the learning lives of children in low- and middle-income country contexts. These approaches are effective because they align with the experimental findings from cognitive psychology and the science of learning. This psychology research tells us a great deal about how humans process information; how short-term memory works; how learning is chunked and consolidated into long-term memory; how spaced repetition reinforces retention; how being tired or low in calories reduces the rate of learning; how expertise is developed; how we transfer learning from one specialist domain to another (i.e., with great difficulty), and so on (Hattie & Yates, 2013; Kirschner & Hendrick, 2020).

Yes, the META^X studies we reviewed in this chapter are predominantly from high-income nations. And yes, we admit, some cognitive psychology studies over the last decade have suggested that there are differences in what features in the environment that Western vs Eastern vs Indigenous groups attend to when they perceive and process information (Kitayama et al., 2019; Varnum et al., 2010). But it seems perverse to argue that Eastern, (globally) Southern, or Indigenous children's brains are so fundamentally different that the approaches we have outlined above won't work. Does anyone really think it's a *bad* idea to situate learning based on children's prior experiences; explain the purpose of the learning and what success looks like; and then support children to engage in deliberate practice, rehearsal, mnemonics, peer tutoring, the jigsaw method, classroom discussion, and testing, etc.? Our message is that high-impact instructional approaches do travel but they must be situated within and be respectful to local cultural norms and values, and local linguistic and counting conventions.

Now to the less good news. In our helicopter fly-past of the literature on high-impact teaching and learning approaches, we outlined 40+ effective strategies. Much like the way that boiling an egg involves many sub-steps that must also be mastered and deployed at the right time, like filling the kettle; boiling the water; putting the egg in a pan; pouring over the water; lighting the stove, etc., each of the 40+ strategies have layered sub-processes and sub-sub processes. Assuming that there are (on average) 25 'things' that a teacher needs to master to implement each of the 40+ high-impact approaches, that's 1,000+ "balls" that educators need to select from, and then juggle at exactly the right moment. And this is a gross underestimate. For most of the 40+ strategies there is at least one book as long (or longer) than this one, explaining the theory and the complex steps and sub-routines to put it into practice.

Adding to the complexity, as well as knowing when in the learning journey to use each of the "balls", some vary in their impact depending on the age of students. We gave the homework example at the end of the last section. To this, we can add problem-based learning – which is more effective with older students who have already acquired high levels of domain-specific expertise (Walker & Leary, 2009). It works (reasonably) well with university-level students and correspondingly less well as we cycle down the ages. It is too often introduced before students have sufficient surface knowledge to engage in problem-based learning.

Then educators need to weave all these "balls" in with subject knowledge. Whilst, as we outlined in Chapter 5, primary- and lower-secondary-level teachers do not need to be degree-level experts in the subject they teach, they do need to know which of their 1,000+ balls work best with different curriculum topics. Talk to any highly proficient mathematics/science/literacy teacher (or watch a group of them talk together) and you will witness LOTS of dialogue not only on the instructional approaches that relate to the stage of the learning cycle but also about what works best for fractions, the structure of the atom, or past-perfect tense, etc.

Educators need to juggle the balls across stages of the learning cycle, age of the learner, and curriculum content. Three dimensions of juggling: it's hardly any wonder that some balls get dropped. And, as we go on to unpack in the second part of the chapter, this suggests that we need to use the same kinds of approaches to unlock the professional expertise of teachers as we expect teachers to use with their students! It also (perhaps) suggests that we need to automate the pedagogic heavy lifting so that teachers can focus on the moment-by-moment interactions in the classroom.

Integrated programs to reduce teacher cognitive load (a.k.a. automation)

What can we learn from other esteemed professions?

Other professions have tackled the challenge of 'ball juggling' in a variety of ways. In aviation, pilots juggle engines, steering, wing flaps, navigation, communication, emergency procedures, etc. They need to press the right buttons and say the right things at the right time or people die. The industry-wide approach was to standardize the language of the cockpit and the protocols for flying. Key to this is the use of carefully constructed and *mandated* checklists that help aviators manage their cognitive loads: the right ball at the right moment (Gawande, 2010).

Another esteemed profession has gone even further. Only elite actors can join the Royal Shakespeare Company. However, one of the rules is that you CANNOT change any of Shakespeare's lines. Of course, the purpose is not to reduce cognitive load, it's simply a tradition of the genre. But the world-famous actors that deliver the scripts are highly esteemed and receive great praise for their performance: they generate that brilliance *between the lines*.

What are the applications for education?

To us, the learning from the examples presented above is that (some) high-status professions have already explicitly sought to systematize, standardize, and automate the processes that even their most elite operators utilize. Those professionals, in turn, also seem to accept and embrace that this is how it should be done.

If we can apply the same principles to education, then perhaps we can overcome the challenges associated with training teachers to juggle 1,000+ balls. Maybe we can help them to better weave the right approach into the right stage of learning, for the right age of learner. Perhaps we can also help them to account for the fact that certain approaches work better for the water cycle, covalent bonding, the periodic table, electricity and resistance, etc. And maybe the best way of doing this is to automate as much of the heavy lifting as possible?

The good news is that in certain pockets of the global education system we are already quite far down this road. Figures 8.9 and 8.10 summarize data from the META^X in relation to three different levels (or degrees) of standardization and automation:

- **Level 1: Generic frameworks** – these provide a suggested process map/pathway through the various high-impact instructional approaches, outlining the optimal approaches, steps, and sequences for juggling. But they are merely wireframes. Teachers still need to develop the curriculum, curriculum content, scheme of work, lesson plans, student worksheets, and formative assessment tools that embody the (selected) overarching framework (i.e., they need to color it all in).
- **Level 2: Scaffolded programs** – these go further, providing educators with the additional subject-specific teaching, learning, and assessment materials outlined above, rather than expecting teachers to develop these themselves. But there is still considerable leeway in how the teacher delivers the lesson. For example, guidance is provided as 'suggestions' in bullet points, which the teacher interprets and makes relevant to the context of

their students. If educators don't like the proposed activity they (usually) have the leeway to use their professional judgment to swap it out, or even to mix, match, blend, and weave the materials from different scaffolded programs together.

■ **Level 3: Scripted programs** – this is like a Royal Shakespeare Company approach to education. Teachers are provided with a full script that details exactly what it is they should say and do. Some scripted programs are linear – with the teacher simply starting at the beginning and working through to the end, like an actor in a play. Others are branching. The script writers attempt to anticipate the different reactions from the learners, providing pivot points for the teacher to transition to whichever alternative sub-script is then relevant to what is happening in the room. This is bit like a multiple-ending novel, where if you decide to slay the dragon you must then turn to page 56 and face a long walk through the wilderness, but if (alternatively) you decide to befriend the dragon you turn to page 907, finding yourself riding on its back to your next destination, and so on. The difference of course is that it is the students, through their reaction to the unfolding story, that decide the dragon's (or rather the lesson's) fate and direction.

However, we should highlight that reality is a little messier than the levels within Figures 8.9 and 8.10. For most of the relevant influences in the META[x] there are many meta-analyses, which aggregate the findings from many hundreds, and sometimes thousands, of studies. Not all the treatments under a specific influence sit firmly within one of our three proposed levels, and for some, different parts of the treatment straddle different levels, so great care is required in how we interpret.

Level 1 example: Flipped classroom

A Level 1 program provides educators with a suggested wireframe that they use to design their own curriculum, lesson plans, student activities, and assessments. One example is flipped classroom – an explicit set of teaching and learning protocols where students review materials (video of the class, read a text, watch an experiment, etc. – designed/selected by the teacher) before class, and then in class the teacher delves deeper into the topic. Hence, flipped, because this is the reverse of the usual way of doing things (i.e., where you learn in class and then follow this up with homework).

Flipping has been promulgated by many as a revolution in teaching. There are now 42 meta-analyses on the effects of flipped classrooms (based on 1,356 studies), with an average effect size of $d = 0.59$ (which is pretty good) – although the range of effects across these 42 metas spans from $d = 0.19$ to 2.29 (see, e.g., Kapur et al., in review). This points to the critical importance of the differing design features and degree of implementation of different flipped classroom wireframes; and how hard it is to codify teaching strategies without knowing

Influence	Description	No. of Metas	No. of Studies	No. of Students	No. of Effects	Aggregate Effect Size
Integrated Programs – (mainly) Level 1						
Flipped classroom	Students learn the foundation content for a new topic independently at home and then discuss and analyze it in class. More effective for older learners	42	1,359	209,926	1,331	**0.59**
Mastery learning	Involves providing students with formative tests to measure their learning level and appropriate content, then measuring that they have 'mastered it'. Students repeat the content at their own pace until achieving mastery	14	742	11,383	595	**0.61**
Explicit teaching strategies	Highly structured approach that involves instruction/teaching, guided practice by students, and feedback/formative assessment, followed by more teaching and guided practice until students achieve mastery	16	5,784	1,491,369	13,186	**0.57**
Response to intervention programs (RTI)	A systems-level, tiered approach to the early identification of students who are at risk for learning difficulties or problem behavior and the consequent provision of increasingly intensive preventative interventions – an educational equivalent of medical triaging	5	107		332	**1.09**
Conceptual change programs	Programs focused on diagnosing/identifying student misconceptions in specific curriculum areas and re-orienting/changing their understanding	2	112		168	**0.99**
Service learning	Where students engage in community service that links to a curriculum area they are learning about. This enhances both their understanding of the course content as well as contributing to their community	3	39	5,020	45	**0.58**

Figure 8.9 Integrated Programs – (mainly) Level 1

(Adapted from Visible Learning META^X, 2021)

Influence	Description	No. of Metas	No. of Studies	No. of Partici- pants	No. of Effects	Aggregate Effect Size
Integrated Programs – (mainly) Levels 2 and 3						
Visual perception programs	A structured approach to reading comprehension related to organizing and inter- preting the letters on a page	13	497	11,531	1,254	0.63
Phonics programs	Reading comprehension program that focuses on teaching students to phoneti- cally decode written words. Often accompanied with guided and graded reading materials	29	1,102	79,368	7,906	0.60
Repeated read- ing programs	This is where learners re-read short, meaningful passages until a satisfactory level of fluency is reached	66	2,301	457,069	6,673	0.48
Comprehen- sive reading programs	These have a core focus on information processing strategies (e.g., inferential reasoning, summarizing, and chunking text for deeper understanding and stronger retrieval from long-term memory)	38	1,258	288,225	3,288	0.52
Reading recov- ery programs	Structured 1:1 reading intervention programs for students that have been identified as having poor reading skills. However, these interventions are resource intensive	3	68	5,685	1,496	0.53
Spelling programs	Systematic programs focused on improving spelling – including weekly lists of words to memorize, and weekly tests and feedback	1	91	9,341	153	0.58
Science programs	Explicitly structured science programs that have differentiated and scaffolded teaching and learning materials, and which are supported by formative assessment materials	19	1,157	405,573	2,815	0.54
Integrated cur- ricular programs	Structuring the curriculum around exploration of a topic or theme and applying math, literacy, science, etc. specifically to address the topic. Evidence suggests stronger impact during elementary/primary education	3	89	13,298	108	0.47
Creativity programs	Programs that explicitly teach creative thinking skills and provide learners with scaf- folded strategies to apply these to different curriculum/domain areas	16	853	49,621	1,032	0.64
Intelligent tutor- ing systems	Computer-based instruction where students receive a diagnostic test and are then presented with content in their areas of greatest need	5	299	22,700	304	0.51
Direct instruc- tion programs (DI)	DI programs involve 7 major steps: 1. Teacher specifies learning; 2. Teacher knows and communicates success criteria; 3. Build commitment and engagement in learning task (the hook); 4. Lesson design: input, model, check for understanding; 5. Guided practice; 6. Closure; and 7. Independent practice	6	652	42,618	4,691	0.59

Figure 8.10 Integrated Programs – (mainly) Levels 2 and 3

(Adapted from Visible Learning META[x], 2021)

what the program developer means by flipped classrooms, how it was implemented, whether the teacher assessed the students learning from the pre-class and then modified what happened in class or not, whether the effect was primarily due to students' having double the time being exposed to the content (i.e., pre-class + class experience), and more.

It turned out, from our syntheses of these 42 metas, that the typical explanations about flipped classes being effective because they are using deeper methods (e.g., problem based, discovery, enquiry teaching in the class session) was irrelevant; and, where it occurred, the effects were actually lower than using explicit instruction (Kapur et al., in review). Our conclusion, from wading through the 42 metas, was that we needed to deconstruct the elements of flipped classrooms that lead to higher effects, and reframe the methods related to specific aspects of the learning cycle. In other words, none of the existing wireframes was (yet) a sufficient Level 1 guide-frame for teachers to implement flipped classroom with fidelity and impact.

A better Level 1 guide-frame needed to start by recognizing that students often come to a new topic with various conceptions and misconceptions, errors of understanding, or simply no knowledge of the specific topic. Not knowing is the norm – indeed, if they know it, then it is too easy, and why be inefficient and spend more time teaching them what they know. Yes, scaffolding on prior achievement is critical. As Ausubel (1968) famously noted, the most important single factor influencing learning is what the learner already knows. The first aim of flipped learning relates to activating relevant prior knowledge even if students produce sub-optimal or incorrect solutions. Second, help the students notice their inconsistencies and misconceptions, which in turn makes them aware of the gaps and limits of their knowledge. Third, prior knowledge activation affords students opportunities to compare and contrast their solutions with the correct solutions during subsequent instruction, thereby increasing the likelihood of students' noticing and encoding critical features of the new concept. Finally, besides the cognitive benefits, problem-solving prior to instruction also has affective benefits of greater learner agency, as well as engagement and motivation to learn the targeted concept. Hence, the argument is a four-step flipped model:

1 **Fail** – providing opportunities for the instructor and the student to diagnose, check, and understand what was and was not understood
2 **Flip** – pre-exposure to the ideas in the upcoming class (as simple as providing video of the class)
3 **inForm** – a class where these misconceptions are explored, and an opportunity to re-engage in learning the ideas and a traditional lecture is efficient to accomplish this
4 **Feed** – feedback to the students and instructor about levels of understanding and where to next directions.

If you are confused by the discussion above, then that's the point. It highlights that Level 1 generic frameworks have the potential to add value but only if:

- The specific framework you select has evidence of impact (with flipped classrooms alone we mapped more than 29 different varieties of flipping – with differing levels of impact)
- The stages, steps, and sub-steps within the selected framework are clearly articulated, easy to understand and follow, and not open to misinterpretation (they need be almost like a Jamie Oliver cookery book)
- Ideally, there is also additional guidance about how to connect these processes to the target curriculum area and age range of learners you happen to be teaching.

Therefore, simply providing teachers with training and scaffolding in the form of (loose) Level 1 tips and tricks and then leaving them to figure out the appropriate stages in the learning journey to embed these is likely to be counter-productive if we want them to quickly master the tradecraft of teaching. This is (arguably) where Level 2 and 3 programs come in!

Level 2: Scaffolded programs

The next level down involves *more* prescription about the sequencing of teaching and learning activities and much *more* dovetailing, or at least signposting and linkage, to the curriculum. One of the most lauded developing country education interventions is *Teaching at the Right Level* (TaRL), which was pioneered by Pratham, an Indian non-governmental organization. Positive evaluations of various iterations of TaRL include Banerjee et al., 2007; Banerjee et al., 2010; Banerji & Chavan, 2016; Global Education Evidence Advisory Panel, 2020. Whilst there is variation across the treatment arms, TaRL starts to move us much more toward Level 2. Although, as we shall show, even in its most recent iterations, different bits of it straddle different levels – with higher and lower degrees of scaffolding and prescription. However, the program is specifically designed to improve children's reading and mathematics skills (generally) in grades 3 to 5; and the focus is on children that have fallen behind and who might not subsequently be able to catch up because their grade-level understanding and skills do not match their age, meaning that as they progress up the grades they inevitably fall further and further behind – eventually dropping out altogether.

The TaRL protocols include:

1 **Using formative assessment instruments to diagnose what children already know and can do in literacy and mathematics**. The idea is to identify (with precision) their gaps in foundational knowledge; and, therefore, their actual mathematics and literacy 'age'.

2   **Grouping by levels rather than age**. For a proportion of each school day, children are re-grouped based on their current level of understanding rather than their age/grade/form.

3   **Learning at the right level**. This sees mixed age groups from grades 3–5 working together and being taught together – with the content knowledge (and teaching and learning materials) being appropriate to their collective current level of understanding.

4   **Re-evaluating**. This is about going back to (1) and using formative assessment instruments to diagnose where to next, i.e., which group and what learning. The outcome is that the children are (again) re-grouped and (again) undertake learning relevant to their current level of understanding.

During implementation, educators are provided with high levels of support via a standardized school and teacher activation process.

We shouldn't be surprised that TaRL evaluations have been positive. It's not a million miles from Fail, inForm, and Feed; and is pretty close to *Response to Intervention* (RTI), which is outlined in Figure 8.9. Across five metas of 107 studies, RTI generates an aggregate effect size of 1.09 (see, e.g., Burns et al., 2005; Torres, 2016). Like TaRL, RTI involves the use of formative assessment to identify students at risk of falling behind and providing them with additional targeted support. As with TaRL, this often involves bringing students with similar needs/progress levels together for a proportion of the day to address and support those shared needs. It also involves a further level of 1:1 tuition for students that have not 'caught up'. The fact that TaRL and RTI are independently invented, but similar, suggests that design features which generate impact can travel across cultures. Indeed, as we said earlier in the chapter, human brains are broadly the same the world over in terms of cognition, working memory, attention, etc.

Although, our interpretation is that during stage 3 of TaRL (i.e., the bit where teachers are delivering their lessons), it is still largely left to the local discretion of individual educators. They are provided with exemplars and suggestions for teaching and learning materials, but the teachers are still (often) developing their own lessons from scratch. This means that whilst some elements and aspects of TaRL are more Level 2 (e.g., the assessment and grouping protocols; and school activation and training systems), what teachers then do in their classrooms is (more) toward the Level 1 generic wireframe modality.

Level 3: Scripted programs

The final level down brings us to the Royal Shakespeare Company model of education. Each night, millions of teachers make critical decisions about their lesson plans for the next day – often developing them from scratch. Surely this is among the most inefficient/anti-Lean, evidence-free cottage industries that sucks up time, intellect, and resources in the business of teaching? Yes, there are multitudes of lesson plans on the internet already (for those that can access it), but many teachers argue that their class is unique, and thus they need the autonomy to develop their own lesson plans and resources. We understand this claim, as it is the moment-by-moment adjustments to the planning that are core to the success of much teaching.

But what if there was an evidence base of lessons where there are ratings as to the alignment to curricula, rigor of the lesson, focus on knowing that and/or knowing how, and an opportunity for teachers having used the resource to rate the impact on the students. US-based *EdReports* (https://www.edreports.org/) has some components of these ratings, and building such an evidence database across other countries could save much time and energy, and link teachers into a professional community where they can learn from each other about the rigor, value, and impact of lessons. Then the focus of teachers could be on the adaptations, the adjustments, the moment-by-moment decisions that are core to the success of teaching. However, even this approach arguably only takes us to Level 2.5 – still leaving teachers to select which lesson plans, which sequence, and what to swap in or out. The airline equivalent would be making the checklists 'recommended but optional best practice' rather than the 'mandatory way we do things around here'.

The research suggests that a more impactful (and more Level 3) approach is for experts to craft a universal (but culturally localized) script for each curriculum area that integrates the right pedagogics in at the right time and then to test, refine, and continually iterate it with teachers and learners in the classroom (a.k.a. scripted direct instruction). This scripted direct instruction approach was first pioneered in 1960s America by Siegfried Engelmann. It involved students being placed into within-class ability groups and teachers following a (field-tested) scripted manual that provided them with the exact word-for-word lesson content – both for the whole class and for their differentiated interactions with the various ability sub-groups. Again, this sounds a lot like *teaching at the right level* – albeit with more guard rails and far greater prescription.

Whilst a common objection to scripted direct instruction is that it de-professionalizes teachers – turning them into little more than actors that merely read their lines – there is evidence of positive impact on student test scores in high-income country contexts. Quality implementation requires teachers to 'read between the lines'.

We have identified six meta-analyses that collectively aggregate the findings from 652 studies, involving more than 42,000 participants, relating to the implementation of direct instruction methods (Adams & Engelmann, 1996; Borman et al., 2003; Coughlin, 2010; Haas, 2005; Stockard et al., 2018; White, 1988). The mean average effect size across these six meta-analyses is $d = 0.59$, which again is not to be sniffed at. The systematic reviews that we catalogued in Chapter 3 also found strong evidence of impact for scripted/(or at least) structured lesson plans and aligned student learning materials in low- and middle-income country contexts (e.g., Angrist et al., 2020; Conn, 2017; Ganimian & Murnane, 2016; Glewwe & Muralidharan, 2016; Kremer & Holla, 2009; Krishnaratne et al., 2013; Snilstveit et al., 2016). And in sub-Saharan Africa we are aware of several private school operators that have embraced scripted direct instruction approaches, providing teachers in their schools with a pre-loaded tablet that contains their lines. So more evidence is being collected about the impact potential in low- and middle-income contexts by the day.

However, simply lifting programs off the shelf from one country/culture and transplanting them to another is not likely to be terribly effective. Instead, the materials need to be reviewed in the context of the local theory of change, taken apart, recontextualized/adapted, and put back together in the context that they will be used – with the language and examples/stimulus material being aligned to that local cultural context. This process also needs to include careful piloting – involving the collection of formative evaluation data that can be used to iterate the approaches to implementation. This also links to a cognitive bias called *The Ikea Effect*: we have greater love for things we were involved in building, or at least localizing (Norton et al., 2011). We will return to scripted approaches in the next chapter – because through the use of technology we can increase the ease of use, or at least reduce some of the friction!

But integrated programs also require teacher training (at all levels)

The next challenge is in how we train educators to implement these (Level 1, 2, or 3) programs with fidelity – especially as in Chapter 5 we highlighted the inefficiency of many types of teacher training.

To recap and link these two areas of research together our interpretation is that:

- **Pre-service initial teacher training programs that occur largely away from the school setting are unlikely to have very much impact on teaching quality and learning outcomes.** From a Lean perspective, this training could either stop, be significantly reduced, or be embedded within schools – if it is to continue.
- **Teachers do not need to hold degree-level qualifications in the subjects they teach** – they merely need to understand the content knowledge up to the level that they are required to teach at. From a Lean perspective, this means that it is not essential to invest in degree-level scientists to teach school-level science (at least not for primary and lower-secondary, anyway), etc.

BUT:

- **In-service training is much more likely to be effective in equipping educators with the pedagogic content knowledge, skills, and enthusiasm to implement (localized) integrated programs if it is:**
  - Spaced;
  - Involves developing an understanding of why the specific integrated program works;
  - Involves modelling, practice, and hearing expert teachers thinking and making evaluative judgments while teaching; and
  - Involves peer collaboration and (high-quality) coaching.
- Even more so if those delivering the training were also part of the localization/design team that developed the integrated program.

One way of thinking about this teacher expertise development continuum is as outlined in Figure 8.11.

Modality	Mode A	Mode B	Mode C	Mode D
A.K.A.	Osmosis	Scripted/ Prescriptive	Professional Expertise	Systematic Enquiry
Way of acting	Unstructured learning on the job – by osmosis	Teachers follow a script developed by experts	Teachers learn many classroom protocols and mix these intuitively based on their reading of the classroom context	Teachers use the scientific method to develop hypotheses and conduct experiments to measure and enhance their impact
Way of training	No training provided, and limited personal reflection required	Training in how to effectively execute branching scripts and eventually to graduate to become a script writer	Training in new pedagogies that teachers can add to their repertoire – leaving the selection largely down to the teacher's professional judgment	Training in scientific inquiry to enable educators to (clinically) conduct inquiry cycles to enhance their impact
Way of thinking	Narrow and implicit	Narrow and explicit for 'actors' but wide, deep, and evidence-based for 'script writers'	Wide but often intuitive/gut feeling-based; pattern recognition	Wide, deep, evaluative, and evidence-based

Figure 8.11 The Teacher Expertise Development Continuum

(Authors' analysis)

Each of these approaches work to some degree – although we would expect to see higher effect sizes from the scripted/prescriptive (Mode B) and evaluative thinking approaches (Mode D), which highlights that to make progress sometimes you end up taking a step backwards along the way (Mode C)! Indeed, 17th-century surgeons thought that they were displaying professional expertise, but without systematic inquiry to evaluate the efficacy of their treatments, they had no way of knowing that their mercury and lead-based tinctures were highly poisonous.

We can use the explanations that underlie effective teaching strategies from the Visible Learning interpretations to help bring focus of the underlying skills. There are seven big ideas:

1 Teachers working together as evaluators of their impact   1.22
2 All having high expectations   0.90
3 All moving toward explicit success criteria   0.77
4 Using the Goldilocks principle of challenge   0.74

5	Welcoming errors and high trust as opportunities to learn	0.72
6	Maximizing the feedback to teachers about their impact	0.72
7	A focus on learning the right proportions of surface and deep	0.69

Source: Hattie (2012)

Hence the importance of finding time and resources such that teachers (and/or script writers) can work together to evaluate their impact – asking the three impact questions: impact about what, for whom, and how much? This amount then relates to the nature of expectations teachers have about what a year's growth for a year's input means, and needs robust discussions based around evidence of growth (reviewing students' work over time, using effect-size growth measures, etc.). These sessions highlight the evaluative thinking, the appropriate high expectations, and are powerful professional learning (moving beyond sharing resources, having deficit thinking about students, and focusing on the teaching more than the impact of the teaching). When these high expectations are transparent to students (via success criteria) this helps the students know when good is good enough, know how to interpret the lessons and feedback as aides to knowing their progress toward success, and engages them in the excitement of challenge – providing the Goldilocks principle that these success criteria should not be too hard, too easy, or too boring is followed.

When success criteria are used in the class, there is a gap between what the students know and can do now, and where they need to be, and this gap must be seen as a positive. Hence, errors, not knowing, and seeking help should be seen as opportunities to learn and not indicators of failure. Indeed, high trust classes see failure as a learner's best friend, and students need to be taught about the delightful struggle to learn – there are specific learning strategies they need to be taught as well as knowing when is optimal to use the various strategies. When teachers are listening, using assessment and questioning, and gathering student voice, they can hear more about their impact on students and thus make the adjustments, move to the next levels of learning, and increase their impact on their students' progress and achievement.

These seven big ideas transcend subject domains, ages of students, abilities (bright or otherwise), national boundaries (low-, middle- and high-income nations), and show the critical nature of the evaluative thinking that underlines the expertise of teachers (and script writers). Without investment in developing these skills (and/or scaffolding them through Level 1–3 type interventions), there is far less likelihood of return on investment in schooling. Yes, we will have solved the *easier* problem, but the *hard* problem shall remain.

Conclusion

In this chapter we have explored the applications of the global research on high-impact teaching and learning approaches. Unlike the previous four chapters, where we identified multiple Jenga blocks for the removal/hollowing out/not adding, we instead found many, many, many things worth adding. Our hope is that the META^X data provides a metaphorical torch that can illuminate the (Lean-est) path. That path starts with what we know about how our brains learn; maps back to the high-impact instructional approaches; then back further to how we support teachers and students to develop expertise in these effective strategies; and then, finally, to the school/system features that buttress, scale, and sustain impact. In other words, from brains, to learning strategies, to teachers, to classrooms, to schools, to systems. NOT the other way round.

Through a Lean lens, we might draw the following tentative conclusions (with attendant health warnings) from the META^X research:

Tentative Lean Conclusions	Health Warnings/Side Effects
• High-impact instructional approaches generate the highest impact when teachers know when and how to sequence them	• Effective sequencing is extremely challenging as it requires juggling the "balls" of surface, deep, and transfer learning across what works for different ages and different curriculum areas • Leaving the sequencing decisions to teachers is good for their notion of professional competency and autonomy but may result in sub-optimal outcomes. Therefore, integrated programs may offer a better alternative
• Integrated programs have very strong potential for enhancing the quality of teaching and learning, and potentially at moderate cost (especially if they are scripted/scaffolded and contain clear instructions for teachers to follow while still allowing for the moment-by-moment evaluative thinking and adjustments in the implementation)	• Do not attempt to plug in and play. Look carefully at how the program will need to be adapted for the local ecosystem, and drop it if it there is evidence it is not having the desired impact
• Select programs that have robust evidence of impact in similar contexts	• There is no guarantee that the program will work in your context. But take heart that if it has been built from cognitive psychology research findings there is a far higher probability of effectiveness, given that human brains store and retrieve information through broadly the same neurological processes the world over!
• Establish local design groups to take these programs apart, localize them, and put them back together	• This will almost certainly require capacity-building if a cadre of program designers is not already available within the local context

(Continued)

Tentative Lean Conclusions	Health Warnings/Side Effects
• Pilot carefully and iteratively evaluate before attempting national/regional rollout, paying extra careful attention to the most effective approaches for inducting and upskilling teachers	• It can be seductive to skip evaluation and assume that your program will work or to cherry-pick anecdotes and testimonials that suggest successful implementation and impact. Formative evaluation is crucial to iterative improvement

Returns from education technology

In the preceding chapters we explored the various Jenga blocks that can be removed, not added, hollowed out, and occasionally inserted in relation to teachers, structures, accountability drivers, and high-impact instructional approaches. However, many of the interventions that we investigated within these categories are not new. State management of teacher recruitment and training has existed for more than 300 years (Gray, 2013; Vincent, 2019). Ditto state coordination of school building programs. And various approaches to accountability and motivation can be traced back at least as far as the Romans – including the carrots of victory titles and financial awards, and the sticks of decimation and crucifixion (Watson, 1969).

The focus of this chapter, however, is on a type of education intervention that has only really existed post-1960: education technology. More specifically, electrically powered digital devices and/or the software that runs on these. A potential theory of change, which we will go on to test and interrogate, is as follows:

Theory of change

Assumptions:

1 Student success is influenced by a wider range of variables than simply their own individual characteristics and socio-economic status
2 In particular, the quality of teaching that students receive has a *significant* impact on accelerating their learning outcomes
3 Teaching quality can be significantly enhanced through technological aides that: (a) **monitor** whether educators are in class and teaching; (b) **amplify** and enhance their instructional approaches; and (c) **save them time** that they can reinvest in self-evaluation and deliberate practice

DOI: 10.4324/9781003166313-12

4 Learning outcomes can also be significantly increased through **students' direct engagement with appropriate forms of technology** (i.e., complementing/enhancing learner's engagement with teachers).

Therefore, invest in the following **inputs**:

1 **Access** to technology for BOTH teachers and students
2 Use of technology to **monitor teacher activity** (a.k.a. techno-accountability)
3 Use of EdTech tools that **enhance the quality of teaching** (e.g., technology-enhanced teacher training and technology-enhanced instruction – including scaffolded or even scripted solutions)
4 Provision of **student self-access to intelligent tutoring systems** to enhance and extend classroom instruction and/or to compensate for absentee teachers
5 Technology that generates **process efficiencies** (e.g., automation of human capital-intensive processes such as school timetabling, homework marking, parental reporting, and development of personalized learning pathways for students – N.B. none of the data we have identified explicitly explores the question of saving teachers' time).

The **outcome** of this investment will be:

1 Enhanced teacher performance
2 Enhanced learning outcomes for students.

Technology in developing contexts

Before we get into the 'what works best' data, it is worth noting that all the technology-related interventions we will discuss require electricity, and many also need the internet. Whilst many countries are nearing universal access to electricity, in sub-Saharan Africa, penetration rates are only at 47% (World Bank Open Data, 2020a). Across Nigeria, Ethiopia, and the Democratic Republic of Congo, the proportion of population with access to an electrical supply is 55%, 48%, and 19% respectively. This leaves approximately 175 million people without access to power – across just these three countries alone (Rodriguez-Segura, 2020). The next hurdle is internet, with more than 50% of the global population still not connected (World Bank Open Data, 2020b).

In jurisdictions where access to electricity and the internet are more widespread, there is still often a shortage of digital devices in schools. For example, in India, less than 20% of schools have hardware for individual use (Sampson et al., 2019); and across Africa, data from the EdTech Hub (Crawfurd, 2020) suggests that only 19 million out of 450+ million children are using any kind of digital education technology, and most of this is limited to children watching educational television programs.

However, there are grounds for considerable optimism, including:

- **Declining costs:** in 1965, Gordon Moore – co-founder of Intel – noticed that the number of transistors per square inch of an integrated circuit board had exponentially doubled every year. He predicted that this trend would continue for, at least, several decades. It has, and is now known as Moore's Law (Moore, 1965). This has resulted in an explosion of computational processing power, and lower and lower costs (Schneider, 2017).
- **"Free" electricity:** in low-income contexts there has been no sudden and miraculous installation of power stations or electricity distribution grids. But recent advances in both renewable/solar energies and battery technology have meant that this is (often) no longer necessary. And, as with Moore's Law, we expect the cost of solar generators to decline and the amount of electrical energy that they can produce to significantly increase (Arndt et al., 2019; Shubbak, 2019).
- **Satellite internet:** several corporations, including Amazon and SpaceX, are already launching armadas of satellites, with the intention that they be used to provide high-speed 5G wireless internet from space that will be accessible from any part of the planet (Giuliari et al., 2020). However, we are unlikely to see fully operational systems before 2030.

The confluence of cheaper devices and access to both electricity and internet without the need to lay costly infrastructure offers the prospect of more democratized availability of education technology. However, the question for right here and right now, from our Lean perspective, is whether EdTech is worth the investment in the present.

META^X EdTech data: An overview

In Figure 9.1 we present relevant META^X data. We have divided this into 'baskets' related to access to hardware and then to various usage contexts linked to the already presented theory of change. This gives us 206 meta-analyses of more than 14,000 individual studies, involving more than four million study participants, albeit that these are primarily from high-income country contexts, so we must be *extremely cautious* in how we interpret the research.

Influence	No. Metas	No. Studies	Effect Size d =
Access to Hardware			
One-on-one laptops	1	10	**0.16**
Use of calculators	5	222	**0.27**
Clickers (feedback)	2	81	**0.22**
Mobile/touch devices/tablets	8	368	**0.48**
Presence of mobile phones in classroom	1	39	**−0.34**
Teacher Accountability Technology			
???	???	???	**???**
Teacher Enhancing Technology			
Micro-teaching/video review of lessons	4	402	**0.88**
Direct instruction programs (DI)	6	652	**0.59**
Student and Teacher Enhancing Technology			
Webinars	1	15	**0.33**
Gaming/simulations	27	1,634	**0.34**
Interactive video	6	372	**0.54**
Online and digital tools	9	344	**0.33**
Technology in distance education	2	28	**0.01**
Use of PowerPoint	1	12	**0.26**
Intelligent tutoring systems	5	299	**0.51**
Web-based learning	4	163	**0.33**
Audiovisual methods	8	452	**0.36**
Programmed instruction	8	1,889	**0.23**
FaceTime and social media	3	72	**−0.07**
Usage Context			
Technology with elementary students	6	264	**0.44**
Technology with high school students	9	681	**0.30**
Technology with college students	16	2,636	**0.45**
Technology in mathematics	19	898	**0.33**
Technology in science	6	391	**0.23**
Technology in reading/literacy	15	652	**0.29**
Technology in writing	3	70	**0.42**
Technology in other subjects	3	96	**0.55**
Technology with learning needs students	4	114	**0.57**
Technology in small groups	3	193	**0.21**
Television at home	3	37	**−0.18**
Distance Education	18	1,143	**0.14**
Process Efficiency Technology			
???	???	???	**???**
	Metas	**Studies**	**Mean d =**
Totals	**206**	**14,229**	**N/A**

Figure 9.1 Education Technology META^X Data

(Adapted from Visible Learning META^X, 2021)

However, the good news is that only three of the 30 listed technology interventions in Figure 9.1 show the potential for negative impact that harms or reverses learning. These are:

1 **Overconsumption of television outside of school hours** (Neuman, 1986; Razel, 2001; Williams et al., 1982). This appears to be more harmful to adolescents than to younger students, perhaps because the former is more likely to be given homework that TV watching interferes with. Although we note that in many low-income contexts, access to TV within the home is extremely limited. This is (perhaps) good news, and an example of less being more. However, during COVID-19, television (and radio) broadcasts were one of the only means of providing education in low- and middle-income countries during school lockdowns.

2 **Use of social media as a teaching and learning tool**, because of its potential to distract learner focus and to be used as a conduit for cyber bullying (Huang, 2017; Liu et al., 2017; Marker et al., 2018). Although we need to be careful here, as this is but one (prevalent) use of social media, as we shall see below.

3 **Presence of smartphones in the classroom**, again, because of their ability to distract students from learning (Kates et al., 2018). We note that in many low- and middle-income country contexts, access to smartphones is on the rise. If harnessed correctly, these devices can be used to 'transmit' high-quality teaching and learning content and assessments to enhance learning (and all without education systems having to pay for the technology!) But if schools do not plan how to leverage students' devices in a positive manner, there is the clear danger that they will simply be used to download an endless stream of cat videos that reduce task focus and learning outcomes.

When we turn our attention to the remaining 27 types of education technology interventions catalogued in the META[X], none of these reverses learning. Each will result in a better outcome than doing nothing. However, better than nothing is not the correct benchmark as the technology is generally being embedded within existing school ecosystems (i.e., something), and in many cases, the time and infrastructure cost of adoption and implementation means that some existing activities and interventions within that ecosystem need to be displaced; however, the things being displaced might generate a higher effect size than the technology that is usurping it!

The current mean average effect size for all the technology interventions listed in Figure 9.1 is $d = 0.31$, which is an improvement on the average effect size from research conducted in the 1960s (Kulik & Kulik, 1987). But the needle has not swung significantly upwards since the 1970s, when the available education technology was still very rudimentary. Do you remember those terminals with green screens and attached tape decks? Apparently they generated similar learning gains to contemporary devices. And, as we vector in on the total number of interventions that are above the $d = 0.40$ effect size, only 11 out of the 30 make the grade (i.e., slightly above one third). Let's get to some interpretations!

Interpreting the implications of META^X data for low- and middle-income countries

We start by reviewing the returns from access (i.e., what happens when you just give devices to students and teachers and leave them to get on with it?) We then explore the research on technology for teacher monitoring and accountability purposes; then, for enhancing what teachers do in the classroom; and, finally, for students to use independently in their learning.

Access to hardware

Here we have 17 metas, which aggregate the findings of 720 studies, involving almost 195,000 participants. Broadly, these explore the outcomes for student learning of distributing different types of digital hardware to schools for use by teachers and learners. We unpack the findings below.

Providing individual laptops to students

Zheng et al. (2016) synthesize the findings of ten studies exploring the impact of providing individual laptops to students in the US, where all the students in a class, grade, school, or district were given a computer to use throughout the school day and, sometimes, also at home. Student computer usage largely involved writing and revising assignments, undertaking research on the internet, and using educational software or tools for personalized instruction. The aggregate effect size was $d = 0.16$ – which, whilst positive, is significantly below our proposed hinge point of $d = 0.40$.

Ironically, we note that investment in one-child-laptop policies have become priorities for many donors and governments operating in low- and middle-income contexts (Kozma & Surya Vota, 2014). However, in line with the Zheng et al. (2016) high-income nation meta, none of the impact evaluations from low- and middle-income country contexts have been particularly encouraging either. In Latin America, the findings from Colombia (Barrera-Osorio & Linden, 2009), Peru (Beuermann et al., 2015; Cristia et al., 2010, 2017), Uruguay (de Melo et al., 2014), and Costa Rica (Meza-Cordero, 2017) found no significant gains in student achievement from merely distributing technology. And in Honduras, where the cost of implementation was also carefully accounted for (Bando et al., 2017), the findings were that the transition to laptops not only had no statistically significant impact on learner outcomes but that it cost almost US$50 *more* per student than the pre-existing use of printed workbooks and activity sheets. Perhaps there is little surprise here, as distributing laptops and expecting miracles is like building classrooms and hoping great teaching and learning will happen. This is magical thinking. It is what we do *with* the technology that matters, and often there is little investment in this aspect of laptop distribution.

Providing calculators

The META^X contains five meta-analyses on the use of handheld calculators in mathematics (Ellington, 2000; Hembree & Dessart, 1986; Nikolaou, 2001; Smith, 1996), which aggregate the findings from 222 studies that explored the relationship between the presence or absence of calculators and student achievement. The mean effect size across all five metas is $d = 0.27$, which whilst below the $d = 0.40$ hinge point, is achievable for a cost of less than US$1 per student. However, we note significant heterogeneity in the effect sizes between the metas (lowest: 0.14; highest: 0.49) and this divergence is explained by differences in teacher instructional approach – which presumably incurs additional investment in the enhancement of teacher mathematical pedagogic content knowledge. However, even without additional teacher training, we see some level of improvement in student learning outcomes. This is because calculators help students to reduce their cognitive load and give them the space to think about the best way of solving a mathematic problem without being doubly encumbered with undertaking manual calculations (and calculation checking) alongside (Ellington, 2000). Unlike other forms of education technology, however, calculators have limited utility outside STEM instructional contexts.

Clicker feedback tools

Two metas of 81 studies involving 26,000+ students explore the deployment of clicker hardware within schools (Chien et al., 2016; Hunsu et al., 2016). Clickers are handheld remote devices that are distributed to children in the classroom. Students use these tools to vote in quizzes or surveys conducted by the teacher – with the results being visible on an interactive whiteboard and/or the teacher's personal computer. The idea is that clickers provide a quick and unobtrusive way of collecting 'pulse data' during lessons.

The aggregate effect size is $d = 0.22$, which is (again) significantly below our $d = 0.40$ hinge point. Three things make us lukewarm about investing in clickers: (1) the unit cost can be relatively high at US$20+ per unit; (2) implementation requires investment in wider hardware, i.e., a teacher laptop and electronic whiteboard/data projector; and (3) from the research showcased in Chapter 8 we know that there are a variety of high-impact instructional approaches that cost nothing, or just a fraction of what it costs to implement clickers, but which achieve the same (or better) results. These include giving children traffic light cards to hold up to show their current level of understanding (Green = I'm ready to move on; Yellow = I'm getting the hang of it; Red = I'm stuck), getting children to raise their hand, or asking open questions, with deliberate pauses, to gauge current levels of understanding.

Mobile/touch devices/tablets and presence of mobile phones in the classroom

We have identified eight metas that review access to mobile/tablet device usage in classroom contexts (Cassil, 2005; Cho et al., 2018; Fabian et al., 2016; Mahdi, 2018; Petersen-Brown et al., 2019; Sung et al., 2016; Tamin et al., 2017; Tingir et al., 2017). These aggregate 368 studies, involving 19,735 participants. The mean average effect size across all these studies is $d = 0.48$, which is above our proposed $d = 0.40$ hinge point. This suggests, on the surface, that touch devices may be worth investing in.

However, we remain skeptical that it is mere access to the devices that drives this effect size. The technology is near identical to laptops, which generate exceedingly little impact. Whilst, yes, the smaller device size increases ease of transportation, the smaller screens and lack of a physical keyboard also reduce the usage contexts. We note considerable heterogeneity of effect sizes amongst the metas (highest: $d = 0.73$ and lowest: $d = 0.29$). Our interpretation: it isn't the mere presence of mobile/tablet devices that are directly unlocking impact. It's about *how* they are used. We see greater returns when they are leveraged for inquiry, collaboration, cooperative learning, and for deployment of intelligent tutoring software. But all of these can be implemented without access to tablet devices or any kind of digital technology (even intelligent tutoring software, as we shall explore below).

As discussed earlier, we also note that the presence of mobile phones in classrooms can significantly hinder learning progression. Kates et al. (2018) meta, which reviewed 39 studies involving 149,000 students, records an effect size of $d = -0.34$. Where students have access to mobile technology in the class, this can act as a distractor, with children monitoring their social media feeds rather than engaging in learning. We know from the research on multitasking that our working memory can only attend to one task at a time (Gopher et al., 2000; Mayr & Kliegl, 2000). When we continually switch between tasks there is a corresponding loss of mental productivity, which explains this whopping negative effect size.

Summary: Returns from access to hardware

Our interpretation of 17 meta-analyses on access to technology is that it is magical thinking to suppose that the mere act of distributing devices will lead to tangible improvements in student learning outcomes. For an investment in digital devices to bear fruit, we must traverse six hurdles:

1 the devices end up in the hands of the intended recipients
2 the recipients *know* how to use them
3 the recipients *do* use them
4 the use has an educational purpose (i.e., not cat videos or social media)
5 the educational purpose leverages and *significantly* amplifies a high-impact instructional approach

6   (from a Lean perspective) the cost of implementation is no higher than the status quo.

In short, usage context is king. We will now go on to explore relevant data on the educational returns from different types of deployment. We start with teacher accountability, then move to teacher enhancement technology, and finally, to independent use of technology by students.

Teacher accountability technology

In Chapter 7 we discussed the thorny issue of teacher absenteeism – from both the school (bottleneck 1) and the classroom (bottleneck 2). We also reviewed evidence on various incentive-oriented approaches to encourage greater participation from teachers in the learning lives of children. One sub-set of accountability drivers is the use of technology as a mechanism to encourage greater teacher attendance – either through surveillance or behavioral nudges. The $META^X$ cannot help us to answer questions about the effectiveness of such approaches as we have been unable to locate even a single meta-analysis on the subject. We do, however, see some evidence of impact from smaller-scale low- and middle-income country studies, including:

- Aker and Ksoll (2019), which reviewed the impact of a randomized mobile phone monitoring initiative in Niger. The treatment involved teachers, students, and village chiefs being called on a weekly basis for a 'monitoring call', over a 6-week period. For schools in the treatment group, student literacy outcomes increased by up to $d = 0.30$ and math outcomes up to $d = 0.15$.
- Duflo et al. (2012), which evaluated the impact of camera monitoring teacher attendance and linking teacher salary payments to their presence in school and class in India. This involved a designated student photographing the teacher at the start and end of the school day – using a camera with a tamper proof data/ time stamp function. During the 30-month program, teacher absenteeism decreased by 21% and there was a $d = 0.17$ increase in student test scores. A similar treatment in Indonesia (Gaduh et al., 2020) also successfully increased the percentage of time that teachers were present in class and teaching.
- Vakis and Farfan (2018), which analyzed the impact of sending timed SMS nudges to teachers' mobile phones in Peru. These included reminders about deadlines and motivational messages. The impact on classroom behavior and student learning outcomes were however inconclusive, as the study's main measure was changes in teacher perceptions.

Our interpretation is that it may be challenging to scale and maintain the human capital-intensive mobile phone monitoring protocols that were implemented in the Niger study. The SMS nudges implemented in the Peru study had a much lower time and economic cost, with each SMS message costing US$0.03 and with the system being scalable to any teacher with a personal device. However, we need to understand more about how quickly teachers' become immune to and then ignore these types of messages, the optimum frequency of communication, and tone/call to action, etc. The same goes for the Indian camera monitoring study – where one of the risks is that it simply creates perverse incentives for teachers to be present at the start and end of the school day but not in-between, or to be present in class without doing much teaching (bottleneck 3). And, as discussed in Chapter 7, we remain deeply pessimistic about the impact of these approaches for unlocking the collaborative expertise of teachers and significantly improving what they do in their classrooms. For this, we (perhaps) need to look more to the strategies of successful cult-like organizations.

Teacher enhancing technology

In Chapter 8 we introduced four meta-modes of thinking about teaching, which we recap in Figure 9.2.

At the far right of our ways of thinking about teaching is (mode D) *systematic enquiry*. This is about educators using the scientific/evaluative methods to develop hypotheses, to then conduct 'experiments' and collect evidence to measure their impact. This approach (or at least aspirations toward it) is common within high-income country contexts. The idea is that teachers *think* like evaluators or research scientists and that they continuously conduct (clinical) inquiry cycles to enhance their impact (Rickards et al., 2020). This aligns with collective teacher efficacy, which we explored in Chapter 5. Education technology can also help to unlock mode 4, particularly the use of video-based teacher performance analytics, as we discuss next.

Micro-teaching/video-based teacher performance analytics (meta-mode D)

The 402 studies catalogued within the META^X review the impact of video recording in both pre-service initial teacher training and for experienced teachers who are

Mode A	Mode B	Mode C	Mode D
Osmosis	**Scripted/ Prescriptive**	**Professional Expertise**	**Systematic Enquiry**
Unstructured learning on the job – by osmosis	Teachers follow a script developed by experts	Teachers learn many classroom protocols and mix these intuitively based on their reading/implicit pattern recognition of the classroom context	Teachers use the scientific method to develop hypotheses and conduct experiments to measure and enhance their impact

Figure 9.2 Four Meta-Modes of Thinking About Teaching

already in the classroom (Bennett, 1988; Butcher, 1981; Metcalf, 1993; Yeany & Padilla, 1986). The aggregate effect size across all these studies is $d - 0.88$ – which is extremely high. In fact, the use of video to record and review teaching is the highest impact technology intervention that we have identified.

However, being prepared to video yourself and to watch the playbacks takes a significant act of courage. Watching yourself on the small screen for the first time can be exceedingly cringe-worthy as you realize that your self-concept of how you stand, walk, talk, look, and act is often very different from what you see staring back at you on the video. Many Hollywood actors apparently report that they assiduously avoid watching their own work for fear that they won't like what they see! So, for teachers, the first hurdle is to get them to willingly film themselves and the second is to then watch the actual films. Similarly, those reviewing the videos need to be mindful to not let biases about voice, clothes and such interfere with evaluations of the quality of the teaching on student learning.

There is also a third challenge. The research tells us that whilst recording and privately reviewing videos of one's own classroom teaching results in improved pedagogical skills and enhanced student learning outcomes, much stronger benefits come when teachers review and comment on each other's videos! However, this requires an extremely strong trust culture within the school and a commitment from everyone to use the data for collective improvement rather than accountability and blame. This culture of collaborative trust links to self and collective teacher efficacy, which we discussed in Chapters 5 and 7. Our hunch is that the video analytics technology is more of an enabler of already highly efficacious teachers.

The approaches to the use of teacher video analytics/micro-teaching that show most impact involve:

- **Regular collection and self-review of video footage, with the film being re-wound over and over** – so that teachers can review and re-review from a range of different stances (e.g. teacher talk time, open vs closed questions, students time on task, clarity of the learning objectives, response to classroom behavioral issues, etc.)
- **Filming from multiple angles** – particularly from the perspective of the learners so that inferences can be made about their level of engagement and their reaction to the classroom approaches being deployed
- **Collaborative review of videos** – using questioning tools or lesson observation rubrics to scaffold the peer review and feedback process.

The strongest approaches to implementation of micro-teaching involve video footage being collected on a regular basis, with the video being stopped and re-wound over and over so that teachers can (collaboratively) home in on specific micro-practices and review them. Visible Learning is about teachers seeing learning through the eyes of the students, so it also makes sense for the recording to be of the learners as well as the teachers.

However, implementation requires access to technology – although this is arguably easier now, even in low-income contexts like sub-Saharan Africa where an estimated one third of mobile phone users have a smartphone equipped with video recording technology (GSMA, 2020; World Bank Open Data, 2020c). It may now be more feasible to think about how using such mobile technologies may lead to better training, coaching, and professional learning, as well as enabling communities of teachers across sites to work together to improve their impact on students. Beyond the technology, educators require access to suitable rubrics to facilitate collaborative lesson review and support/training to build the trust to share their classroom videos with one another. Therefore, we think that this has high potential for impact but far more modest potential for rapid scaling.

Digital scripted direct instruction (meta-mode B)

In Chapter 8 we reviewed the evidence on high-impact instructional approaches on student achievement. The clear and consistent findings across the research are that pedagogies that leverage the findings from cognitive psychology about memory, retention, forgetting, reinforcement, attention, cognitive load, and domain specificity are more likely to generate deeper and longer learning outcomes for children.

The challenge, however, is that different pedagogical approaches work better for different phases of the learning cycle, for different age groups, and also for different topic and sub-topic areas. It is extremely challenging for teachers to consistently pick and weave the best approaches together, if they are left to use their own discretion (i.e., mode 3 in our meta-modes of thinking about teaching). The research suggests that a more impactful approach is for experts to craft a universal (but culturally localized) script for each curriculum area that integrates the right pedagogics at the right time, and then to test, refine, and continually iterate it with teachers and learners in the classroom (a.k.a. scripted direct instruction). This sits within mode B of our meta-modes of thinking about teaching.

As we explained in Chapter 8, this scripted direct instruction (DI) approach was first pioneered in 1960s America by Siegfried Engelmann. It involved students being placed into within-class ability groups and teachers following a scripted manual that provided them with the exact word-for-word lesson content – both for the whole class and for their differentiated interactions with the various ability sub-groups. Whilst a common objection to direct instruction is that it de-professionalizes teachers – turning them into little more than actors that merely read their lines – there is extremely robust evidence of positive impact on student test scores.

We have identified six meta-analyses that collectively aggregate the findings from 652 studies, involving more than 42,000 participants, relating to the implementation of direct instruction methods, as discussed in Chapter 8. The mean average effect size across these six meta-analyses is $d = 0.59$, which is above our proposed hinge point. The 57 developing country systematic reviews that we catalogued in Chapter 3 also found strong evidence of impact for scripted/structured lesson plans and aligned student learning materials in low- and middle-income country contexts (e.g., Angrist et al., 2020; Conn, 2017; Ganimian & Murnane, 2016; Glewwe & Muralidharan, 2016; Kremer & Holla, 2009; Krishnaratne et al., 2013; Snilstveit et al., 2016).

Since the advent of (relatively cheap) digital devices, we have witnessed the migration of these scripted direct instruction approaches from paper-based manuals to teacher-held tablets. This digital direct instruction has the potential to significantly enhance process efficiency by:

- **Enabling teaching scripts to be rapidly and regularly updated and pushed out to all networked devices**, without having to undertake fresh print and physical distribution runs.
- **Tracking teacher pace through the content** to ensure that they are neither going too fast nor too slow, and to ensure that they are actually in school and class teaching (which can be tracked through GPS monitoring or taking timestamped photos at the start and end of each lesson).
- **Augmenting teacher instruction with video content and/or (pre-recorded and live) beamed-in teachers**. This means that the role of the classroom teacher is a little like a "TV Anchor", that acts as the continuity thread and curator between different "Reporters".
- **Enabling student achievement data to be automatically captured and aggregated**, e.g., via optical character recognition of multiple-choice test responses via a smartphone camera (the data can then be used by the script writers to identify areas where all students are underperforming and, therefore, where script enhancements may be required through the next push update).
- **Enabling teachers to also record student attendance** seamlessly within the same teaching app.

We see these digital process efficiencies as evolution rather than revolution and we note the (as yet) lack of systematic data on whether digitized vs paper manual-based direct instruction results in significantly higher student learning outcomes. But we see no reason why it would reverse the paper-based DI effect sizes, so long as it is implemented with fidelity. We also note some promising recent evaluations of these types of digital direct instruction-like approaches in, for example, Guatemala (Blimpo et al., 2020); Pakistan (Beg et al., 2019); Paraguay (Näslund-Hadley et al., 2014); and the Mindspark program in India, which also incorporated elements of computer-assisted instruction (Muralidharan et al., 2019).

Student enhancement technology: Intelligent tutoring systems

Paper-based programs that enable children to progress through an individualized curriculum at their own pace have been with us for 70+ years. Examples include Japanese-invented Kumon (Ukai, 1994) and the Secondary Mathematics Individualized Learning Experiment (SMILE), which was used in London schools (Martini, 1987). These programs involve an initial assessment to see what children already know. The teacher then selects appropriate activity cards, from a bank of 1,000s, that children independently complete. Arran was a SMILE 'guineapig'. For 5 years he received no math instruction – only the activity cards!

Both SMILE and Kumon allow for high fidelity of instruction – much like the scripted direct instruction approaches already described. They also enable students to progress by level rather than age/grade. Although there is an 'art' to how teachers design the learner pathways through the cards, which is human-capital (or teacher) intensive – educators must interpret the outputs from the initial diagnostic tests, then set activity cards and continually assess student progress to decide 'where to next' for each individual learner.

Intelligent tutoring systems do the same as Kumon and SMILE, albeit without much input from teachers. Students access these systems through a tablet/laptop and undertake an initial diagnostic assessment so that the system (rather than the teacher) determines the child's literacy or numeracy level. The system then decides which learning objects (or lessons) should be served up, makes a probability inference about whether students have learned the concept or topic based on their responses to ongoing formative assessment tests, and then decides where they should go to next.

The best systems also carefully track whether tasks are too difficult and then either provide carefully scaffolded hints and/or swap out the learning episode for something of a lower (and more appropriate) level of difficulty. Some of the (even) better systems also draw on the cognitive psychology research on memory and forgetting – requiring students to retake learning episodes that they have already successfully completed, after around 6 weeks, to reinforce their prior learning and deepen the retention (this links to the surface learning consolidation strategies we discussed in Chapter 8). Educators are also able to measure student progress through a digital teachers' dashboard, which gives insights about which topic areas specific students are struggling with and where there are common misconceptions or misunderstandings across many students.

The data from five (high-income country) meta-analyses of 299 individual intelligent tutoring system research studies, involving 22,700 study participants, generates an aggregated effect size of $d = 0.51$ (see, e.g., Gerard et al., 2015; Kulik & Fletcher, 2016; Ma et al., 2014; VanLehn, 2011). This is worth investing in and intelligent tutoring systems are more viable than ever – even in low-income country contexts – because of cheaper digital devices and more readily available solar-generated electricity. There is also a growing range of low- and middle-income country studies that suggest evidence of impact, including Chile (Araya et al., 2019), India (Banerjee et al., 2007; Hirshleifer, 2016), Ecuador (Carrillo et al., 2011), Cambodia (Ito et al., 2019); and Malawi (Pitchford et al., 2018). Many of the systematic reviews we surveyed in Chapter 3 also highlighted computer-assisted instruction (a.k.a. intelligent tutoring systems) as high-impact interventions (e.g., Asim et al., 2015; Conn, 2017; Evans & Popova, 2015; Global Education Evidence Advisory Panel, 2020; Kremer et al., 2013; Kremer & Holla, 2009; McEwan, 2015; Spink et al., 2018).

The evidence of impact for intelligent tutoring is currently strongest for numeracy, science, and, to a lesser extent, literacy. And, apart from the requirement to localize the learning content to the local language and cultural context, these systems are far easier to implement and have the potential to generate much faster impact (with much greater fidelity) than any/many of the other interventions we have discussed thus far. They can be implemented as parallel/stand-alone initiatives that simply require teachers to make time in the school day for children to login and engage, before switching back to more traditional teaching approaches.

However, with aligned teacher professional development the impact on student learning can be significantly enhanced. Teachers can be trained to interpret the diagnostic data at both individual student and class/cohort level to identify how and where they could improve. And in contexts where teachers also have access to cheap projectors, many of these intelligent tutoring systems also contain a 'teaching mode', enabling the whole class to work through one of the system's learning episodes together.

With advances in biometrics (cheap wearable devices that can measure heart rate, galvanic skin response, and even brain waves) and parallel improvements in deep learning AI (algorithms that continuously assess their effectiveness and iterate their protocols to self-learn), we expect to see further significant improvements to intelligent tutoring systems over the next decade. Students may be able to wear cheap and unobtrusive derma patches that stream real-time data back to the system. In turn, the system will be able to make inferences about whether the students are bored, excited, cognitively overloaded, etc. The AI will also be able to track breathing rate; what the child is saying out-loud as they undertake a task, via the device's in-built microphone; and where on the device's screen the student is gazing, via eye tracking software that leverages the in-built digital camera within the tablet or smartphone. All of this will help the AI to make inferences about how to personalize the learning and also about how to improve the common content bank for all learners.

It is possible that deep learning AI will also accelerate the potential of intelligent tutoring systems over the coming decades – enabling the systems to both provide real-time guidance (through verbal discussion) as students undertake research and craft their arguments, and formative assessment against rubrics and model/exemplar answers. Eventually, as software platforms evolve, we think this interaction and feedback could (consistently) become as good as that from the very best human teachers.

EdTech: Where next?

Whilst we are relatively underwhelmed by the student impact data for *most* of the categories of current education technology, several existing and experimental technologies offer the prospect for deep impact to student and lifelong learning in the coming decades. We summarize some of these in Figure 9.3.

Technology	Status	Description
5G	Already invented – requires rollout	5th generation wireless internet – offering data transfer speeds of up to 20GB per second
Smart lenses/ smart glasses	Already invented – requires improvement	Contact lenses or glasses that contain an augmented reality/virtual reality display, moving the world of the internet from the palm of your hand (i.e., smartphone) to direct and ongoing contact with your retina through a 'heads-up' display
Haptics	Already invented	Wearables that vibrate, giving the illusion of touch, resistance, and feeling
Biometrics	Already invented	Monitoring of heart rate, galvanic skin response, breathing rate, and brainwaves via miniature devices that can be attached to the body and remotely monitored
Brain– computer interfaces	Early stage of development	Embedding digital circuitry into the brain to enable two-way data transfers
Genetic engineering	Early stage of development	Using, for example, the CRISPR-Cas9 process to genetically modify embryos and people to enhance traits (e.g., working memory, IQ, lifespan, etc.)
Deep learning AI	Already invented	Algorithms that 'self-learn' by reviewing training data, recalibrating, and evaluating – including fields like language learning/translation

Figure 9.3 The Education Technology Future Pipeline

Adapted from Hamilton & Hattie (2021)

In the near- and longer-term, some of the interesting Lean education applications of the technologies in Figure 9.3 could include virtual schooling, the end of foreign language learning, genetic engineering, and brain–computer interfaces. We discuss these below.

Virtual schooling

With the combination of cheaper, faster, and better broadband; virtual reality-enabled lenses/glasses; and haptic wearables, it may soon be possible to enter virtual worlds that are almost indistinguishable from reality. This would enable the creation of digital school campuses – allowing children to learn without leaving their homes and significantly reducing capital expenditure costs, as schools literally dematerialize. In the short-term, these will still be teacher directed. The presence of a warm and caring person knowledgeable in teaching may be needed in some form for a long time.

One of the disadvantages of existing face-to-face teaching is that it often socializes students into compliance, getting everything 'right', and being embarrassed to acknowledge their struggles (Davies, 2012; Davies & Merchant, 2014). However, it seems that students are more willing to speak openly on existing social media platforms to their teachers and peers about what they do not know, their errors and misconceptions, and engage in dialogue to clarify their misunderstandings via social media. We can see potential for reducing this loss of face by using social media. For example, there could be the educational equivalent of the Catholic Confessional, where students can anonymously enter a digital 'booth' and seek support from teachers or peers on areas where they are struggling.

The end of foreign language learning?

Deep learning AI is getting extremely good at language translation, with the potential for it to achieve native speaker 'fluency' by 2030. In many middle- and high-income countries, smartphone apps are already being used for real-time translation. By combining this ever-improving technology with smart lenses and earpieces, we predict that it will soon be possible to use augmented reality to both lip-synch and to synthesize speech patterns – giving the illusion that the person you are speaking with is talking back to you in the same language (Hamilton & Hattie, 2021). As this technology advances, we wonder whether anyone would bother to learn foreign languages? We also see strong globalization potential, as language will no longer be as much of a barrier for young people anywhere to participate, collaborate, and innovate.

Genetic engineering

Longer-term, we foresee the potential for genetic engineering to enhance working memory, IQ, and grit – although the regulatory/ethical constraints and the practical challenge of isolating the correct combination of genes to edit/manipulate means that we are unlikely to see widespread use for at least several decades (Plomin & von Stumm, 2018). Depending on how this is deployed, it could theoretically 'level-up' the biological capacity of everyone to learn. Although it sounds like we are building the students we want, not dealing with the students we get.

Brain–computer interfaces

Brain–computer interfaces might become less risky to implant and be able to connect meaningfully with more parts of the brain (Musk & Neuralink, 2019; Royal Society, 2019; Shanahan, 2015). This offers the (eventual) possibility of brain-to-brain and brain-to-cloud Bluetooth. This could (literally) result in the end of schooling, as you might be able to download new skills from an appstore in seconds. However, we do not expect widespread access to this technology before 2070 and suspect it will create yet another North–South divide.

Conclusion

In this chapter we explored the current and potential impact for technology to enhance the learning lives of children in developing countries. Through a Lean lens, we might draw the following tentative conclusions (with attendant health warnings):

Tentative Lean Conclusions	Health Warnings/Side effects
• Simply procuring and distributing digital devices in the hope that this will result in enhanced teaching and learning is magical thinking • Only invest in devices where they form part of an evidence-driven theory of improvement; and note that (often) paper-based systems can generate the same impact as digital devices at a fraction of the cost	• Large-scale digital device procurement offers opportunity for extraction (a.k.a. kickbacks), and may therefore be a tempting policy option in systems where corruption is rife, irrespective of evidence of impact • Devices are another poor proxy for learning – along with reducing class sizes, enhancing school infrastructure, etc.
• Technology for accountability can increase teacher attendance at school	• Monitoring alone is unlikely to enhance the instructional approaches teachers use in the classroom
• Use of micro-teaching/teacher video performance analytics can significantly enhance 'mode D' teacher practices, resulting in improved student learning outcomes	• Requires locally available video capture technology • Great care is required to build trust so that teachers have confidence to video their lessons and collaboratively review, otherwise technology ceases to be used after novelty wears off • When used for accountability purposes, the positive 'mode D' benefits are likely to be diminished
• Digitally scripted direct instruction approaches have the potential to significantly increase the quality and consistency of 'mode B' teaching, and the level of differentiation	• Need to carefully address educator beliefs about the nature of the teaching profession (i.e., fears of being relegated to the status of an actor) • These approaches do not require technology to be effective. Paper-based scripts work just as well; although technology can enhance the speed of distribution/updating, and also integrate with intelligent tutoring systems (see below)

Tentative Lean Conclusions	Health Warnings/Side effects
• Intelligent tutoring systems have strong potential to remediate numeracy and literacy outcomes for students	• Requires careful localization to the target language and culture • Mitigation strategies also need to be put in place to ensure that the devices remain within schools and are used for the intended purpose • The tools are currently more effective for remediation and reinforcement than as a replacement for teachers • Careful dosage is required. Many studies attest to the law of diminishing returns where students use systems for more than 90 minutes per week
• In the longer-term, (currently) experimental technology is far more likely to be more transformative to education outcomes than any of the enhancements identified and discussed in Part 2 of the Manifesto	• Technology timelines are always longer than we anticipate • Some of the more controversial technologies like genetic engineering and brain–computer interfaces may (eventually) render the whole business of schooling obsolete

Friends, we have now reached the end of Part 2 of the Manifesto. In Part 3 we get all practical, exploring tools and processes that you can use to turn evidence into action that generates deep and wondrous impact.

Evidence into action

10

From provocation to implementation

In Part 1 of the Manifesto, we made the case that the global massification of education has been one of the greatest successes of the modern era. Schools have been built, teachers recruited, and children taught at ever-increasing rates. There are, however, still significant gaps in both access to education (the *easier* problem) and quality of provision (the *hard* problem) – particularly for low- and middle-income countries. Whilst increased resources might help, we made the case for learning to leverage more from less: getting Lean. But for system leaders to get Lean, they need access to good quality data about (lower-cost and higher-impact) interventions that have been effective in other contexts.

However, the pool of available research from low- and middle-income contexts is relatively slender. By our count, there are 57 systematic reviews aggregating a gross 3,912 studies. With duplicates removed, the net number of high-quality studies is closer to (a more meager) 2,500 – with the findings often pulling in different directions. We therefore suggested the Visible Learning META^X as a sort of 'stop-gap'. The META^X, which catalogues 1,700+ meta-analyses of 100,000+ studies, involving 300m+ students, is arguably the largest 'what works best' for education database in the world. Most of the data does come from high-income countries, however, so we must interpret with great care. We therefore also narrowed our focus to 856 metas of 50,000+ studies, i.e., the ones that had the most relevance to developing country contexts; giving us a total of 913 systematic reviews of 53,219 studies when the developing country research is also blended in.

In Part 2 of the Manifesto, we leveraged the META^X to identify educational Jenga blocks that could potentially be removed, hollowed out, not added, and (occasionally) inserted. Some of our provocative recommendations included reducing investment in pre-service initial teacher training; not requiring teachers to have degrees in the subjects they teach; reducing the length of the school day/year (i.e., quality not quantity); not reducing class size; multi-age classes; instructional leadership about impact; teaching to level rather than grade; scaffolded or scripted curricula; enhanced in-service professional development; and intelligent tutoring systems.

DOI: 10.4324/9781003166313-14

Evidence into action?

Across the five chapters of Part 2 of the Manifesto, we made 30+ recommendations about initiatives to stop/avoid starting, water down, and (occasionally) throw fresh funds at. However, one thing we are extremely conscious of is the challenge of turning recommendations into actions and, of those actions, subsequently delivering educational impact. As we survey the lists of recommendations in various glossy reports produced by donors, NGOs, and think tanks, we are continually struck by how difficult it would be to do anything meaningful with these shopping lists of 'best' and 'worst' buys.

Knowing that a particular recommendation 'worked' somewhere is not enough. We need to determine whether it is relevant to our local context, i.e., does it help to solve a problem (or contribute to a goal) that we have? Then, we need to understand the specific (and detailed) steps required during implementation to achieve the same ballpark effect size. It's obvious to us that nothing we have written thus far in the Manifesto is of the slightest practical use in helping ministries to select activities/interventions that are appropriate for their contexts, fashion instruments, implement, evaluate, iterate, sustain, and scale.

Partly, the challenge is 'just' that education improvement is exceedingly complex. Almost 40 years ago, Larry Cuban likened it to a storm at sea:

> The surface is agitated and turbulent, while the ocean floor is calm and serene (if a bit murky). Policy churns dramatically, creating the appearance of major changes . . . while deep below the surface, life goes on, largely uninterrupted.
> (Cuban, 1984, p. 234)

As we illustrate in Figure 10.1, there are at least six layers of Cuban-like ocean floor that our Lean recommendations need to percolate to turn evidence into actions that generate deep impact.

The problem with the suggestions that we make in Part 2 of the Manifesto is that education systems do not operate in vacuums. Our recommendations are only relevant if they help policymakers and practitioners address their Level 1 local big picture policy goals. Each of our suggestions operates at Level 2, and there is much subsequent devil in the detail after deciding, say, to implement scripted direct instruction (DI) and this achieving a meaningful legacy effect at Level 6. At Level 3, for example, there are a host of design and implementation questions that need to be addressed, including:

- Will scripted DI will be introduced for every subject area or just for some?
- Will the materials be locally developed, imported, or hybridized?
- Will it be fully scripted or merely scaffolded?
- Will it be paper or tablet-based?
- Will there will be aligned student learning and formative assessment materials?

Layer	Description
Level 1: Goals	The locally agreed purpose of education, which might include a mixture of: - **Noble drivers** (e.g., basic human rights, closing the equity gap, prosperity, health and wellbeing etc.) - **Grey drivers** (e.g., nation-building, human capital development, etc.) - **Dark drivers** (e.g., political patronage, rent seeking, extraction, etc.) - **Progressing specific priorities** (e.g., low access to education/literacy/numeracy outcomes for girls/special needs/indigenous, etc.) I.e., what is it that principal stakeholders want to achieve and why?
Level 2: Instruments	The tools that are leveraged to achieve the Level 1 big picture policy goals, including: - Education funding - Facilities - Curriculum - School governance structures - Assessment systems - Teacher recruitment and training processes - Data monitoring systems, - Class size - Length of school day - Teacher professional development - Level of centralization vs decentralization, etc.
Level 3: Implementation	How the selected tools are used in practice, including: - Design features and setting levels - Dosage, i.e., how much, how frequently, and for whom - Fidelity vs adaptation vs localization considerations - Implementation and scaling methodology.
Level 4: Impact	The impact that implementation has on the operation of schools and the activities undertaken by teachers within classrooms (e.g., changes in their beliefs, behaviors, and instructional approaches).
Level 5: Outcomes	The degree to which changes in service delivery at Level 4 enhances student access, participation, and achievement; ultimately, whether there is any increase in children's neurons firing and wiring together.
Level 6: Legacy	The level of long-term contribution that schooling makes in equipping young people with skills for life versus the impact of other formal and informal mechanisms for learning (e.g., environmental context, family, peers, voluntary associations, etc.). — And the fadeout/degradation of learning over time (i.e., how much of what children learn in school is useful and used?)

Figure 10.1 Six Layers of 'Ocean Floor'

(Adapted from Hamilton & Hattie, 2021a)

- Will it operate on a grade-based system (children segregated by age), a levels-based system (children grouped by ability), or a hybrid response to intervention approach (where children sit in age-based classrooms but are pulled out for remedial support as needed)?
- Will teacher beliefs be addressed during implementation and, if so, how?
- What kind of teacher training will support implementation (e.g., cascade training vs coaching vs apprenticeship model vs none)?
- Will teachers receive incentives to implement with fidelity and, if so, of what size and frequency? Also, how will monitoring be undertaken, if at all?
- What high-impact instructional approaches will be leveraged and at what stages of the learning journey?

There are multiple answers or setting levels for each of these design questions/features, ranging from turning the dial to maximum or right down to zero. And all the different dial settings can work – depending on the local context and the interplay with the position of the other dials and features of the wider system. Then, once our agreed scripted direct instruction approach is implemented, we need to see/ensure that it results in Level 4 behavioral changes in how educators deliver classroom instruction; Level 5 changes in the rate of student learning; and Level 6 changes in the preparedness of children for work and life. And we need to assume that we won't get it all right first time. There will be lots of snakes and ladders along the way.

Finally, it is worth us highlighting that scripted direct instruction is just one example of an approach that *might* be suitable, practical, and viable in your context. There are many others with very different theories of change – including Teaching at the Right Level and Escuela Nueva – that also have strong evidence of impact in developing country contexts. We make this point here because in Chapter 11 we will come back to scripted direct instruction and use it, again, as an example to illustrate our suggested activity design and implementation tools. However, we don't want you to think that we have a pet preference for scripted DI or that we are subliminally trying to sell it to you. What might work best for you will very much depend on your Level 1 policy goals and on the beliefs and capabilities that currently reside on your system; these provide you with the foundation from which to build and grow.

Toward an implementation science for education?

In the parallel fields of health and international development, "implementation science" has had a reasonably long history. Frameworks for healthcare reforms have been with us since the 1960s (Pressman & Wildavsky, 1984; Wandersman et al., 2008); and, ditto, international development, where the US Agency for International Development (USAID) created the Logframe Model in the same era (World Bank, 2000). These approaches emerged because policymakers and funders realized that it was not enough simply to say, "all children shall have a polio vaccine" or "all adults should have the COVID-19 vaccine", and then expect it to magically get done. Even something (seemingly) as simple as vaccination required robust, and often iterative, processes to get from Level 1 policy aspirations, to a Level 4 sugar-cube swallowed/shot in the arm, and then Level 6, "no more polio".

The research from healthcare and international development suggests that:

1 **The implementation processes are often just as important as the thing being implemented in determining whether there is an impact** (Kelly, 2012; Meyers et al., 2012). So, how you go about it really matters.

2 **In healthcare, there is a potent relationship between the beliefs of healthcare professionals and the outcomes of implementation.** Where a new intervention aligned with pre-existing beliefs, it was more likely to be implemented enthusiastically (Aarons et al., 2012). This perhaps explains why, back in the 1860s, Joseph Lister had much trouble convincing his colleagues to wash their hands prior to surgery: they didn't believe in germ theory (Barry, 2018).

3 **Implementation is less likely to be successful where frontline practitioners are left to do it alone.** Better results are more likely to be achieved when researchers/program developers work in tandem with on-the-ground practitioners (Meyers et al., 2012).

Within education, implementation science has had a much shorter history. The *Handbook of Implementation Science for Psychology in Education*, edited by Kelly and Perkins, was published in 2012. This was the first major education sector-specific tome on the psychology and methodology of implementation. There are now, however, several implementation and improvement methodologies being utilized across a range of education contexts. We summarize some of these in Figure 10.2.

As we attempt to unpick the similarities and differences between these implementation frameworks, we find it useful to distinguish between the following dimensions:

- **Adding vs subtracting.** An additive process is about introducing something new to enhance outcomes: another Jenga block. Subtracting is about sharpening or chiseling away at an existing process to make it more efficient. Lean is an example of the latter. All the other frameworks we outline in Figure 10.2 can be used for efficiency but are more likely to be used for the development and rollout of new things.

- **Innovation scaling vs local needs-driven.** Innovation-scaling means that the methodology focuses on the development of novel products. Once developed, implementation is about convincing stakeholders they need this new 'hammer' to solve their local problem of 'banging nails'. None of the approaches outlined in Figure 10.2 is specifically about the development and mass-scaling/selling of innovative products to address needs that stakeholders might not even be aware

Methodology	Description	Key Reference
Logical Framework Approach (LFA)	Created in 1969 for the US Agency for International Development (USAID), this toolkit is used for: (1) designing, (2) managing, and (3) evaluating international development projects by, for example, the World Bank. The LogFrame approach specifies the inputs, activities, outputs, and (expected) impact for a project design. **Verdict:** Forces project designers to explicitly map the mediators and moderators of project success but can become a (cumbersome) static and linear tool that does not enable rapid, iterative, and adaptive improvement to the project design during implementation (Bell, 2000; Biggs & Smith, 2003; Gasper, 2000; Hailey & Sorgenfrei, 2004; Hubbard, 2001).	World Bank (2000)
Getting to Outcomes (GTO)	A ten-stage results-based approach for getting to agreed outcomes: (1) focus, (2) target, (3) adopt, (4) adapt, (5) resources, (6) plan, (7) monitor, (8) evaluate, (9) improve, and (10) sustain. **Verdict:** A highly structured approach that tends to assume interventions will be built out from an existing program that is adapted to the local context. More suited to large-scale/system-wide improvement than smaller-scale/local changes. Less focus on stakeholder beliefs than some other models. The GTO program developers found that detailed manuals, training, technical assistance, and external quality assurance were necessary for implementation of the processes with fidelity (Wandersman et al., 2012)	Wandersman (2014)
Problem-Driven Iterative Adaptation (PDIA) – Building State Capability (BSC)	A design-thinking oriented approach that: (1) reverse engineers from problems/goals to instruments, (2) develops (multiple) designs, (3) implements, (4) evaluates, and (5) iterates. Specifically designed for international development projects. **Verdict:** Starts with the (reasonable) assumption that program designs may not be effective and that significant iteration will be required to generate impact, and has a strong focus on processes for getting and maintaining 'upstream' authorization from senior stakeholders. However, limited focus on 'downstream' authorization/buy-in/beliefs; and limited attention to specific implementation, monitoring, or evaluation processes. Also, tends toward problem/deficit-theorizing rather than strengths-based/appreciative-focused thinking.	Andrews et al. (2017)

Figure 10.2 Landscape Analysis of Implementation Frameworks

Methodology	Description	Key Reference
Deliverology	Focuses on scaled implementation of an already agreed intervention, with fidelity. Designed to be used across sector areas (i.e., within and beyond education). **Verdict:** Strong emphasis on governance, implementation, scalability, monitoring, and project management processes. Less focus on how to select an appropriate problem/goal, how to design appropriate interventions, and how to iterate and adapt during delivery. Also, top-down oriented, with less focus on the psychology of beliefs and habit change (Birch & Jacob, 2019).	Barber et al. (2011)
Positive Deviance	A framework for grass-roots exploration and fact finding to detect positive outliers or 'deviants' that buck whatever issue stakeholders seek to resolve. The idea is to catalogue positive outlier behaviors that can be replicated and scaled. **Verdict:** Useful for identifying innovations that already exist in the community and for piloting scale-up. But limited attention to how stakeholders select their focus area/problem in the first place and how they should subsequently scale.	LeMahieu, Nordstrum, & Gale (2017); Pascale et al. (2010)
Spiral of Inquiry	Provides educators with six processes to enhance student learning outcomes: (1) scanning, (2) focusing, (3) developing a hunch, (4) learning, (5) taking action, and (6) checking. **Verdict:** Specifically developed for the education sector. Supports the identification of local improvement priorities and the implementation of local action research projects to implement and measure improvement. Strong focus on stakeholder beliefs and their role in enabling/disabling change. More suited to agile school-led/bottom-up improvement than top-down scaling.	Timperley et al. (2014)
Reduce Change to Increase Improvement – Open to Learning Conversations	Proposes a highly selective improvement focus and offers protocols for coaches to engage with and understand stakeholder beliefs around change. Suggests that where the proposed changes are misaligned with existing stakeholder beliefs about what works, change efforts are less likely to be successful. **Verdict:** Strongly focused on 'less being more' and on effective approaches for engaging with rather than bypassing educators' beliefs. Less coverage of the explicit processes for implementing, evaluating, and scaling up improvement. Developed and implemented in high-income country contexts.	Robinson (2018)

Figure 10.2 (Continued)

Methodology	Description	Key Reference
Hexagon Tool	A six-part planning tool for schools to identify local needs and then evaluate pre-built programs and their suitability for the local context. Focus areas are: (1) need, (2) fit, (3) resources, (4) evidence, (5) readiness, and (6) capacity. **Verdict:** A useful cost–benefit analysis framework to support individual schools to select pre-built evidence-based programs. Does not specifically address implementation and evaluation, nor system-wide scaling.	Blase et al. (2013)
Learning to Improve (LTI)/ Networked Improvement Communities	LTI offers a framework for: (1) the identification of areas for improvement, (2) improvement hypothesis development, and (3) agile-oriented improvement cycles. **Verdict:** A powerful set of tools with a strong focus on starting local and then scaling. LTI also proposes involvement of external researchers/coaches to work alongside those implementing improvement.	Bryk et al. (2017)
Lean Improvement	As outlined in Chapter 2, this provides a methodology for iterative efficiency-oriented improvement cycles. **Verdict:** More suited to efficiency improvements in existing processes than to the development of new products/services or interventions.	Womak & Jones (2013)
Appreciative/ Strengths-based Inquiry	Centers on identifying, celebrating, and leveraging existing strengths rather than searching for problems to fix and deficit theorizing. Proposes a 4D approach: (D1) discover, (D2) dream, (D3) design, and (D4) destiny. **Verdict:** Raises important philosophical and psychological questions about mental priming/framing. However, it is more focused on the process of gathering stakeholder insight and designing alternative futures than the processes of implementation, evaluation, iteration, and scaling. Evidence of impact from implementation is currently mixed (Bushe & Kassam, 2005).	Cooperrider & Srivastva (1987)

Figure 10.2 (Continued)

they have. Instead, they all come from a local needs-driven perspective. They do this by asking "what goal or problem do we need to address?" and "what is the best way of doing it?".

- **Bottom-up vs top-down.** The former is community-driven and about local stakeholders selecting local goals and then designing and implementing activities for their specific context. The latter is about scaling the implementation of pre-agreed national priorities, with fidelity (e.g., rolling out a standardized performance-related pay approach for teachers or establishing a national school inspectorate). Deliverology is an example of a top-down policy-driven approach, whereas most of the other frameworks are compatible with either stance.

- **Linear vs adaptive implementation.** This is about whether the methodology has explicit feedback loops to continually evaluate and iterate during implementation or whether protocols are more rigid, with a long cycle of implementation followed by summative evaluation. The Logical Framework Approach is (arguably) more linear, whereas Problem-Driven Iterative Adaptation and Learning to Improve are explicitly iterative – starting with the assumption that the initial prototype is unlikely to be effective and several rounds of heavy refinement will be required before we see deep impact.

- **Blank-sheeting vs localization.** This is about whether the methodology emphasizes building a new activity from scratch to meet unique local needs, or whether it is about the search for pre-built products/programs for localization. Learning to Improve tilts (more) toward blank-sheeting, whereas the Hexagon Tool and Getting to Results are more predicated to the identification and implementation (with localization) of pre-built solutions (i.e., finding and deploying the 'right' hammers, saws, and drills for local needs).

- **Governance vs beliefs focus.** Governance-focused frameworks pay stronger attention to processes for establishing a dedicated implementation structure, responsibilities, and accountabilities frameworks, and getting authorization from senior stakeholders. Beliefs-focused frameworks are more interested in whether the proposed intervention aligns with or bypasses existing stakeholder beliefs (much like the way that Lister's handwashing advice did not align with prevailing beliefs about how infection was transmitted). These two implementation stances are not mutually exclusive, although Viviane Robinson's (2018) *Reduce change to increase improvement* is the framework most heavily predicated to explicitly grappling with beliefs.

- **Analytic vs agile.** Analytic-focused approaches spend time gathering data, weighting options, and reviewing evidence of impact in other settings prior to authorizing a high-probability intervention. Agile approaches, on the other hand, are concerned about the potential for analysis-paralysis: the danger that by undertaking a lengthy review process, everyone will have lost interest and impetus in change by the time they get to implementation. Logical Frameworks, Getting to Outcomes, and Learning to Improve operate at the more analytic end of the spectrum, whereas Spiral of Enquiry is more agile. It is designed to be used at school level and for much faster and hunch/heuristic-based improvement cycles.

- **Problem-driven vs strengths-based.** Problem-driven approaches are ultra-focused on things that have gone wrong and that urgently need to be fixed. They start by identifying appropriate problems and then move to mapping the causes of disfunction, to design interventions or treatments that will bring relief or improvement. Strengths-based approaches, on the other hand, start by mapping and appreciating existing organizational capabilities and then leverage these to build momentum for 'moonshot thinking' and the implementation of inspirational goals. Most of the catalogued frameworks in Figure 10.2 implicitly adopt a problem-centered approach. Problem-Driven Iterative Adaptation (PDIA) explicitly leverages this stance, whereas Appreciative/Strengths-based Inquiry explicitly banishes the search for problems.

In short, there is much diversity of philosophy and emphasis across the surveyed implementation methodologies. Ouch, indeed.

But can we find *some* commonalities?

In the preceding section we surveyed 11 different 'flavors' of methodology for the identification of priority goals, and the design, implementation, evaluation, iteration, and scaling of high-probability initiatives. Many of the frameworks that we outlined emphasized or privileged extremely different success factors or areas of focus. But fear not: we have identified 23 key processes that are (relatively) common across all the methodologies (inspired by Greenhalgh et al., 2004; Meyers et al., 2012; Moullin et al., 2015; Tabak et al., 2012). And below we unpack these into five phases of activity:

Phase 1: Problem/need/goal identification

1   Conducting a problem/needs/goals diagnostic assessment
2   Building a theory of the cause of the problem/need (i.e., mapping the causal drivers and/or mapping existing strengths)
3   Agreeing what success looks like (i.e., the success map or results framework)
4   Commencing an evaluation plan related to this success
5   Gaining authorization and resources to proceed to Phase 2.

Phase 2: Solution/activity design

6   Inductive solutions/opportunities scanning (i.e., identifying pre-built programs that could be deployed)
7   Deductive solution/opportunities development (i.e., using a logic framework to build multiple intervention/activity models from scratch)

8 Ranking solutions/opportunities by, for example, capability to implement, cost–benefit, ease of implementation, whether they engage vs bypass stakeholder beliefs, possibility for adaptation, early vs late adopter potential

9 Stress-testing preferred designs by, for example, mapping the various possible design features and setting levels, and different dosage and fidelity levels

10 Agreeing preferred solutions/opportunities – including design features and setting levels

11 Identifying potential enablers and barriers to implementation, and the risk mitigations to these

12 Building implementation capacity (e.g., recruiting and training a central backbone team)

13 Developing a full monitoring and evaluation plan, including developing ways to assess fidelity of implementation and being particularly focused on local adaptations and their effects

14 Gaining authorization and resources to proceed to Phase 3.

Phase 3: Implementation

15 Creating implementation plans
  a Implementing program management processes
  b Developing product/output descriptors and acceptance criteria
  c Ensuring an evaluative plan is in continual process.

16 Creating implementation teams – ensuring there is a mixture of research, evaluation, project management, and local context expertise

17 Undertaking implementation

18 Monitoring implementation (i.e., milestones, products, budget, timelines, outputs, outcomes).

Phase 4: Evaluation

19 Ongoing collection of impact data during implementation

20 Identification and agreement on areas to iterate (i.e., crawl and learn (or agreement to stop), including dosage, fidelity, adaption, and quality (using Phase 2 processes)

21 Go back to Phase 3 and/or forward to Phase 5.

Phase 5. Re-iterating, scaling, and sustaining

22 Developing a plan to re-iterate/scale/sustain using data from steps 18–20 and tools and processes from steps 6–13

23 Go back to Phase 3.

Five phases and 23 core activities to generate sweet impact!

Conclusion

Recognizing the danger that the Manifesto simply becomes (yet) another list of unimplementable "policy recommendations", in this chapter we expanded our search to identify viable methodologies for turning evidence into action.

We started by examining the six layers of 'ocean floor' that any new activity/intervention must traverse to achieve impact: from selecting (appropriate) goals, leveraging (suitable) instruments, and implementing (with fidelity), which should lead to (noticeable) improvements in service delivery and then (hopefully) to short and longer-term impact on students.

To cut (or wade?) through these six layers of floor, we then mined the world of implementation methodologies both within and beyond the education. We identified a range of strongly codified approaches, including Deliverology, Getting to Outcomes, Appreciative Inquiry, Problem-Driven Iterative Adaptation, Spiral of Inquiry, and, of course, Lean. Each of these privilege different success factors. Some emphasized problems, others moonshot goals. Some were top-down and others more bottom-up. Most were additive, apart from Lean – with its explicit focus on subtraction.

To add to the confusion, there is currently very little systematic data to tell us which of these implementation approaches is most effective. The major difficulty is in untangling the *process* of implementation from the *thing* being implemented. Therefore, as an interim measure, we mapped the areas of agreement across all 11 surveyed implementation approaches – identifying five phases and 23 (relatively) common processes.

But we don't think this is enough to support you in turning evidence into action: it's still too high level. Therefore, in the next chapter we go deeper still, introducing *Leaning to GOLD* – our proposed framework for helping you to bring the 23 processes to life. Our hope is that this will help you identify goals worth progressing and activities/interventions that are worth considering, and lead to the implementation that generates tangible impact – so that the storm raging on the surface also churns the waters deep below.

11

Leaning to GOLD

In Chapter 10, we mapped existing frameworks, processes, and toolkits for effective implementation of education improvement at scale. Whilst there were *significant* differences across the methodologies, they all highlighted the importance of explicitly and systematically:

1   Selecting an appropriate area for improvement
2   Identifying or developing activities to bring about positive change
3   Implementing the agreed activities using project management systems and tools
4   Evaluating impact to identify either how implementation can be further enhanced or jettisoned
5   Scaling and sustaining successes to generate system-wide impact.

To use the language of Lant Pritchett, Salimah Samji, and Jeffrey Hammer (2013, p. 2), this is about slowly "crawl[ing] the design space" to move forward, test, iterate, and scale high probability approaches. We also think it is equally about identifying pre-existing activities that are value-subtracting (or at least non-value adding) and inching backwards through design space to de-implement them, test the impact, and then carefully dismantle a bit more, i.e.:

6   Lean improvement processes, of the kind we outlined in Chapter 2, to identify and remove sources of waste (a.k.a. *muda*).

Therefore, in this chapter we fashion these six broad baskets into an explicit education improvement methodology that we call *Leaning to GOLD*, which is illustrated in Figure 11.1. Its purpose is to help you turn evidence into action that generates deep impact.

The GOLD part is about moving (or crawling) forward. This involves inventing (or borrowing) and deploying new tools and approaches to progress challenging goals. And it builds on our earlier paper *Getting to GOLD* (Hamilton & Hattie,

G.O.L.D. Improvement				
1. **GOAL Hunting**	2. **OPPORTUNITY Searching**	3. **LIFTOFF**	4. **DOUBLE Back**	5. **D*OUBLE Up**
Agreeing a *compelling cause* worthy of TOTAL commitment	Systematically investigating mechanisms for improvement to agree the local best-fit approach	Implementing the agreed improvement strategies	Explicitly and scientifically measuring the impact and agreeing where to next	Expanding the scale of implementation to generate sustained system-wide impact
LEAN Improvement				
E. **Agree Where to next**	D. **Evaluate Future State**	C. **Pilot Future State**	B. **Future State Analysis**	A. **Current State Analysis**
Scaling-up/ scaling-back and searching for new sources of waste/*muda*	Carefully reviewing the impact of waste/*muda* elimination	Implementing controlled elimination of waste/*muda*	Identifying waste for elimination (*muda*)	Mapping the existing value stream

Figure 11.1 Leaning to GOLD

2021a). Lean on the other hand is about judicious use of the rearview mirror. It's about giving permission to find existing things to stop or thin out and then testing what happens after pilot dismantling, i.e., delicately removing those Jenga blocks.

Whilst Figure 11.1 is presented as two arrows pointing in different directions, the thinking or activity is not likely to be linear. We tried to illustrate this by making the lines wavy but even this does not convey the messy and complex world of implementation. We also need to fess up that, philosophically, many of the showcased processes come from the problem-driven end of the spectrum. They are more geared toward identifying crises, burning platforms, catastrophes, and galvanizing solution-oriented action. And whilst, yes, this way of thinking can be highly motivational to system leaders and funders, by lensing activity as a response to a pressing cause and then 'milking the crisis'; it is likely to be much less motivational to grassroots stakeholders. In environs where there is a relatively low level of local resource or capability, focusing on everything that's 'wrong' is only likely to generate despondency and despair; whereas starting with everything that's right, appreciating it, and identifying opportunities to build and grow atop is likely to be more invigorating and empowering. In delivery, our teams and collaborators have sought to balance this tightrope better than we are able to convey below: talking to ministers, ministries, and funders about 'the learning *crisis*' and to schools and communities about 'the learning *opportunity*'.

It's also worth adding that it may be cognitively challenging to think and act from an additive and subtractive perspective simultaneously. You may want two separate teams: one working on GOLD inquiry and the second on Lean improvement – although it's important that they talk regularly or one might be dismantling infrastructure that the other is banking on being able to leverage!

Finally, for avoidance of all doubt, *Leaning to GOLD* is in no way revolutionary. We have merely "borrowed" the best third-party tools and processes from the improvement and implementation methodologies that we reviewed in Chapter 10, combining these with the Lean processes we introduced in Chapter 2. We have also blended these with the trial-and-error insights that our teams and collaborators have gained from direct involvement in large-scale education improvement initiatives across low-, middle-, and high-income country contexts.

In the next part of the chapter, we unpack the five stages of GOLD and present a range of tools that can be used to support your inquiry – see Figure 11.2

G.O.L.D. Improvement				
1. **GOAL** Hunting	2. **OPPOR-TUNITY** Searching	3. *LIFTOFF*	4. *DOUBLE* Back	5. *D^{x}OUBLE* up
Agreeing a *compelling cause* worthy of TOTAL commitment	Systematically investigating mechanisms for improvement to agree the best-fit approach	Implementing the agreed improvement strategies	Explicitly and scientifically measuring the impact and agreeing where to next	Expanding the scale of implementation to generate system-wide impact
G1: Establish GOLD team **G2:** Map the education landscape **G3:** Agree the *compelling cause* **G4:** Build a theory of the present **G5:** Set the provisional improvement goal	**O1:** Search for opportunities in design space **O2:** Develop a logic model **O3:** Iterate your logic model **O4:** Develop a success map	**L1:** Establish delivery office **L2:** Develop implementation plans using project management tools **L3:** Implement **L4:** Collect monitoring and evaluation data	**D1:** Review monitoring and evaluation data **D2:** Identify 'where to next?' using O1–O4 tools **D3:** Resume liftoff with revised logic model	**D^{x}1:** Build in intention to scale from the get-go **D^{x}2:** Use scaling strategies **D^{x}3:** Back to O3 and then to liftoff **D^{x}4:** Evaluate for fidelity at scale and identify 'where to next'

Figure 11.2 Digging Deeper into GOLD

for an overview of the key waypoints. We then re-introduce the Lean processes explored in Chapter 2, making them relevant to education improvement in low- and middle-income countries.

GOLD inquiry

GOLD stage 1: Goal hunting (a.k.a. finding the *compelling cause*)

GOLD starts with goal hunting, which is about identifying and agreeing *compelling cause* that is worth everyone's ongoing time, effort, and commitment. Note that we mean 'cause' in the sense of mission/purpose/goal/end/crusade/quest and not as in cause-and-effect. Ergo, a *compelling cause* is a vigorous, relentless, and ongoing campaign for positive change – at scale. It consumes a high proportion of your mental energy and your action – possibly all of it. You pursue your *cause* because you are *compelled* to: you are convinced it's really, really important. It isn't, by contrast, a halfhearted aspiration you bury in your national education strategy that you hope everyone will forget about or where you think/hope that you will have moved on and that it will become someone else's problem.

In the sub-sections below we outline explicit processes and activities that you could consider during the goal hunting phase.

G1: Establish the GOLD team

Education improvement rarely happens by osmosis. More often, it requires the establishment of a backbone team that works in concert to agree the priority area(s) for improvement; design activities to meet these needs; then implement, evaluate, scale, and sustain the processes. There is, however, something a bit chicken-and-egg about the establishment of a backbone. On the one hand, senior stakeholders are unlikely to want to invest in this unless they can already smell smoke (i.e., the whiff of a 'problem') or they are deeply inspired by the potential of a pet moonshot opportunity. On the other hand, however, there is strong value in the team having wide parameters so that they can codify and validate (or otherwise) the implicit theory of change of the sponsors. This means giving them the leeway and confidence to say, "we know you wanted us to head North by boat, but we think South East via hot air balloon might be a more realistic strategy".

Our assumption is that your backbone team, its resourcing, and terms of reference are authorized/mandated by sponsors at the highest level in the national/regional/district-level education system. During the goal hunt phase, the team is likely to comprise a sponsor, guiding coalition, and an inquiry team that does the actual work. The inquiry team might include ministry officers, university researchers, and external technical assistance, for example. We think you are looking for people with a balance of knowledge and expertise in global-local education research, program design, program evaluation, and deep local knowledge of on-the-ground realities. It also helps if these people are trained in how to use the various tools and if they share a common language of improvement and implementation.

We also need to stress that a successful team is more than just having the right governance model and people with the right job titles. It's also about how the team operates – its explicit understanding of cognitive biases and the messy iterative process of learning and implementing; and about thinking positively about the world of wondrous possibilities.

G2: Map the education landscape

To bring about meaningful education improvement you need to select your *compelling cause* with great care. The first key step is to map the local education landscape. This involves gaining a deep and appreciative understanding of the starting point and strengths that currently reside in your system. One common approach is to harvest and analyze metric data. A whole global industry has sprung up of education information management systems (eMIS) and indicators: this can be an obvious place to start your system mapping – reviewing data on, for example, student access, student achievement, student inclusion, teacher attendance, teacher utilization rates, types and frequency of teacher training, per pupil funding levels, etc. There is also strong value in comparing and benchmarking these findings to global averages and to regional or similar system averages. The World Bank's SABER Initiative (Systems Approach for Better Education Results) supports this type of benchmarking, which can help ministries of education to understand where their system resides on the continuum of effective policies, processes, and practice (Klees et al., 2020; World Bank, 2016). As can the use of open-source lesson observation tools like *Teach*, which was specifically designed to lift the lid on classroom practices in low- and middle-income contexts (www.worldbank.org/education/teach).

However, one of the challenges with these types of assessment is that it can be *deeply* disheartening to view your country or school data plotted on comparative rubrics and charts, especially if it shows your system to be in the 'latent' (a.k.a. starting) phase for many kinds of policies, processes, activities, and outcomes. If you cast your mind back to our discussion in Chapter 7, we highlighted that where teachers believed that they had the agency to transform children's learning outcomes, they did. And when students believed that their success was down to their hard work and goal commitment – rather than fate or innate talent – it was.

Cooperrider et al. (2008) have found much the same in their organizational improvement work across different sectors and settings. They discovered that where organizational inquiry was framed from the perspective of "what is the problem?", it consistently generated negativity and defensiveness from respondents. Thinking from the perspective of "wrong", "deficit", or "broken" immediately leads stakeholders to thoughts of *their* ineffectiveness and to justifications about why they can do no different within the constraints of the current system.

These are not useful, empowering, or generative discussions. They lead to people barricading themselves into their minds, their classrooms, and digging down yet further into their existing ways.

Instead, as your inquiry team engages with schools, communities, parents, teachers, and businesses, they are more likely to get to generative discussions if they inquire about (Cooperrider et al., 2008):

- **Personal highpoints**, i.e., times and circumstances where stakeholders felt *alive* and *energized* within their organizations
- **What they most value** about their work, their school, and their education system
- What they believe are the **key strengths** that give their school and education system life and that could be leveraged further
- What they **aspire for their school or education system to be** in 10 years:
  - ○ What is different?
  - ○ How have *they* contributed to that difference?

By asking stakeholders to think reflectively and appreciatively about what is already good and strong, positive and powerful stories and narratives often emerge. Even in the most challenging of contexts there is always something affirmative and inspiring that can be latched onto and leveraged. Our teams and collaborators have adopted these strengths-based approaches in, for example, indigenous Pacific Island contexts – using theatre, dance, art, and storytelling to harvest and build on community narratives of deep, deep pride. And these positive and appreciative discussions also keep your backbone team energized and engaged in the world of brilliant possibilities.

G3: Agree the compelling cause

Once you have mapped the present, you will very likely have a long list of both 'problems' from your empirical/data-driven inquires and 'opportunities' from your appreciative inquiry. However, the challenge with long lists is that if you attempt to progress it all you very often end up achieving nothing at all. We have seen this many times, attending Ministerial launches of complex blueprints with 20 to 30 key priorities and sometimes as many as 100 pre-designed programs or initiatives that are expected to be implemented simultaneously. It's just too complex to explain, deliver, monitor, evaluate, or iterate so much. Quickly, everyone tires from initiative fatigue (a.k.a. initiativitis) and people just end up going through the motions, then cherry-pick data to try and show that something has improved. Even if it's just that the schools have got a new lick of paint. And, as implementation steams ahead, everyone has forgotten what the original purpose of the reform initiative was anyway.

To avoid the risk that you overcommit and underdeliver, the obvious solution is to select your *compelling cause* with great care. Note, too, that we say cause in the singular and not the plural. The key is to identify ONE single, central area of focus that everyone (or at least the majority) can vigorously get behind and in front of. And you can approach this distillation process from both a problem-driven and appreciative inquiry perspective.

Problem-driven distillation

If you have adopted a problem-driven perspective what you want to know is which of the 'issues' that you have identified are worth 'solving'. For each potential *compelling cause,* you might want to ask carefully, deliberately, and provocatively:

■ Does this really matter? Does it truly compel us?
■ What is the worst that could happen if we did absolutely nothing?
■ Should we really care?

This may sound shockingly cruel (and yes it needs to be managed *extremely* carefully to avoid causing offense with stakeholders), but the idea is to take as many of the potential causes *off* the table as possible. In challenging contexts where many worthy causes are competing for very limited resources, tough questions have to be asked. Unpleasant as it might be, to not ask them would be a neglection of duty.

When you ask whether it really matters all that much that 19% of 15-year-olds can't read or write and the reaction from assembled stakeholders is utter incredulity (i.e., a burning pitchfork moment), then you just might have vectored in on a *cause* that people care enough about to want to act on. And the idea is to narrow down the causes to the smallest number, until you get to the point that large numbers of people refuse to ignore a particular *cause*. In Figure 11.3, we illustrate this potentially uncomfortable process in action.

Appreciative distillation

Of course, as we have already highlighted, one of the potential challenges of presenting quantitative and, at times, bleak-looking 'deficiencies' is that whilst they raise blood pressure and anger, they can also raise despondency and helplessness. From your appreciative mapping, you have already asked stakeholders what they aspire for their school or education system to be in 10 years. Rich, powerful, and positive narratives will almost certainly be captured from this dialogue. In addition, many of the problem-oriented statements can easily be re-lensed into appreciative aspirations. Problem statements like, "19% of 15-year-olds are functionally illiterate" become empowering goal orientations – "We aspire for a system that equips all children with the literacy and numeracy skills they need for adult life". However, the crucial next step is the selection of your most *compelling cause.*

Synthesis and selection of THE compelling cause

We offer no hard and fast rules about how many *compelling causes* you whittle down to; but overall, less is more. ONE would be ideal and any more than two or three would (likely) get you back into *initiativitis.* If the inquiry team and wider stakeholders are struggling to narrow down, then processes like community preference

GOAL HUNTING

Potential *Compelling Cause* Areas (Problem-driven perspective)	Does it really Matter? i.e. the 'So what?' *Provocation*	What's the worst that could happen if we did nothing? i.e. where is the evidence? And how strong is the evidence?	Should we care? i.e. is this our most important *mega-challenge?*
On average, 22% of teachers are absent from school on any given teaching day	Is there a strong relationship between teacher attendance/hours of instruction and student learning?	• Children will continue to spend an average of 1.6 hours a day in school without supervision • Teachers will be paid a cumulative $830m for days they are absent	It *might* be the case that even with 8-hour per week teacher shortfall per child, enough instruction is already being supplied. Requires deeper investigation.
27% of children have dropped out of school by grade 5	Maybe four years of education are enough?	Primary school dropouts in our context are: • 5x more likely to be in low paying jobs • 3.2x more likely to serve jail time • 3.4x more likely to die before age 60	Yes. But we need to understand more about whether there are differences in outcome for children that are already literate by grade 5 and drop out vs those that are not.
19% of 15-year-olds are functionally illiterate	Is it essential that everyone is literate? Can we live with 79%?	Illiterate adults in our context are: • 4x more likely to be in low paying jobs • 2.7x more likely to be convicted of a criminal offense • 3x more likely to die before age 60 • 6x more likely to have dropped out of school by grade 5	This is an utter catastrophe. It might also be that other identified problems like low teacher attendance and high student dropout are contributing to this.
School buildings are shabby	Is there a relationship between the quality of infrastructure and student attendance/ achievement?	There is no statistically significant difference in learning outcomes or attendance between new-build and 'traditional' schools	Not right now. But we might need to explain to community stakeholders why they should worry less, too.
Difficulty in recruiting qualified mathematics and science teachers – 76% do not have an advanced qualification in the subject they teach	Do teachers really need to have an advanced qualification in the subject they teach?	Mathematics and science teachers with an advanced qualification are, on average, $d = 0.10$ more effective (if they turn up to school)	No. This is probably not big enough to warrant the investment, for now.

Figure 11.3 Identifying *Compelling Causes* from a Problem-Driven Perspective

voting or consensus seeking on matched pairs may help to break the deadlock. We want to be frank: if you cannot find a potential cause that convincingly passes the 'so what?' test, you should disband your GOLD team and leave individual schools to progress their education improvement agendas locally.

However, if you successfully identify a *compelling cause* for which there is a high level of consensus, then we recommend that you define this with greater precision. If, for example, your cause is about addressing the fact that 19% of 15–year–olds are functionally illiterate, you will want to determine whether there are any hotspots within the data and break your cause down into smaller parts. We illustrate this in Figure 11.4.

G4: Build a theory of the present

To make progress with your *compelling cause* you need to design and implement activities that generate improvement. However, these designs are more likely to be effective if they are rooted in a deep understanding of the local context. Therefore, you need to build a theory of the present. This is not dissimilar to the mapping activity that you will have already undertaken in G2, but the focus is narrower.

Compelling Cause	
We aspire for a system that equips all children with the literacy and numeracy skills they need for adult life ***Present situation:*** *19% of 15-year-olds are functionally illiterate*	
Present Breakdown Structure	**Commentary**
Functionally literate is defined as achieving a grade 3 or higher in national literacy assessment	External consultants have recently benchmarked our national assessments and suggested they are of low validity and reliability – the situation could actually be much worse (!!!)
52% of 15-year-old's not meeting the standard have not actually sat the assessment	Can we assume that all those that have not sat the assessment would have failed to achieve grade 3?
Students that have not sat the assessment are: • Disproportionately girls (68%) • Disproportionately rural (74%) • Disproportionately low SES (83%) • Have not been attending school for more than 4 years (23%)	Is this a consequence of poorer school quality in our rural districts or of lower levels of community engagement/aspiration?
Of the students who sat the assessment and did not achieve grade 3: • Disproportionately boys (57%) • Disproportionately rural (63%) • Disproportionately low SES (83%)	Can we find any data on teacher demographics, e.g., are these students more likely to be taught by less experienced teachers or are their teachers more frequently absent?

Figure 11.4 *Compelling Cause* Breakdown Structure

> **We aspire for a system that equips all children with the literacy and numeracy skills they need for adult life**
> **Present situation:** *19% of 15-year-olds are functionally illiterate.*
> **Why is this?**
>
> —
>
> **Why 1:** Because they have dropped out of school
> **Why 2:** Because they don't like school
> **Why 3:** Because they find it boring
> **Why 4:** Our teachers are not providing instruction that they find meaningful or enjoyable
> **Why 5:** Our teachers have not been trained or supported to implement more effective instructional approaches

Figure 11.5 The Five Whys Approach

Instead of holistically exploring and mapping your entire education system, you are focusing in on mapping your agreed cause. And you can do this from a problem-based or an appreciative perspective; or both.

If you have adopted a problem-based perspective, you are looking for 'solutions' to your agreed priority 'problem'. But to craft suitable interventions you need to understand the drivers of the problem. Often system reformers and local improvers skip this step and rely on (implicit) folk theory to explain why their problem exists. The reason this isn't good enough is that if we don't diagnose effectively, then there is a strong likelihood that we will prescribe and implement entirely the wrong 'treatments'.

One simple but effective approach to diagnosis is *The Five Whys*, which was developed by Sakichi Toyoda and was used within the Toyota Motor Corporation (Ohno, 1988). It involves continually asking why X is the case. We illustrate this in Figure 11.5.

The basic idea is that the inquiry team asks as many 'why?' questions as possible and uses the outputs to build a causal model. Depending on the composition, worldviews, and beliefs of the team and wider stakeholders, it's likely you will come up with multiple *Five Whys*, all telling different potential stories. Some stories might be about lack of teacher motivation, others might be about poor-quality instructional materials, and yet others about economic costs to parents of sending their children to school. In Figure 11.6 we illustrate how these different stories can be woven together into a path analysis (a.k.a. theory of the present). However, you will notice that in our illustration we have only peeled back three layers of 'why' in any given direction. This is, therefore, far from being a complete map.

However, what you have mapped and presented is merely an untested theory or a 'just so' story. You now need to collect empirical data to validate whether what you have mapped is a plausible explanation of your *cause* area. Your sources of data might include eMIS, learning walks, stakeholder interviews, and surveys. This is

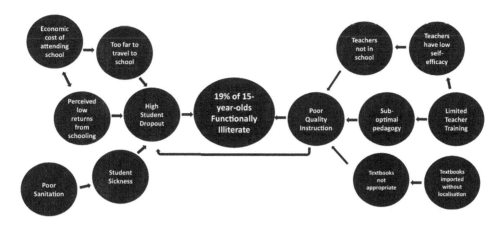

Figure 11.6 Problem-Driven Path Analysis

Influences	Causal Hypothesis	Sources of Verification Data	Outcome of Verification	Variable Remains?
Teachers not in school/ class	Students are in class unsupervised and are therefore not engaging in high-quality learning	Spot audit of 25 randomly selected schools in the district	**Verified.** Mean average of 22% of classrooms had teacher missing during learning walk audits	**Remains**
Poor quality instruction	Students are not attending school because they do not enjoy their classes and do not believe what they study is relevant	Student voice Lesson observations Curriculum review	**Verified.** Students consistently reported that they found lessons unengaging. Lesson observations also suggested disengagement	**Remains**
Perceived low returns from schooling	Students and parents do not fully understand the lifechanging power of education	Student voice and parental interviews of students that have exited the system	**Not verified.** Both parents and children predominantly report that they are aware of returns from schooling, including previous participation in information/ awareness campaigns in 87% of cases	**Removed**

Figure 11.7 Validating the Path Analysis

very much like the process a police detective uses to test each piece of evidence before presenting it in court, and we illustrate this in Figure 11.7.

Current Situation	'To be' Situation	By When	Measured How
19% of 15-year-olds are functionally illiterate	88% of 15-year-olds are functionally literate	December 2025	Percentage of total school-age population that achieves grade 3 threshold in national literacy assessment
Justification of Selection of 'To be' Values			
Review of regional comparator data suggests that an average of 90% students achieve functional literacy in those other contexts.			

Figure 11.8 Setting the Provisional Improvement Goal

The team redraws the path analysis to remove influences that have not been verified, add influences that emerged from on-the-ground research, and re-jiggle the position of arrows between the respective influences. This is not an exact science: it's more an art informed by systematic data collection. However, the finalized path analysis is a crucial foundational platform for the identification of initiatives that slow, block, or reverse each of the identified influences. We should add that if you are undertaking this mapping at district level, one map may do it. However, at regional or national level, you might end up with several maps that reflect variations across, for example, urban vs rural areas or indigenous vs dominant cultural contexts.

From an appreciative perspective, you will likely cover similar ground and vector in on similar drivers. However, the way you frame the inquiry is much more positive and empowering. It may be that your GOLD team flips back and forth between these two perspectives and that the latter appreciative framing is what is used for engagement, communication, and validation with grassroots stakeholders.

G5: Set the provisional improvement goal

Now that you have agreed your *compelling cause* and mapped the drivers, the final step in the goal hunting stage is to set success criteria. We illustrate this in Figure 11.8.

At this stage, the targets are merely provisional – they will be further chiseled and refined during the opportunity sifting phase. But it gives you an (initial) tangible goal to keep in mind as you progress to stage 2.

GOLD stage 2: Opportunity searching (a.k.a. designing the activities)

Opportunity searching is about identifying appropriate activities to advance your *compelling cause*. You are sifting through the various opportunities in design space to select the one(s) with the highest probability of impact; and then working these up into prototype initiatives to subsequently test, iterate, and scale. In the sub-sections below, we outline explicit processes and activities that you could consider during the opportunity searching phase.

O1: Search for opportunities

The first task is to go back to the path analysis that was developed in process G4 (Figure 11.6) to identify all the different types of opportunities or options for improvement in each 'bubble' marked on that map. There are (at least) three places that you can look to identify appropriate interventions:

(1) External to the system

Here, the idea is to search for and harvest interventions that have been successfully tried in other places to support similar goals, and which should (theoretically) work in your context. In addition to the META^X, other excellent sources of data include:

- **Developing country-focused:** The Campbell-UNICEF Child Well-being Mega Map; EPPI-Centre; RISE Program; J-PAL; African Education Research Database
- **'Developed' county-focused:** What Works Clearing House (US); Education Endowment Foundation (UK); Iterative Best Evidence Synthesis Programme (New Zealand); Best Evidence Encyclopedia (US); and Education Resources Information Center (US).

These data repositories can help you to make probability estimates about good bets for implementation, however they rarely provide detailed blueprints.

(2) Internal to the system: Positive outliers

Here you are looking for schools, educators, or wider stakeholders that for whatever reason already seem to be doing extremely well. In the context of our literacy example, these might be schools that already meet or even exceed the 'To Be' aspirational target that you set in step G5. You might use quantitative methods to identify these 'deviants' and then go down to the ground and use qualitative methods to try and understand what they are doing differently and the degree to which it can be replicated. We illustrate this in Figure 11.9.

Outlier Stakeholder	Outlier Outcome	Outlier Behaviors	Replication Potential
Who are they?	How do their outcomes buck the general trend?	What do they seem to be doing differently?	How easy would it be for other stakeholders to replicate the outlier behaviors?

Figure 11.9 Mapping Positive Outliers

(3) Internal to the system: Existing practice

Here the idea is to catalogue what currently happens on the ground and to sense check how far away these existing behaviors, processes, and activities are from either the positive outliers and/or the evidence about successful approaches that have been implemented external to the system.

Combining (1), (2), and (3) to sift the opportunities in design space

Through analysis of (1) highly effective practice external to the system; (2) positive outliers within the system; and (3) existing practice within the system, the next step is to develop a list of potential activities (or opportunity sketches) for each of the identified path analysis 'bubbles'. In the case of "student sickness", you might identify a range of potential activities, including vaccinations, deworming, WASH facilities, and school-based health screening, etc.

For "poor quality instruction" you might identify intelligent tutoring systems, scripted direct instruction, teacher coaching programs, teacher surveillance systems, and curriculum by level not grade, etc.

Each of these activities has a different theory of improvement. Intelligent tutoring systems bypass poor quality instruction; scripted direct instruction and teacher coaching programs are designed to enhance teacher effectiveness; surveillance systems are designed to make sure educators are in the classroom, but do not guarantee they are teaching; and curriculum by level is about ensuring that children do not fall behind and drop out – because the pace is personalized to them. Ergo, whilst each of these activities can (in theory) support a particular 'bubble' on the path analysis, it does so in a different way, with a different theory of improvement.

It's unlikely you will have the resource to implement all the potential opportunity sketches simultaneously, so you need to vector in on those that have a higher probability of impact. Some of the criteria that you might include are illustrated in Figure 11.10.

As you rank the opportunity sketches, it is likely that a small number have higher probability for impact than the rest, and these are the interventions/activities that will be carried forward to the next stage in the GOLD process.

02: Develop a logic model

Having identified the opportunities with higher potential for impact, you now need to plan how you will bundle them together into a cohesive program design to achieve that impact. One tool for doing this is called a program logic model, which was created in 1969 for the US Agency for International Development (World Bank, 2000). As illustrated in Figure 11.11, this provides a structured framework to explore answers to the following questions:

1 What is our *compelling cause*? (E.g., the 'problem' we are trying to resolve and/ or the positive outcome we seek)
2 What resources do we need to deploy to implement each agreed opportunity sketch? (E.g., people, time, budget, etc.)

Factor	Criteria
Evidence of impact	• Outcomes achieved in other contexts (e.g. effect size) • Number of studies and population of studies (e.g. in the Visible Learning META[x] we include a confidence ranking for each influence) • Similarities between the context of the studies and your local environment
Ease of replicability	• Is the intervention 'productized' or do you need to build it yourself? • Are the steps easy to follow or open to wildly different interpretations? • Was it developed for your cultural/linguistic context and/or has it already been localized?
Local capacity to implement	• Do you have access to high-quality internal or third-party technical assistance to support implementation? • Is there buy-in from stakeholders/does the intervention model conform with local stakeholder beliefs/theory of action? • Do stakeholders have sufficient time to engage/participate at the levels required for success? • Do local stakeholders have the skills to implement the new approach/how easy will it be to upskill them?
Cost of implementation	• Total cost ÷ Total number of *Direct Beneficiaries*

Opportunity Sketches	Evidence of Impact 1–5 [5 = strong evidence]	Ease of Replicability 1–5 [5 = high ease]	Local Capacity to Implement 1–5 [5 = high capacity]	Cost of Implementation 1–5 [5 = low cost]	Total
Intelligent tutoring systems	5	3.5	2	3	13.5/25
Scripted direct instruction	5	2.5	1	4	12.5/25

Figure 11.10 Ranking Opportunity Sketches

(Adapted from Hamilton & Hattie, 2021a)

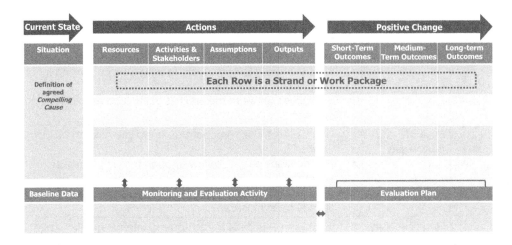

Figure 11.11 Program Logic Model Template

3 What activities will be implemented through use of this resource to generate improvement in the cause area?

4 What assumptions are we making about how and why 2 and 3 will work?

5 What will be the outputs of all this activity? (E.g., the artifacts created; the number of people that have received training or have access to an intelligent tutoring platform, deworming tablets, etc.)

6 What measurable outcomes do we expect to see from implementing the intervention over the short, medium, and longer term?

7 How will we collect data and measure for monitoring and evaluation purposes? And what types of data will we collect?

However, rather than developing one single program logic model and then moving on to implementation, there are strong benefits to developing multiple models so that you can (carefully) consider all the different ways that you can design and implement your improvement initiative (i.e., you need to conduct iteration thought experiments), which we outline below.

03: Iterating your logic model

Design features and setting levels

Whilst program logic models have been used on international development projects since the 1970s and have also become popular in education improvement in high-income nations during the last decade, on their own, they do not enable us to uncover and map the deeper hidden wiring. Every activity/intervention has a range of *design features*. Some of these are generic considerations that will be relevant to all types of intervention, including:

- **Dosage** (i.e., how much is administered)
- **Duration** (i.e., how long does the treatment last for)

- **Target group** (i.e., who is selected for treatment)
- **Delivery group** (i.e., who implements the initiative)
- **Fidelity** (i.e., how much variation is allowed in how the treatment is delivered locally?)

In addition to these generic considerations, there will also be a range of intervention-specific design features. In the case of a scripted direct instruction curriculum, for example, these might include:

- Technology usage
- Level of localization
- Breadth of coverage
- Initial teacher training
- Ongoing teacher professional development
- Selection of instructional approaches
- Curriculum content
- Level of localization.

And for each design feature there are several *setting options*. Some features can be switched off entirely, so the initial decision is about whether to activate or exclude them. And then, for all the active design features, there are decisions to be made about how far (up or down) to turn the dial.

In our work, we have found it useful to map and explore all the key *design features* and *setting options/levels* as explicitly as possible, and in Figure 11.12 we outline how you might map and record your options and your selected settings.

This is merely a worked example. For the 'average' activity/intervention, it might be that there are 25 or more *design features* that you can switch on or off. And for each one that you switch on, there might be 10 or more individual *setting options* or levels that you can choose between. This amounts to at least 250 different positions that the collection of 'switches' can be placed in (i.e., 25 x 10); add to this the fact that your logic model likely includes more than one initiative (e.g., maybe you have opted for scripted direct instruction + teacher surveillance + teacher incentives + parental cash transfers) and the number of combinations across all your treatments becomes phenomenally large.

You are never going to be able to test all those different combinations of design features and setting levels out in the field, but it is important that you explicitly identify them and consider the implications of each position before you reach lift-off. Even seemingly small decisions can have significant potential to moderate the level of impact. Let's say, for example, you choose to distribute your scripted direct instruction materials to teachers in loose-leaf binders. Your rationale for doing this might be that educators can remove the pages they need for the lesson and bring them to class and that this will cause less implementation friction than having to lug an unwieldy instruction bible. But it may be that teachers then forget to put the sheets back into the binder after class and that those sheets then become jumbled or misplaced by year two, and this then means that the activity basically stops.

Activity: Scripted Direct Instruction Program					
	Design Feature 1: Breadth of Coverage	**Design Feature 2: Degree of Scripting**	**Design Feature 3: Distribution Strategy**	**Design Feature 4: Student Materials**	**Design Feature 5: Assessment for Learning**
Setting 1	Whole curriculum	Teacher flexibility – materials are provided for guidance only	Paper-based booklets	None	None
Setting 2	Mathematics, science, and literacy	Scripted but flexible – areas where teachers can adapt are clearly delineated	Paper-based ring-binders, enabling materials to be extracted	Textbooks linked to teaching materials	Multiple choice tests without follow-up
Setting 3	Literacy	Fully scripted	Tablet devices	Workbooks	Multiple choice tests with differentiated response to instruction materials
Setting 4	Mathematics				
Setting 5	Science				
Analysis					
	We need to pilot in one subject area. Literacy is highest priority for improvement	Our teachers require high levels of scaffolding	No local infrastructure to support and maintain ICT devices	Limited budget for the pilot	Setting 3 likely to have most impact but let's start at Setting 1 to reduce complexity and cost
Conclusion					
	Literacy	**Fully scripted**	**Paper-based booklets**	**None**	**None**

Figure 11.12 Design Features and Settings Level Mapping

Many program/initiative designers only work down as far as the high-level program logic model. But given how much complexity lies beneath, in the selection of design features and setting levels, our message is that the devil really is in the detail. You need to explicitly record the options you have selected and why, and also consider which design features and setting levels could be augmented in delivery if, once you liftoff, you find that the impact is not quite at the level you expected.

Stress testing

We are both inherently optimistic – particularly about the power of education to transform lives and the overall quality of living. However, after you have selected your design features and setting levels, it helps if you get exceedingly pessimistic and look for and unpick every possible way that, in implementation, your initiative could go wrong. In other words, you need to stress test.

Some of the areas that you might want to explore during your stress testing review include:

1 **Stakeholder beliefs**. From implementation science research, in healthcare and education, we know that stakeholder's pre-existing beliefs are a crucial determinant of whether your program logic model will generate impact (Knoster, 1991; Robinson et al., 2009; Robinson, 2018). In the last chapter we discussed the challenges that Joseph Lister had in convincing surgeons to wash their hands because they did not believe in germ theory (Barry, 2018). The same goes for education interventions. If you are planning on implementing scripted direct instruction, educators may hold the belief that "*teaching isn't acting*" or "*scripting de-professionalizes my expertise*." Conversely, if you are going to implement a student-led inquiry model, parents may say "we sacrifice a lot to be able to send our children to school, but with this new approach the teacher isn't doing any teaching!" Where beliefs and interventions are misaligned, you are unlikely to generate (as much) impact. And you will need to decide whether to abandon interventions that are too far from current beliefs about what works and what is acceptable, or whether you need to also include additional design features that focus on re-orienting those beliefs.

2 **Motivation.** If your proposed activity requires stakeholders to do something that is radically different from existing practice you need to confront the Papay and Kraft (2015) research that we discussed in Chapter 5. Early on in a teacher's career, when they are novices, they are highly motivated to learn whatever high-impact instructional approaches are thrown at them. However, when educators have mastered enough tradecraft to get by, the opportunity–cost of engaging in deliberate, effortful, and mentally tiring practice to learn how to do something differently may no longer seem worth the payoff. So, you need to assume that mid-career teachers (and beyond) might not be terribly motivated to engage, and you may need to include design features that counteract (or bypass) this.

3 **Friction.** Online retailers have learned that the more clicks required to complete a transaction the more likely that the online shopping cart gets left abandoned part way through the process. Clicks are hurdles and hurdles cause friction. The same principle applies to your program logic model. So, from a Lean perspective, you want to ask how many "clicks" (processes/steps) there are in what you are asking people to do; how you can reduce this number; and how your new processes can help reduce friction in other parts of your target group's lives.

4 **Maintenance.** Research in the field of human nutrition tells us that whilst losing weight is hard, maintenance is even more challenging – with up to 80% of dieters rebounding to their prior weight within 5 years (Wing & Phelan, 2005). The process of maintaining a habit (whether this be healthy weight or a new instructional approach) requires a permanent change in behavior without backsliding/relapsing. You need to carefully consider whether what you are asking people to do is easy for them to (1) commit to and (2) maintain over time, and therefore (3) whether you need additional support mechanisms to amplify their initial and ongoing willpower.

5 **Mutation.** Reviews of the implementation of student-centered 'progressive' instructional approaches in the US have found that even though many teachers believed that they were implementing the key features of the new approach, in many cases they had merely cherry-picked the features that they liked and blended these with their existing practice (Cuban, 1990; Elmore, 1996). In your activity design you will need to consider whether fidelity of implementation matters and, if it does, what countermeasures you can put in place to reduce the probability of mutation.

6 **Voltage drop.** In healthcare implementation research, a common finding is that pilot interventions where the researchers/program designers work closely with on-the-ground practitioners are more likely to generate positive outcomes than scaled implementation without close involvement of the developers. As the number of clinics/hospitals/practitioners increase, there is often a corresponding decline in the implementation quality of the activity. This has been termed "voltage drop" (Kilbourne et al., 2007). It is reasonable to assume it will be the same for education. So, as you scale from 10 schools to 100, or even 1,000, are there any design features that might mitigate this reduction in 'electrical current' or do you/can you accept the voltage drop?

—

Assuming you undertake steps O2 and O3 with gusto (and we recommend that you do), you will likely end up with multiple program logic models with different proposed activities; and for each logic model, multiple variations in the design features and setting levels for each of those interventions. You now need to select the logic model(s), activities, design features, and setting levels that you think will have the highest probability of impact and implement one or more of these.

However, whether you will generate impact is uncertain. You will only know for sure once you press "play". So, you also need to develop a success map that you can monitor (during liftoff and double back) to decide what to dial up, dial down, and what to stop.

04: Developing a success map

Things that get measured are more likely to get improved. Therefore, the final part of opportunity searching involves identifying, selecting, and setting quantifiable improvement goals and indicators. You might start by making a long list of all the potential indicators; possibly identifying 20+, which link to different parts of your program logic model and to your assumptions about the appropriate design features and settings. Once you have your longlist you will then (likely) want to narrow it down to a smaller subset of indicators that:

■ Most directly and explicitly link to your *compelling cause*
■ Are easier to collect data for
■ Are valid (i.e., measure the right thing) and reliable (i.e., measure the thing in a consistent way)
■ Give you a mixture of leading indicators (i.e., quick data) and lagging indicators (i.e., slow data) which more directly measures your mega-challenge.

For each of your agreed indicators, you will then want to set baseline values and a proposed improvement trajectory over time. The outputs are then fed into your program logic model (i.e., outputs; and short-, medium-, and long-term outcomes).

You will also need to consider whether the act of measuring creates any potential for perverse incentives. For example, we know of one middle-developing nation that decided to use student performance in the OECD *Programme for International Student Assessment* (PISA) as their lagging indicator (and target) of success in their widely promoted national education transformation program. System leaders publicly announced both the indicator and the target: to be in the top-XX percent of PISA performers. In the next round of assessments, there were serious questions about the validity of their PISA scores. The allegation was that the ministry had "massaged" the protocols by only collecting/submitting data from high-performing schools. We think you need to be extremely pessimistic (or realistic?) and assume that whatever measures you select will create some sort of perverse incentives and that you need to plan for how you will either counteract or accommodate/leverage this.

GOLD stage 3: Liftoff

Now that you have identified and mapped your *compelling cause*; built multiple program logic models; explored the implications of various design features and settings, selecting those with the highest probability of impact; and developed your success map, it is time to liftoff. Whether you do this by selecting your best design and throwing everything at it or by running parallel pilots on several plausible designs will depend on the resources you have at hand.

Liftoff/delivery is more likely to be effective when:

1 There is a dedicated GOLD delivery team that has clear roles, responsibilities, and accountabilities (i.e., a delivery office)
2 The delivery team utilizes a systematic project/program management methodology
3 The delivery team fully implements the selected project/program management methodology
4 The delivery team regularly draws on data to review whether they are doing the things they set out to do and whether those things are resulting in impact and improvement (monitoring and evaluation)
5 The delivery team is supported by a trained project/program manager(s) who oversees points 1–4.

We have relatively little to say about the explicit project management processes used during liftoff/delivery. From the involvement of our own teams in education improvement projects in 30+ countries, we have found that most ministries of education (sorta) know how to do this bit. They (usually) know how to produce project initiation documents, project plans, risk registers, issues logs, communications plans, product acceptance criteria, and lessons learnt logs. In fact, without these processes (even if only embryonic) they would not have been able to recruit, train, and pay teachers, or build and maintain schools in the first place. Yes, there is always room for improvement; and, yes, ongoing debates about whether PRINCE2, Critical Chain, Agile, Waterfall, etc. provide the best tools and processes. There are also differences in how rigid or flexible each of these frameworks is. For the purposes of liftoff, however, all we are interested in is that the delivery office can monitor the budget; schedule and monitor inputs, resources, activities, and outputs; and measure whether all of this has resulted in the agreed outputs and outcomes.

There is, of course, a major difference between a project/program successfully achieving all its deliverables and this actually making progress toward the *compelling cause*. This is the difference between generating outputs (i.e., ticking-off deliverables) vs outcomes (achieving impact). To ensure you generate the latter, you need to embed evaluation processes for doubling back after liftoff. And you need to double back frequently.

GOLD stage 4: Double back (a.k.a. evaluation)

You are more likely to make meaningful progress toward your *compelling cause* when:

1   There is an explicit attempt to evaluate whether the initiatives have generated meaningful impact
2   The evaluation methodology and protocols are agreed ★*before*★ the project commences, rather than tacked on as an afterthought
3   An appropriate evaluation methodology is selected, and indicators are base-lined prior to project commencement and then tracked over time
4   The evaluation design measures what has been done (i.e., monitoring) and whether it resulted in the intended impact (i.e., evaluation)
5   The outcomes of evaluation are regularly used to refine/iterate the delivery of the project – to enhance/amplify impact – with checkpoint review gates that are used to explicitly decide and agree 'where to next?'

In other words, we need to double back to confirm and enhance our impact; and the reason we need to double back is because implementation is complex. Activities that have worked in other, similar, contexts often fail when plugged into new settings. Sometimes they can be downright harmful. In science this is known as the *replication crisis* (Staddon, 2017). Some of the reasons for this inability to replicate include:

■   **That the ecosystems are profoundly different** – even if they generate similar needs/goals. This means that different types of activities, design features, and settings may have been far more effective.
■   **That the activity/program/process was not delivered 'properly'**. This may be because of some of the reasons we outlined in stress–testing, including mutation, voltage drop, or misaligned stakeholder beliefs.

Whilst, through careful opportunity sifting, we can mitigate and reduce the probability of implementation failure, we can only know for sure whether there will be impact by looking for it (or the lack of it) after the fact. In other words, we only know when we know!

During the earlier stages of GOLD, we already embedded a range of processes that help to ensure that meaningful evaluation can take place, which we will illustrate in Figure 11.13.

By doubling back, we can understand:

■   **WHETHER** implementation resulted in impact. For example, are literacy rates and teacher and student attendance, etc., actually going up?
■   **WHY** impact was (or wasn't) achieved. We can then better understand whether to stop completely, carry on as is, or whether we need to iterate by cycling different interventions, design features, or setting levels.

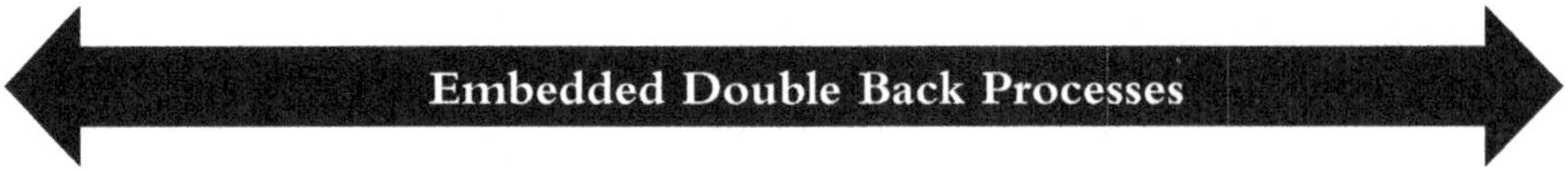

Goal Hunting	Opportunity Seeking	Liftoff
G2 and 3: by searching for and ranking potential *compelling causes* you are pre-evaluating which are most worthy of progressing **G4:** by developing a path analysis you are building a theory of the present **G5:** by setting provisional improvement goals you are collecting baseline data and setting improvement targets	**O1:** by sifting global research data, local positive outliers, and existing local practice, you are pre-evaluating which overarching activities have the highest probability of generating impact **O2 and 3:** by systematically reviewing all the different design features, setting levels, and undertaking stress testing, you are pre-evaluating the design features most likely to generate impact **O4:** by developing G5 into a full success map that identifies the key indicators, targets, and data collection protocols, you have ready measuring sticks for evaluation	Through use of project management and evaluation tools you will be able to measure: - **Milestones/outputs/deliverables** (i.e., are we doing the things we said we would do, and are these being delivered on time/budget/to the agreed quality standard?) - **Evidence of impact** (i.e., are the things we are doing resulting in tangible improvement in our O4 leading and lagging indicators?

Figure 11.13 Embedded Double Back/Evaluation Processes

There are many existing 'how to guides' on designing and undertaking evaluations in low- and middle-income country contexts (see, for example, Gertler et al., 2016; Nkwake, 2020; Vaessen et al., 2020). What methodology, tools, and evaluation protocols you select will vary depending on your implementation context and budget. Our only counsel is about the importance of being clear on the *purpose* of evaluating. Most of the peer reviewed research within the META^{X} (and many of the international development initiative reviews) evaluate for *summative* purposes. They principally want to know whether the intervention 'worked'. They collect pre- and post-intervention data to calculate effect size; and they often also compare the treatment group outcomes to a control group to confirm that it was the treatment that generated the effect, not chance.

However, our suggestion is that during implementation of your GOLD initiatives you want to evaluate for *formative* purposes. You want to know whether your intervention is generating impact and also *why* (or why not). You need to know

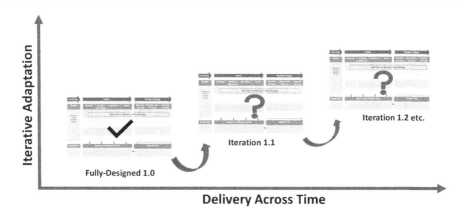

Figure 11.14 Iterative Adaptation

this so that you can 'wiggle' the design features and setting levels during further rounds of implementation to increase effectiveness. This means that during liftoff and double back you continue with the thought experiments you started during your initial program logic modeling; you continually ask, "what would happen if we switched off this design feature or changed its setting level?". You are not doing this simply to naval gaze – you are doing it to identify features that you are going to adjust and then monitor to determine whether they generated more/less/the same amount of impact. We illustrate this in Figure 11.14.

By reviewing formative evaluation data and using it to iterate your implementation, you are more likely to overcome the great replication crisis and generate impact. You are also more likely to explore and develop countermeasures for features that do not scale as you grow from a handful of pilot schools/settings to regional or national impact.

GOLD *stage 5: Double up* (a.k.a. scaling)

Our assumption is that stakeholders *want* to scale their impact (or double up). Many researchers of implementation define scale in terms of widespread use of a program or intervention (Adelman & Taylor, 1997; Fullan, 2000; Sloane, 2005; Stringfield & Datnow, 1998). Some go even further. Michael Fullan (2000), for example, defines scale as a *minimum* of 20,000 students across 50 schools. We prefer to be less explicit/prescriptive, leaving it to GOLD teams to agree what scale means in their local contexts. However, to scale, you need to:

1   Select a *compelling cause* that responds to a pervasive need/goal. You can only scale improvement if the thing you are trying to address is widespread (G2)
2   Thoroughly map your ecosystem to understand whether the environmental context is uniform or whether it varies significantly from setting to setting, including between schools in the same neighborhood (G3)

3   Build multiple program logic models to respond to identified differences across your different settings (O2)

4   Pre-iterate your program logic models through exploration of design features and setting levels, and stress testing (O3) – prior to liftoff

5   After liftoff, double back to formatively evaluate the mediators and moderators of impact, identifying design features and settings to iteratively adapt – particularly those that might support effective scaling

6   Have a plan about how you will scale. For example, will you:
    - **"Go-big"** – and seek to uniformly roll out an activity/program across all schools/settings; or
    - **"Snowball"** – testing and refining your program logic model and gradually sucking more schools/settings into the orbit of your program; or
    - **"Go flexible"** – having a handful of pre-validated implementation models for different types of contexts; and/or
    - **"Go meta-flexible"** – giving schools the tools to design and evaluate their own local initiatives?

Our counsel is that if you get the earlier parts of the GOLD equation right, then double up should take care of itself. That isn't to say that doubling up is easy (it isn't); but you will have designed, implemented, and evaluated for it from the get-go. However, in addition to the (O3) stress testing considerations related to beliefs, motivation, friction, maintenance, and voltage drop, we outline some additional scaling considerations below.

D^x perspective 1: Grain size

This is about the extent of required change in each school/setting for the improvement to be implemented effectively. Here we delineate between fine grain, coarse grain, and rock (Hamilton & Hattie, 2021a):

- **Fine grain.** This is a relatively self-contained change that is (theoretically) easier to implement. It might take only a few minutes per day and require very few steps or 'clicks' to execute. Taking a student attendance register at the start of the school day is an example. It can be easily explained to teachers, requires minimal training, takes only a few minutes each day to action, and simple monitoring/auditing can be leveraged to measure compliance. Therefore, it (should) scale more easily.

- **Coarse grain.** This takes longer to execute (either more minutes or more required repetitions throughout the day) and requires a greater number of 'clicks' to implement each repetition with fidelity. It may also involve more local discretion about when, where, and how to execute the new protocols. Introducing success criteria as a system-wide instructional approach would be an example of this. As we discussed in Chapter 8, success criteria involves clearly displaying/explaining to learners at the start of each lesson what is expected of them and what they will be able to do by the end of the learning episode. When implemented with fidelity, success criteria generates an effect size of $d = 0.88$, which is extremely high. Whilst (arguably) it does not take much longer than taking an attendance register to introduce success criteria at the start of each lesson, it needs to be repeated with greater frequency throughout the day. And the criteria also need to be contextualized to the specific learning objectives of the lesson. Therefore, we should expect more implementation friction and therefore more required support/scaffolding.

- **Rock.** This is a significant level of change that involves more routines, more minutes and repetitions per routine, more clicks, and possibly also more discretion. An example might be the decision to mandate five high-impact instructional approaches across all schools, e.g., success criteria ($d = 0.88$) + cognitive task analysis ($d = 1.29$) + feedback ($d = 0.57$) + Jigsaw method ($d = 1.20$) + differentiation ($d = 0.68$). Even if teachers are provided with sizable amounts of training, on-the-job coaching, and scaffolded implementation materials, this represents a profound level of change to the routines and expectations of the existing day job. It also flags considerable risk for mutation, voltage drop, and (lack of) maintenance.

D^x perspective 2: Transmission mechanism

This is about the processes utilized to engage with stakeholders to bring about fine grain, coarse grain or rock-type changes. Here, we distinguish between viral transmission, replication, and adaptation (Morel et al., 2019):

- **Viral transmission**. This happens when a new process, tool, or idea is gradually and organically transmitted through the system by word of mouth, testimonials/case studies from early adopters, and endorsements by figures of authority – gradually becoming accepted. One example is Bloom's Taxonomy, which moved from fringe circles in the 1950s to widespread usage in assessment, curriculum development, and classroom instruction (Schneider, 2014). In the healthcare sector there is a relatively new sub-field called *Implementation Science*, which specifically explores how findings from research can be bundled and transmitted (or marketed) to healthcare institutions. The rise of educational what works institutes like the Education Endowment Foundation (UK), What Works Clearing House (US), and the African Education Research Database arguably serve a similar purpose (i.e., as education research "marketing agencies"). Although it is still left to the discretion of individual schools which pieces of research/tools they pick up and what they do with them. Therefore, the returns from viral transmission are highly variable.
- **Replication.** This is about explicitly designing a highly structured intervention/activity that can be activated and scaled with fidelity. It might be done through testing a range of designs, design features, and setting levels (as per GOLD); and "productizing" or codifying the most effective variants. Productization levers might include:
  - ○ **Process standardization.** E.g., by providing explicit steps to be undertaken during implementation. This might be scaffolded (i.e., recommended

processes/checklists with discretion about how and when to use) or it might be scripted (i.e., mandated processes that are delivered with fidelity)

- ○ **Process simplification.** E.g., by reducing the number of clicks or points of friction in implementation of the new standard work protocols
- ○ **Stakeholder capacity-building.** E.g., gradual release support, including training; spaced learning; modelling; coaching; feedback, etc.
- ○ **Staged implementation.** E.g., successfully juggle one ball and then graduate to two, etc.
- ○ **Stakeholder motivation.** E.g., beliefs/hearts and minds vs incentives (carrot) vs sanctions (stick)
- ○ **Stakeholder by-pass.** E.g., using intelligent tutoring systems to automate instructional processes.

- ■ **Adaptation.** This is about scaled implementation that allows local stakeholders to adjust the processes to make them more workable locally (Clarke & Dede, 2009; Fishman, 2005; Means & Penuel, 2005; Sisken, 2016; Wiske & Perkins, 2005). However, the challenge with adaptation is that it can morph into a mutation that retains the superficial form but none of the essential substance of the original treatment. Lant Pritchett (2013, p. 12) refers to it as *isomorphic mimicry*. Our advice is that if you opt to allow implementation with variation, that you do not leave the areas that can be adapted to chance. As you iterate your program logic model(s) (step O3), you can explicitly map and tag:
  - ○ **Mandatory processes/design features.** I.e., those that cannot be deviated from at all and that need to be locked in
  - ○ **Flexible processes/design features.** I.e., those that need to be implemented but where the tolerance for local discretion/variation is high (e.g., whether school attendance is taken in assembly for the whole year group or whether teachers do it in their individual form rooms, and what it is that children shout out to signal their presence during rollcall may not really matter. It only matters that the attendance data is accurately captured.)
  - ○ **In-built areas for localization.** I.e., explicit design features for local stakeholders to "decorate" and make personal to increase buy-in/ownership and unlock the IKEA effect. This might be as simple as adding the school logo and vision to the front of a nationally standardized document; or it might be as complex as a scripted direct instruction program that highlights areas of delivery that can be localized to be more relatable to students' lives, with suggested examples of how this could be done.

We class GOLD as a form of meta-adaptation. It is a set of suggested processes, which can be varied but that have been crafted to help education system leaders to discover an appropriate *compelling cause*, search the opportunities for appropriate activities, liftoff, double back, and double up.

LEAN improvement

For a book called *The Lean Education Manifesto* you might be thinking that the GOLD processes we spent so much time unpacking seem remarkably additive, rather than subtractive. You would be right. GOLD is principally about identifying new Jenga blocks to insert to build on the existing educational structures and making their impact stronger. However, even GOLD has hues of (parsimoniously) Lean thinking embedded:

1   By selecting the smallest number of *compelling causes* and by continually asking the "so what/so why?" question, we avoid the temptation of dismantling and rebuilding the entire Jenga tower simultaneously. Instead, we vector in on a minimal number of challenge blocks or agendas (GOLD process G2 and G3).
2   By selecting activities with the highest probability of impact/return on investment and explicitly mapping the design features and settings prior to liftoff we increase the likelihood of efficient and effective intervention (GOLD processes O1–4).
3   By starting small, evaluating, iterating, and growing, we mitigate the potential that we bet the farm on white elephants; and we hold at bay our cognitive biases for cherry picking, sunk cost, optimism, and plan continuation (see Hattie & Hamilton, 2021).

However, we also suggest simultaneous exploration of things that you can stop, reduce, or make more efficient through Lean-oriented processes. In Chapter 2, we already introduced Lean. So, in the remainder of this chapter, we will explore how it can be implemented in education contexts; Figure 11.15 recaps the process.

LEAN Improvement				
E. AGREE Where to next	**D. EVALUATE** Future State	**C. PILOT** Future State	**B. FUTURE** State Analysis	**A. CURRENT** State Analysis
Scaling-up/ scaling-back and searching for new sources of waste/*muda*	Carefully reviewing the impact of waste/*muda* elimination	Implementing controlled elimination of waste/*muda*	Identifying waste for elimination (*muda*)	Mapping the existing value stream

Figure 11.15 Lean Improvement

Establishing a Lean team

To undertake a Lean investigation, you need a Lean team. As we outlined in the introduction to this chapter, expecting your GOLD team to think and act from both an additive and subtractive perspective simultaneously might be too high a burden on their cognitive load. Therefore, you could establish a second team, specifically for Lean forays. As with GOLD teams, your Lean taskforce is likely to comprise: Lean Sponsor, Lean Guiding Coalition, Lean Leader, Lean Investigators, and involve collaboration with wider stakeholders across the system.

However, we think that the task of the Lean team may be more challenging. Not in terms of processes. Value stream mapping and the subsequent identification of activities and steps to deactivate are (arguably) easier than building out a new activity or intervention. Where we think Lean investigations are likely to be considerably harder is in terms of the willpower to follow-through on removing superfluous or over-engineered Jenga blocks. This is because of:

- **Rent seeking, extraction, and patronage reduction potential.** In systems where the educational political economy is oriented toward extraction and patronage, Lean means fewer new contracts awarded – and possibly also fewer staff – through a gradual process of attrition. This perhaps makes it more challenging for political actors to continue to 'feed their base' (Kingdon et al., 2014).
- **Electoral suicide potential.** Where service users judge quality by input metrics like teacher–student ratios, length of the school day/year, number of years of schooling, class size, etc., explicitly chiseling away at any of these is likely to create a perception that the quality of service has declined – even if student attendance and achievement go up in parallel. (Of course, they won't go up in parallel because they are lagging indicators that require a lot of breath-holding before the needle starts to move. This makes it even more difficult.)
- **Teacher mutiny potential.** If someone turned up at your workplace with a stopwatch and followed you around all day making copious notes, you would probably get suspicious and alert your union representative. In fact, in Kenya, when (Lean) Contract Teacher initiatives were introduced that involved hiring and deploying minimally qualified teachers on much lower rates of remuneration, the predictable result was strike action by the Kenya National Union of Teachers (Duflo et al., 2015).

For these reasons, we think that *Hard Lean* – where stakeholders boldly, deliberately, and gleefully search for fat to cut – is likely to be an extremely challenging political agenda. Except in circumstances where sizable fiscal deficits and declining tax revenues make the current contours of the national education system difficult to fund, and/or where everyone is aggressively questioning why their taxes are resulting in so little gains in student learning.

However, we think that *Soft Lean* – where the focus is not on reducing people's rice or cassava bowls but on increasing the returns from each existing minute of activity – is likely to be more palatable. In fact, in many jurisdictions, teachers (reasonably) complain that their workloads are too high (OECD, 2019c) – with a consequence that this increases their stress and reduces their health and the likelihood of them remaining in the profession. For example, across OECD countries, lower-secondary school teachers report spending an average of 57% of their time on non-teaching activities (*ibid.*). Yes, some of this will be about planning lessons, undertaking formative assessment, and professional development. But some of it will (likely) be on non-value adding or not sufficiently value-adding activity (a.k.a. 'busy work' that makes not one iota of difference to the learning lives of children).

Therefore, if it is made explicit that the focus of Lean inquiry is to make teachers lives easier AND to help children learn more – without job cuts or reductions in service standards – we think stakeholders might come to positively embrace Lean. However, it requires an unambiguous commitment from the Lean Sponsor about what is on and off the table (e.g. we are focusing on making teachers' lives less stressful; we are not touching your terms and conditions of employment, etc.). And it (likely) also requires co-opting teaching unions and parental peak associations into the guiding coalition; and for them to participate in designing the parameters and terms of reference for the Lean taskforce.

We also believe that Lean processes can be effective at the individual school level. This might, for example, involve setting up a Professional Learning Community of teachers who agree to conduct an in-house 'time and motion study' to collect metrics on what they spend most of their time doing. They would then select and agree one thing to stop doing, implement the stop, and then see if it has any impact on student learning (positive or negative). And they would continue this process over and over.

With this preamble out of the way, we now unpack the suggested Lean improvement steps, from A to E.

(A) Current state analysis

Once your Lean team is assembled, their first task is to map the existing value chain to understand what it is that everyone spends their time on. There are several ways that you can do this, including:

- **Time logging.** This involves the group closely recording what they are doing throughout the day. You might start by identifying the key categories of activity. You can then ask stakeholders to record the time they spend doing each of these tasks. There are already free mobile apps to support this, which are often used by, for example, lawyers and management consultants to facilitate (by-the-minute) client billing. You can use the outputs of this analysis to provide a high-level overview of the percentage of time devoted to different categories of task and the number of task repetitions per day. And for full coverage, you also want stakeholders to record work-related activities that they undertake outside their official working hours.

■ **Micro-process mapping.** For each major activity type, you might undertake a process walk. This involves recording all the major steps and sub-steps (or clicks) traversed in implementation of the process. These can be recorded in lists, through the use of post-it notes, or through process mapping software, if available.

■ **Macro-process mapping.** From Chapter 2, you will remember that Lean is not just about improvement within a single organization. It's about exploring the contours of the entire value chain. This means that if you are operating at system-level, in addition to school-level processes, you are also interested in the upstream activities like initial teacher recruitment and training, school construction, and student recruitment and transportation – basically any process that happens outside the school gates (which the ministry/department of education can influence) that has an impact on what happens inside. What you are interested in is whether these 'raw inputs' have been 'overprocessed' prior to use.

■ **eMIS data review.** You may also have electronic data (or logbooks) that enable you to identify and analyze averages, such as hours in the classroom, teacher/student absence rates, teacher–student ratios, etc.

(B) Future state analysis

Now that you have mapped the existing value chain, the next step is to identify potential areas of waste/*muda* for elimination. As we illustrate in Figure 11.16, there are at least five approaches that you could adopt.

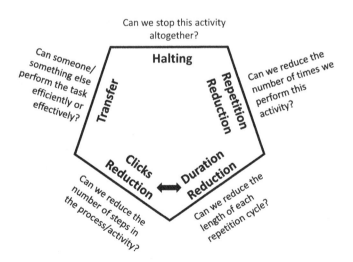

Figure 11.16 Five Approaches for Waste/Muda Reduction

Let's say, for example, that in your current state analysis you identify that marking student homework is taking up a significant proportion of teacher time, and that teachers are regularly sitting up until 11pm or later undertaking formative assessment. Your Lean options include:

- **Halting.** Your first potential approach is simply to administer no further homework. The META^X contains data from 8 meta-analyses of 217 studies on the impact of homework on student achievement (Bas et al., 2017; Cooper, 1989; Cooper, 1994; Cooper et al., 2006; DeBaz, 1994; Fan et al., 2017; Hendricks et al., 2014; Paschal et al., 1984). The mean effect size across all these metas is $d = 0.28$. However, there are marked differences between the impact on students in basic education versus those in secondary schooling ($d = 0.15$ vs $d = 0.65$). This suggests that in primary schools it might well be a viable strategy to halt but that in secondary education, this would be ill-advised.
- **Repetition reduction**. Your second potential approach is to keep giving homework but to reduce the number of instances (i.e., the frequency rate). In primary education this might be an initial reduction from five nights a week to four, three, or fewer. In secondary schooling, it might involve a shift from daily to weekly homework per subject area.
- **Duration reduction.** Your third potential option is to reduce the intensity of each repetition. You might still give homework with the same level of frequency, but you might reduce the size of each assignment and therefore the time it takes for teachers to prepare it and then formatively assess. In fact, there is some evidence suggesting that the duration of homework may be inversely proportional to the level of impact on student achievement (i.e., short and sweet is better) (Trautwein et al., 2002).
- **Clicks reduction.** Your fourth potential option involves the step-by-step review of what it is teachers and students are actually doing during the end-to-end homework process. You would look at how the homework is designed and distributed; how students undertake it and for how long; how it is collected and transported; how much time is spent assessing each task; how the outcomes of assessment are record/reported back to students; and what students are subsequently doing with this information. Through a click review you might, for example, identify that teachers are spending five minutes per child writing personalized feedback that isn't subsequently read by the students; and that, perhaps, an easier to complete dashboard sheet might be both quicker and have more feedback value.
- **Transfer.** Your final potential option is to see whether someone or something else can take on the task at no extra cost and at no reduction in current outcomes. This may sound like magical thinking, but it is worth exploring. In the case of homework, could older/more advanced students be trained to assess their younger/less advanced peers? Can this activity be sold to them/ their parents as actually enhancing their own learning? Can intelligent tutoring

systems completely replace homework? Obviously, there is additional cost to the latter.

The idea is that you develop a longlist of potential options and you can rank these based on the factors that we outline in Figure 11.17.

(C) Pilot future state

Once you have decided which Lean initiative you are going to progress, the next step is to design your treatment and then to pilot it. Many of the tools that we introduced in GOLD are also relevant to the design aspect:

- **Path analysis** – although in this case you are actually mapping the existing process, rather than hypothesizing the causal landscape of a *compelling cause*, and proposing changes for efficiency and effectiveness gains
- **Program logic modelling** – the key difference is that you are outlining existing things to halt, reduce, or re-engineer rather than new initiatives to start
- **Design features and settings mapping** – as above you are looking for features that can be switched off and/or alternative features that contain less clicks, reduced duration, or decreased repetition

Factor	Criteria/Commentary
Evidence of impact	• What does the global, regional, and local evidence tell us about the importance (or lack thereof) of this process or activity? • What is the size of the current evidence base/our confidence in it? • How similar are the characteristics of our learners to those analyzed in the peer reviewed research (e.g., age, demographic, etc.)
Ease of implementation	• Halting and repetition reduction are arguably the easiest to implement • Duration, clicks reduction, and transfer all require 'lifting the lid' on the existing process and some degree of process analysis and process re-engineering, followed by training for all parties that are expected to implement the new process
Stakeholder engagement	• Is implementation an 'easy sell' to affected stakeholders or will they perceive it as a reduction in service quality, and/or will implementors be concerned that the transition is more complex than the status quo
Cost of implementation	• Total cost of implementation vs future financial and time savings

Figure 11.17 Framework for Assessing Lean Initiative Potential

- **Success mapping** – to identify appropriate metrics to monitor during implementation. In the case of student homework, you will likely want to be tracking the revised minutes per day that teachers are spending on formative assessment-related tasks, and leading and lagging indicators on student progress and achievement
- **Program management tools** – including project plan, risk register, and monitoring and evaluation plan.

You can then use project management tools and processes to implement your designs.

(D) Evaluate future state and (E) agree where to next

Here, the processes draw on the frameworks and tools of GOLD double back. As you implement your agreed Lean intervention you are collecting leading and lagging data to help you determine whether your intervention really does:

- Save time
- Reduce cost
- Achieve the same student outcomes (or ideally better).

The idea is that you use the data to determine whether you should continue with (and scale) your de-implementation or whether you should stop. And if the decision is to continue, you can use the evaluation data to help you identify any design features or settings that can be wiggled more to further enhance the level of Lean impact.

Conclusion

In Part 3 of the Manifesto, we sought to move beyond abstract recommendations to practical processes that you can use to unleash local impact. We outlined tools for crawling forward through design space (i.e., GOLD) to trial and scale new education improvement activities; and process for mapping backwards (i.e., Lean) to incrementally chisel away at existing Jenga blocks and accomplish more (or at least the same) with less.

We recognize there is much more to be done to further evaluate the effectiveness of implementation tools. But our overarching hope is that, through judicious use of existing developing context research, the META^{X}, and the *Leaning to GOLD* framework, we will see ever-greater improvement in the learning lives of children in low- and middle-income countries – so that every child, no matter their geographic location, will receive a year's teaching input and, from it, at least a years' worth of delicious growth will emerge.

12

Conclusions

Friends, our time together is almost at an end. And whilst we are sad to write these last words, the message of the Manifesto is one of great optimism. Our species has existed an estimated 200,000 years and for 99%+ of this had no systematic approach to maintaining, growing, and passing-on our collective learnings. The last 300 years, however, have witnessed a marvel greater than the Pyramids, the Taj Mahal, or the Great Wall of China. Never in the field of human endeavor have so many been mobilized to increase the life chances of so, so many more, and with such profoundly positive impact. The educational Big Bang that erupted has spread far and wide; albeit with (still) many black holes.

The core focus of the Manifesto has been on those remaining black holes and on how we can shore them up. The consequences of their continued existence are an estimated 258 million children that have no access to schooling (UNESCO UIS, 2019, 2020); and a further 617 million that dutifully attend class each day but who learn little and then enter adulthood functionally illiterate (UNESCO UIS, 2017). This 617 million represents more than one-third of the current school-aged population.

This picture is, however, pre-COVID-19. In 2020, 195 countries implemented nationwide closures (UNESCO, 2020c), impacting 99% of the global school population or around 1.72 billion children (World Bank, 2021b). In mid-2021, the access to schooling situation was a little better, but with more expected twists and turns and the potential for a long-lingering legacy. Many high- and upper-middle-income countries are, therefore, focusing on strategies to enable their children to 'catch-up' on their lost learning. Whereas, for low- and lower-middle-income nations the danger is that many children will be lost to learning forever, exiting the system to early marriage and childrearing, or even to child armies.

Before the pandemic there was already a significant financial gap between what low- and lower-middle-income nations could raise from domestic taxation and what they needed to fund high-quality education. The youth bulge in low-income nations further exacerbated this. However, one of the immediate consequences of

DOI: 10.4324/9781003166313-16

the pandemic has been declining tax revenues and projected declines in official development assistance. Countries everywhere are confronting the potential long-term impact of lost student learning but with less access to resources to plug the growing black hole. Difficult choices may need to be made, and for quite some time.

Admittedly, the long-term implications of the pandemic for education outcomes will take time to see. Researchers of the impact of the so-called 'Spanish Flu' of 1918 are still busily collecting, analyzing, and interpreting the data 100+ years later (e.g., Aassve et al., 2021; Lilley et al., 2020). So, we expect that bands of epidemiologists, sociologists, criminologists, and educationalists will be reviewing, researching, and tracing the long-term impact of COVID-19 in 2121 and beyond.

However, in the near-term, we suspect that ministries of education, international development organizations, and providers of technical assistance and capacity-building may be increasingly tasked with doing and achieving more with less. In other words, they may need to get Lean. Although, even without COVID-19 there are still strong arguments for a greater ongoing focus on *efficiency of impact* in education. So, our message and our provocations are for the longer term: they are not pandemic- specific.

Our guiding metaphor throughout the Manifesto has been the game of Jenga. In the world of the game, players build a tower from uniform wooden blocks and then take turns to carefully remove blocks from the middle and bottom; re-placing them on the top – over and over. By implication, the tower is overengineered. The middle block from each layer can be easily removed without any risk to the structure. Although, as the game progresses, the options for safe extraction become fewer and the tower becomes increasingly warped, unstable, and ultimately (always) tumbles. However, we don't want the (educational) tower to fall. Instead, our aim is to build it strong with the least number of blocks; and in the case of already over-towering towers, identify blocks to gently tease out. As a minimum, it's about achieving more with the same. But, ideally, we want more from less.

We need to loudly scream that we would love more funding. Combined with the Lean strategy, more could touch an increasing number of young people. But this has been the premise for so long – give us more – but the evidence, as outlined throughout the Manifesto, is that this increase does not necessarily lead to improved learning. Our mantra has been to focus on the interventions that truly make the greatest difference, and be efficient and Lean in the cost of these, so we can touch more lives.

The Manifesto originally started life as a short think-piece, although as we added and added we realized there was a book in the making. We had to go back to our publisher after we (seriously) busted the agreed word limit. Yes, not very Lean! Given that we have covered so much ground we now think it's worthwhile doing what most people do in their book conclusions: recap, recap, recap. So, let's get on with it.

Part 1 was about scene setting and laying the foundations. We started, in Chapter 1, by undertaking a global education stock-take. From Big Bang, to Guttenberg

Press, to 84 million teachers, and (near?) universal primary education. Like Hans Rosling (2018) and Steven Pinker (2018), our intention was to start by celebrating how much has already been achieved. Imagine taking a time machine to the mid-1700s and telling people from that era that the Prussian education experiment would soon be rolled out globally; that most boys and *girls* would be able to access *free* education; and that almost 90% of adults across the world would be literate. It would not have sounded credible. But it has been *in*credibly done. It's 'just' that, now, we need to mop-up the remainder and profoundly increase the quality of service for all. And those remainders are more concentrated in low- and middle-income countries – everyone is worth educating.

However, it can be tempting to think that the best way of enhancing both access to education (what we call the *easier* problem) and quality of education (what we call the *hard* problem) is to harvest more resource and add more blocks to the Jenga tower. In Chapter 2 we explored the relationship between resources and outcomes, and investigated what level of resourcing is likely to be available over the next half decade. In terms of the former, whilst we readily accept that education systems need money, there is no empirical evidence that continually adding more leads to greater outcomes. We noted several examples of systems that punched well above their financial 'weight' – squeezing every last drop of education returns from relatively modest inputs.

More speculatively, we also reviewed the potential financial implications of COVID-19 on both education funding requirements and the availability of both domestic funds and official development assistance. Our conclusion was that systems would (likely) need to accomplish more but also (likely) have less resource to hand. This is where the Lean thinking can potentially help. In the second half of Chapter 2, we introduced both the history of Lean and the key processes. We explained that whilst Lean had not yet been embraced by educators, many other sectors have found utility in the unrelenting focus on efficiency of outcome. Obviously, schools are not car factories, but there is no reason why we shouldn't at least *consider* an explicitly efficiency-oriented approach to education.

There is, of course, a danger that by attempting to wiggle and remove random Jenga blocks we pull out the wrong ones, and that after they are out the expertise to reinsert them has also evaporated. Therefore, we must select our targets for removal (or for not adding in the first place) with great care. We need to be guided by *empirical* evidence rather than hunch or random tugging. In Chapter 3 we harvested and explored the currently available evidence on 'what works best' in low- and middle-income country contexts. We identified and interrogated 57 systematic reviews (28 narrative reviews, 9 vote counts, and 20 meta-analyses). Between them, they synthesized the data from 3,912 experimental and quasi-experimental studies (or around 2,500 unique studies – after duplicates were removed). Across these, we found reasonable consistency of interpretation for what works best for access to education (a.k.a. the *easier* problem). We also found relatively successful strategies for getting teachers to turn up regularly.

However, when we turned to effective strategies for enhancing the quality of education (the *hard* problem) there were remarkably few common golden threads across the 57 systematic reviews. And in the areas where some consensus existed (e.g., pedagogy, teacher training, intelligent tutoring systems) it was extremely difficult to unpick or visualize how these could be put into action. Our conclusion was that whilst 57 systematic reviews of an estimated 2,500 unique studies is clearly better than a stick in the eye, as the principal divining rod to decide which Jenga blocks to remove/add, we would be in for a (fairly) hairy-scary ride.

Enter stage left the Visible Learning META^X, which we introduced and outlined in Chapter 4. This is (probably) the largest 'what works best' database for education in the world. It aggregates the findings from 1,700+ meta-analyses of 100,000+ studies, involving 300 million+ students. However, whilst the META^X is 40x bigger than the developing country systematic reviews that we outlined in Chapter 3, one of its (many) downsides is that most of the data comes from high- and upper-middle-income contexts and may, therefore, not travel well. The other downsides are that the underlying studies use a variety of methodologies or measuring instruments (the *apples with oranges problem*); positive studies tend to be (over-) published and negative ones tend to perish (the *file-drawer problem*); and the META^X only catalogues what researchers chose to investigate and what meta-analysist subsequently hoovered up (the *rearview mirror problem*). Yet further downsides are that it merely aggregates the average effect sizes across metas investigating similar areas (sometimes these can vary as much as $d = 1.0$); and whilst it can (roughly) tell you what has worked there are no guarantees this can be replicated; and (generally) the metas do not provide sufficient detail to tell you *how* to replicate. That's why we call Chapter 4 the Visible Learning 'stop gap': we acknowledge that what we really need is more developing country research and we are basically saying that, until we have this, let's try and see what (tentative) conclusions we can draw from this much bigger but 'developed' country-centric dataset.

Part 2 is the 'meat' of the Manifesto. It's where we got busy applying the META^X data to education improvement. Across the five chapters in Part 2, there was a bit of a formula. Each chapter presented a theory of change that detailed how investing in certain types of inputs and activities *might* enhance education outcomes. You will notice that in the previous sentence 'might' is italicized. In three-and-a-half out of our five meat chapters the theory of change proved to be what academics often call a 'straw man', or what Agatha Christie would call a 'red herring'. In other words, something that has surface appeal but when fully interrogated proves to be a faulty theory of how we can best harvest and pull energy through the system, turning this into sweet momentum.

In each 'meat' chapter, we then presented a table of relevant META^X data followed by pages of interpretation about potential opportunities for removing (or not adding) Jenga blocks, plus suggestions for blocks that really should be added/enhanced. Finally, we concluded each of these chapters with a table of provocations and health warnings. The provocations were meant to be provocative – like metaphorical hand-grenades – whereas the health warnings outlined the potential side effects or (anticipated) unanticipated consequences of implementation, building on Yong Zhao's (2018) notion that *what works may hurt* (i.e., if you pull the pin this will create heat, but it could also blow your fingers off).

Our first 'meat' chapter, Chapter 5, focused on teacher selection, recruitment, and pre-service and in-service training. It presented a theory of change of the 'red herring' variety – suggesting that educators were more likely to be effective if they have comprehensive pre-service training and licensing, and if they have an advanced qualification in the subject(s) they teach. However, after interpretation of the META^X data and relevant developing country studies we let loose our (pyrotechnic) grenades, suggesting that pre-service teacher training/licensing *could* be stopped/not started. We also suggested that, at least until upper-secondary/high school education, there seemed to be no particularly strong reason for educators to hold advanced qualifications in the subjects they teach – another block to withdraw (or not add).

For avoidance of all doubt, we were NOT saying that teachers require no training/professional development. We see considerable returns from carefully designed in-service training once teachers are already on the job. The best kinds of in-service training follow the surface-to-deep-to-transfer protocols, which we subsequently outlined in Chapter 8 as being effective for *students*. No surprises that high-impact approaches for children are also effective for adults! Effective in-service professional development for teachers is carefully sequenced and involves spaced learning, presentation of a theory, modelling, deliberate practice in the target context, coaching, and peer collaboration. It also has a strong focus on pedagogic content knowledge (i.e., the best way to sequence learning to aid children's understanding; mapping to the struggles children often have with specific concepts, ideas, or content; and connecting to specific approaches to bridge their understanding on each type of learning challenge).

We also, more controversially, suggested that there *could* be utility in leveraging psychometric tools, working memory and/or IQ tests, and classroom simulations to select candidates for teaching that have a higher probability of staying in the profession and turning up to work each day, and to evaluate and enhance their impact. We do not think education systems are (yet) ready to rely on such tools in teacher hiring decisions, but we think that more teacher selection assessment tool testing, longitudinal performance tracking, and inference-making by deep learning AI *could* make for a powerful longer-term prediction engine.

Then, in Chapter 6, we shifted our focus, exploring the structures that educators operate within. Once again, we presented a fishy theory of change suggesting that more funding, better school buildings, smaller schools, smaller class sizes, same age classes, longer school days and years, and grade repetition for unsuccessful students would enhance the quality of teaching and learning. And yet again, we presented META^X and developing country research data suggesting it was possible to generate enhanced learner outcomes from the exact opposite. Instead, we suggested a number of Lean efficiencies, including multi-age open-space classrooms, with children working by level rather than grade; students peer tutoring one another; and, perhaps controversially, we also suggested that the length of the school day and year *could* also be significantly reduced – allowing triple-shift schools to cater to more learners and/or to enable teachers to have more time for professional development, so enhancing their impact across each of those reduced hours of contact. And, as we review the global data on learning loss because of COVID-related school closures, we will have many more data juxtapositions on 'how low we can go' with the duration of the school day and year before we see negative long-term outcomes for learners.

Accountability was our area of focus for Chapter 7. Many reams have already been penned on this by development economists and in our theory of change we presented more of the 3-day-old variety of fish. This sub-species of unpick-led herring suggested that we needed teacher performance-related pay; system-level accountability drivers like school inspections, league tables, and performance standards for teachers; and lashings of public–private partnerships to create competition and choice. To be fair, some of these are relatively effective at addressing a perennial problem for some low- and lower-middle-income countries: teacher attendance. Interventions like camera surveillance, daily bonuses for showing up, and community monitoring have been reasonably successful at getting teachers into their classrooms. However, addressing this is at the more basic end of the education 'supply-side' challenge spectrum. Once teachers are in classrooms, we then need to be far more interested in whether these accountability mechanisms also enhance student learning – the evidence suggests they principally encourage perverse incentives and extrinsic motivation (i.e., comparing notes on how to game the system to collect the cash prize). We also found no strong evidence that public–private partnerships offer silver bullets/garlic/crucifixes/magic beans that (once scaled-up) are significantly more effective than state-managed education systems.

We also suggested that focus on 'carrot' and 'stick' accountability approaches are likely barking up the wrong tree – and possibly in the wrong forest. They come from the rational actor school of behavioral economics, whereas perhaps we have more to learn from the research on collective teacher efficacy and Visible Learning mind frames, where the emphasis is on building teachers' beliefs that:

- **ALL children can learn**
- **ALL children have the right to learn**
- **Teachers make the BIGGEST difference**
- **Teachers must know and grow their IMPACT.**

Of course, we need to pay teachers a decent living and pay them on time. But after we have done so, further buttressing this with performance measures, monitoring, bonuses, league tables, inspections et al. are only likely to get us to the *illusion* of performance – *belief* in the mission is what counts. In our work we have consistently found that what teachers think makes a profound difference. Where educators see their role as being an evaluator of their own impact on student learning and when they believe all students can improve, they are far more likely to invest in the *right* mission. And if they are invested in that mission, they are obviously more likely to turn up to school – sans the stick of CCTV monitoring and carrot additional cash payments.

Putting this into context, we didn't work on this book because it was written into our performance objectives, and our overlords, in turn, did not monitor our daily output of keystrokes or publish a league table comparing our production speed with other researchers to encourage us to type faster. And we suspect that carrot and stick drivers are also not why you are reading these words. We doubt anyone is paying you by the chapter. Instead, we are on a shared mission to enhance the quality of education for all. And we have a shared *belief* in the power of education to transform lives.

In Chapter 8 we (finally) moved away from herring and toward approaches that really do enhance the quality of education. We outlined 40+ approaches to teaching and learning that each generate an effect size greater than the $d = 0.40$ hinge point. Each of these approaches will generate significant impact on student learning. The challenge, however, is that each have a time and place. Some are better for *starting* a new lesson, topic, or inquiry cycle; others for *surface acquisition* and *surface consolidation* of learning; yet others for *deep acquisition* and *deep consolidation*; and yet, yet others for *transfer* of learning to new domains. By our (conservative) estimate, this adds up to at least 1,000 protocols or "balls" that educators must master and then juggle at the right time to deliver high-quality instruction. There are also additional complexities. Some of these approaches work well with younger learners but not older – and others vice versa. We then need to factor in pedagogic content knowledge. For example, some approaches are better than others for teaching number, place value, percentages, fractions, and so on. Ditto concepts in literacy, science, history, geography, or music.

Expecting teachers to learn the 1,000+ and to also know when and how to deploy them seems, to us, challenging. That's why in the second half of the chapter we explored approaches that scaffold and support teachers to do this effectively. We introduced three levels of support – ranging from a Level 1 generic framework, to a Level 2 scaffolded program, to a Level 3 scripted program. Level 1 provides educators with a generic set of sequenced protocols that they can use to design their own teaching and learning programs; Level 2 provides pre-built programs but gives educators the flexibility to mix and adapt these to local needs; Level 3 provides a prescribed and scripted set of materials for teachers to follow like Shakespearian actors. Each can be effective, albeit with different tradeoffs. The Level 1 generic framework enables teachers to maintain full professional autonomy but requires more effort and expertise from educators to build their schemes of work, lesson plans, and student learning materials from scratch. There is also much greater risk that the outcomes weave together the wrong balls juggled at the wrong time. The Level 2 scaffolded program slightly reduces the autonomy of the teacher by providing a recommended pathway, but with the ability to still make local decisions and, still, the risk that those decisions involve selection of the wrong balls.

The Level 3 scripted program, however, is akin to a train glued to specific tracks, with stops at different pre-agreed stations – and to a pre-set speed of travel.

Each of these ways *can* work. Which path you choose will be influenced by your local context, your local needs, your local theory of change, and your local *beliefs*. Our advice is that you select carefully, explore all the different design and setting features, prototype, pilot, evaluate, iterate, and then slowly scale. In Chapter 8, we also looped back to our discussions on teacher training and professional development from Chapter 5. We introduced four meta-modes of thinking about what kind of profession teaching is and therefore how teachers should be trained and supported to undertake their role. These modes were: *(A) osmosis* (which requires no training and is not recommended); *(B) acting* (which requires support to follow a branching script); *(C) professional expertise* (which requires professional development to master the 1,000+ balls but results in variable fidelity); and *(D) systematic inquiry* (which is more akin to scientific research: setting hypothesis, collecting data, evaluating impact). These modes also clearly link to our three levels of support – generic framework through to scaffolded or scripted program.

Then, in Chapter 9, we explored the impact of education technology, where the evidence is extremely mixed and largely depends on *what* the technology is being used for, how it is deployed, and whether its utilization is more cost/time effective than previous practices. Where the theory of improvement is that providing teachers and students with access to technology – in the form of laptops and tablets – will result in enhanced learning outcomes, we saw no corresponding uplift. Here, the *six hurdles (H) of the apocalypse* negate impact, i.e., whether *(H.1)* stakeholders actually receive the devices; *(H.2)* they know how to use them; *(H.3)* they do use them; *(H.4)* the use has a carefully designed educational purpose; *(H.5)* the educational purpose significantly amplifies a high-impact instructional approach; and *(H.6)* the cost of implementation is no higher than the status quo.

Where the purpose of EdTech is teacher surveillance, we see impact in getting teachers into their classes but next to none on enhancing their instructional approaches. However, when the purpose is specifically on enhancing teacher capabilities, we do see pockets of high-probability approaches. Firstly, the use of video to record classroom teaching and learning to then re-wind and review, frame-by-frame, to evaluate the impact of one's own instruction generates the highest effect size of all the techno tools ($d = 0.88$) – particularly when the review is done to listen also to other teachers' interpretations and feedback. However, it is not easy to implement. It works better when teachers collaboratively review one another's videos, and it serves no (instructionally) useful purpose when the videos are used for accountability rather than developmental purposes. Second, it is also likely that the use of teacher tablets and of automated marking systems *can* generate process efficiencies in the deployment of scripted direct instruction teaching models. Although the scripted-DI approach can be implemented perfectly well without tablet computers.

There is also growing evidence on the benefits of intelligent tutoring systems. These are highly effective for identifying gaps in students prior learning and remediating those gaps through surface-level drill and spaced repetition. They are also highly scalable (with fidelity) if suitable technology is available locally. Although intelligent tutoring systems currently work best for mathematics, science, and literacy, and they have more limited utility in the deep or transfer phases of learning – so not a panacea for all ills.

However, as we explore experimental technology, we suspect that EdTech will become much more of a gamechanger to education in the longer term. Three of the (many) areas we have our eyes on are:

1 **Virtual schooling.** This would effectively be the next generation version of Zoom-based schooling that was implemented in high-income nations during the pandemic – with teachers and students collaborating synchronously over the web. The key difference is that it will likely become a more immersive experience, with teachers and students donning cheap smart lenses/glasses and haptic gloves that enable them to 'port' into immersive virtual schools that look and feel like the real thing. This would allow the physical campus to dematerialize or for it to serve more learners that each come in for fewer days and undertake a portion of their studies from home; offering a Leaner way of expanding access to secondary education in times of austerity. If the use of these Zoom-like tools proliferates, perhaps teachers will talk less, listen more to students, and engage in triage (prioritizing the next best learning step for learners). We see this as near-term technology – it will (likely) be with us by 2030, or sooner.

2 **Brain–computer interfaces**. These have already been around for decades to remediate epilepsy and control robotic limbs. However, the longer-term leap will likely be in injectable nanobots that cross the blood–brain barrier and latch on to neurons. With enough of these in place it may be possible to transmit data from the outside world directly to the brain and vice versa. If you wanted to learn Kung Fu or how to pilot an Airbus you might be able to download the knowledge, skills, and muscle memory from an app store and be ready to go in seconds. This is (likely) longer term – beyond 2070 – if the ethics is ever sorted out.

3 **Genetic engineering.** The recent discovery of the CRISPR–Cas9 gene editing technology may mean that over the next few decades humans increasingly experiment with re-writing their own source code. This could result in humans with much larger working memories and much longer lifespans, although the outcome could well be a genetic Global North and Global South. The implementation of this technology seems longer-term but could be with us in one to two decades, or less. The possible side effects and ethical issues could be immense.

We highlight these forms of technology because, whilst most types of EdTech have generated consistently below average effect sizes since the 1970s, we think these three areas have the capability of being completely game changing to how we think of and approach teaching and learning in the next century.

Putting the *Star Trek* futurism to one side and getting back to practical interventions that can be implemented today to enhance education outcomes in the low- and middle-income countries, throughout the Manifesto we occasionally highlighted new Jenga blocks that were worth investing in to build and add to the tower. The hottest of these hot blocks is the 1,000+ high-impact instructional "balls" from Chapter 8 and the supporting implementation mechanism of the (L1) generic framework, (L2) scaffolded or (L3) scripted program. The next hottest blocks were effective approaches to teacher professional development that operate in lockstep with these support frameworks to facilitate effective juggling of the 1,000+ balls. Our final hot block is in moving from rational actor/carrot and stick modes of motivation to collective teacher efficacy, supported by instructional leadership about impact and the Visible Learning mind frames. And, if you have a few spare coins, you could possibly also consider investing in teacher support technology that links to your selected meta-mode (e.g., video analytics software or tablet-driven scripted direct instruction). You might also consider intelligent tutoring systems for students.

Our original intention was to finish the book at the end of Part 2. But it struck us that there was already a burgeoning pile of developing country-oriented publications stuffed with "policy recommendations". The only difference between these and our "Lean provocations" is that the former are less likely to make you fall off the back of your chair. They are normally about adding new funds, new programs, or new bells and whistles to existing things. It seemed painfully obvious to us that Part 1 and Part 2 of the Manifesto would not help education system leaders to select the provocations that were most appropriate for their context or to work these up (or down) into prototypes that could be tested in actual schools. We kept thinking back to the two case studies we included in the introduction and to a host of other case studies we didn't include because of confidentiality covenants. And we kept asking, "is this particular provocation relevant for a country like Liberia AND for a middle-income Asian country?" And, "are there differences in where we would start and how we would implement across these very different contexts?" The answers were invariably: maybe, yes, and yes.

This led us to *Part 3* – which was intended as an implementation toolkit for ministries of education, funders, and deliverers to select appropriate provocations, start small, and grow big. We started the process in Chapter 10, where we surveyed a range of existing approaches to organizational improvement and implementation across international development, healthcare, business, and education. We owe a huge intellectual debt to Lant Pritchett, Michael Barber, Abraham Wandersman, Paul LeMahieu, Helen Timperley, Viviane Robinson, Sugata Mitra, Russell Bishop, Michael Fullan, David Cooperrider, and Rukmini Banerji. From our analysis of their ideas, tools, and frameworks (and approaches in the relatively new health field of implementation science) we were able to identify 23 (relatively) common processes – delivered across five distinct phases of implementation.

Then in Chapter 11, which is by far the longest in the whole Manifesto, we outlined a process for moving from provocation to action, and ultimately impact.

We call this *Leaning to* GOLD, and there are two directions of travel. You can use the GOLD tools to slowly move forward in design space – identifying new Jenga blocks to insert, prototyping, piloting, evaluating, and then either iterating and scaling or hitting the ejector switch. Or you can use the Lean process to move backwards in design space – identifying blocks to remove, piloting their removal, assessing the impact, and then scaling the dematerialization. Our hope is that these tools will help you to select *compelling causes* that are worth your time; develop a theory of the present; design multiple interventions or de-interventions; implement those with the highest probability; and make a profound difference to the learning lives of children.

We constantly marvel at how far humanity has come during these short 300 years. The exponential growth of schooling; and its contribution to the spread of enlightenment values, democracy, progress, the rule of law, health, the scientific method, and the baton-passing of brilliant ideas between the living, the dead, and the yet to be born. Education is our species' greatest invention. A gift that keeps on giving. Our hope is that the Manifesto helps us to collectively make this even stronger – equipping our children for a world of tomorrow that will be fundamentally different from the world of today.

So, dear reader, what will you *take* from the Manifesto and what will you *do* with it to grow the power of education to transform lives? The baton is now with you.

Appendix: High-level summary of 57 developing country 'what works best' for education systematic reviews

Authors	Research Question	Method-ology	No. Studies	Key Findings
Systematic Reviews of 'Everything' (i.e. all intervention types, stages of education, and geographies)				
Angrist, Evans, Filmer, Glennerster, Rogers, & Sabarwal (2020)	Approaches that increase access to and quality of education	Meta-analysis	150	**For increasing time in school:** • Providing information on returns to schooling • School links to village councils **For improving student learning outcomes:** • Teacher training – to target instruction to student learning level rather than grade • Structured teacher lesson plans and linked student materials • Contract teachers • Tracking students
Global Education Evidence Advisory Panel (2020)	Approaches that increase access to and quality of education	Not disclosed but largely adapted from Angrist et al. (2020)	Not disclosed	**Great buys:** • Giving information on the benefits, costs, and quality of education **Good buys:** • Structured lesson plans with linked materials and ongoing teacher monitoring and training • Target teaching instruction by learning level not grade

(Continued)

Authors	Research Question	Method-ology	No. Studies	Key Findings
				• Reducing travel times to schools • Merit-based scholarships to disadvantaged children • Intelligent tutoring software • Pre-primary interventions for 3–5-year-olds **Bad buys:** • Additional inputs alone without addressing wider ecosystem • ICT hardware alone • Cash transfers to improve learning outcomes
Damon, Glewwe, Wis-niewski, & Sun (2019)	Approaches that increase time in school and improve learning outcomes in developing contexts	Vote counting	114	**For increasing time in school:** • Building new schools • Conditional cash transfers **For improving student learning outcomes:** • Merit-based scholarships • Remedial instruction • Reducing class size • Building new schools
Evans & Popova (2015)	What enhances student learning outcomes in develop-ing country contexts?	Narrative review	227	• **Pedagogical interventions** – includ-ing computer assisted instruction • **Repeated teacher training interventions** – linked to pedagogical enhancement • (In some contexts) **improving accountability** through the use of performance incen-tives or contract teachers
Ganimian & Murnane (2016)	Approaches that enhance access and quality in developing contexts	Narrative review	119	**For increasing access to schooling:** • Cash transfers • Scholarships • School building programs • Information to parents on returns from schooling **For improving quality:** • Enhancing teacher pedagogy • Teacher and student incen-tives (in some contexts)

Authors	Research Question	Method-ology	No. Studies	Key Findings
Glewwe & Muralidharan (2016)	Approaches that enhance access and quality in developing contexts	Vote counting	118	**For increasing access to schooling:** • Conditional cash transfers • Information to parents • Merit-based scholarships **For improving quality:** • Pedagogic interventions • Remedial instruction • Governance and teacher accountability measures
Kremer, Brannen, & Glennerster (2013)	Approaches that enhance access and quality in developing contexts	Meta-analysis	39	**For increasing access to schooling:** • Conditional cash transfers • Merit scholarships • Deworming in low-income contexts • Information to parents and students on returns from schooling **For improving quality:** • Computer-assisted instruction • Contract teachers • Tracking/streaming • Camera monitoring of teachers and teacher incentives for attendance (although does not directly enhance the quality of instruction)
Krishnaratne, White, & Carpenter (2013)	Approaches that enhance access and quality in developing contexts	Meta-analysis	69	**For increasing access to schooling:** • Conditional cash transfers • School buildings **For improving quality:** • Teacher enhancement materials • Teaching resources
Samoff, Leer, & Reddy (2016)	Whether developing country evaluation data provides generalizable insights	Narrative review	40	**For increasing access to schooling:** • Cash transfers • Providing information on returns from education **For improving quality:** • Local ownership of the education improvement design and implementation process

(Continued)

Authors	Research Question	Methodology	No. Studies	Key Findings
Snilstveit et al. (2015) & (2016)	Approaches that enhance access and quality in developing contexts	Meta-analysis	420	**For increasing access to schooling:** • Cash transfers • School buildings **For improving quality:** • Structured pedagogy programs • Community-based monitoring
Masino & Niño-Zarazúa (2016)	Approaches that enhance access and quality in developing contexts	Narrative review	38	Found that none of the supply-side, demand-side, and institutional reform-side baskets of drivers worked effectively on their own. Higher probability of impact where two or more sets of these drivers are deployed in concert.
Spink, Cassity, & Rorris (2018)	Approaches that enhance access and quality in developing contexts	Vote counting	18	**For increasing access to schooling:** • Cash transfers **For improving quality:** • Provision of literacy materials – particularly in mother tongue • School management and school improvement training • Teacher professional development • Curriculum materials • Computer-assisted instruction • Teacher recruitment and selection reforms • Teacher performance-based contracts

Authors	Research Question	Method-ology	No. Studies	Key Findings
Kremer & Holla (2009)	Approaches that enhance access and quality in developing contexts	Narrative review	Not stated	**For increasing access to schooling:** • Conditional cash transfers • Merit scholarships • School health programs • Providing information on returns from schooling **For improving quality:** • Computer-assisted instruction • Tracking/ability grouping • Teacher pedagogical enhancement • Contract teachers • Voucher systems
Glewwe, Hanushek, Humpage, & Ravina (2014)	Improving education outcomes in developing contexts	Vote counting	43	**For improving quality:** • Availability of desks for students • Teacher knowledge of the subjects they teach • Teacher level of absence/absence reduction
Saran, White, Albright, & Adona (2020)	Evidence gap map	Vote counting	83	**Areas where more research is required:** • Child safety • Equity • Economic impact
Muralidharan (2017)	Review of RCTs	Narrative review	Not stated	**Promising areas where more research is required:** • Teacher pedagogy • Secondary education
Systematic Reviews with a Specific Regional or Phase of Education Focus				
Conn (2017)	Enhancing education outcomes in sub-Saharan Africa	Meta-analysis	56	• **Pedagogical interventions** – especially when combined with computer-assisted instruction • **Increasing instruction time** • **Student incentives** – particularly micro cash payments that are linked to attendance and grade performance

(Continued)

Authors	Research Question	Method-ology	No. Studies	Key Findings
Asim, Chase, Dar, & Schmillen (2015)	South Asian Focus – access and quality	Meta-analysis	29	**For increasing access to schooling:** • Cash transfers • Building schools **For improving quality:** • Contract teachers • Enhanced curriculum materials • Computer-assisted instruction
McEwan (2015)	Enhanc-ing student learning outcomes in primary settings for developing countries	Meta-analysis	77	**For improving quality:** • Computers or instructional technology • Teacher training • Smaller classes • Smaller learning groups within classes, or ability grouping • Contract or volunteer teachers • Student and teacher perfor-mance incentives • Instructional materials
Banerjee, Glewwe, Powers, & Wasserman (2013)	Enhanc-ing student learning outcomes in post-primary settings for developing countries	Narrative review	56	**For increasing access to schooling:** • Conditional cash transfers • Information on benefits of education **For improving quality:** • Self-paced curricula (i.e., levels rather than grades)
Systematic Reviews on Access to Education				
Petrosino et al. (2012)	Effective strategies to improve student enrollment	Meta-analysis	73	• Found significant varia-tion on effect size of most interventions, across dif-ferent geographies. Only **new school buildings and infrastructure** were consistently effective in all locations
Kabeer, Piza, & Taylor (2012)	Condi-tional cash transfers	Meta-analysis	46	• Reports strong evidence for **conditional cash transfers** in reducing child labor and increasing school attend-ance rates

Authors	Research Question	Method-ology	No. Studies	Key Findings
Saavedra & García (2012)	Condi-tional cash transfers	Meta-analysis	42	• Conditional cash transfers more effective in secondary education enrollment than primary • Positive correlation between ($) size of trans-fer amount and increased enrollment
Baird, Fer-reira, Özler, & Woolcock, (2014)	Conditional vs uncondi-tional cash transfers	Meta-analysis	35	• Both conditional and unconditional cash transfers increase the odds of child enrollment, with conditional cash transfers achieving larger attendance rates • Highest impact on attend-ance comes where programs are explicitly conditional, monitor compliance, and penalize non-compliance • Cash transfers (either con-ditional or unconditional) have marginal impact on improving student test scores
Jasper, Le, & Bartram (2012)	School sanitation	Vote counting	47	• Positive correlation between access to clean water and school attend-ance/reduction in the number of non-attendances due to diarrheal and gas-trointestinal diseases and menstruation
Rao et al. (2014)	Early childhood interventions	Narrative review	111	**For increasing access to schooling:** • Family income supple-ments/conditional cash transfers • Parental education programs
J-PAL Policy Bulletin (2017)	Effective strategies to improve student enrollment	Meta-analysis	58	**For increasing access to schooling:** • Build new schools • Scholarships • Conditional cash transfers

(*Continued*)

Authors	Research Question	Method-ology	No. Studies	Key Findings
Adelman, Gilligan, & Lehrer (2008)	School feeding programs	Narrative review	27	Positive impact on access/ participation when this is low but limited impact on children already attending school regularly.
Lawson (2012)	School feeding programs	Narrative review	26	School feeding programs increase children's gross calorie intake.
Bakhshi, Kett, & Oliver (2013)	Disabled students	Narrative review	89	Inconclusive due to heterogeneity of contexts and interventions.
Systematic Reviews on Girls' Education				
Evans & Yuan (2019)	Access and outcomes for girls	Meta-analysis	177	Concludes that most of the interventions that improve outcomes for girls also do the same for boys. Highest impact interventions: • **Increasing access for girls** (and boys): Cash transfer programs • **Quality education for girls** (and boys): Teacher pedagogy enhancements
Sperling, Winthrop, Kwauk, & Yousafzai (2016)	Access and outcomes for girls	Narrative review	138	• **Increasing access for girls:** scholarships, conditional cash transfers, building schools closer to home, flexible school schedules to accommodate girls' work • **Retention for girls:** school meals; water, sanitation, and hygiene infrastructure • **Quality education for girls:** hire more qualified teachers, increase teacher attendance, improve teacher pedagogy

Authors	Research Question	Method-ology	No. Studies	Key Findings
Unterhalter et al. (2013)	Access and outcomes for girls	Vote counting	177	• **Strong evidence:** conditional cash transfers to families; information to families about the returns from schooling; provision of additional schools in underserved areas; training teachers in gender-sensitive pedagogy; group learning pedagogies in classrooms; women's literacy programs • **Promising evidence:** deworming; school feeding programs; involving women in school governance; gender mainstreaming • **Limited/more evidence required:** single sex vs co-educational schools; employment of women teachers; school choice programs; interventions to tackle gender-based violence
Birdthistle, Dickson, Freeman, & Javidi, (2011)	Gender segregated toilets	Narrative review	73	• More important variable was whether there were *enough* toilets and whether these were of sufficient quality/effectiveness, rather than gender segregation
Dickson & Bangpan (2012)	Economic assets	Meta-analysis	18	• Positive impact on girls' attendance from parental conditional cash transfer programs
Systematic Reviews on Governance and Accountability Drivers				
Bruns, Filmer, & Patrinos (2010)	Accountability reforms to increase service delivery quality	Narrative review	22	• **Emerging/promising evidence** on contract teachers and teacher incentives • **Inconclusive evidence** on information reforms and school-based management/decentralization

(Continued)

Authors	Research Question	Method-ology	No. Studies	Key Findings
Best, Knight, Lietz, Lockwood, Nugroho, & Tobin (2013)	Participation in standard-ized student assessment	Narrative review	54	• Review of how participating in national and international student assessment pro-grams impacts on country-level education policies. **Inconclusive findings.**
Kingdon et al. (2014)	Political economy and education	Narrative review	64	Highlights the following nega-tive drivers in *some* contexts: • Rent-seeking/patronage politics • Teaching unions **Concludes that resourcing differences are not a key driver of student outcomes.** The key driver appears to be how the system uses the resources.
Eddy-Spicer, Ehren, Bangpan, Khatwa, & Perrone (2016)	Accountabil-ity systems	Narrative review	68	Review of impact of: • High stakes testing • Monitoring • School inspections Data across all three domains showed **limited evidence of improved service delivery**, system efficiency, or student learning outcomes. In many cases the initiatives resulted in perverse incentives and unin-tended consequences.
Guer-rero, Leon, Zapata, Sugimaru, & Cueto (2012)	Increas-ing teacher attendance	Meta-analysis	9	Promising interventions: • Teacher monitoring sys-tems when combined with rewards for increased attendance • Community monitoring programs
Morgan, Petrosino, & Fronius (2013)	School voucher programs	Narrative review	2	Review of programs in Colom-bia and Pakistan with the fol-lowing outcomes: • Enrollment increased • Lower costs of service delivery Evidence base too small to generalize from.

Authors	Research Question	Method-ology	No. Studies	Key Findings
Day Ashley et al. (2014)	Private schools	Vote counting	59	• **Strong evidence** that private schools generated better student learning outcomes than comparator state schools (but studies do not always adequately factor in student background/ socio-economic status) • **Moderate evidence** that private schools are more cost effective than state schools • **Weak evidence** on whether private schools drive competition and choice, thereby enhancing state school quality
Barakat, Hardman, Rohwerder, & Rzeszut (2014)	Low-cost private schools in South West Asia	Narrative review	44	**Weak evidence base** from which to determine the impact of low-cost private schools but suggests: • Low-cost private schools can offer lower cost and higher quality education outcomes, but they are not scalable or sustainable in all contexts • Whilst low-cost private schools increase enrollment, they may do so at the cost of also increasing education inequality
Westhorp et al. (2014)	Community account-ability	Narrative review	140	Citizen voice + teacher monitoring resulted in significantly enhanced teacher and student attendance
Carr-Hill, Rolleston, & Schendel (2016)	School-based management/ decentralization	Meta-analysis	35	Reforms that decentralize budget management, school administration, and pedagogic decision-making to school level have limited impact in increasing teacher attendance, the quality of instruction, or student learning outcomes in low-income countries. However, decentralization *might* generate greater impact in middle-income countries.

(Continued)

Authors	Research Question	Method-ology	No. Studies	Key Findings
Carr et al. (2011)	Increasing teacher salaries	Narrative review	1	Identified an increase in Brazilian student grades when their teacher salaries were raised – but not clear why/if this was purely coincidental or whether effect was maintained over time.
Systematic Reviews on Quality of Education				
Westbrook et al. (2013)	Teacher pedagogy	Narrative review	54	**Review of effective classroom pedagogies and teacher professional development strategies.** Concluded that the overall developing-world evidence base on pedagogy was, at best, **'moderate'** – with few studies measuring the impact of different approaches on student learning outcomes.
Orr et al. (2013)	Teacher pedagogy	Narrative review	23	**No single strategy independently improved the quality of teaching.** High-impact strategies included: • Changing the pedagogical approach of untrained teachers through a mixture of theory, demonstration, modelling, and practice • Coaching by highly experienced teachers (although this incurs high cost)
Nag, Chiat, Torgerson, & Snowling (2014)	Enhancing children's literacy	Narrative review	260	**Culturally embedded approaches that assimilate indigenous methods** and that co-opt parents and community to design literacy curriculum have higher potential for impact.
Kingdon et al. (2013)	Contract teachers	Narrative review	17	**Contract teachers are generally more effective at enhancing student achievement than regular teachers** but the magnitude of the effect is low and also depends on contextual factors such as who employs them (e.g., NGOs (higher impact) vs government (lower impact)).

Authors	Research Question	Methodology	No. Studies	Key Findings
Aslam et al. (2016)	Enhancing teacher effectiveness	Narrative review	15	Reviewed contract-teacher programs, pre-service/in-service teacher training, teacher certification, and teacher monetary incentives – with **inconclusive findings**.
Miscellaneous Systematic Reviews				
Hawkes & Ugur (2012)	Education and human capital development	Meta-analysis	33	Finds positive correlation between increased education expenditure, access to schooling, years of schooling, graduation, and economic outcomes (both private returns and overall GDP).
Novelli, Higgins, Ugur, & Valiente (2014)	Education in post-conflict/ fragile contexts	Narrative review	69	**Education is often marginalized in post-conflict environments**, with humanitarian and security-related drivers taking precedent (e.g., a security first agenda).
Rodriguez-Segura (2020)	Education technology	Narrative review	67	Technology that enables self-led learning (e.g., **intelligent tutoring systems**) generates the strongest impact for student learning. Access to technology alone (e.g., **one laptop per child programs**) is not sufficient on its own to improve learning outcomes.
Joshi & Amadi (2013)	Water, sanitation, and hygiene interventions	Vote count	15	Increased access to WASH facilities resulted in significantly reduced diarrhea outbreaks.
Spier et al. (2016)	Family and community interventions	Meta-analysis	10	Found that educational radio/ television programs designed to support parents to equip their children with school readiness skills enhanced children's literacy outcomes.
Kristjansson et al. (2007)	School feeding programs	Meta-analysis	18	School feeding programs, in low-income countries, resulted in weight (but not height) gain, and increases in attendance and mathematics achievement. Minimal impact in high-income contexts.

References

Aarons, G. A., Green, A. E., & Miller, E. (2012). Researching readiness for implementation of evidence-based practice: A comprehensive review of the evidence-based practice attitude scale (EBPAS), in Kelly, B., & Perkins, D. F. (Eds), *Handbook of implementation science for psychology in education,* New York: Cambridge University Press, 150–164.

Aassve, A., Alfani, G., Gandolfi, F., & Le Moglie, M. (2021). Epidemics and trust: The case of the Spanish Flu. *Health Economics*, 30(4), 840–857, doi: 10.1002/hec.4218.

Abrami, P. C., Leventhal, L., & Perry, R. P. (1982). Educational seduction. *Review of Educational Research*, 52(3), 446–464.

Adams, G. L., & Engelmann, S. (1996). *Research on direct instruction: 20 years beyond DISTAR.* Seattle, WA: Educational Achievement Systems.

Adelman, H. S., & Taylor, L. (1997). Addressing barriers to learning: Beyond school-linked services and full-service schools. *American Journal of Orthopsychiatry*, 67(3), 408–421.

Adelman, S. W., Gilligan, D. O., & Lehrer, K. (2008). How effective are food for education programs?: A critical assessment of the evidence from developing countries. *Food Policy Reviews 9*. Washington D.C.: International Food Policy Research Institute (IFPRI).

Ahn, S., & Choi, J. (2004, April). *Teachers' subject matter knowledge as a teacher qualification: A synthesis of the quantitative literature on students' mathematics achievement.* Paper presented at the American Educational Research Association, San Diego, CA.

Aker, J. C., & Ksoll, C. (2019). Call me educated: Evidence from a mobile phone experiment in Niger. *Economics of Education Review*, 72, 239–257, doi: 10.1016/j.econedurev.2019.05.001

Allen, C. S., Chen, Q., Willson, V. L., & Hughes, J. N. (2009). Quality of research design moderates effects of grade retention on achievement: A meta-analytic, multilevel analysis. *Educational Evaluation and Policy Analysis*, 31(4), 480–499, doi: 10.3102/0162373709352239

Alloway, T. P. (2006). How does working memory work in the classroom? *Educational Research and Reviews*, 1, 134–139, doi: 10.5897/ERR.9000188

Aloe, A. M., & Becker, B. J. (2009). Teacher verbal ability and school outcomes: Where is the evidence? *Educational Researcher*, 38(8), 612–624, doi: 10.3102/0013189X09353939

Al-Samarrai, S., Cerdan-Infantes, P., & Lehe, J. (2019). *Mobilizing resources for education and improving spending effectiveness establishing realistic benchmarks based on past trends.* Policy Research Working Paper 8773. Washington D.C.: World Bank Group.

Al-Samarrai, S., Cerdan-Infantes, P., Bigarinova, A., Bodmer, J., Vital, M. J. A., Antoninis, M., Barakat, B., & Fouad, M. Y. (2021). *Education finance watch 2021* (English). Washington, D.C.: World Bank Group. http://documents.worldbank.org/curated/en/226481614027788096/Education-Finance-Watch-2021

Altinok, N., Angrist, N., & Patrinos, H. A. (2018). *Global data set on education quality (1965–2015).* Policy Research Working Paper 8314. Washington D.C.: World Bank Group. https://openknowledge.worldbank.org/handle/10986/29281

Anderson, B. (1991). *Imagined communities: Reflections on the origin and spread of nationalism.* London: Verso.

Andrews, M., Pritchett, L., & Woolcock, M. (2017). *Building state capability evidence, analysis, action.* Oxford: Oxford University Press.

Angrist, N., Evans, D., Filmer, D., Glennerster, R., Rogers, H., & Sabarwal, S. (2020). *How to improve education outcomes most efficiently? A comparison of 150 interventions using the new learning-adjusted years of schooling metric.* Washington D.C.: World Bank Group

Araya, R., Arias Ortiz, E., Bottan, N. L., & Cristia, J. P. (2019). *Does gamification in education work?: Experimental evidence from Chile.* Washington D.C: Inter-American Development Bank, doi: 10.18235/0001777

Arndt, C., Arent, D., Hartley, F., Merven, B., & Mondal, A. H. (2019). Faster than you think: Renewable energy and developing countries. *Annual Review of Economics*, 11(1), 149–168, doi: 10.1146/annurev-resource-100518-093759

Aronson, J., Zimmerman, J., & Carlos, L. (1998). *Improving student achievement by extending school: Is it just a matter of time?* San Francisco: WestEd.

Arteaga, I., & Glewwe, P. (2014). *Achievement gap between indigenous and non-indigenous children in Peru: An analysis of young lives survey data.* Working Paper 130. Oxford: Young Lives.

ASER Centre. (2017). *Annual status of education report (rural).* New Delhi: ASER Centre.

Asiedu, E., & Nandwa, B. (2007). On the impact of foreign aid in education on growth: How relevant is the heterogeneity of aid flows and the heterogeneity of aid recipients? *Review of World Economics*, 143(4), 631–649, doi: 10.1007/s10290-007-0125-9

Asim, S., Chase, R. S., Dar, A., & Schmillen, A. (2015). *Improving education outcomes in South Asia: Findings from a decade of impact evaluations.* Policy Research Working Paper 7362. Washington DC: World Bank.

Aslam, M., Rawal, S., Kingdon, G., Moon, B., Banerji, R., Das, S., Banerji, M., & Sharma, S. K. (2016). *Reforms to increase teacher effectiveness in developing countries.* London: EPPI-Centre, Social Science Research Unit, UCL Institute of Education, University College London.

Ausubel, D. P. (1968). *Educational psychology: A cognitive view.* New York: Holt, Rinehart, & Winston.

Azevedo, J. P., Hasan, A., Goldemberg, D., Aroob, S., & Geven, I. K. (2020). *Simulating the Potential impacts of covid-19 school closures on schooling and learning outcomes: A set of global estimates.* Washington D.C.: World Bank Group. https://thedocs.worldbank.org/en/doc/798061592482682799-0090022020/original/covidandeducationJune17r6.pdf

Baird, S., Ferreira, F., Özler, B., & Woolcock, M. (2014). Conditional, unconditional and everything in between: A systematic review of the effects of cash transfer programmes on schooling outcomes. *Journal of Development Effectiveness,* 6(1), 1–43, doi: 10.1080/19439342.2014.890362

Baker, A., Traub, J., Mills, P., & Young, C. (2020). *Recovery from the COVID-19 crisis: What role will tax policy play?* London: Deloitte. https://www2.deloitte.com/content/dam/Deloitte/global/Documents/Tax/dttl-tax-recovery-from-covid-19-crisis-what-role-tax-policy-play-supporting-recovery-1.pdf

Baker, G. (2001). The romantic and radical nature of the 1870 Education Act. *History of Education,* 30(3), 211–232, doi: 10.1080/00467600010029320

Bakhshi, P., Kett, M., & Oliver, K. (2013). *What are the impacts of approaches to increase the accessibility to education for people with a disability across developed and developing countries and what is known about the cost-effectiveness of different approaches?* London: EPPI-Centre, Social Science Research Unit, Institute of Education, University of London.

Bando, R., Gallego, F., Gertler, P., & Romero Fonseca, D. (2017). Books or laptops? The effect of shifting from printed to digital delivery of educational content on learning. *Economics of Education Review,* 61, 162–173, doi: 10.1016/j.econedurev.2017.07.005

Banerjee, A. V., & Duflo, E. (2011). Why aren't children learning. *Development Outreach,* 13(1), 36–44, doi: 10.1596/1020–797X_13_1_36

Banerjee, A. V., Banerji, R., Berry, J., Duflo, E., Kannan, H., Mukerji, S., Shotland, M., & Walton, M. (2017). From proof of concept to scalable policies: Challenges and solutions, with an application. *Journal of Economic Perspectives,* 31(4), 73–102. https://www.nber.org/papers/w22746

Banerjee, A. V., Banerji, R., Duflo, E., Glennerster, R., & Khemani, S. (2010). Pitfalls of participatory programs: Evidence from a randomized evaluation in education in India. *American Economic Journal: Economic Policy,* 2(1), 1–30, doi: 10.1257/pol.2.1.1

Banerjee, A. V., Cole, S., Duflo, F.., & Linden, L. (2007). Remedying education: Evidence from two randomized experiments in India. *The Quarterly Journal of Economics*, 122(3), 1235–1264, doi: 10.1162/qjec.122.3.1235

Banerjee, A., Glewwe, P., Powers, S., & Wasserman, M. (2013). *Expanding access and increasing student learning in post-primary education in developing countries: A review of the evidence*. Abdul Latif Jameel Poverty Action Lab (J-PAL) Post-Primary Education Initiative Review Paper. Cambridge, MA: J-PAL.

Banerji, R. (2000). Poverty and primary schooling: Field studies from Mumbai and Delhi. *Economic and Political Weekly*, 35(10), 795–802.

Banerji, R., & Chavan, M. (2016). Improving literacy and math instruction at scale in India's primary schools: The case of Pratham's Read India program. *Journal of Educational Change*, 17(4), 453–475, doi: 10.1007/s10833-016-9285-5

Barakat, S., Hardman, F., Rohwerder, B., & Rzeszut, K. (2014). *The evidence for the sustainable scale-up of low-cost private schools in South West Asia*. London: EPPI-Centre, Social Science Research Unit, Institute of Education, University of London.

Barber, M., & Mourshed, M. (2007). *How the world's best-performing education systems came out on top*. New York: McKinsey & Co.

Barber, M., Kihn, P., & Moffit, A. (2011). *Deliverology 101: A field guide for educational leaders*. Thousand Oaks, CA: Corwin Press.

Bardach, L., & Klassen, R. (2020). Smart teachers, successful students? A systematic review of the literature on teachers' cognitive abilities and teacher effectiveness. Teacher Selection Project Working Paper. *Educational Research Review*, 30(100312), doi: 10.1016/j.edurev.2020.100312

Barker, G. (2009). *The agricultural revolution in prehistory: Why did foragers become farmers?* Oxford: Oxford University Press.

Barnard, H. C. (1961). *A history of English education from 1760*. London: University of London Press.

Barrera-Osorio, F., & Linden, L. L. (2009). *The use and misuse of computers in education: Evidence from a randomized experiment in Colombia*. Policy Research Working Paper 4836. Washington D.C.: World Bank Group

Barro, R. J., & Lee, J-W. (2013). A new data set of educational attainment in the world, 1950–2010. *Journal of Development Economics*, 104, 184–198, doi: 10.1016/j.jdeveco.2012.10.001

Barry, R. R. (2018). From barbers and butchers to modern surgeons: How Joseph Lister's application of germ theory revolutionized surgery in the mid-19th century. *Distillations*, 4(1), 40–43.

Bas, G., Senturk, C., & Cigerci, F. M. (2017). Homework and academic achievement: A meta-analytic review of research. *Issues in Educational Research*, 27(1), 31–50. www.iier.org.au/iier27/bas.pdf

Batdi, V. (2014). Jigsaw tekniğinin öğrencilerin akademik başarilarina etkisinin meta-analiz yöntemiyle incelenmesi. *EKEV Akademi Dergisi*, 58(58), 699–714.

Batts, K. B. (2010). *Mentoring beginning teachers for cognitive growth*. [Dissertation] University of North Carolina Wilmington.

Baugh, F., & Thompson, B. (2001). Using effect sizes in social science research: New APA and journal mandates for improved methodology practices. *Journal of Research in Education*, 11(1), 120–129.

Beatty, A., & Pritchett, P. (2012*). From schooling goals to learning goals: How fast can student learning improve?* CGD Policy Paper 012. Washington D.C.: Center for Global Development. www.cgdev.org/content/publications/detail/1426531. Updated January 29, 2013.

Becker, G. S. (1993). *Human capital: A theoretical and empirical analysis, with special reference to education* (3rd ed.). Chicago: University of Chicago Press.

Beg, S., Lucas, A., Halim, W., & Saif, U. (2019). *Beyond the basics: Improving post-primary content delivery through classroom technology* (No. w25704; p. w25704). National Bureau of Economic Research, doi: 10.3386/w25704

Bell, S. (2000). Logical frameworks, Aristotle and soft systems: A note on the origins, values and uses of logical frameworks, in reply to Gasper. *Public Administration and Development*, 20(1), 29–31, doi: 10.1002/1099–162X(200002) 20:1%3C29::AID-PAD98%3E3.0.CO;2–2

Bénabou, R., & Tirole, J. (2003). Intrinsic and extrinsic motivation. *The Review of Economic Studies,* 70(3), 489–520, doi: 10.1111/1467–937X.00253

Bennett, N. (1988). The effective primary school teacher: The search for a theory of pedagogy. *Teaching and Teacher Education*, 4(1), 19–30, doi: 10.1016/0742–051X(88)90021–2

Bertua, C., Anderson, N., & Salgado, J. F. (2005). The predictive validity of cognitive ability tests: A UK meta-analysis. *Journal of Occupational and Organizational Psychology*, 78(3), 387–409, doi: 10.1348/096317905x26994

Best, M., Knight, P., Lietz, P., Lockwood, C., Nugroho, D., & Tobin, M. (2013). *The impact of national and international assessment programmes on education policy, particularly policies regarding resource allocation and teaching and learning practices in developing countries. Final report.* London: EPPI-Centre, Social Science Research Unit, Institute of Education, University of London.

Béteille, T. (2009*). Absenteeism, transfers and patronage: The political economy of teacher labor markets in India.* [Dissertation] Stanford University, California.

Betts, J. R., & Tang, Y. E. (2011). *The effect of charter schools on student achievement: A meta-analysis of the literature.* Seattle, WA: Center on Reinventing Public Education.

Beuermann, D. W., Cristia, J., Cueto, S., Malamud, O., & Cruz-Aguayo, Y. (2015). One laptop per child at home: Short-term impacts from a randomized experiment in Peru. *American Economic Journal: Applied Economics*, 7(2), 53–80, doi: 10.1257/app.20130267

Bhalotra, S., & Clarke, D. (2013). *Educational Attainment and Maternal Mortality*. Paper commissioned for EFA Global Monitoring Report 2013/4. Paris: UNESCO

Bhalotra, S., Harttgen, K., & Klasen, S. (2013). *The impact of school fees on the intergenerational transmission of education.* Background paper commissioned for EFA Global Monitoring Report 2013/4. Paris: UNESCO.

Biggs, S., & Smith, S. (2003). A paradox of learning in project cycle management and the role of organizational culture. *World Development*, 31(10), 1743–1757.

Birch, L., & Jacob, S. (2019). "Deliverology" and evaluation: A tale of two worlds. *Canadian Journal of Program Evaluation/La Revue canadienne d'évaluation de programme*, 34(2), 303–328, doi: 10.3138/cjpe.53365

Birdthistle, I., Dickson, K., Freeman, M., & Javidi, L. (2011). *What impact does the provision of separate toilets for girls at schools have on their primary and secondary school enrolment, attendance and completion?: A systematic review of the evidence.* London: EPPI-Centre, Social Science Research Unit, Institute of Education, University of London.

Bishop, A. R., Berryman, M., Wearmouth, J., & Peter, M. (2012). Developing an effective education reform model for indigenous and other minoritized students. *School Effectiveness and School Improvement*, 23(1), 49–70, doi: 10.1080/09243453.2011.647921

Blase, K., Kiser, L., & Van Dyke, M. (2013). *The hexagon tool: Exploring context.* Chapel Hill, NC: National Implementation Research Network, FPG Child Development Institute, University of North Carolina at Chapel Hill.

Blimpo, M. P., Gajigo, O., Owusu, S., Tomita, R., & Xu, Y. (2020). *Technology in the classroom and learning in secondary schools.* Policy Research Working Paper 9288. Washington D.C.: World Bank Group.

Bocquet-Appel, J.-P. (July 29, 2011). When the world's population took off: The springboard of the neolithic demographic transition. *Science*, 333(6042), 560–561, doi: 10.1126/science.1208880

Bold, T., Filmer, D., Martin, G., Molina, E., Stacy, B., Rockmore, C., Svensson, J., & Wane, W. (2017). *What do teachers know and do? Does it matter? Evidence from primary schools in Africa.* Policy Research Working Paper 7956. Washington D.C.: World Bank Group.

Bold, T., Kimenyi, M., Mwabub, G., Ng'ang', A., & Sandefur, J. (2018). Experimental evidence on scaling up education reforms in Kenya. *Journal of Public Economics*, 168, 1–20, doi: 10.1016/j.jpubeco.2018.08.007

Bonner, S., & Sprinkle, G. (2002). The effects of monetary incentives on effort and task performance: Theories, evidence, and a framework for research. *Accounting, Organizations and Society*, 27, 303–345, doi: 10.1016/S0361-3682(01)00052-6

Booij, A. S., Leuven, E., & Oosterbeek, H. (2017). Ability peer effects in university: Evidence from a randomized experiment. *The Review of Economic Studies*, 84(2), 547–578, doi: 10.1093/restud/rdw045

Borenstein, M., Hedges, L. V., Higgins, J. P., & Rothstein, H. R. (2011). *Introduction to meta-analysis.* Chichester: John Wiley & Sons.

Borman, G. D., Hewes, G. M., Overman, L. T., & Brown, S. (2003). Comprehensive school reform and achievement: A meta-analysis. *Review of Educational Research*, 73(2), 125–230, doi: 10.3102/00346543073002125

Bray, M. (2008). *Double-shift schooling: Design and operation for cost-effectiveness.* London: Commonwealth Secretariat.

Bray, M., & Lykins, C. (2012). Shadow education: Private supplementary tutoring and its implications for policy makers in Asia. Metro Manila: Asian

Development Bank. https://www.adb.org/publications/shadow-education-private-supplementary-tutoring-and-its-implications-policy-makers-asia

Breierova, L., & Duflo, E. (2004). *The impact of education on fertility and child mortality: Do father's really matter less than mothers?* Cambridge, MA: National Bureau of Economic Research (NBER).

Bruns, B., Filmer, D., & Patrinos, H. (2010). *Making schools work: New evidence on accountability reforms.* Washington D.C.: World Bank Group.

Brunsek, A., Perlman, M., Falenchuk, O., McMullen, E., Fletcher, B., & Shah, P. S. (2017). The relationship between the Early Childhood Environment Rating Scale and its revised form and child outcomes: A systematic review and meta-analysis. *PLoS One*, 12(6), e0178512, doi: 10.1371/journal.pone.0178512

Brydges, C. R., Landes, J. K., Reid, C. L., Campbell, C., French, N., & Anderson, M. (2018). Cognitive outcomes in children and adolescents born very preterm: A meta-analysis. *Developmental Medicine & Child Neurology*, 60(5), 452–468. https://doi.org/10.1111/dmcn.13685

Bryk, A. S., Gomez, L. M., Grunow, A., & LeMahieu, P. G. (2017). *Learning to improve: How Americas schools can get better at getting better.* Cambridge, MA: Harvard Education Press.

Buonanno, P., & Leonida, L. (2006). Education and crime: Evidence from Italian regions. *Applied Economics Letters*, 13, 709–713, doi: 10.1080/13504850500407376

Burns, M. K., Appleton, J. J., & Stehouwer, J. D. (2005). Meta-analytic review of responsiveness-to-intervention research: Examining field-based and research-implemented models. *Journal of Psychoeducational Assessment*, 23(4), 381–394, doi: 10.1177/073428290502300406

Bushe, G. R., & Kassam, A. F. (2005). When is appreciative inquiry transformational? A meta-case analysis. *Journal of Applied Behavioral Science*, 41(2), 161–181, doi: 10.1177/0021886304270337

Butcher, P. M. (1981). *An experimental investigation of the effectiveness of value claim strategy unit for use in teacher education.* [Unpublished M.A.] Macquarie University, Sydney.

Call, K. (2018). Professional teaching standards: A comparative analysis of their history, implementation and efficacy. *Australian Journal of Teacher Education*, 43(3), 93–108, doi: 10.14221/ajte.2018v43n3.6

Cameron, D. B., Mishra, A., & Brown, A. N. (2016). The growth of impact evaluation for international development: How much have we learned? *Journal of Development Effectiveness*, 8(1), 1–21, doi: 10.1080/19439342.2015.1034156

Campaniello, N., Gray, R., & Mastrobuoni, G. (2016). Returns to education in criminal organizations: Did going to college help Michael Corleone? *Economics of Education Review*, 54(C), 242–258, doi: 10.1016/j.econedurev.2016.03.003

Caplan, B. (2018). *The case against education: Why the education system is a waste of time and money.* Princeton: Princeton University Press.

Carr, S. C., Leggatt-Cook, C., Clarke, M., MacLachlan, M., Papola, T. S., Pais, J., Thomas, S., McAuliffe, E., & Normand, C. (2011). *What is the evidence of the impact of increasing salaries on improving the performance of public servants, including teachers, doctors/nurses, and mid-level occupations, in low and middle-income countries: Is it time to give pay a chance?* London: EPPI-Centre, Social Science Research Unit, Institute of Education, University of London.

Carr-Hill, R., Rolleston, C., & Schendel, R. (2016). The effects of school-based decision-making on educational outcomes in low- and middle-income contexts: A systematic review. *Campbell Systematic Reviews*, 12(1), 1–169, doi: 10.4073/csr.2016.9

Carrell, S. E., Maghakian, T., & West, J. E. (2011). A's from Zzzz's? The causal effect of school start time on the academic achievement of adolescents. *American Economic Journal: Economic Policy*, 3, 62–81, doi: 10.1257/pol.3.3.62

Carrillo, P. E., Onofa, M., & Ponce, J. (2011). *Information technology and student achievement: Evidence from a randomized experiment in Ecuador.* IDB Working Paper, 78, doi: 10.2139/ssrn.1818756

Cassil, K. (2005). *A meta analysis: The effectiveness of the use of mobile computers on the attitude and academic outcomes of k-12 students.* [Dissertation] Auburn University. http://etd.auburn.edu/handle/10415/756

Chabbott, C., & Chowdhury, M. (2015). *Institutionalizing health and education for all global goals, innovations, and scaling up.* New York, NY: Teachers College Press.

Chauhan, S. (2017). A meta-analysis of the impact of technology on learning effectiveness of elementary students. *Computers & Education*, 105, 14–30, doi: 10.1016/j.compedu.2016.11.005

Cheng, A., Hitt, C., Kisida, B., & Mills, J. N. (2017). "No excuses" charter schools: A meta-analysis of the experimental evidence on student achievement. *Journal of School Choice*, 11(2), 209–238, doi: 10.1080/15582159.2017.1286210

Chien, Y. T., Chang, Y. H., & Chang, C. Y. (2016). Do we click in the right way? A meta-analytic review of clicker-integrated instruction. *Educational Research Review*, 17, 1–18, doi: 10.1016/j.edurev.2015.10.003

Childs, T. S., & Shakeshaft, C. (1986). A meta-analysis of research on the relationship between educational expenditures and student achievement. *Journal of Education Finance*, 12(2), 249–263.

Chin, J. M. C. (2007). Meta-analysis of transformational school leadership effects on school outcomes in Taiwan and the USA. *Asia Pacific Education Review*, 8(2), 166–177, doi: 10.1007/BF03029253

Cho, K., Lee, S., Joo, M. H., & Becker, B. (2018). The effects of using mobile devices on student achievement in language learning: A meta-analysis. *Education Sciences*, 8(3), 105, doi: 10.3390/educsci8030105

Chrisomalis, S. (2009). The origins and co-evolution of literacy and numeracy, in Olson, D., & Torrance, N. (Eds), *The Cambridge handbook of literacy*, Cambridge: Cambridge University Press, 1–16.

Çiftçi, Ş. K., & Cin, F. M. (2017). The effect of socioeconomic status on students' achievement, in *The factors effecting student achievement*. New York: Springer, Cham, 171–181.

Clark, H. (2002). *Building education: The role of the physical environment in enhancing teaching and research.* London: Institute of Education.

Clark, M., Isenberg, E., Liu, A., Makowsky, L., & Zukiewicz, M. (2017). *Impacts of the Teach For America Investing in Innovation scale-up.* Princeton: Mathematica Policy Research.

Clarke, J., & Dede, C. (2009). Design for scalability: A case study of the River City curriculum. *Journal of Science Education and Technology*, 18(4), 353–365, doi: 10.1007/s10956-009-9156-4

Coe, R. (2002). *It's the effect size, stupid: What effect size is and why it is important.* Paper presented at the British Educational Research Association Annual Conference, Exeter, England. www.cem.org/attachments/ebe/ESguide.pdf

Çoğaltay, N., & Karadağ, E. (2017). The effect of collective teacher efficacy on student achievement, in Karadağ, E. (Ed.), *The Factors Effecting Student Achievement*, New York: Springer, Cham, 215–226.

Cohen, J. (1988). *Statistical power analysis for the behavioural sciences* (2nd ed.). Hillsdale, NJ: Erlbaum.

Cohen, J., & Goldhaber, D. (2016). Building a more complete understanding of teacher evaluation using classroom observations. *Educational Researcher*, 45(6), 378–387, doi: 10.3102/0013189X16659442

Conn, K. (2017). Identifying effective education interventions in sub-Saharan Africa: A meta-analysis of impact evaluations. *Review of Educational Research*, 87(5), 863–898, doi: 10.3102/0034654317712025

Coombs, P. H. (1985). *The world crisis in education: The view from the eighties.* Oxford: Oxford University Press.

Cooper, H. (1989). Synthesis of research on homework. *Educational Leadership*, 47(3), 85–91.

Cooper, H. (1994). *Homework research and policy: A review of the literature.* Center for Applied Research and Educational Improvement. Retrieved from the University of Minnesota Digital Conservancy. https://hdl.handle.net/11299/140536

Cooper, H., Robinson, J. C., & Patall, E. A. (2006). Does homework improve academic achievement? A synthesis of research, 1987–2003. *Review of Educational Research*, 76(1), 1–62, doi: 10.3102/00346543076001001

Cooper, H., Valentine, J. C., Charlton, K., & Melson, A. (2003). The effects of modified school calendars on student achievement and on school and community attitudes. *Review of Educational Research*, 73(1), 1–52, doi: 10.3102/00346543073001001

Cooperrider, D. L., & Srivastva, S. (1987). Appreciative inquiry in organizational life, in Woodman, R. W., & Pasmore, W. A. (Eds), *Research in organizational change and development*, vol. 1, Stamford, CT: JAI Press, 129–169.

Cooperrider, D., Whitney, D. D., & Stavros, J. (2008). *The appreciative inquiry handbook: For leaders of change.* Berrett-Koehler Publishers.

Cornel, A., Knutsen, C. H., & Teorell, J. (2020). Bureaucracy and growth. *Comparative Political Studies*, 53(14), 2246–2282, doi: 10.1177/0010414020912262

Cornelius-White, J. (2007). Learner-centered teacher–student relationships are effective: A meta-analysis. *Review of Educational Research*, 77(1), 113–143, doi: 10.3102/003465430298563

Coughlin, C. (2011). *Research on the effectiveness of Direct Instruction (NIFDI Technical Report 2011–4)*. Eugene, OR: National Institute for Direct Instruction.

Crawfurd, L., (2020, May 18). *Why the COVID Crisis Is Not Edtech's Moment in Africa*. [Blog post]. Center for Global Development. https://www.cgdev.org/blog/why-covid-crisis-not-edtechs-moment-africa

Cristia, J., Czerwonko, A., & Garofalo, P. (2010). *Does ICT increate years of education? Evidence from Peru*. Inter-American Development Bank Working Paper: OVE/WP-01/10. Washington D.C.: Inter-American Development Bank.

Cristia, J., Ibarrarán, P., Cueto, S., Santiago, A., & Severín, E. (2017). Technology and child development: Evidence from the one laptop per child program. *American Economic Journal: Applied Economics*, 9(3), 295–320, doi: 10.1257/app.20150385

Cuban, L. (1984). *How teachers taught: Constancy and change in American classrooms, 1890–1980*. New York: Longman.

Cuban, L. (1990). Reforming again, again, and again. *Educational Researcher*, 19(1), 3–13, doi: 10.3102/0013189X019001003

Curlette, W., Hendrick, R., Ogletree, S., & Benson, G. (2014). Student achievement from anchor action research studies in high-needs, urban professional development schools: A meta-analysis, in Ferrara, J., Nath, J., & Guadarrama, I. (Eds), *Creating visions for university–school partnerships*, Charlotte, NC: Information Age Publishing, 61–72.

Damon, A., Glewwe, P., Wisniewski, S., & Sun, B. (2019). What education policies and programmes affect learning and time in school in developing countries? A review of evaluations from 1990 to 2014. *Review of Education*, 7(2), 295–387, doi: 10.1002/rev3.3123

Darling-Hammond, L., & Youngs, P. (2002). Defining "highly qualified teachers": What does "scientifically-based research" actually tell us? *Educational Researcher*, 31, 13–25, doi: 10.3102/0013189X031009013

Davies, J. (2012). Facework on Facebook as a new literacy practice. *Computers & Education*, 59(1), 19–29, doi: 10.1016/j.compedu.2011.11.007

Davies, J., & Merchant, G. (2014). Digital literacy and teacher education, in Benson, P., & Chik, A. (Eds), *Popular culture, pedagogy and teacher education: International perspectives*. New York: Routledge.

Davis, R. (2007). *Shipbuilders of the Venetian arsenal: Workers and workplace in the preindustrial city*. Baltimore: The Johns Hopkins University Press.

Davis-Beggs, K. D. (2013). *The effects of school resources on student achievement*. [Unpublished PhD thesis] Lincoln Memorial University.

Day Ashley, L., Mcloughlin, C., Aslam, M., Engel, J., Wales, J., Rawal, S., Batley, R., Kingdon, G., Nicolai, S., & Rose, P. (2014). *The role and impact of private schools in developing countries: A rigorous review of the evidence. Final report*. Education Rigorous Literature Review. London: Department for International Development.

de Melo, G., Machado, A., & Miranda, A. (2014). *The impact of a one laptop per child program on learning: Evidence from Uruguay*. IZA, Discussion Paper 8489. Bonn: IZA.

De Pelijt, A. M. (2019). Human capital formation in the long run: Evidence from average years of schooling in England, 1300–1900. *Cliometrica*, 12, 99–126, doi: 10.1007/s11698-016-0156-3

de Ree, J., Muralidharan, K., Pradhan, M., & Rogers, H. (2018). Double for nothing? Experimental evidence on an unconditional teacher salary increase in indonesia. *The Quarterly Journal of Economics*, 133(2), 993–1039, doi: 10.1093/qje/qjx040

DeBaz, T. P. (1994). *Meta-analysis of the relationship between students' characteristics and achievement and attitudes toward science.* [Doctoral Dissertation] Ohio State University.

Diamond, J. M. (2012). *The world until yesterday: What can we learn from traditional societies?* New York: Viking.

Dickson, K., & Bangpan, M. (2012). *Providing access to economic assets for girls and young women in low-and-lower-middle-income countries. A systematic review of the evidence.* London: EPPI-Centre, Social Science Research Unit, Institute of Education, University of London.

Dietrichson, J., Bøg, M., Filges, T., & Klint Jørgensen, A-M. (2017). Academic interventions for elementary and middle school students with low socioeconomic status: A systematic review and meta-analysis. *Review of Educational Research*, 87(2), 243–282, doi: 10.3102/0034654316687036

Dignath, C., Buettner, G., & Langfeldt, H.-P. (2008). How can primary school students learn self-regulated learning strategies most effectively?: A meta-analysis on self-regulation training programmes. *Educational Research Review*, 3(2), 101–129, doi: 10.1016/j.edurev.2008.02.003

Doemeland, D., & Trevino, J. (2014). *Which World Bank reports are widely read?* Policy Research Working Paper 6851. Washington, D.C.: World Bank Group.

Donker, A. S., De Boer, H., Kostons, D., Van Ewijk, C. D., & van der Werf, M. P. (2014). Effectiveness of learning strategy instruction on academic performance: A meta-analysis. *Educational Research* Review, 11, 1–26, doi: 10.1016/j.edurev.2013.11.002

Donohoo, J. (2016). *Collective efficacy: How educators' beliefs impact student learning.* Thousand Oaks: Corwin Press.

Draney, K., & Wilson, M. (1992, April). *The impact of design characteristics on study outcomes in retention research: A meta-analytic perspective.* Paper presented at the Annual Meeting of the American Educational Research Association, San Francisco, CA.

Druva, C. A., & Anderson, R. D. (1983). Science teacher characteristics by teacher behavior and by student outcome: A meta-analysis of research. *Journal of Research in Science Teaching*, 20(5), 467–479.

Duflo, E., Dupas, P., & Kremer, M. (2015). School governance, teacher incentives, and pupil–teacher ratios: Experimental evidence from Kenyan primary schools. *Journal of Public Economics*, 123, 92–110.

Duflo, E., Dupas, P., & Kremer, M. (2019). *The impact of free secondary education: Experimental evidence from Ghana.* Working Paper. Washington. D.C: J-Pal.

https://www.povertyactionlab.org/evaluation/returns-secondary-schooling-ghana [accessed 26/02/21].

Duflo, E., Dupas, P., & Kremer, M. (2021). *The impact of free secondary education: Experimental evidence from Ghana*. Working Paper. https://economics.mit.edu/files/16094

Duflo, E., Hanna, R., & Ryan, S. P. (2012). Incentives work: Getting teachers to come to school. *American Economic Review*, 102(4), 1241–1278, doi: 10.1257/aer.102.4.1241

Eddy-Spicer, D., Ehren, M., Bangpan, M., Khatwa, M., & Perrone, F. (2016). *Under what conditions do inspection, monitoring and assessment improve system efficiency, service delivery and learning outcomes for the poorest and most marginalised? A realist synthesis of school accountability in low- and middle-income countries.* London: EPPI-Centre, Social Science Research Unit, UCL Institute of Education, University College London.

Education Commission. (2016). *The learning generation: Investing in education for a changing world.* New York: International Commission on Financing Global Education Opportunity.

Eells, R. J. (2011). *Meta-analysis of the relationship between collective teacher efficacy and student achievement.* [Dissertation] Loyola University Chicago. https://ecommons.luc.edu/luc_diss/133

Ellington, A. J. (2000). *Effects of hand-held calculators on precollege students in mathematics classes: A meta-analysis.* [Doctoral dissertation] University of Tennessee. https://www.learntechlib.org/p/127244/

Elmore, R. (1996). Getting to scale with good educational practice. *Harvard Educational Review*, 66(1), 1–27, doi: 10.17763/haer.66.1.g73266758j348t33

Erickson, M. J. (2013). *Examining a decade of reading and mathematics student achievement among primary and secondary traditional public school and charter school students: A meta-analytic investigation.* [Doctoral dissertation] Youngstown State University.

Ericsson, A., & Pool, R. (2016). *Peak: Secrets from the new science of expertise.* Boston, MA: Houghton Mifflin Harcourt.

Ericsson, K., Hoffman, R., Kozbelt, A., & Williams, A. (Eds). (2018). *The Cambridge handbook of expertise and expert performance* (2nd ed., Cambridge handbooks in psychology). Cambridge: Cambridge University Press, doi: 10.1017/9781316480748

Evans, D., & Popova, A. (2015). *What really works to improve learning in developing countries? An analysis of divergent findings in systematic reviews.* Policy Research Working Paper WPS 7203. Washington, D.C.: World Bank Group.

Evans, D. K., & Yuan, F. (2019). *What we learn about girls' education from interventions that do not focus on girls.* World Bank Policy Research Working Paper 8944. Washington D.C.: World Bank Group.

Evans, D., Yuan, F., & Filmer, D. (2020). *Are teachers in Africa poorly paid? Evidence from 15 countries.* Working Paper 9358. Washington D.C.: World Bank Group.

Fabian, K., Topping, K. J., & Barron, I. G. (2016). Mobile technology and mathematics: Effects on students' attitudes, engagement, and achievement. *Journal of Computers in Education*, 3(1), 77–104, doi: 10.1007/s40692-015-0048-8

Fan, H., Xu, J., Cai, Z., He, J., & Fan, X. (2017). Homework and students' achievement in math and science: A 30-year meta-analysis, 1986–2015. *Educational Research Review*, 20, 35–54, doi: 10.12691/education-5–4-5

Filges, T., Sonne-Schmidt, C. S., & Nielsen, B. C. V. (2018). Small class sizes for improving student achievement in primary and secondary schools: A systematic review. *Campbell Systematic Reviews*, 14(1), 1–107, doi: 10.4073/csr.2018.10

Fisher, K. (2001). *Building better outcomes: The impact of school infrastructure on student outcomes and behaviour*. Canberra: Department of Education, Training and Youth Affairs.

Fisher, R. A. (1971) [1935]. *The design of experiments* (9th ed.). London: Macmillan.

Fishman, B. J. (2005). Adapting innovations to particular contexts of use: A collaborative framework, in Dede, C., Honan, J. P., & Peters, L. C. (Eds), *Scaling up success: Lessons from technology-based educational improvement*. San Francisco: Jossey-Bass, 48–66.

Forth, G. (2018). Rites of passage, in Callan, H. (Ed.), *The international encyclopedia of anthropology*. London: John Wiley & Sons.

Franklin, B. (2017). *The art of virtue*. New York: Skyhorse.

Friedman, M. (1955). The role of government in education, in Solo, R. A. (Ed.), *Economics and the public interest*. New Brunswick, New Jersey: Rutgers University Press, 123–144.

Fryer, R., & Dobbie, W. (2011). Are high-quality schools enough to increase achievement among the poor? Evidence from the Harlem children's zone. *American Economic Journal: Applied Economics*, 3(3), 158–187, doi: 10.1257/app.3.3.158

Fuchs, D., & Fuchs, L. S. (1986). Test procedure bias: A meta-analysis of examiner familiarity effects. *Review of Educational Research*, 56(2), 243–262, doi: 10.3102/00346543056002243

Fuchs, D., Fuchs, L. S., Mathes, P. G., Lipsey, M. W., & Roberts, P. (2002). Is "learning disabilities" just a fancy term for low achievement? A meta-analysis of reading differences between low achievers with and without the label, in Bradley, R., Danielson, L., & Hallahan, D. P. (Eds), *Identification of learning disabilities: Research to practice. The LEA series on special education and disability*. Mahwah, NJ: Lawrence Erlbaum Associates, 737–762.

Fullan, M. (2000). The return of large-scale reform. *Journal of Educational Change*, 1, 5–28.

Gaduh, A., Pradhan, M., Priebe, J., & Susanti, D. (2020). *Scores, camera, action? Incentivizing teachers in remote areas. RISE* Working Paper Series, 20(035), doi: 10.35489/BSG-RISE-WP_2020/035

Galloway, A. M. (2003). *Improving reading comprehension through metacognitive strategy instruction: Evaluating the evidence for the effectiveness of the reciprocal teaching procedure*. ETD collection for University of Nebraska - Lincoln. AAI3092542. https://digitalcommons.unl.edu/dissertations/AAI3092542

Galton, M., & Pell, T. (2012). Do class size reductions make a difference to classroom practice? The case of Hong Kong primary schools. *International Journal of Educational Research*, 53, 22–31, doi: 10.1016/j.ijer.2011.12.004

Ganimian, A., & Murnane, R. (2016). Improving education in developing countries: Lessons from rigorous impact evaluations. *Review of Educational Research*, 86(3), 719–755, doi: 10.3102/0034654315627499

Gasper, D. (2000). Evaluating the "logical framework approach" towards learning-oriented development evaluation. *Public Administration and Development*, 20(1), 17–28, doi: 10.1002/1099–162X(200002)20:1<17::AID-PAD89>3.0.CO;2–5

Gawande, A. (2010). *The checklist manifesto: How to get things right*. New York: Picador.

Gayle, B. M., Preiss, R. W., & Allen, M. (2006). How effective are teacher-initiated classroom questions in enhancing student learning?, in Gayle, B. M., Preiss, R. W., Burrell, N., & Allen, A. (Eds), *Classroom communication and instructional processes: Advances through meta-analysis*. Mahwah: Lawrence Erlbaum Associates Publishers, 279–293.

Gerard, L. F., Matuk, C. F., McElhaney, K. W., & Linn, M. C. (2015). Automated, adaptive guidance for K-12 education. *Educational Research Review*, 15, 41–58, doi: 10.1016/j.edurev.2015.04.001

Gertler, P. J., Martinez, S., Premand, P., Rawlings, L. B., & Vermeersch, C. M. J. (2016). *Impact evaluation in practice* (2nd ed.). Washington, D.C.: Inter-American Development Bank and World Bank.

Giaconia, R. M., & Hedges, L. V. (1982). Identifying features of effective open education. *Review of Educational Research*, 52(4), 579–602, doi: 10.3102/00346543052004579

Gilbert, J. K., Bulte, A. M. W., & Pilot, A. (2011). Concept development and transfer in context-based science education. *International Journal of Science Education*, 33(6), 817–837, doi: 10.1080/09500693.2010.493185

Giuliari, G., Klenze, T., Legner, M., Basin, D., Perrig, A., & Singla, A. (2020). Internet backbones in space. *SIGCOMM Computer Communication Review*, 50(1), 25–37, doi: 10.1145/3390251.3390256

Glass, G. V. (1976). Primary, secondary, and meta-analysis of research. *Educational Researcher*, 5(10), 3–8, doi: 10.3102/0013189X005010003

Glewwe, P., & Muralidharan, K. (2016). Improving education outcomes in developing countries: Evidence, knowledge gaps, and policy implications, in Machin, S., Woessmann, L., & Hanushek, E. A. (Eds), *Handbook of the economics of education*. Amsterdam: Elsevier, 653–743, doi: 10.1016/B978–0–444–63459–7.00010–5

Glewwe, P., Hanushek, E. A., Humpage, S. D., & Ravina, R. (2014). School resources and educational outcomes in developing countries: A review of the literature from 1990 to 2010, in Glewwe, P. (Ed.), *Education policy in developing countries*. Chicago, IL: University of Chicago Press, 13–64.

Global Education Evidence Advisory Panel. (2020). *Cost-effective approaches to improve learning: What does recent evidence tell us are "smart buys" for improving learning in low- and middle-income countries?* Washington D.C.: World Bank Group.

Gopher, D., Armony, L., & Greenspan, Y. (2000). Switching tasks and attention policies. *Journal of Experimental Psychology: General,* 129, 308–339, doi: 10.1037//0096–3445.129.3.308

Gould, E., Mustard, D., & Weinberg, B. (2002). Crime rates and local labor market opportunities in the United States: 1977–1997. *Review of Economics and Statistics,* 84, 45–61, doi: 10.1162/003465302317331919

Graff, H. J. (1995). *The labyrinths of literacy: Reflections on literacy past and present* (Revised Edition). Pittsburgh: University of Pittsburgh Press.

Gray, P. (2013). *Free to learn: Why unleashing the instinct to play will make our children happier, more self-reliant, and better students for life.* New York: Basic Books.

Greenhalgh, T., Robert, G., Macfarlane, F., Bate, P., & Kyriakidou, O. (2004). Diffusion of innovations in service organizations: Systematic review and recommendations. *The Milbank Quarterly,* 82(4), 581–629, doi: 10.1111/j.0887–378X.2004.00325.x

Grogger, J. (1996). Does school quality explain the recent Black/White wage trend? *Journal of Labor Economics,* 14(2), 231–253.

GSMA. (2020). *The state of mobile internet connectivity 2020.* London: GSM Association. https://www.gsma.com/r/wp-content/uploads/2020/09/GSMA-State-of-Mobile-Internet-Connectivity-Report-2020.pdf

Guerrero, G., Leon, J., Zapata, M., & Cueto, S. (2013). Getting teachers back to the classroom. A systematic review on what works to improve teacher attendance in developing countries. *Journal of Development Effectiveness,* 5(4), 466–488, doi: 10.1080/19439342.2013.864695

Guerrero, G., Leon, J., Zapata, M., Sugimaru, C., & Cueto, S. (2012). *What works to improve teacher attendance in developing countries? A systematic review.* London: EPPI-Centre, Social Science.

Guirguis-Blake, J. M., Evans, C. V., Senger, C. A., Rowland, M. G., O'Connor, E. A., & Whitlock, E. P. (2015). *Aspirin for the primary prevention of cardiovascular events: A systematic evidence review for the U.S. preventive services task force.* Rockville, MD: Agency for Healthcare Research and Quality (US). Report No.: 13–05195-EF-1. PMID: 26491760.

Gunter, T., & Shao, J. (2016). Synthesizing the effect of building condition quality on academic performance. *Education Finance and Policy,* 11(1), 97–123, doi: 10.1162/EDFP_a_00181

Gupta, S., Davoodi, H. R., & Tiongson, E. (2000). *Corruption and the provision of health care and education services.* Washington, D.C.: International Monetary Fund.

Haas, M. (2005). Teaching methods for secondary algebra: A meta-analysis of findings. *Nassp Bulletin,* 89(642), 24–46, doi: 10.1177/019263650508964204

Hailey, J., & Sorgenfrei, M. (2004). *Measuring success: Issues in performance management.* Occasional Paper Series, 44. Oxford: INTRAC. https://www.intrac.org/wpcms/wp-content/uploads/2018/11/OPS44Final.pdf

Hall, J. F. (2019). *A multi-level meta-analysis to determine the association of school district consolidation on student performance on state assessments.* [Unpublished doctoral dissertation] Youngstown State University.

Hallinger, P., Hosseingholizadeh, R., Hashemi, N., & Kouhsari, M. (2018). Do beliefs make a difference? Exploring how principal self-efficacy and instructional leadership impact teacher efficacy and commitment in Iran. *Educational Management Administration & Leadership*, 46(5), 800–819, doi: 10.1177/1741143217700283

Hallinger, P., Walker, A., Nguyen, D. T. H., Truong, T., & Nguyen, T. T. (2017). Perspectives on principal instructional leadership in Vietnam: A preliminary model. *Journal of Educational Administration*, 55(2), 222–239, doi: 10.1108/JEA-11–2015–0106

Hamilton, A., & Hattie, J. (2021a). *Getting to G.O.L.D. The Visible Learning approach to unleashing education improvement.* Thousand Oaks: Corwin Press.

Hamilton, A., & Hattie, J. (2021b). *Not all that glitters is gold: When will education technology finally deliver?* Thousand Oaks: Corwin.

Hansard. (1947). House of Commons, *November 11 Debate (Series 5 Vol. 444 Col. 207).* https://api.parliament.uk/historic-hansard/commons/1947/nov/11/parliament-bill

Hansford, B. C., & Hattie, J. A. (1982). The relationship between self and achievement/performance measures. *Review of Educational Research*, 52(1), 123–142, doi: 10.3102/00346543052001123

Hanushek, E. (1971). Teacher characteristics and gains in student achievement: Estimation using micro data. *American Economic Review*, 61(2), 280–288.

Hanushek, E. A. (2020). Financing schools, in Hattie, J., & Anderman, E. M. (Eds.), *Visible Learning guide to student achievement.* New York: Routledge, 92–97.

Hanushek, E. A., & Wößmann, L. (2006). Does educational tracking affect performance and inequality? Differences-in-differences evidence across countries. *The Economic Journal*, 116(510), C63–C76, doi: 10.1111/j.1468–0297.2006.01076.x

Harari, Y. N. (2015). *Sapiens: A brief history of humankind.* New York: HarperCollins.

Harari, Y. N. (2019). *21 lessons for the 21st century.* London: Vintage.

Harris, A., Jones, M., Cheah, K. S. L., Devadason, E., & Adams, D. (2017). Exploring principals' instructional leadership practices in Malaysia: Insights and implications. *Journal of Educational Administration*, 55(2), 207–221, doi: 10.1108/JEA-05–2016–0051

Harris, D. N., & Sass, T. R. (2011). Teacher training, teacher quality and student achievement. *Journal of Public Economics*, 95(7–8), 798–812.

Harris, W. V. (1989). *Ancient literacy.* Cambridge, MA: Harvard University Press.

Harwell, M., Maeda, Y., Bishop, K., & Xie, A. (2017). The surprisingly modest relationship between SES and educational achievement. *The Journal of Experimental Education*, 85(2), 197–214, doi: 10.1080/00220973.2015.1123668

Hattie, J. A. C. (2003). *Teachers make a difference: What is the research evidence?* Australian Council for Educational Research Annual Conference on Building Teacher Quality. Auckland: University of Auckland.

Hattie, J. A. C. (2006). The paradox of reducing class size and improved learning outcomes. *International Journal of Education Research*, 42, 387–425, doi: 10.1016/j.ijer.2006.07.002

Hattie, J. A. C. (2009). *Visible learning: A synthesis of over 800 meta-analyses relating to achievement.* New York: Routledge.

Hattie, J. A. C. (2012). *Visible learning for teachers.* New York: Routledge.

Hattie, J. A. C. (2015). *What doesn't work in education: The politics of distraction.* London: Pearson.

Hattie, J. A. C. (2016). The right question in the debates about class size: Why is the (positive) effect so small?, in Blatchford, P. Chan, K. W., Galton, M., Lai, K. C., & Lee, J. C. L. (Eds), *Class size: Eastern and Western perspectives.* London: Routledge, 105–118.

Hattie, J. A., & Donoghue, G. M. (2016). Learning strategies: A synthesis and conceptual model. *Science of Learning*, 1(16013).

Hattie, J. A., & Hamilton, A. (2020). *Real gold vs. fool's gold: The Visible Leaning methodology for finding what works best in education.* Thousand Oaks, CA: Corwin Press.

Hattie, J. A., & Hamilton, A. (2021). *As good as gold: Why We Focus on the Wrong Drivers in Education.* Thousand Oaks: Corwin.

Hattie, J. A. C., & Yates, G. (2013). *Visible Learning and the science of how we learn.* New York: Routledge.

Hattie, J. A. C., & Zierer, K. (2018). *10 mindframes for Visible Learning: Teaching for success.* London: Routledge.

Hawkes, D., & Ugur, M. (2012). *Evidence on the relationship between education, skills and economic growth in low-income countries: A systematic review.* London: EPPI-Centre, Social Science Research Unit, Institute of Education, University of London.

Haystead, M. W. (2009). *Meta-analytic synthesis of studies conducted at Marzano Research Laboratory on instructional strategies.* Englewood, CO: Marzano Research Laboratory.

Hedges, L. V., & Olkin, I. (1985). *Statistical methods for meta-analysis.* Orlando, FL: Academic Press.

Hedges, L. V., Laine, R. D., & Greenwald, R. (1994). An exchange: Part I: Does money matter? A meta-analysis of studies of the effects of differential school inputs on student outcomes. *Educational Researcher*, 23(3), 5–14, doi: 10.2307/1177220

Hembree, R., & Dessart, D. J. (1986). Effects of hand-held calculators in precollege mathematics education: A meta-analysis. *Journal for research in mathematics education*, 17(2), 83–99, doi: 10.2307/749255

Hendriks, M. A., Scheerens, J., & Sleegers, P. J. C. (2014). *Effects of evaluation and assessment on student achievement: A review and meta-analysis.* Enschede: University of Twente.

Hetzel, D. C., Rasher, S. P., Butcher, L., & Walberg, H. J. (April 1980). *A quantitative synthesis of the effects of open education.* Paper presented at the annual meeting of the American Educational Research Association, Boston, MA.

Hincapie, D. (2016). *Do longer school days improve student achievement? Evidence from Colombia.* IDB Working Paper Series, No. IDB-WP-679. Washington D.C.: InterAmerican Development Bank (IDB), doi: 10.18235/0000268

Hinrichs, P. (2011). When the bell tolls: The effects of school starting times on academic achievement. *Education*, 6, 486–507, doi: 10.1162/EDFP_a_00045

Hirshleifer, S. R. (2016). *Incentives for effort of outputs? A field experiment to improve student performance.* Working Papers 201701. University of California at Riverside, Department of Economics.

Hjalmarsson, R., & Lochner, L. (2012). *The impact of education on crime: International evidence.* CESifo DICE Report, ISSN 1613–6373, ifo Institut - LeibnizInstitut für Wirtschaftsforschung an der Universität München, München, 10(2), 49–55, http://hdl.handle.net/10419/167078

Hjalmarsson, R., Holmlund, H., & Lindquist, M. (2011). *The effect of education on criminal convictions and incarceration: Causal evidence from micro-data.* Research Discussion Paper 8646. London: Centre for Economic Policy Research (CEPR).

HM Treasury. (2020). *2020 Spending Review.* London: Her Majesty's Stationery Office https://assets.publishing.service.gov.uk/government/uploads/system/uploads/attachment_data/file/938054/SR20_print.pdf

Huang, C. (2017). Time spent on social network sites and psychological well-being: A meta-analysis. *Cyberpsychology, Behavior, and Social Networking*, 20(6), 346–354, doi: 10.1089/cyber.2016.0758

Hubbard, M. (2001). Shooting the messenger: Log frame abuse and the need for a better planning environment – A comment. *Public Administration and Development*, 21(1), 25–26, doi: 10.1002/pad.168

Hume, D., & Millican, P. F. (2007 [1748]). *An enquiry concerning human understanding.* Oxford: Oxford University Press.

Hunsu, N. J., Adesope, O., & Bayly, D. J. (2016). A meta-analysis of the effects of audience response systems (clicker-based technologies) on cognition and affect. *Computers & Education*, 94, 102–119, doi: 10.1016/j.compedu.2015.11.013

IbisWorld. (n.d.). *The 10 global biggest industries by revenue in 2021.* https://www.ibisworld.com/united-states/industry-trends/biggest-industries-by-revenue/ [accessed 24/01/21].

ICRW (International Center for Research on Women). (2006). *Too young to wed: Education and action toward ending child marriage, brief on child marriage and domestic violence.* Washington: ICRW.

Inter-Agency Network for Education in Emergencies (INEE). (2011). *Education and fragility in Liberia.* Paris: International Institute for Educational Planning. https://www.imf.org/~/media/Files/Publications/covid19-special-notes/en-special-series-on-covid-19-challenges-in-forecasting-tax-revenue.ashx [accessed 8/2/21].

International Labour Organisation (ILO). (2021). *ILO Monitor: COVID-19 and the world of work.* Seventh edition Updated estimates and analysis. 27 January. Geneva: ILO. https://www.ilo.org/wcmsp5/groups/public/—-dgreports/—-dcomm/documents/briefingnote/wcms_767028.pdf [accessed 8/2/21].

International Monetary Fund (IMF). (2020a). *World economic outlook: A long and difficult ascent.* Washington D.C.: IMF.

International Monetary Fund (IMF). (2020b). *A year like no other: IMF annual report 2020.* Washington D.C.: IMF.

International Monetary Fund (IMF). (2020c). *Fiscal affairs: Challenges in forecasting tax revenue.* Washington, D.C.: IMF.

International Monetary Fund (IMF). (2021). *Fiscal monitor: Strengthening the credibility of public finances.* Washington D.C.: IMF.

Ito, H., Kasai, K., & Nakamuro, M. (2019). *Does computer-aided instruction improve children's cognitive and non-cognitive skills? Evidence from Cambodia.* Discussion Papers 19040. Tokyo: Research Institute, Trade and Industry (RIETI). https://ideas.repec.org/p/eti/dpaper/19040.html

Ivaschenko, O., Rodriguez C. P., Novikova, M., Romero, C., Bowen, T., & Zhu, L. (2018). *The state of social safety nets 2018 (English).* Washington, D.C.: World Bank Group.

Jabbar, H., Fong, C. J., Germain, E., Li, D. Sanchez, J. D., Sun, W. L., & DeVall, M. (2017, April). *The competitive effects of school choice on student outcomes: A systematic review and meta-analysis.* Paper to be presented at the Annual Meeting of the American Education Research Association, San Antonio, TX.

Jasper, C., Le, T. T., & Bartram, J. (2012). Water and sanitation in schools: A systematic review of the health and educational outcomes. *International Journal of Environmental Research and Public Health,* 9(8), 2772–2787, doi: 10.3390/ijerph9082772

Jeynes, W. H. (2012). A meta-analysis on the effects and contributions of public, public charter, and religious schools on student outcomes. *Peabody Journal of Education,* 87(3), 305–335, doi: 10.1080/0161956X.2012.679542

Johnson, P. (1947). *Mies van der Rohe.* New York: Museum of Modern Art. https://assets.moma.org/documents/moma_catalogue_2734_300062055.pdf

Jones, K. L., Tymms, P., Kemethofer, D., O'Hara, J., McNamara, G., Huber, S., Myrberg, E., Skedsmo, G., & Greger, D. (2017). The unintended consequences of school inspection: The prevalence of inspection side-effects in Austria, the Czech Republic, England, Ireland, the Netherlands, Sweden, and Switzerland. *Oxford Review of Education,* 43(6), 805–822, doi: 10.1080/03054985.2017.1352499

Joshi, A., & Amadi, C. (2013). Impact of water, sanitation, and hygiene interventions on improving health outcomes among school children. *Journal of Environmental and Public Health,* 984626, doi: 10.1155/2013/984626

Joyce, B., & Showers, B. (2002). *Student achievement through staff development* (3rd ed.). Alexandria, VA: Association for Supervision and Curriculum Development.

J-PAL Policy Bulletin. (2012). *Deworming: A best buy for development.* Cambridge, MA: Abdul Latif Jameel Poverty Action Lab.

J-PAL Policy Bulletin. (2017). *Roll call: Getting children into school.* Cambridge, MA: Abdul Latif Jameel Poverty Action Lab.

Kabeer, N., Piza, C., & Taylor, L. (2012). *What are the economic impacts of conditional cash transfer programmes? A systematic review of the evidence. Technical report.* London: EPPI-Centre, Social Science Research Unit, Institute of Education, University of London.

Kane, T. J., & Staiger, D. O. (2012). *Gathering feedback for teaching: Combining high-quality observations with student surveys and achievement gains.* Seattle, WA: Bill and Melinda Gates Foundation.

Kant, I. (1996 [1784]). An answer to the question: What is enlightenment?, in Gregor, M. J. (Ed.), *Practical philosophy. The Cambridge edition of the works of Immanuel Kant.* Cambridge: Cambridge University Press, doi: 10.1017/CBO9780511813306.005

Kapur, M., Hattie, J., Grossman, I., & Sinha, T. (in review). *Fail, flip, inForm, and feed – Rethinking flipped learning by trying productive failure: A review of meta-analyses and a subsequent meta-analysis.* Working Paper. Zürich: ETH Zürich.

Kates, A. W., Wu, H., & Coryn, C. L. S. (2018). The effects of mobile phone use on academic performance: A meta-analysis. *Computers and Education*, 127, 107–112, doi: 10.1016/j.compedu.2018.08.012

Kelley, P., & Camilli, G. (2007). *The impact of teacher education on outcomes in center-based early childhood education programs: A meta-analysis.* New Brunswick, NJ: National Institute for Early Education Research, Rutgers University.

Kelly, B. (2012). Implementation science for psychology in education, in Kelly, B., & Perkins, D. F. (Eds), *Handbook of implementation science for psychology in education.* New York: Cambridge University Press, 3–12.

Kelly, B., & Perkins, D. (Eds). (2012). *Handbook of implementation science for psychology in education.* New York: Cambridge University Press.

Kfir, I. (2019). Australia and the European Union promoting a normative security agenda in the South Pacific Islands. *Global Affairs*, 5(4–5), 539–549, doi: 10.1080/23340460.2020.1714471

Khokhar, T., & Srajuddin, U. (2015). Should we continue to use the term "developing world"? *World Bank Blogs.* 16 November 2015. https://blogs.worldbank.org/opendata/should-we-continue-use-term-developing-world [accessed 9/2/21].

Kilbourne, A. M., Neumann, M. S., Pincus, H. A., Bauer, M. S., & Stall, R. (2007). Implementing evidence-based interventions in health care: Application of the replicating effective programs framework. *Implementation Science*, 2, 42, doi: 10.1186/1748–5908–2-42

Kim, D., Kim, B. N., Lee, K., Park, J. K., Hong, S., & Kim, H. (2008). Effects of cognitive learning strategies for Korean learners: A meta-analysis. *Asia Pacific Education Review*, 9(4), 409–422, doi: 10.1007/BF03025659

Kim, J. P. (1996). *The impact of the nongraded program on students' affective domains and cognitive domains.* [Unpublished Ed.D.] University of Georgia, GA.

Kim, J. S. (2002). *A meta-analysis of academic summer programs.* [Unpublished Ed.D.] Harvard University, MA.

Kim, K. R., & Seo, E. H. (2018). The relationship between teacher efficacy and students' academic achievement: A meta-analysis. *Social Behavior and Personality: An international journal,* 46(4), 529–540, doi: 10.2224/sbp.6554

Kim, S. H. (2015). A meta-analysis on the effects of differentiated instruction in mathematics. *The Mathematical Education,* 54(4), 335–350, doi: 10.7468/mathedu.2015.54.4.335

Kim, S. W., Cho, H., & Kim, L. Y. (2019). Socioeconomic status and academic outcomes in developing countries: A meta-analysis. *Review of Educational Research,* 89(6), 875–916, doi: 10.3102/0034654319877155

Kingdon, G., & Muzammil, M. (2013). The school governance environment in Uttar Pradesh: Implications for teacher accountability and effort. *Journal of Development Studies,* 49(2), 251–269, doi: 10.1080/00220388.2012.700397

Kingdon, G., Aslam, M., Rawal, S., & Das, S. (2013). *Are contract teachers and para-teachers a cost-effective intervention to address teacher shortage and improve learning outcomes?* London: EPPI-Centre, Social Science Research Unit, Institute of Education, University of London.

Kingdon, G. G., Little, A., Aslam, M., Rawal, S., Moe, T., Patrinos H., Béteille T., Banerji, R., Parton, B., & Sharma, S. K. (2014). *A rigorous review of the political economy of education systems in developing countries. Final Report.* Education Rigorous Literature Review. London: Department for International Development.

Kirschner, P. A., & Hendrick, C. (2020). *How learning happens: Seminal works in educational psychology and what they mean in practice.* New York: Routledge.

Kitayama, S., Karasawa, M., Grossmann, I., Na, J., Varnum, M. E. W., & Nisbett, R. (2019, October 28). East–West differences in cognitive style and social orientation: Are they real? *PsyArXiv,* doi: 10.31234/osf.io/c57ep

Klassen, R. M., & Tze, V. M. (2014). Teachers' self-efficacy, personality, and teaching effectiveness: A meta-analysis. *Educational Research Review,* 12, 59–76, doi: 10.1016/j.edurev.2014.06.001

Klees, S. J., Ginsburg, M., Anwar, H., Robbins, M. B., Bloom, H., Busacca, C., Corwith, A., Decoster, B., Fiore, A., Gasior, S., Le, H. M., Primo, L. H., & Reedy, T. D. (2020). The World Bank's SABER: A critical analysis. *Comparative Education Review,* 64(1), 46–65, doi: 10.1086/706757

Knoster, T. (1991, June). Factors in managing complex change. *Material presentation at TASH conference,* Washington D.C.: The Association for People with Severe Disabilities.

Konstantopoulos, S. (2007). *How long do teacher effects persist?* IZA Discussion Paper 2893. https://ssrn.com/abstract=1000142

Kozma, R. B., & Vota, W. S. (2014). ICT in developing countries: Policies, implementation, and impact, in Spector, J. M., Merrill, M. D., Elen, J., & Bishop,

M. J. (Eds), *Handbook of research on educational communications and technology*. Springer: New York, 885–894.

Kraft, M. A., Blazar, D., & Hogan, D. (2018). The effect of teacher coaching on instruction and achievement: A meta-analysis of the causal evidence. *Review of Educational Research*, 88(4), 547–588, doi: 10.3102/0034654318759268

Kremer, M., & Holla, A. (2009). Improving education in the developing world: What have we learned from randomized evaluations? *Annual Review of Economics*, 1, 513–542, doi: 0.1146/annurev.economics.050708.143323

Kremer, M., Brannen, C., & Glennerster, R. (2013). The challenge of education and learning in the developing world. *Science*, 340, 297–300, doi: 10.1126/science.1235350

Kremer, M., Chaudhury, N., Rogers, H., Muralidharan, K., & Hammer, J. (2005). Teacher absence in India: A snapshot. *Journal of the European Economic Association*, 3, 658–667, doi: 10.1162/jeea.2005.3.2–3.658

Krishnaratne, S., White, H., & Carpenter, E. (2013). *Quality education for all children? What works in education in developing countries?* Working Paper 20. New Delhi: International Initiative for Impact Evaluation (3ie).

Kristjansson, B., Petticrew, M., MacDonald, B., Krasevec, J., Janzen, L., Greenhalgh, T., Wells, G. A., MacGowan, J., Farmer, A. P., Shea, B., Mayhew, A., Tugwell, P., & Welch, V. (2007). School feeding for improving the physical and psychosocial health of disadvantaged students. *Cochrane Database of Systematic Reviews*, 1, CD004676, doi: 10.1002/14651858.CD004676.pub2

Krowka, S., Hadd, A., & Marx, R. (2017). "No excuses" charter schools for increasing math and literacy achievement in primary and secondary education. *Campbell Systematic Reviews*, 9. Oslo: Campbell Collaboration, doi: 10.4073/csr.2017.9

Kulik, J. A., & Fletcher, J. D. (2016). Effectiveness of intelligent tutoring systems: A meta-analytic review. *Review of Educational Research*, 86(1), 42–78, doi: 10.3102/0034654315581420

Kulik, J. A., & Kulik, C.-L. C. (1987). *Computerbased instruction: What 200 evaluations say*. Ann Arbor: University of Michigan, Center for Research on Learning and Teaching.

LaRocque, N. (2008). *Public–private partnerships in basic education: An international review*. Reading: CfBT Education Trust.

Lauer, P. A., Akiba, M., Wilkerson, S. B., Apthorp, H. S., Snow, D., & Martin-Glenn, M. (2004). *The effectiveness of out-of-school-time strategies in assisting low-achieving students in reading and mathematics: A research synthesis*. Washington, D.C.: Institute of Education Sciences, Department of Education. https://dpi.wi.gov/sites/default/files/imce/sspw/pdf/ostfullsum.pdf

Lavery, L. (2008). *Self-regulated learning for academic success: An evaluation of instructional techniques*. [Unpublished doctoral dissertation] The University of Auckland, Auckland.

Lavy, V. (2015). Do differences in schools' instruction time explain international achievement gaps? Evidence from developed and developing countries. *The Economic Journal,* 125(588), doi: 10.1111/ecoj.12233

Lawson, T. M. (2012). *Impact of school feeding programs on educational, nutritional, and agricultural development goals: A systematic review of literature.* [Graduate Research Master's Degree] Plan B Papers 142466. Michigan: Michigan State University, Department of Agricultural, Food, and Resource Economics.

Leão, L. D., & Eyal, G. (2019). The rise of randomized controlled trials (RCTs) in international development in historical perspective. *Theory and Society,* 48(3), 383–418, doi: 10.1007/s11186-019-09352-6

Lee, J. (2008). Is test-driven external accountability effective? Synthesizing the evidence from cross-state causal-comparative and correlational studies. *Review of Educational Research,* 78(3), 608–644, doi: 10.3102/0034654308324427

Lee, J.-W., & Lee, H. (2016). Human capital in the long run. *Journal of Development Economics,* 122(C), 147–169, doi: 10.1016/j.jdeveco.2016.05.006

Leithwood, K., & Jantzi, D. (2009). A review of empirical evidence about school size effects: A policy perspective. *Review of Educational Research,* 79(1), 464–490, doi: 10.3102/0034654308326158

LeMahieu, P., Nordstrum, L., & Gale, G. (2017). Positive deviance: Learning from positive anomalies. *Quality Assurance in Education,* 25(1), 109–124, doi: 10.1108/QAE-12-2016–0083

LeMahieu, P. G., Nordstrum, L. E., & Greco, P. (2017). Lean for education. *Quality Assurance in Education: An International Perspective,* 25(1), 74–90.

Leuven, E., & Oosterbeek, H. (2018). Class size and student outcomes in Europe. *European Expert network on Economics of Education Analytical Report,* 33. www.eenee.de/dms/EENEE/Analytical_Reports/EENEE_AR33.pdf

Levin, H. (2001). Waiting for Godot: Cost-effectiveness analysis in education. *New Directions for Evaluation,* 90, 55–68, doi: 10.1002/ev.12

Levin, H. M., Bowden, A. B., Shand, R., McEwan, P. J., & Belfield, C. R. (2018). *Economic evaluation in education: Cost-effectiveness and benefit-cost analysis.* Los Angeles: SAGE.

Liao, Y. K. C., & Chen, Y. H. (2018, October). Effects of integrating computer technology into mathematics instruction on elementary schoolers' academic achievement: A meta-analysis of one-hundred and sixty-four studies from Taiwan, in *E-Learn: World Conference on E-Learning in Corporate, Government, Healthcare, and Higher Education.* Waynesville: Association for the Advancement of Computing in Education (AACE), 165–173.

Lilley, A., Lilley, M., & Rinaldi, G. (May 2, 2020) *Public health interventions and economic growth: Revisiting the Spanish flu evidence.* https://ssrn.com/abstract=3590008 or doi: 10.2139/ssrn.3590008

Liu, D., Kirschner, P. A., & Karpinski, A. C. (2017). A meta-analysis of the relationship of academic performance and social network site use among adolescents and young adults. *Computers in Human Behavior,* 77, 148–157, doi: 10.1016/j.chb.2017.08.039

Liu, J., & Bray, M. (2020). Private subtractory tutoring: The negative impact of shadow education on public schooling in Myanmar. *International Journal of Educational Development,* 76, 102213, doi: 10.1016/j.ijedudev.2020.102213

Lleras-Muney, A. (2005). The relationship between education and adult mortality in the United States. *Review of Economic Studies, 72,* 189–221, doi: 10.1111/0034–6527.00329

Lomos, C., Hofman, R. H., & Bosker, R. J. (2011). Professional communities and student achievement – a meta-analysis. *School Effectiveness and School Improvement, 22*(2), 121–148, doi: 10.1080/09243453.2010.550467

Lusher, L., & Yasenov, V. (2016). Double-shift schooling and student success: Quasi-experimental evidence from Europe. *Economics Letters,* 139(C), 36–39, doi: 10.1016/j.econlet.2015.12.0090165–1765

Ma, W., Adesope, O. O., Nesbit, J. C., & Liu, Q. (2014). Intelligent tutoring systems and learning outcomes: A meta-analysis. *Journal of Educational Psychology,* 106(4), 901, doi: 10.1037/a0037123

Machin, S., Marie, O., & Vujic, S. (2011). The crime reducing effect of education. *Economic Journal,* 121, 463–484, doi: 10.1111/j.1468–0297.2011.02430.x

Madamba, S. R. (1981). *Meta-analysis on the effects of open and traditional schooling on the teaching–learning of reading.* Dissertation Abstracts International Section A: Humanities and Social Sciences, 41(8-A), 3508.

Mahdi, H. S. (2018). Effectiveness of mobile devices on vocabulary learning: A meta-analysis. *Journal of Educational Computing Research,* 56(1), 134–154, doi: 10.1177/0735633117698826

Manning, M., Garvis, S., Fleming, C., & Wong, G. T. (2017). The relationship between teacher qualification and the quality of the early childhood care and learning environment. *Campbell Systematic Reviews,* 2017, 1, doi: 10.4073/csr.2017.1

Marker, C., Gnambs, T., & Appel, M. (2018). Active on Facebook and failing at school? Meta-analytic findings on the relationship between online social networking activities and academic achievement. *Educational Psychology Review,* 30, 651–677, doi: 10.1007/s10648-017-9430-6

Markussen-Brown, J., Juhl, C. B., Piasta, S. B., Bleses, D., Højen, A., & Justice, L. M. (2017). The effects of language and literacy-focused professional development on early educators and children: A best-evidence meta-analysis. *Early Childhood Research Quarterly,* 38, 97–115, doi: 10.1016/j.ecres q.2016.07.002

Martini, R. (1987). *Research and statistics report: SMILE examination results.* London: Inner London Education Authority.

Marton, F. (2006). Sameness and difference in transfer. *Journal of the Learning Sciences,* 15, 499–535, doi: 10.1207/s15327809jls1504_3

Marzano, R. J. (1998). *A theory-based meta-analysis of research on instruction.* Washington D.C.: Mid-Continent Regional Educational Lab.

Marzano, R. J., Pickering, D., & Pollock, J. E. (2001). *Classroom instruction that works: Research-based strategies for increasing student achievement.* Alexandria, VA: Association for Supervision and Curriculum Development.

Masino, S., & Niño-Zarazúa, M. (2016). What works to improve the quality of student learning in developing countries? *International Journal of Educational Development,* 48, 53–65, doi: 10.1016/j.ijedudev.2015.11.012

Massachusetts Board of Education. (1844). *Seventh annual report of the Board of Education: Together with the Seventh annual report of the Secretary of the Board*. Boston: Dutton and Wentworth.

Mastropieri, M. A., & Scruggs, T. E. (1989). Constructing more meaningful relationships: Mnemonic instruction for special populations. *Educational Psychology Review*, 1(2), 83–111, doi: 10.1007/BF01326638

Mayr, U., & Kliegl, R. (2000). Task-set switching and long-term memory retrieval. *Journal of Experimental Psychology: Learning, Memory, and Cognition*, 26, 1124–1140, doi: 10.1037/0278–7393.26.5.1124

Mbiti, I. (2016). The need for accountability in education in developing countries. *Journal of Economic Perspectives,* 30(3), 109–132, doi: 10.1257/jep.30.3.109

McCowan, T., & Unterhalter, E. (2015). Introduction, in McCowan, T., & Unterhalter, E. (Eds), *Education and international development: An introduction*. London: Bloomsbury Academic Publishing.

McEwan, P. (2015). Improving learning in primary schools of developing countries: A meta-analysis of randomized experiments. *Review of Educational Research*, 85, 353–394. doi: 10.3102/0034654314553127

Means, B., & Penuel, W. R. (2005). Scaling up technology-based educational innovations, in Dede, C., Honan, J. P., & Peters, L. C. (Eds), *Scaling up success: Lessons learned from technology-based educational improvement* (1st ed.). San Francisco: Jossey-Bass, 176–197.

Meghir, C., Palme, M., & Schnabel, M. (2011). *The effect of education policy on crime: An intergenerational perspective*. Research Papers in Economics 2011:23. Stockholm: Department of Economics, Stockholm University.

Melby-Lervåg, M., & Hulme, C. (2013). Is working memory training effective? A meta-analytic review. *Developmental Psychology*, 49, 270–291, doi: 10.1037/a0028228

Metcalf, K. K. (1993). Critical factors in on-campus clinical experiences: Perceptions of preservice teachers. *Teaching Education*, 5(2), 163–174.

Meyers, D. C., Durlak, J. A., & Wandersman, A. (2012). The quality implementation framework: A synthesis of critical steps in the implementation process. *American Journal of Community Psychology*, 50(4), 462–480, doi: 10.1007/s10464–012–9522-x

Meza-Cordero, J. A. (2017). Learn to play and play to learn: Evaluation of the one laptop per child program in Costa Rica. *Journal of International Development*, 29(1), 3–31, doi: 10.1002/jid.3267

Miller, G. (1956). The magical number seven, plus or minus two: Some limits on our capacity for processing information. *The Psychological Review*, 63, 81–97, doi: 10.1037/h0043158

Ministry of Education – Liberia. (2016). *Liberia Education Sector Analysis*. Monrovia: Ministry of Education, Republic of Liberia.

Miron, G., & Nelson, C. (2001). *Student academic achievement in charter schools: What we know and why we know so little*. Occasional Paper No. 41. New York:

National Center for the Study of Privatization in Education Teachers College, Columbia University. https://ncspe.tc.columbia.edu/working-papers/OP41.pdf

Mitlin, D., & Satterthwaite, D. (2013). *Urban poverty in the Global South: Scale and nature*. New York: Routledge.

Mizunoya, S., Mitra, S., & Yamasaki, I. (2016). *Towards inclusive education: The impact of disability on school attendance in developing countries.* Innocenti Working Paper 2016–03. Florence: UNICEF Office of Research.

Moore, G. (1965). Cramming more components onto integrated circuits. *Electronics*, 38(8). https://newsroom.intel.com/wp-content/uploads/sites/11/2018/05/moores-law-electronics.pdf

Morel, R. P., Coburn, C., Catterson, A. K., & Higgs, J. (2019). The multiple meanings of scale: Implications for researchers and practitioners. *Educational Researcher*, 48(6), 369–377, doi: 10.3102/0013189X19860531

Morgan, C., Petrosino, A., & Fronius, T. (2013). *A systematic review of the evidence of the impact of school voucher programmes in developing countries.* London: EPPI-Centre, Social Science Research Unit, Institute of Education, University of London.

Mosteller, F., Light, R. J., & Sachs, J. A. (1996). Sustained inquiry in education: Lessons from skill grouping and class size. *Harvard Educational Review*, 66(4), 797–843.

Moullin, J. C., Sabater-Hernández, D., Fernandez-Llimos, F., & Benrimoj, S. (2015). A systematic review of implementation frameworks of innovations in healthcare and resulting generic implementation framework. *Health Research Policy and Systems,* 13(16), doi: 10.1186/s12961–015–0005-z

Mueller, P. A., & Oppenheimer, D. M. (2014). The pen is mightier than the keyboard: Advantages of longhand over laptop note taking. *Psychological Science*, 25(6), 1159–1168. doi: 10.1177/0956797614524581

Mullis, I. V. S., Martin, M. O., Foy, P., & Arora, A. (2012). *TIMSS 2011 international results in mathematics: International Association for the Evaluation of Educational Achievement (IEA)*. Boston: Lynch School of Education, Boston College.

Muralidharan, K. (2017). Field experiments in education in developing countries, in Banerjee, A. V., & Duflo, E. (Eds), *Handbook of economic field experiments*, Vol. 2. Amsterdam, Netherlands: North-Holland, an imprint of Elsevier, 323–388.

Muralidharan, K., Das, J., Holla, A., & Mohpal, A. (2017). The fiscal cost of weak governance: Evidence from teacher absence in India. *Journal of Public Economics*, 145, 116–135, doi: 10.1016/j.jpubeco.2016.11.005

Muralidharan, K., Singh, A., & Ganimian, A. J. (2019). Disrupting education? Experimental evidence on technology aided instruction in India. *American Economic Review*, 109(4), 1426–1460, doi: 10.1257/aer.20171112

Murdock, T. A. (1987). It isn't just money: The effects of financial aid on student persistence. *The Review of Higher Education*, 11(1), 75–101.

Murphy, P. K., Wilkinson, I. A., Soter, A. O., Hennessey, M. N., & Alexander, J. F. (2009). Examining the effects of classroom discussion on students' comprehension of text: A meta-analysis. *Journal of Educational Psychology*, 101(3), 740–764, doi: 10.1037/a0015576

Musk, E., & Neuralink. (2019). An integrated brain–machine interface platform with thousands of channels. *Journal of Medical Internet Research*, 21(10), e16194, doi: 10.1101/703801

Nag, S., Chiat, S., Torgerson, C., & Snowling, M. J. (2014). *Literacy, foundation learning and assessment in developing countries: Final report.* Education Rigorous Literature Review. London: Department for International Development.

Näslund-Hadley, E., Parker, S., & Hernandez-Agramonte, J. M. (2014). Fostering early math comprehension: Experimental evidence from Paraguay. *Global Education Review*, 1(4), 135–154. https://eric.ed.gov/?id=EJ1055163

Nathan, M. J., & Petrosino, A. (2003). Expert blind spot among preservice teachers. *American Educational Research Journal*, 40(4), 905–928, doi: 10.3102/00028312040004905

Neber, H., Finsterwald, M., & Urban, N. (2001). Cooperative learning with gifted and high-achieving students: A review and meta-analyses of 12 studies. *High Ability Studies*, 12(2), 199–214, doi: 10.1080/13598130120084339

Neuman, S. B. (1986). *Television and reading: A research synthesis.* Washington D.C.: Institute of Education Sciences. https://eric.ed.gov/?id=ED294532

Nguyen, T. (2013). *Information, role models and perceived returns to education experimental evidence from Madagascar.* Washington, D.C.: World Bank Group.

Nietzsche, F. (2008). *Nietzsche's thus spoke Zarathustra: Before sunrise.* (J. Luchte, Ed.). New York: Continuum.

Nikolaou, C. (2001). *Hand-held calculator use and achievement in mathematics: A meta-analysis.* [PhD Thesis] Georgia State University. https://www.learntechlib.org/p/119548/

Nkwake, A. M. (2020). *Working with assumptions in international development program evaluation.* Cham, Switzerland: Springer.

Norton, M. I., Mochon, D., & Ariely, D. (2011). The IKEA effect: When labor leads to love. *Journal of Consumer Psychology*, 22(3), 453–460, doi: 10.1016/j.jcps.2011.08.002

Novelli, M., Higgins, S., Ugur, M., & Valiente, V. (2014). *The political economy of education systems in conflict-affected contexts: A rigorous literature review.* London: Department for International Development.

Nuthall, G. (2007). *The hidden lives of learners.* Wellington: NZCER Press.

Ohno, T. (1988). *Toyota production system: Beyond large-scale production.* Portland, OR: Productivity Press.

Ones D. S., Dilchert S., & Viswesvaran C. (2012). Cognitive ability, in Schmitt N., (Ed.), *Oxford handbook of personnel assessment and selection.* Oxford: Oxford University Press, 179–224.

Organization for Economic Cooperation and Development (OECD). (2013a). *Learning standards, teaching standards and standards for school principals: A comparative study.* OECD Education Working Papers 99. Paris: OECD, doi: 10.1787/5k3tsjqtp90v-en

Organization for Economic Cooperation and Development (OECD). (2013b). *Synergies for better learning: An international perspective on evaluation and assessment.* OECD Reviews of Evaluation and Assessment in Education. Paris: OECD.

Organization for Economic Cooperation and Development (OECD). (2019a). *Education policy outlook 2019: Working together to help students achieve their potential.* Paris: OECD.

Organization for Economic Cooperation and Development (OECD). (2019b). TALIS: Tables I.5.36 and I.5.40. Paris: OECD, doi: 10.1787/1d0bc92a-en

Organization for Economic Cooperation and Development (OECD). (2020a). *Enhancing equal access to opportunities for all.* Paris: OECD.

Organization for Economic Cooperation and Development (OECD). (2020b). *TALIS 2018 results (volume II): Teachers and school leaders as valued professionals.* Paris: TALIS, OECD, doi: 10.1787/19cf08df-en

Organization for Economic Cooperation and Development (OECD). (2020c). *PISA 2018 results (volume V): Effective policies, successful schools.* Paris: PISA, OECD, doi: 10.1787/ca768d40-en

Organization for Economic Cooperation and Development (OECD). (2020d). *Revenue statistics in Asian and Pacific economies 2020.* Paris: OECD, doi: 10.1787/d47d0ae3-en.

Organization for Economic Cooperation and Development (OECD). (2021a). Education spending (indicator), doi: 10.1787/ca274bac-en

Organization for Economic Cooperation and Development (OECD). (2021b). OECD.Stat. http://stats.oecd.org/Index.aspx?datasetcode=CRS1

Orr, D., Westbrook, J., Pryor, J., Durrani, N., Sebba, J., & Adu-Yeboah, C. (2013). *What are the impacts and cost-effectiveness of strategies to improve performance of untrained and under-trained teachers in the classroom in developing countries?* London: EPPI-Centre, Social Science Research Centre, Institute of Education, University of London.

Owen, S. M. (2020). Improving Kiribati educational outcomes: Capacity-building of school leaders and teachers using sustainable approaches and donor support. *Journal of Adult and Continuing Education*, 26(2), 221–241, doi: 10.1177/1477971419892639

Pahlke, E., Hyde, J. S., & Allison, C. M. (2014). The effects of single-sex compared with coeducational schooling on students' performance and attitudes: A meta-analysis. *Psychological Bulletin*, 140(4), 1042–1072, doi: 10.1037/a0035740

Papay, J. P., & Kraft, M. A. (2015). Productivity returns to experience in the teacher labor market: Methodological challenges and new evidence on long-term career improvement. *Journal of Public Economics*, 130, 105–119, doi: 10.1016/j.jpubeco.2015.02.008

Parandii, K. (2020). *Is development aid a victim of the EU budget deal?* London: Centre for European Reform. https://www.cer.eu/sites/default/files/insight_KP_15.9.20.pdf

Pascale, R., Sternin, J., & Sternin, M. (2010). *The power of positive deviance: How unlikely innovators solve the world's toughest problems.* Cambridge, MA: Harvard Business Review.

Paschal, R. A., Weinstein, T., & Walberg, H. J. (1984). The effects of homework on learning: A quantitative synthesis. *The Journal of Educational Research*, 78(2), 97–104.

PASEC (Programme d'Analyse des Systèmes Éducatifs de la Confemen). (2015). *PASEC 2014: Education system performance in francophone Africa, competencies and learning factors in primary education.* Dakar, Senegal: PASEC.

Patall, E. A., Cooper, H., & Allen, A. B. (2010). Extending the school day or school year. *Review of Educational Research*, 80(3), 401–436, doi: 10.3102/0034654310377086

Patrinos, H. A., Barrera-Osorio, F., & Guáqueta, J. (2009). *The role and impact of public–private partnerships in education.* Washington D.C.: World Bank Group.

Pearson, K. (1904). Report on certain enteric fever inoculation statistics. *BMJ*, 2(2288), 1243–1246, doi: 10.1136/bmj.2.2288.1243

Petersen-Brown, S. M., Henze, E. E., Klingbeil, D. A., Reynolds, J. L., Weber, R. C., & Codding, R. S. (2019). The use of touch devices for enhancing academic achievement: A meta-analysis. *Psychology in the Schools*, 56(7), 1187–1206, doi: 10.1002/pits.22225

Peterson, P. L. (1980). Open versus traditional classrooms. *Evaluation in Education*, 4, 58–60.

Petrakis, P. E., & Stamatakis, D. (2002). Growth and educational levels: A comparative analysis. *Economies of Education Review*, 21(5), 513–521.

Petrosino, A., Morgan, C., Fronius, T. A., Tanner-Smith, E. E., & Boruch, R. F. (2012). Interventions in developing nations for improving primary and secondary school enrollment of children: A systematic review. *Campbell Systematic Reviews*, 19, doi: 10.4073/csr.2012.19

Pham, L. D., Nguyen, T. D., & Springer, M. G. (2017, June). *Teacher merit pay and student test scores: A meta-analysis.* Paper presented at the annual conference of the Association for Education Finance and Policy Annual Meeting, Washington, D.C.

Pinker, S. (2018). *Enlightenment now: The case for reason, science, humanism, and progress.* London: Penguin.

Pischke, J. (2007). The impact of length of the school year on student performance and earnings: Evidence from the German short school years. *The Economic Journal*, 117(523), 1216–1242, doi: 10.1111/j.1468–0297.2007.02080.x

Pitchford, N. J., Kamchedzera, E., Hubber, P. J., & Chigeda, A. L. (2018). Interactive apps promote learning of basic mathematics in children with special educational needs and disabilities. *Frontiers in Psychology*, 9, 262.

Planck Collaboration. (2020). Planck 2018 results. VI. Cosmological parameters. *Astronomy & Astrophysics*, 641, doi: 10.1051/0004–6361/201833910.

Plomin, R., & von Stumm, S. (2018). The new genetics of intelligence. *Nature Reviews Genetics*, 19(3), 148–159, doi: 10.1038/nrg.2017.104

Pratt, J. G., Rhine, J. B., Smith, B. M., Stuart, C. E., & Greenwood, J. A. (1940). *Extra-sensory perception after sixty years: A critical appraisal of the research in extra-sensory perception.* New York: Henry Holt.

Pressman, J. L., & Wildavsky, A. (1984). *Implementation: How great expectations in Washington are dashed in Oakland; or, why it's amazing that federal programs work at all: This being a saga of the economic development administration*. Berkeley, CA: University of California Press.

Pritchett, L. (2013). *The rebirth of education: Schooling ain't learning*. Washington D.C.: Center for Global Development.

Pritchett, L., Samji, S., & Hammer, J. (2013). *It's all about meE: Using structured experiential learning ("e") to crawl the design space*. CGD Working Paper 322. Washington, DC: Center for Global Development. www.cgdev.org/publication/its-all-about-mee

Psacharopoulos, G. (1981). Returns to education: An updated international comparison. *Comparative Education*, 17(3), 321–341.

Psacharopoulos, G. (1985). Returns to education: A further international update and implications. *Journal of Human Resources*, 20(4), 583–604.

Psacharopoulos, G., & Patrinos, H. A. (2004). Returns to investment in education: A further update. *Education Economics*, 12(2), 111–134.

Psacharopoulos, G., & Patrinos, H. (2018). *Returns to investment in education: A decennial review of the global literature*. Policy Research Working Paper 8402. Washington D.C.: World Bank Group.

Psacharopoulos, G., Collis, V., Patrinos, H. A., & Vegas, E. (2021). The COVID-19 cost of school closures in earnings and income across the world. *Comparative Education Review*, 65(2), 271–287.

Psacharopoulos, G., Tan, J-P., & Jimenez, E. (1986). *Financing education in developing countries: An exploration of policy options*. Washington D.C.: World Bank.

Qian, H., Walker, A., & Li, X. (2017). The west wind vs the east wind: Instructional leadership model in China. *Journal of Educational Administration*, 55(2), 186–206, doi: 10.1108/JEA-08–2016–0083

Qu, Y., & Becker, B. J. (2003, April). *Does traditional teacher certification imply quality? A meta-analysis*. Paper presented at the Annual Meeting of the American Educational Research Association, Chicago, IL.

Raab, D. (2020). *Official Development Assistance (ODA) spending for 2020: First Secretary of State's letter to the Chair of the Foreign Affairs Committee*. London: Foreign, Commonwealth and Development Office. https://www.gov.uk/government/publications/official-development-assistance-oda-spending-for-2020-first-secretary-of-states-letter

Raas, M., & Riaz, N. (2021). Transforming education by supporting school leaders, in *Pakistan, in connecting classrooms: Unlocking a world of potential: Leading the way*. London: British Council. https://www.britishcouncil.org/sites/default/files/unlocking_a_world_of_potential_report_connecting_classrooms.pdf?_ga=2.142933045.1010556039.1613137716-1070724579.1613137716 [accessed 26/2/2021].

Raghupathi, V., & Raghupathi, W. (2020). The influence of education on health: An empirical assessment of OECD countries for the period 1995–2015. *Archives of Public Health*, 78(20), doi: 10.1186/s13690-020-00402-5

Rao, N., Sun, J., Wong, J. M. S., Weekes, B., Ip, P., Shaeffer, S., Young, M., Bray, M., Chen, E., & Lee, D. (2014). *Early childhood development and cognitive development in developing countries: A rigorous literature review.* London: Department for International Development.

Razel, M. (2001). The complex model of television viewing and educational achievement. *The Journal of Educational Research*, 94(6), 371–379, doi: 10.1080/00220670109598774

Reschly, A. L., Busch, T. W., Betts, J., Deno, S. L., & Long, J. D. (2009). Curriculum-based measurement oral reading as an indicator of reading achievement: A meta-analysis of the correlational evidence. *Journal of School Psychology*, 47(6), 427–469, doi: 10.1016/j.jsp.2009.07.001

Rice, J. K. (2013). Learning from experience? Evidence on the impact and distribution of teacher experience and the implications for teacher policy. *Education Finance and Policy*, 8(3), 332–348, doi: 10.1162/EDFP_a_00099

Rickards, F., Hattie, J., & Reid, C. (2020). *The turning point for the teaching profession growing expertise and evaluative thinking.* New York: Routledge.

Riddell, A., & Niño-Zarazúa, M. (2016). The effectiveness of foreign aid to education. *International Journal of Educational Development*, 48, 23–36, doi: 10.1016/j.ijedudev.2015.11.013

Rizzardo, D., & Brooks, R. (2003). *Understanding Lean manufacturing.* College Park, MD: Maryland Technology Enterprise Institute.

Robertson, E. M., Pascual-Leone, A., & Miall, R. C. (2004). Current concepts in procedural consolidation. *Nature Reviews Neuroscience*, 5, 576–582, doi: 10.1038/nrn1426

Robinson, V. M. J. (2011). *Student-centered leadership.* San Francisco, CA: Jossey-Bass.

Robinson, V. M. J. (2018). *Reduce change to increase improvement.* Thousand Oaks, CA: Corwin.

Robinson, V. M. J., Hohepa, M., & Lloyd, C. (2009). *School leadership and student outcomes: Identifying what works and why. Best Evidence Synthesis iteration (BES).* Wellington: Ministry of Education.

Robinson, V. M. J., Lloyd, C. A., & Rowe, K. J. (2008). The impact of leadership on student outcomes: An analysis of the differential effects of leadership types. *Educational Administration Quarterly*, 44, 635–674, doi: 10.1177/0013161X08321509

Rodriguez-Segura, D. (2020). *Educational technology in developing countries: A systematic review.* EdPolicyWorks Working Paper Series 72. Virginia: University of Virginia.

Romero, M., & Sandefur, J. (2019). *Beyond short-term learning gains: The impact of outsourcing schools in Liberia after three years.* CGD Working Paper 521. Washington, DC: Center for Global Development. https://www.cgdev.org/publication/beyond-short-term-learning-gains-impact-outsourcing-schools-liberia-after-three-years

Romero, M., Sandefur, J., & Sandholtz, W. A. (2020). Outsourcing education: Experimental evidence from Liberia. *American Economic Review*, 110(2), 364–400, doi: 10.1257/aer.20181478

Rosenthal, R., & Rubin, D. B. (1978). Interpersonal expectancy effects: The first 345 studies. *Behavioral and Brain Sciences*, 1(03), 377–386.

Rosling, H., Rosling, O., & Rönnlund, A. R. (2018). *Factfulness: Ten reasons we're wrong about the world – and why things are better than you think.* First edition. New York: Flatiron Books.

Roth, B., Becker, N., Romeyke, S., Schäfer, S., Domnick, F., & Spinath, F. M. (2015). Intelligence and school grades: A meta-analysis. *Intelligence*, 53, 118–137, doi: 10.1016/j.intell.2015.09.002

Rousseau, J.-J. (1991 [1762]). *Emile, or on education.* London: Penguin Classics.

Royal Society. (2019). *iHuman: Blurring lines between mind and machine.* London: The Royal Society. https://royalsociety.org/-/media/policy/projects/ihuman/report-neural-interfaces.pdf [accessed 18 June 2021].

RTI International. (2015). *Status of early grade reading in sub-Saharan Africa.* Washington, DC: U.S. Agency for International Development.

Rubie-Davies, C. M. (2018). *Teacher expectations in education.* London: Routledge.

Rui, N. (2009). Four decades of research on the effects of detracking reform: Where do we stand?—A systematic review of the evidence. *Journal of Evidence-Based Medicine*, 2(3), 164–183, doi: 10.1111/j.1756–5391.2009.01032.x

Saavedra, J. E., & García, S. (2012). *Impacts of conditional cash transfer programs on educational outcomes in developing countries: A meta-analysis.* Working Paper. Washington D.C.: RAND Corporation.

Sabarwal, S., & Abu-Jawdeh, M. (2017). *Understanding teacher effort: Insights from cross-country data on teacher perceptions.* Background Paper. Washington, D.C.: World Bank Group.

Sabarwal, S., & Abu-Jawdeh, M. (2018). *What teachers believe: Mental models about accountability, absenteeism, and student learning.* Policy Research Working Paper 8454. Washington, D.C.: World Bank Group.

Sabarwal, S., Abu-Jawdeh, M., & Kapoor, R. (2021). Teacher beliefs: Why they matter and what they are. *The World Bank Research Observer*, lkab008, doi: 10.1093/wbro/lkab008

Sahlberg, P. (2015). *Finnish lessons: What can the world learn from educational change in Finland?* New York: Teachers College Press.

Salinas, A. (2010). Investing in our teachers: What focus of professional development leads to the highest student gains in mathematics achievement? *Open Access Dissertations.* Paper 393. https://scholarship.miami.edu/esploro/outputs/doctoral/Investing-in-our-Teachers-What-Focus-of-Professional-Development-Leads-to-the-Highest-Student-Gains-in-Mathematics-Achievement/991031447120502976

Samoff, J., Leer, J., & Reddy, M. (2016). *Capturing complexity and context: Evaluating aid to education.* Stockholm: Elanders Sverige AB.

Sampson, R., Johnson, D., Somanchi, A., Barton, H., Ruchika, J., Seth, M., & Shotland, M. (2019). *Insights from rapid evaluations of EdTech products.* The EdTech Lab Series. New Delhi: Central Square Foundation. https://

centralsquarefoundation.org/wp-content/uploads/EdTech%20Lab%20 Report_November%202019.pdf

Sanders, W. L., & Rivers, J. C. (1996). *Cumulative and residual effects of teachers on future student academic achievement (Research Progress Report)*. Knoxville, TN: University of Tennessee Value-Added Research and Assessment Center.

Saran, A., White, H., Albright, K., & Adona, J. (2020). Mega-map of systematic reviews and evidence and gap maps on the interventions to improve child well-being in low- and middle-income countries. *Campbell Systematic Reviews*, 16(4), 1–44, doi: 10.1002/ cl2.1116

Save Our Future. (2020). *Averting an education catastrophe for the world's children*. Save Our Future Campaign. https://saveourfuture.world/white-paper/

Sawilowsky, S. S. (2009). New effect size rules of thumb. *Journal of Modern Applied Statistical Methods*, 8(2), 597–599, doi: 10.22237/jmasm/1257035100

Schmidt, F. (2015). Select on intelligence, in Locke, E. A., (Ed.), *Handbook of principles of organizational behavior: Indispensable knowledge for evidence-based management*. Hoboken, NJ: Wiley, doi: 10.1002/9781119206422.ch1

Schneider, D. (2017). Deeper and cheaper machine learning [Top Tech 2017]. *IEEE Spectrum*, 54(1), 42–43, doi: 10.1109/MSPEC.2017.7802746.

Schneider, J. (2014). *From the ivory tower to the schoolhouse: How scholarship becomes common knowledge in education*. Cambridge, MA: Harvard Education Press.

Schneider, M. (2002). *Do school facilities affect academic outcomes?* Washington D.C.: National Clearinghouse for Educational Facilities.

Schroeder, N. L., Nesbit, J. C., Anguiano, C. J., & Adesope, O. O. (2018). Studying and constructing concept maps: A meta-analysis. *Educational Psychology Review*, 30(2), 431–455, doi: 10.1007/s10648-017-9403-9

Schultz, P. (2002). Why governments should invest more to educate girls. *World Development*, 30 (2), 207–225.

Schunk, D. (2004). *Learning theories: An educational perspective* (4th ed.). Upper Saddle River, NJ: Pearson.

See, B. H., & Gorard, S. (2020). Why don't we have enough teachers?: A reconsideration of the available evidence. *Research Papers in Education*, 35(4), 416–442, doi: 10.1080/02671522.2019.1568535

Shakeel, M., Anderson, K., & Wolf, P. (2021). The participant effects of private school vouchers around the globe: A meta-analytic and systematic review. *School Effectiveness and School Improvement*, doi: 10.1080/09243453.2021.1906283

Shanahan, M. (2015). *The technological singularity*. Cambridge, MA: MIT Press.

Shubbak, M. H. (2019). Advances in solar photovoltaics: Technology review and patent trends. *Renewable and Sustainable Energy Reviews*, 115, 109383.

Sirin, S. R. (2005). Socioeconomic status and academic achievement: A meta-analytic review of research. *Review of educational research*, 75(3), 417–453, doi: 10.3102/00346543075003417

Sisken, L. S. (2016). Mutual adaptation in action. *Teachers College Record*, 118(13), 1–16.

Sitzmann, T., & Ely, K. (2011). A meta-analysis of self-regulated learning in work-related training and educational attainment: What we know and where we need to go. *Psychological Bulletin*, 137(3), 421, doi: 10.1037/a0022777

Slater, H., Davies, N. M., & Burgess, S. (2012). Do teachers matter? Measuring the variation in teacher effectiveness in England. *Oxford Bulletin of Economics and Statistics*, 74(5), 629–645, doi: 10.1111/j.1468–0084.2011.00666.x

Slavin, R. E. (1987). Mastery learning reconsidered. *Review of Educational Research*, 57(2), 175–213.

Slavin, R. E. (2002). Evidence-based education policies: Transforming educational practice and research. *Educational Researcher*, 31(7), 15–21, doi: 10.3102/0013189X031007015

Sloane, F. C. (2005). The scaling of reading interventions: Building multilevel insight. *Reading Research Quarterly*, 40(3), 361–366, doi: 10.1598/RRQ.40.3.4

Smith, B. A. (1996). *A meta-analysis of outcomes from the use of calculators in mathematics education.* [Doctoral dissertation] Texas A & M University, Commerce.

Smith, M. L. (1980). Teacher expectations. *Evaluation in Education*, 4, 53–55.

Smith, M., & McNaughton, B. (2018). *Final report Kiribati Education Improvement Program (KEIP) independent evaluation 2018.* Strategic Development Group. https://dfat.gov.au/about-us/publications/Pages/kiribati-education-improvement-program-2018-independent-evaluation-report-and-management-response.aspx

Snilstveit, B., Stevenson, J., Menon, R., Phillips, D., Gallagher, E., Geleen, M., Jobse, H., Schmidt, T., & Jimenez, E. (2016). *The impact of education programmes on learning and school participation in low- and middle-income countries: A systematic review summary report: 3ie systematic review summary 7.* London: International Initiative for Impact Evaluation.

Snilstveit, B., Stevenson, J., Phillips, D., Vojtkova, M., Gallagher, E., Schmidt, T., Jobse, H., Geelen, M., Pastorello, M., & Eyers, J. (2015). *Interventions for improving learning outcomes and access to education in low- and middle- income countries: A systematic review: 3ie Systematic Review 24.* London: International Initiative for Impact Evaluation (3ie).

Snook, I., O'Neill, J., Clark, J., O'Neill, A. M., & Openshaw, R. (2009). Invisible learnings? A commentary on John Hattie's book: Visible Learning: A synthesis of over 800 meta-analyses relating to Achievement. *New Zealand Journal of Educational Studies*, 44(1), 93–106.

Sparks, K. (2005). *The effect of teacher certification on student achievement.* [Doctoral dissertation] Texas: Texas A&M University.

Spasojevic, J. (2003). *Effects of education on adult health in Sweden: Results from a natural experiment.* [Ph.D Dissertation] New York: City University of New York Graduate Center.

Sperling, G., Winthrop, R., Kwauk, C., & Yousafzai, M. (2016). *What works in girls' education: Evidence for the world's best investment.* Washington D.C.: Brookings Institution Press.

Spier, E., Britto, P., Pigott, T., Roehlkapartain, E., McCarthy, M., Kidron, Y., Song, M., Scales, P., Wagner, D., Lane, J., & Glover, J. (2016). Parental, community, and familial support interventions to improve children's literacy in developing countries: A systematic review. *Campbell Systematic Reviews*, 12(1), 1–98, doi: 10.4073/csr.2016.4

Spink, J., Cassity, E., & Rorris, A. (2018). *What works best in education for development: A super synthesis of the evidence.* Canberra: DFAT.

Staddon, J. (2017). *Scientific method: How science works, fails to work or pretends to work.* New York: Routledge.

Staiger, D., & Rockoff, J. (2010). Searching for effective teachers with imperfect information. *Journal of Economic Perspectives*, 24(3), 97–118, doi: 10.1257/jep.24.3.97

Stockard, J., Wood, T. W., Coughlin, C., & Rasplica Khoury, C. (2018). The effectiveness of direct instruction curricula: A meta-analysis of a half century of research. *Review of Educational Research*, 88(4), 479–507, doi: 10.3102/0034654317751919

Stringfield, S., & Datnow, A. (1998). Introduction: Scaling up school restructuring designs in urban schools. *Education and Urban Society*, 30(3), 269–276, doi: 10.1177/0013124598030003001

Stronge, J. H., Ward, T. J., Tucker, P. D. et al. (2007). What is the relationship between teacher quality and student achievement? An exploratory study. *Journal of Personal Evaluation in Education,* 20, 165–184, doi: 10.1007/s11092–008–9053-z

Sung, Y. T., Chang, K. E., & Liu, T. C. (2016). The effects of integrating mobile devices with teaching and learning on students' learning performance: A meta-analysis and research synthesis. *Computers & Education*, 94, 252–275, doi: 10.1016/j.compedu.2015.11.008

Sutcher, L., Darling-Hammond, L., & Carver-Thomas, D. (2016). *A coming crisis in teaching? Teacher supply, demand, and shortages in the U.S.* Palo Alto, CA: Learning Policy Institute.

Tabak, R. G., Khoong, E. C., Chambers, D. A., & Brownson, R. C. (2012). Bridging research and practice: Models for dissemination and implementation research. *American Journal of Preventative Medicine*, 43, 337–350, doi: 10.1016/j.amepre.2012.05.024

Tamin, R. M., Borokhovski, E., Pickup, D., Bernard, R. M., & Saadi, L. E. (2017). *Tablets and mobile devices in the classroom: Implications from a systematic review and meta-analysis.* Technical Report, Commonwealth of Learning, Canada.

Tanaka, N. (2020). *Additional activities and associated costs for school re-opening under covid-19 pandemic – quick glance based on available information.* Washington D.C.: World Bank Group.

Tegmark, M. (2017). *Life 3.0: Being human in the age of artificial intelligence.* New York: Knopf.

Tilak, J. G. (1988). Foreign aid for education. *International Review of Education*, 34(3), 313–335.

Timperley, H., Kaser, L., & Halbert, J. (2014). *A framework for transforming learning in schools: Innovation and the spiral of inquiry.* Victoria: Centre for Strategic Education.

Timperley, H., Wilson, A., Barrar, H., & Fung, I. (2007). *Teacher professional learning and development: Best evidence synthesis iteration.* New Zealand: Ministry of Education.

Tingir, S., Cavlazoglu, B., Caliskan, O., Koklu, O., & Intepe-Tingir, S. (2017). Effects of mobile devices on K–12 students' achievement: A meta-analysis. *Journal of Computer Assisted Learning*, 33(4), 355–369, doi: 10.1111/jcal.12184

Tofel-Grehl, C., & Feldon, D. F. (2013). Cognitive task analysis–based training: A meta-analysis of studies. *Journal of Cognitive Engineering and Decision Making*, 7(3), 293–304, doi: 10.1177/1555343412474821

Tomlinson, B. R. (2003). What was the Third World? *Journal of Contemporary History*, 38(2), 307–321, doi: 10.1177/0022009403038002135

Torres, M. (2016). *A meta-analysis of research-based reading interventions with English language learners.* [Unpublished doctoral dissertation] University of Denver.

Trautwein, U., Köller, O., Schmitz, B., & Baumert, J. (2002). Do homework assignments enhance achievement? A multilevel analysis in 7th-grade mathematics. *Contemporary Educational Psychology*, 27(1), 26–50, doi: 10.1006/ceps.2001.1084

Tuncer, M., & Dikmen, M. (2017). The effect of cooperative learning on academic achievement: A meta-analysis on the relationship between the study group size and effect size. *Journal of Human Sciences*, 14(1), 473–485.

Twilhaar, E. S., de Kieviet, J. F., Aarnoudse-Moens, C. S., van Elburg, R. M., & Oosterlaan, J. (2018). Academic performance of children born preterm: A meta-analysis and meta-regression. *Archives of Disease in Childhood-Fetal and Neonatal Edition*, 103(4), F322–F330.

Ukai, N. (1994). The Kumon approach to teaching and learning. *Journal of Japanese Studies*, 20(1), 87–113, doi: 10.2307/132785

UNESCO. (2012). *Global Education Digest. Opportunities lost: The impact of grade repetition and early school leaving.* Montreal: UNESCO Institute for Statistics.

UNESCO. (2015a). *Pricing the right to education: The cost of reaching new targets by 2030.* Paris: UNESCO.

UNESCO. (2015b). *SDG4-Education 2030, Incheon Declaration (ID) and Framework for Action. For the implementation of sustainable development goal 4, ensure inclusive and equitable quality education and promote lifelong learning opportunities for all, ED-2016/WS/28.* Paris: UNESCO.

UNESCO. (2018). *Global education monitoring report 2019: Migration, displacement and education – building bridges, not walls.* Paris: UNESCO. https://doi.org/10.18356/22b0ce76-en

UNESCO. (2020a). *Act now: Reduce the impact of COVID-19 on the cost of achieving SDG 4. Global education monitoring report.* Policy Paper 42. Paris: UNESCO. https://en.unesco.org/news/unesco-warns-funding-gap-reach-sdg4-poorer-countries-risks-increasing-us-200-billion-annually [accessed 14/2/21].

UNESCO. (2020b). *Global education monitoring report 2020: Inclusion and education – all means all.* Paris: UNESCO. https://doi.org/10.18356/2ddb782c-en

UNESCO. (2020c). *Press release: 1.3 billion learners are still affected by school or university closures, as educational institutions start reopening around the world, says UNESCO.* https://en.unesco.org/news/13-billion-learners-are-still-affected-school-university-closures-educational-institutions [accessed 8/2/21].

UNESCO. (2021). *UNESCO global monitoring map of school closures.* Paris: UNESCO. https://en.unesco.org/covid19/educationresponse#durationschoolclosures [accessed 24/7/21].

UNESCO Institute for Statistics (UIS) database. (2017). *More than one-half of children and adolescents are not learning worldwide.* Fact Sheet No. 46.UIS/FS/2017/ED/46. Paris: UNESCO.

UNESCO Institute for Statistics (UIS) database. (2019). *New methodology shows that 258 million children, adolescents and youth are out of school.* Fact Sheet No. 56. UIS/2019/ED/FS/56. Paris: UNESCO.

UNESCO Institute for Statistics (UIS). (2020). SDG 4 global data book by target (September 2020 edition). http://tcg.uis.unesco.org/wp-content/uploads/sites/4/2021/01/SDG4_Global_Tables_2020.xlsx [accessed 20/2/21].

Unger, C. (2018). *International development: A postwar history.* London: Bloomsbury Academic.

United Nations Children's Fund (UNICEF). (2020). *Covid-19: Are children able to continue learning during school closures? A global analysis of the potential reach of remote learning policies using data from 100 countries.* New York: UNICEF.

United Nations Development Program Human Rights Development Report (UNDP HDR). (2020). Mean years of schooling (years). http://hdr.undp.org/en/indicators/103006 [accessed 20/2/20].

Unterhalter, E., North, A., Arnot, M., Lloyd, C., Moletsane, L., Murphy-Graham, E., Parkes, J., & Saito, M. (2013). *Interventions to enhance girls' education and gender equality: A rigorous review of literature.* London: DFID.

Vaessen, J., Lemire, S., & Befani, B, (2020). *Evaluation of international development interventions: An overview of approaches and methods.* Independent Evaluation Group. Washington, DC: World Bank.

Vakis, R., & Farfan, G. (2018). Envío de mensajes de texto para incrementar la motivación y satisfacción docente. Policy report. *Evidencias MineduLAB,* 04.

VanLehn, K. (2011). The relative effectiveness of human tutoring, intelligent tutoring systems, and other tutoring systems. *Educational Psychologist, 46*(4), 197–221. doi: 10.1080/00461520.2011.611369

Varnum, M. E., Grossmann, I., Kitayama, S., & Nisbett, R. E. (2010). The origin of cultural differences in cognition: Evidence for the social orientation hypothesis. *Current Directions in Psychological Science,* 19(1), 9–13, doi: 10.1177/0963721409359301

Veenman, S. (1995). Cognitive and noncognitive effects of multigrade and multiage classes: A best-evidence synthesis. *Review of Educational Research,* 65(4), 319–381. doi: 10.3102/00346543065004319

Veenman, S. (1996). Effects of multigrade and multi-age classes reconsidered. *Review of Educational Research*, 66(3), 323–340, doi: 10.3102/00346543066003323

Vegas, E., & Coffin, C. (2015). When education expenditure matters: An empirical analysis of recent international data. *Comparative Education Review*, 59(2), 289–304, doi: 10.1086/680324

Vincent, D. (2019). The modern history of literacy, in Rury, J. L., & Tamura, E. (Eds), *The Oxford handbook of the history of education*. Oxford: Oxford University Press, 507–522.

Visible Learning META^x. (2021). Visible Learning META^x. https://www.visible-learningmetax.com/

Walker, A., & Leary, H. (2009). A problem based learning meta analysis: Differences across problem types, implementation types, disciplines, and assessment levels. *Interdisciplinary Journal of Problem-based Learning*, 3(1), 6, doi: 10.7771/1541–5015.1061

Wandersman, A. (2014). Getting to outcomes: An evaluation capacity building example of rationale, science, and practice. *American Journal of Evaluation*, 35(1), 100–106, doi: 10.1177/1098214013500705

Wandersman, A., Chien, V. H., & Katz, J. (2012). Toward an evidence-based system for innovation support for implementing innovations with quality: Tools, training, technical assistance, and quality assurance/quality improvement. *American Journal of Community Psychology*, 50(3–4), 445–459, doi: 10.1007/s10464-012-9509-7.

Wandersman, A., Duffy, J., Flaspohler, P., Noonan, R., Lubell, K., Stillman, L., Blachman, M., Dunville, R., & Saul, J. (2008). Bridging the gap between prevention research and practice: The interactive systems framework for dissemination and implementation. *American Journal of Community Psychology*, 41(3–4), 171–181.

Watson, G. R. (1969). *The Roman soldier: Aspects of Greek and Roman life*. Ithaca, NY: Cornell University Press.

Weinstein, C. S. (1979). The physical environment of the school: A review of the research. *Review of Educational Research*, 49(4), 577–610, doi: 10.2307/1169986

Westbrook, J., Durrani, N., Brown, R., Orr, D., Pryor, J., Boddy, J., & Salvi, F. (2013). *Pedagogy, curriculum, teaching practices and teacher education in developing countries. Final report. Education rigorous literature review*. London: DFID.

Westhorp, G., Walker, D. W., Rogers, P., Overbeeke, N., Ball, D., & Brice, G. (2014). *Enhancing community accountability, empowerment and education outcomes in low and middle-income countries: A realist review*. London: EPPI-Centre, Social Science Research Unit, Institute of Education, University of London.

White, H. (2019). In denial: Defending Australia as China looks south [online]. *Australian Foreign Affairs*, 6, 5–27.

White, W. A. (1988). A meta-analysis of the effects of direct instruction in special education. *Education and Treatment of Children*, 11(4), 364–374. www.jstor.org/stable/42899084 [accessed 27/12/20].

Whitford, D. K., Zhang, D., & Katsiyannis, A. (2018). Traditional vs. alternative teacher preparation programs: A meta-analysis. *Journal of Child and Family Studies*, 27, 671–685, doi: 10.1007/s10826-017-0932-0

Wiliam, D. (2014). *The formative evaluation of teaching performance.* East Melbourne, Victoria: Centre for Strategic Education.

Wiliam, D. (2018). *Creating the schools our children need: Why what we are doing now won't help much (and what we can do instead).* West Palm Beach, FL: Learning Sciences International.

Williams, P. A., Haertel, E. H., Haertel, G. D., & Walberg, H. J. (1982). The impact of leisure-time television on school learning: A research synthesis. *American Educational Research Journal, 19*(1), 19–50.

Willingham, D. T. (2007). Critical thinking: Why is it so hard to teach? *American Educator, 31,* 8–19, doi: 10.3200/AEPR.109.4.21–32

Wilson, J. M. (1995). Henry Ford's just-in-time system. *International Journal of Operations & Production Management, 15*(12), 59–75.

Wing, R., & Phelan, S. (2005). Long-term weight loss maintenance. *The American Journal of Clinical Nutrition, 82*(1), 222S–225S, doi: 10.1093/ajcn/82.1.222S

Wiseman, A. W. (2002). *Principals' instructional management activity and student achievement: A meta-analysis.* Paper presented at the Annual Meeting of the Southwestern Educational Research Association, Austin, TX.

Wiske, M. S., & Perkins, D. (2005). Dewey goes digital: Scaling up constructivist pedagogies and the promise of new technologies, in Dede, C., Honan, J. P., & Peters, L. C. (Eds), *Scaling up success: Lessons from technology-based educational improvement.* San Francisco: Jossey-Bass, 27–47.

Womack, J. P., & Jones, D. T. (2003). *Lean thinking: Banish waste and create wealth in your corporation.* New York: Free Press.

Womak, J. P., & Jones, D. T. (2013). *Lean thinking: Banish waste and create wealth in your corporation – revised and updated.* London: Simon & Shuster.

Womak, J., Jones, D., & Roos, D. (1990). *The machine that changed the world: The story of lean production, Toyota's secret weapon in the global car wars that is now revolutionizing world industry.* New York: Free Press.

Woolner, P., Hall, E., Higgins, S., McCaughey, C., & Wall, K. (2007). A sound foundation? What we know about the impact of environments on learning and the implications for building schools for the future. *Oxford Review of Education, 33*(1), 47–70, doi: 10.1080/03054980601094693

World Bank. (2000). *The logframe handbook.* Washington D.C.: World Bank Group.

World Bank. (2003). *World development report 2004: Making services work for poor people.* Washington D.C.: World Bank Group.

World Bank. (2016). *SABER tools as a framework for education system assessment: SABER in action.* Washington D.C.: World Bank Group. https://openknowledge.worldbank.org/handle/10986/26463

World Bank. (2018). *Global development report 2018: Learning to realize education's promise.* Washington D.C.: World Bank Group.

World Bank. (2019). *Ending learning poverty: What will it take?* Washington D.C.: World Bank Group.

World Bank. (2021a). *Global economic prospects.* Washington, D.C.: World Bank, doi: 10.1596/978–1–4648–1612–3

World Bank. (2021b). *World Bank education COVID-19 school closures map.* https://www.worldbank.org/en/data/interactive/2020/03/24/world-bank-education-and-covid-19 [accessed 8/2/21].

World Bank EdStats. (2020). Government expenditure on education, total (% of GDP), data as at September 2020. https://data.worldbank.org/indicator/SE.XPD.TOTL.GD.ZS [accessed 20/2/21].

World Bank EdStats. (2021a). Teachers in pre-primary/primary/lower secondary/upper secondary education, both sexes (number). https://databank.worldbank.org/

World Bank EdStats. (2021b). *Literacy rate, adult total (% people aged 15 and above; – Liberia.* Data as at September 2020. Washington D.C.: World Bank Group. https://data.worldbank.org/indicator/SE.ADT.LITR.ZS?end=2017&locations=LR&start=1984

World Bank EdStats. (2021c). Proportion of teachers with the minimum required qualifications in pre-primary/primary/lower secondary/upper secondary, both sexes (%); SABER: (Teachers) Policy Goal 3 Lever 1: Are there minimum standards for pre-service teaching education programs?; percentage of teachers in primary/lower secondary/upper secondary who are trained, both sexes (%). https://databank.worldbank.org/

World Bank Open Data. (2020a). World Bank development indicators: Access to electricity (% of population), 2019. https://data.worldbank.org/indicator/EG.ELC.ACCS.ZS

World Bank Open Data. (2020b). World Bank development indicators: Individuals using the Internet (% of population), 2019. https://data.worldbank.org/indicator/IT.CEL.SETS.P2

World Bank Open Data. (2020c). World Bank development indicators: Mobile cellular subscriptions (per 100 people), 2019. https://data.worldbank.org/indicator/IT.CEL.SETS.P2

World Health Organization (WHO). (2019). *Global spending on health: A world in transition.* Geneva: World Health Organization.

Yang, A. (2018). *The war on normal people: The truth about America's disappearing jobs and why Universal Basic Income is our future.* New York: Hachette Books.

Yeany, R. H., & Padilla, M. J. (1986). Training science teachers to utilize better teaching strategies: A research synthesis. *Journal of Research in Science teaching,* 23(2), 85–95, doi: 10.1002/tea.3660230202

Yildirim, I., Cirak-Kurt, S., & Sen, S. (2019). The effect of teaching 'learning strategies' on academic achievement: A meta-analysis study. *Eurasian Journal of Educational Research,* 79, 87–114. https://dergipark.org.tr/en/pub/ejer/issue/42986/520736

Yoon, K. S., Duncan, T., Lee, S., & Shapley, K. (2008). *The effects of teachers' professional development on student achievement: Findings from a systematic review of evidence.* Paper presented at the American Educational Research Association Annual Meeting.

Zeneli, M., Thurston, A., & Roseth, C. (2016). The influence of experimental design on the magnitude of the effect size-peer tutoring for elementary, middle and high school settings: A meta-analysis. *International Journal of Educational Research*, 76, 211–223, doi: 10.1016/j.ijer.2015.11.010

Zhao, Y. (2018). *What works may hurt: Side effects in education.* New York: Teachers College Press.

Zheng, B., Warschauer, M., Lin, C. H., & Chang, C. (2016). Learning in one-to-one laptop environments: A meta-analysis and research synthesis. *Review of Educational Research*, 86(4), 1052–1084, doi: 10.3102/0034654316628645

Zierer, K. (2021). Effects of pandemic-related school closures on pupils' performance and learning in selected countries: A rapid review. *Education Sciences*, 11(6), 252.

Index

Page numbers in *italics* refer to figures.

Made in the USA
Monee, IL
28 August 2022

12756893R00181